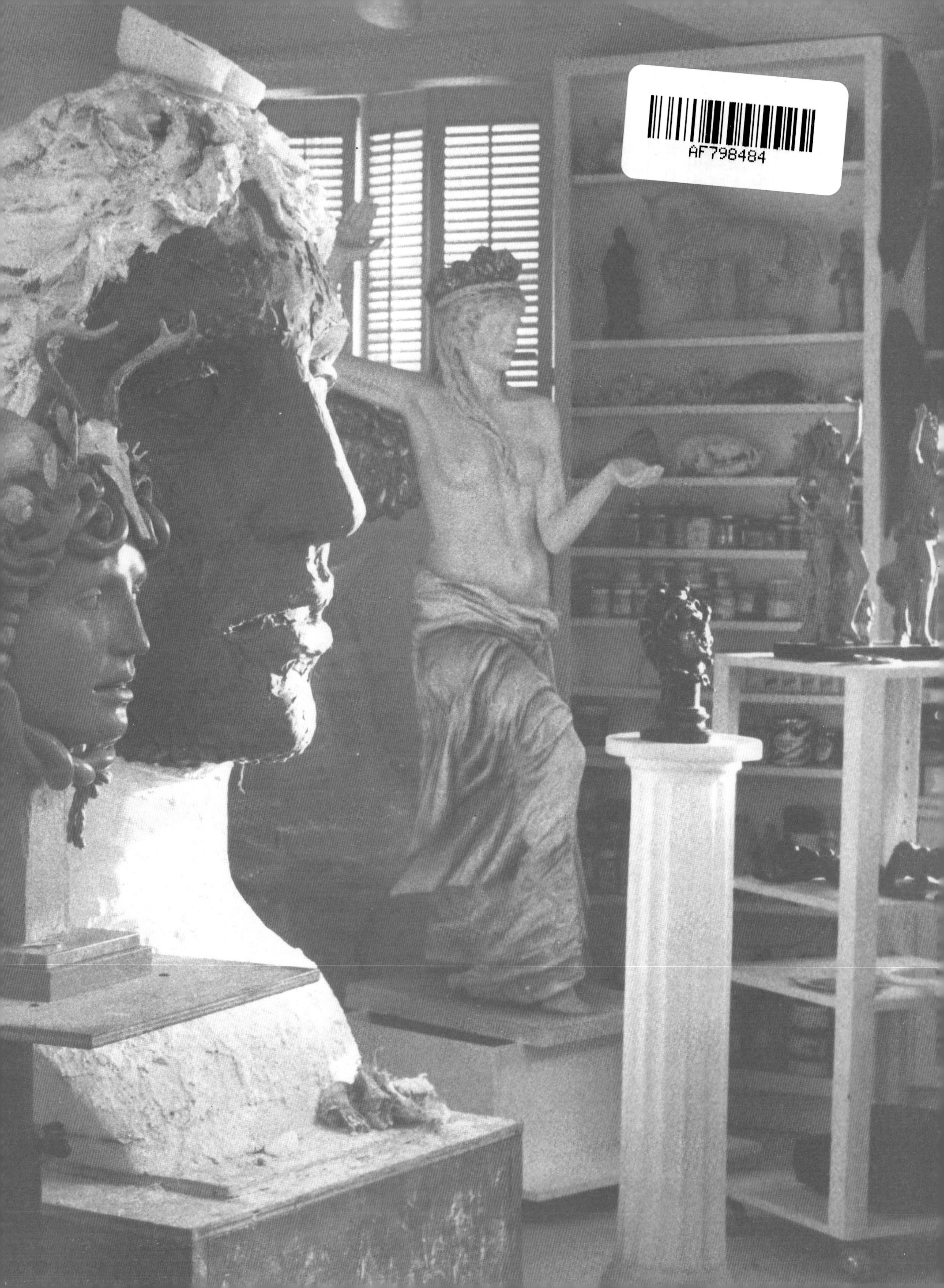

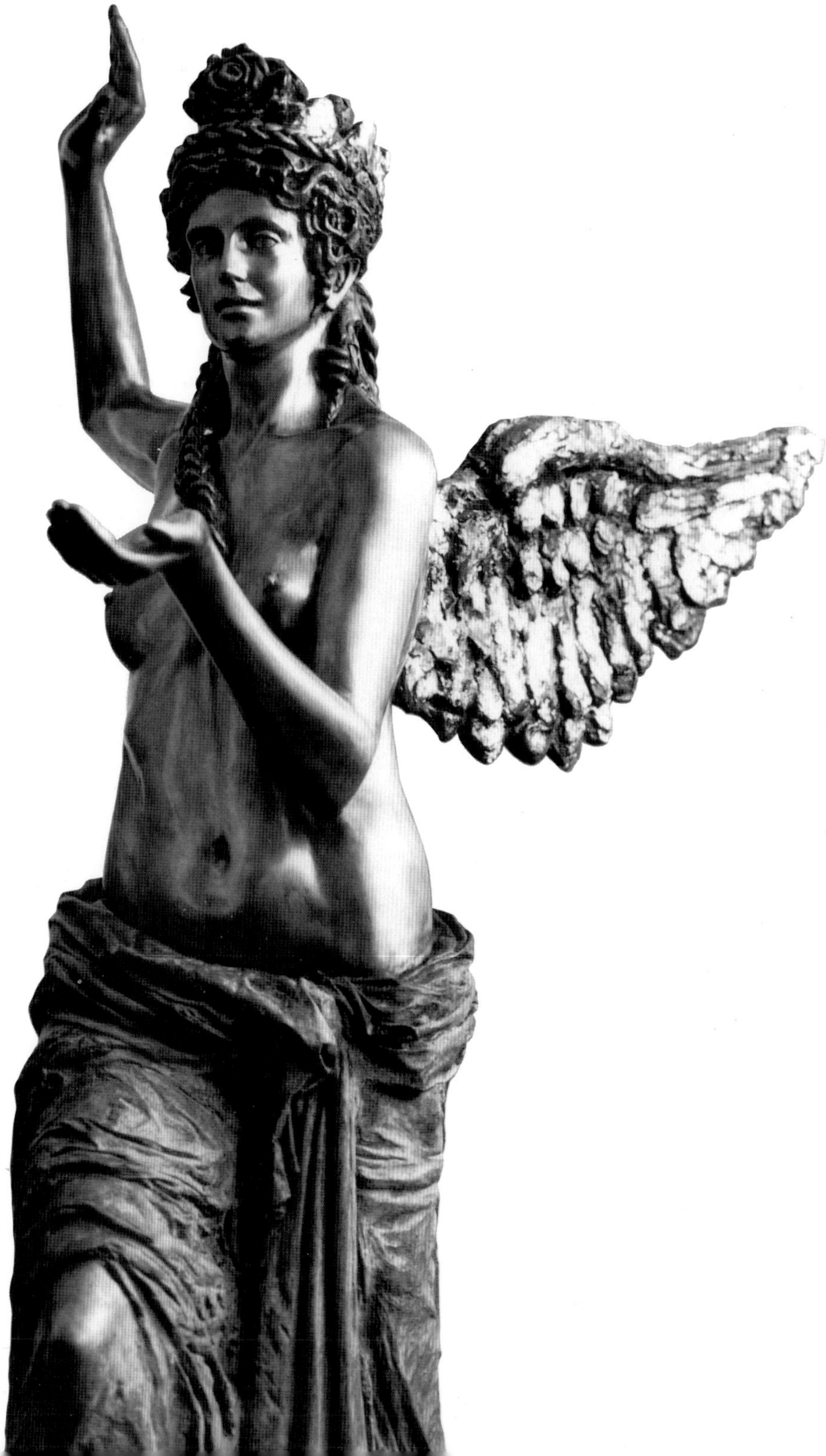

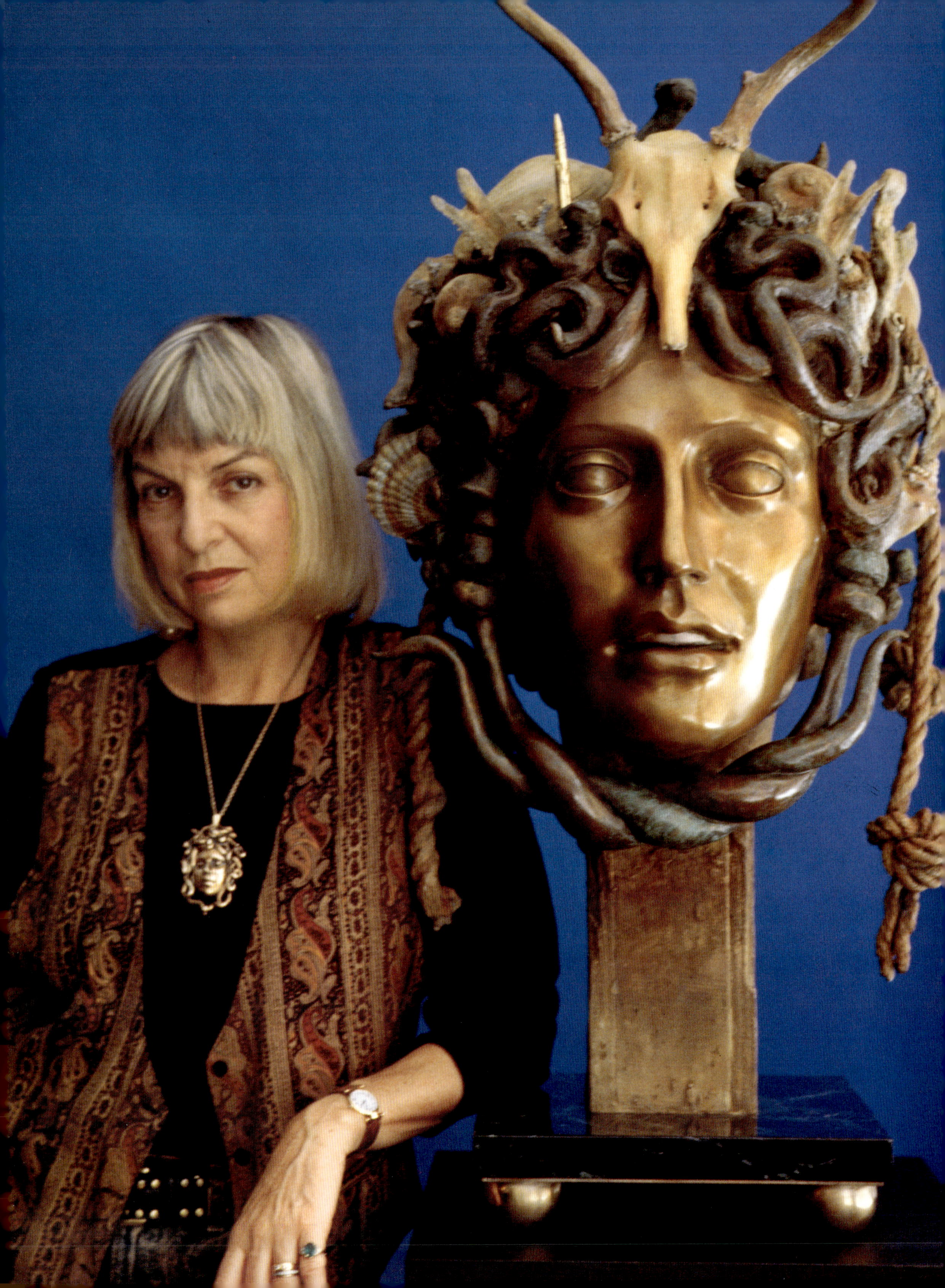

Breaking the Rules

Audrey Flack

A Retrospective 1950–1990

THALIA GOUMA-PETERSON
Curator and Editor

Essays by
PATRICIA HILLS • THALIA GOUMA-PETERSON
LAWRENCE ALLOWAY • SUSAN P. CASTERAS

HARRY N. ABRAMS, INC.
Publishers • *New York*

Breaking the Rules: Audrey Flack, A Retrospective 1950–1990 accompanies an exhibition organized by the J. B. Speed Art Museum, Louisville, Kentucky.

EXHIBITION ITINERARY

Wight Art Gallery, UCLA
March 22–May 17, 1992

Butler Institute of American Art, Youngstown, Ohio
June 28–August 9, 1992

National Museum of Women in the Arts, Washington, D.C.
September 29–December 17, 1992

The J. B. Speed Art Museum, Louisville, Kentucky
January 12–February 28, 1993

EDITOR: *Margaret Rennolds Chace*
DESIGNER: *Judith Michael*

ENDPAPERS: Audrey Flack's sculpture studio
ON PAGE 1: *Islandia: Goddess of the Healing Waters* (detail). 1988.
Patinated and gilded bronze, height 5′9″ (with base).
Collection New York City Technical College, Brooklyn
FRONTISPIECE: Audrey Flack with her sculpture *Colossal Head of Medusa*, 1991, made of patinated and gilded bronze, height 53½″

LIBRARY OF CONGRESS CATALOGING-IN-PUBLICATION DATA
Flack, Audrey.
Breaking the rules: Audrey Flack, a retrospective 1950–1990/
Thalia Gouma-Peterson, curator and editor; essays by Lawrence
Alloway . . . [et al.].
p. cm.
Catalogue of a travelling exhibition held 03/22–05/17/92,
at Wight Art Gallery, UCLA . . . [et al.].
Includes bibliographical references and index.
ISBN 0-8109-3117-6
ISBN 0-961-2276-12 (J. B. Speed Art Museum: pbk.)
1. Flack, Audrey—Exhibitions. I. Gouma-Peterson, Thalia.
II. Alloway, Lawrence, 1926–1989. III. Frederick S. Wight Art
Gallery. IV. Title.
N6537.F53A4 1992
709′.2—dc20 91-33670
CIP

Published in 1992 by Harry N. Abrams, Incorporated, New York
A Times Mirror Company

Printed and bound in Japan

CONTENTS

FOREWORD

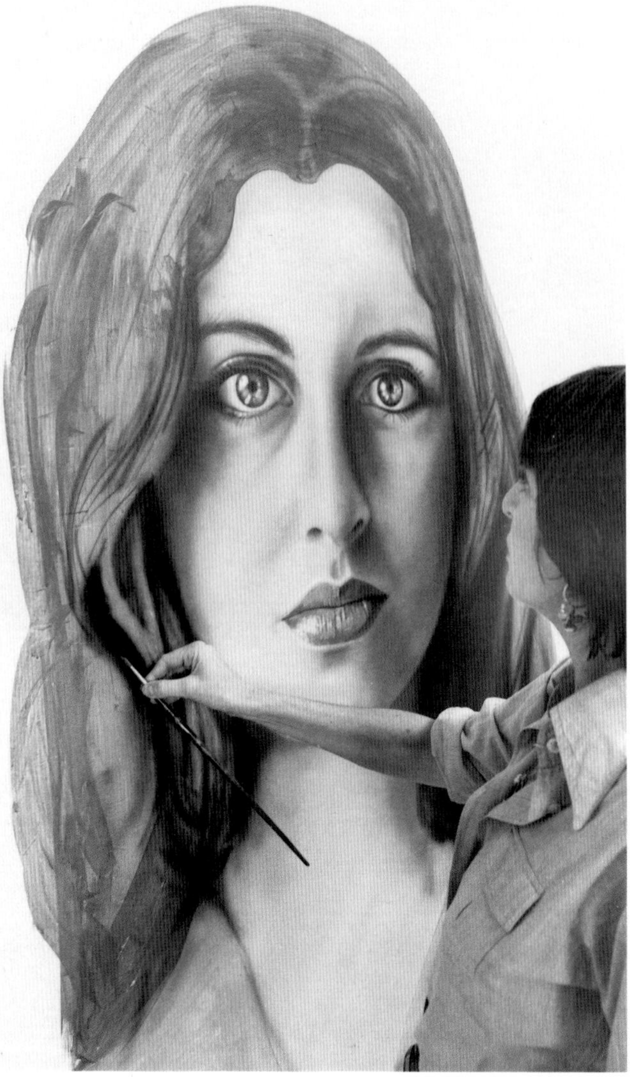

The artist working on
Hannah: Who She Is, c. 1982

The fascination of Audrey Flack's art lies in its originality and independence. She paints and sculpts from conviction, and her relationship to stylistic trends has almost always been tangential. The enduring main currents of her art lie more in subject matter than in style, more in defiance of canons than adherence to them. Abstract Expressionism assumed a prerequisite of painterly good taste, Pop Art insisted on an ironic stance toward commercial icons, Photorealism called for a veneration of the American scene, and recent beaux-arts revivals have tended to reimpose rules of composition. Flack's work has always been rawer, more elemental, and closer to the heart. She upends both the correct decorums of the successive avant-gardes and the broader aspirations to upper-class good taste. She stays teasingly on the edge of risking sentimentality, kitsch, propagandizing, and mock-heroics. What she achieves is artistic honesty, an art of immense power, and very personal monumentality. We are very pleased to have been able to organize this important retrospective and grateful to all of our collaborators, above all, Audrey Flack.

Peter Morrin
Director
J. B. Speed Art Museum

ACKNOWLEDGMENTS

In 1981, when I interviewed Audrey Flack in her home and studio, I saw for the first time a large group of her pre-1970s paintings. I was struck by the scope of her work and the length of her professional career. I knew then that I wanted to organize a retrospective exhibition of her work, to make the wider public aware that she has done much in addition to the Photorealist paintings for which she is so well known. The range and variety of her work demanded, I recognized, a sizable exhibition. Furthermore, during the 1980s Audrey Flack's work took a remarkably new and different direction: she became a sculptor of figural bronzes. Clearly she had reached the point of deserving a serious retrospective, and a record of this achievement was essential. And so this project began.

It is Audrey Flack's faith in my ability to bring the project to fruition that has sustained the energy that has gone into it. She has given generously of her time and her self, and to all of us working on the catalogue and exhibition she has opened her files, her studio—and, indeed, her home. We all thank her for it.

The exhibition would not have been possible without the commitment of the J. B. Speed Art Museum and its Director Peter Morrin and his staff. I especially appreciate the close collaboration of Vallorie Alsup, Coordinator of Exhibitions. Her unflagging steadfastness, happy disposition, diplomatic skills, and untiring willingness to work has seen us through a number of difficult junctures.

I am grateful to the late Lawrence Alloway for his enthusiastic support of the project at its inception and his willingness to write an essay for the catalogue. We are saddened that he is no longer with us to celebrate its successful conclusion.

I also am grateful to Susan P. Casteras, Curator of Paintings at the Yale Center for British Art, and to Professor Patricia Hills of Boston University for their essays and their friendly collegial advice at various times during the preparation of the catalogue. To Professor Carl A. Peterson of Oberlin College I am indebted for his continuous support, counsel, and editorial advice throughout the course of this project. For helpful assistance on many occasions, I thank Louis K. Meisel and the staff of the Meisel Gallery, who has represented Audrey Flack for the last twenty years.

I am delighted that Harry N. Abrams, Inc., has agreed to publish the exhibition catalogue, and I thank Paul Gottlieb for his friendly support. It has been a pleasure to work on the book with Margaret Rennolds Chace, Assistant Managing Editor at Abrams. Her critical insight and discerning eye have been invaluable. Thanks also go to Judith Michael for her sensitivity and intelligence in designing the book.

Finally, I am indebted to a grant from the College of Wooster's Henry Luce III Fund for Distinguished Scholarship that freed me from teaching for one year and enabled me to complete a substantial part of the research and writing for this book.

Thalia Gouma-Peterson, Guest Curator
Professor of Art History
Director, College of Wooster Art Museum

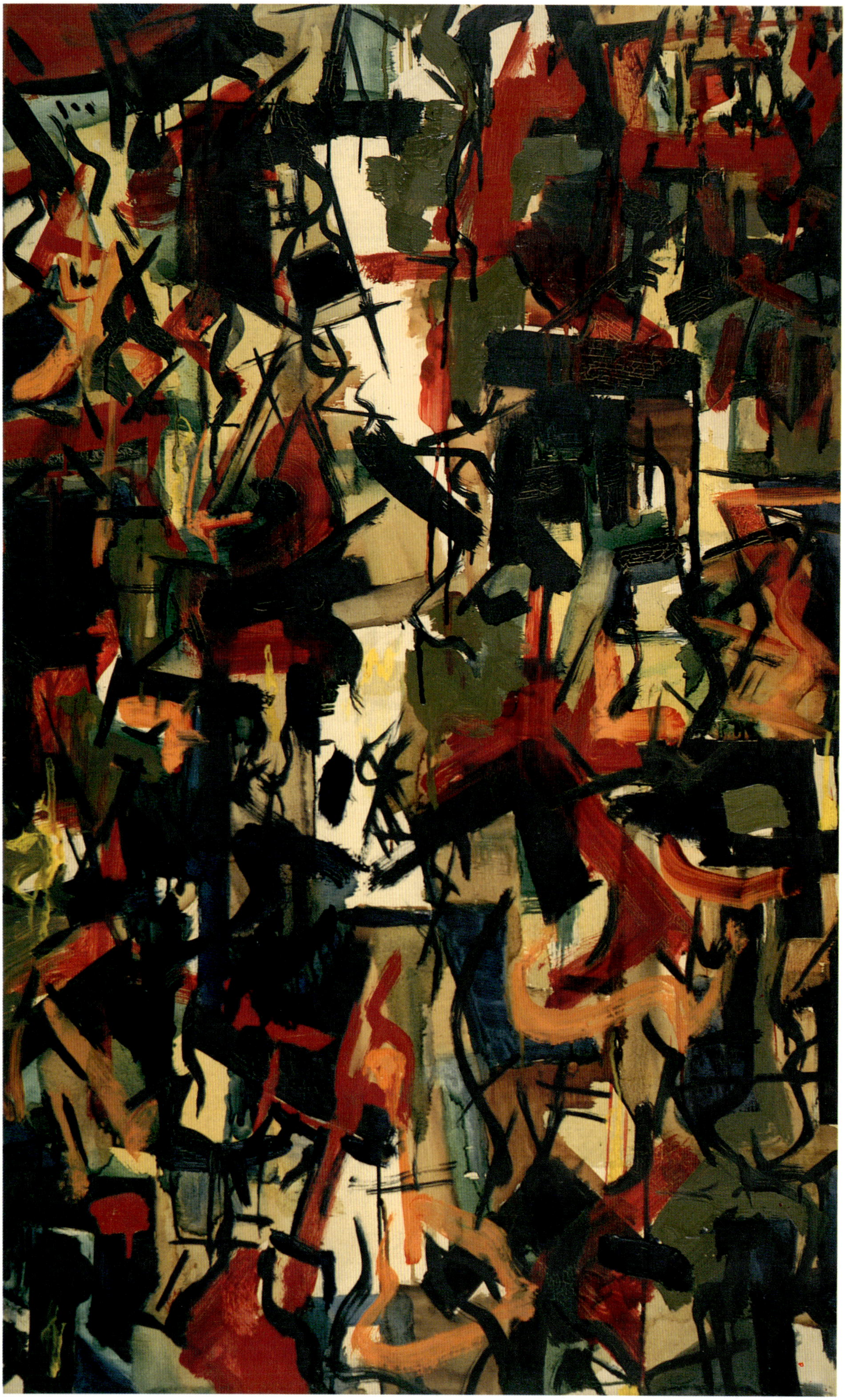

INTRODUCTION: AUDREY FLACK'S SYMBOLIC REALISM

Thalia Gouma-Peterson

Audrey Flack has been identified with Photorealist painting from its inception and throughout the 1970s was a leading figure among that group of artists.[1] But her art of that decade, rich and complex, consisting primarily of still lifes, differs from that of other Photorealists in several significant ways. Her subjects are not, like others, drawn from the contemporary American urban scene nor are they camp deprecations of high art.[2] Her paintings are not detached and in their spatial intricacy and color intensity are "in opposition to the reductive tendencies of American art" of the seventies.[3] In fact, despite her use of contemporary techniques and her strikingly modern color and composition, Flack's still lifes have in their idealized reality and symbolic message much in common with Baroque paintings. Her art is definitely not an offshoot of sixties conceptual art;[4] it is about people and objects the artist cares for and that she often sees as extensions of her own persona. Both her portraits and still lifes have a positive physical and moral presence and a sense of respect for living beings. While updating the traditional subject matter of Baroque still life Flack continues to deal with one of its central themes: the transitoriness of life.

This book accompanies an exhibition spanning the four decades of Audrey Flack's career. Included from the 1950s are large abstract compositions (1950–52), smaller figurative still lifes, and a group of portraits and startling private self-portraits (1952–60). Often painted in thick impasto and dark tones, these early oil paintings such as *Anatomy Lesson*, *Self-Portrait with Anita*, and *Self-Portrait (the Memory)*, clearly show the artist's preoccupation with the figure and with a private symbolic language. They were followed in the early 1960s by a series of public portraits and political paintings based on news

OPPOSITE:
Flashback. 1949–50
Oil on canvas, 45 × 28″
Private collection

OVERLEAF, LEFT:
Black Graph Abstract. 1951
Oil on canvas, 44 × 33″
Collection the artist

OVERLEAF, RIGHT:
Diamonds and Sky (Abstract). 1951
Oil on canvas, 50 × 34″
Collection the artist

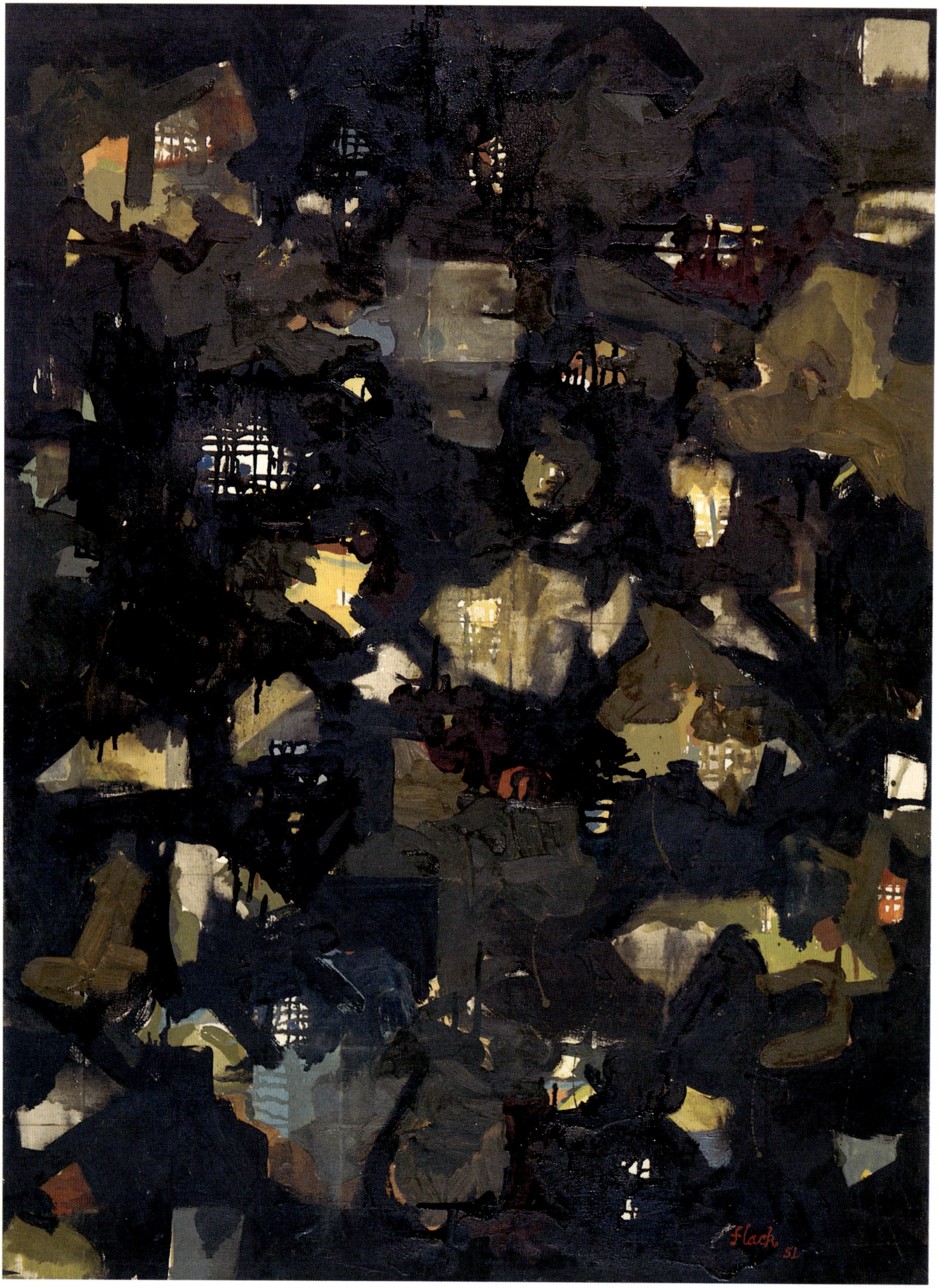
Flach
51

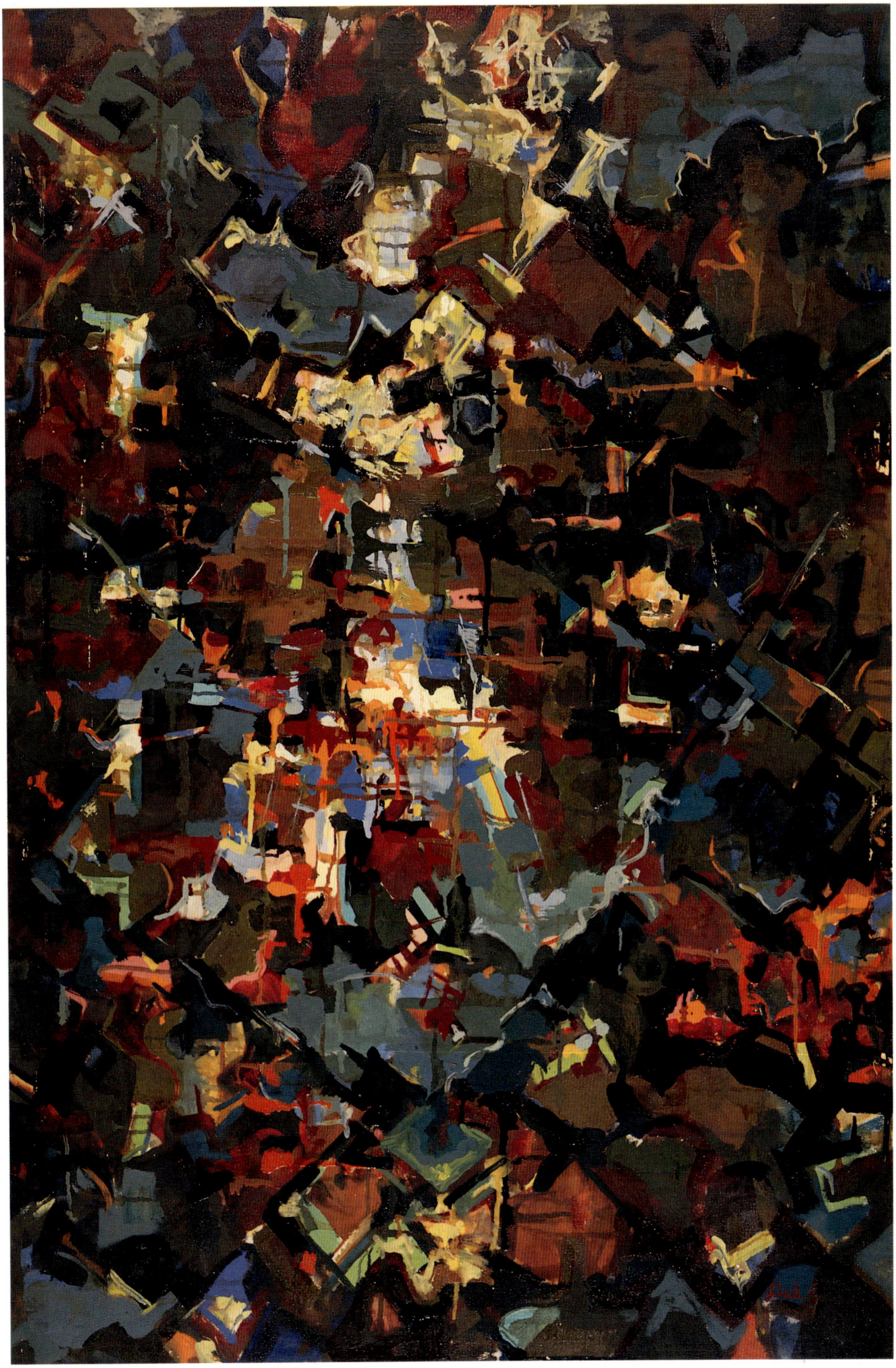

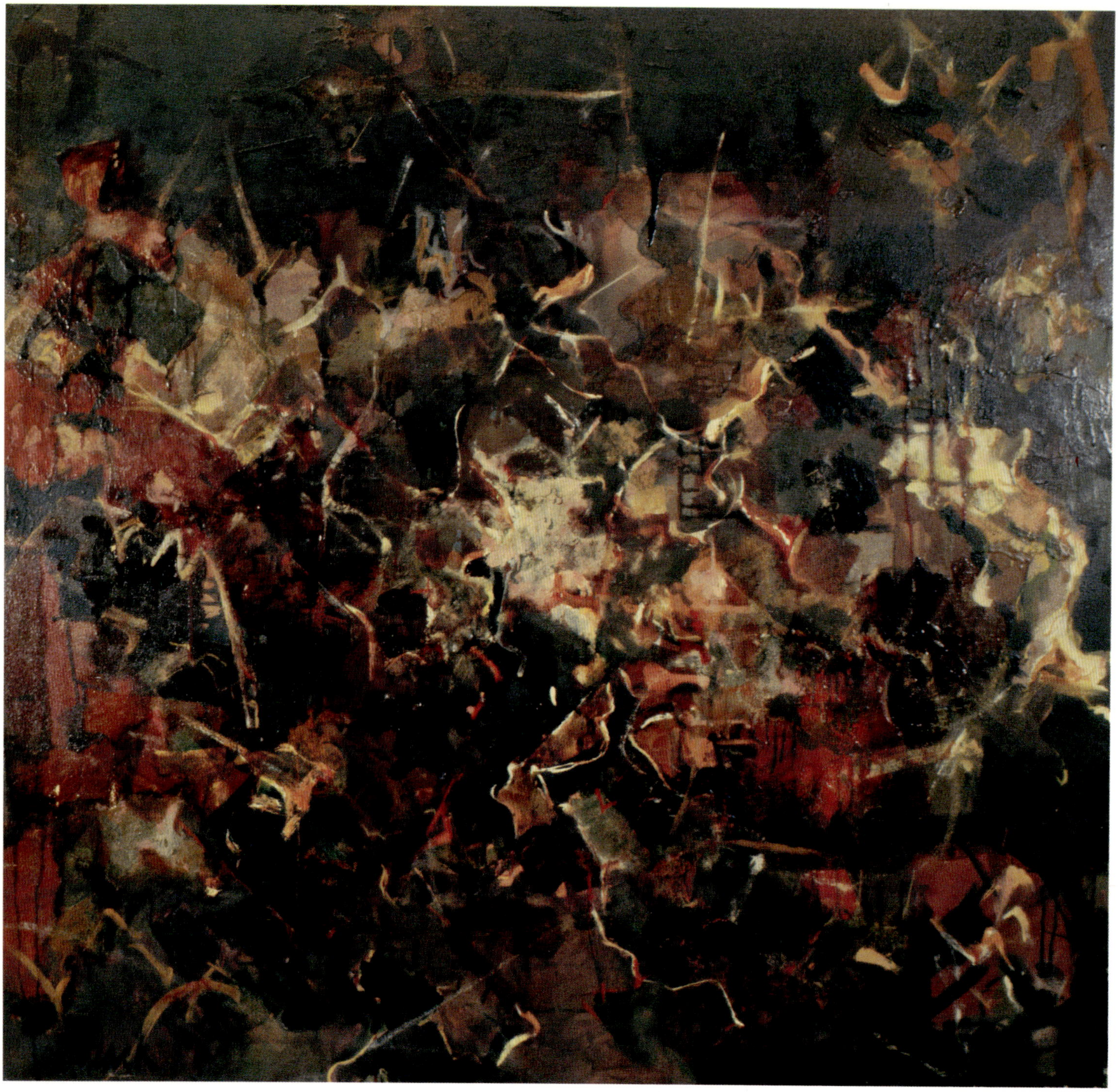

Galaxies: Dark Brown Abstract. 1951
Oil on canvas, 40 × 42″
Collection the artist

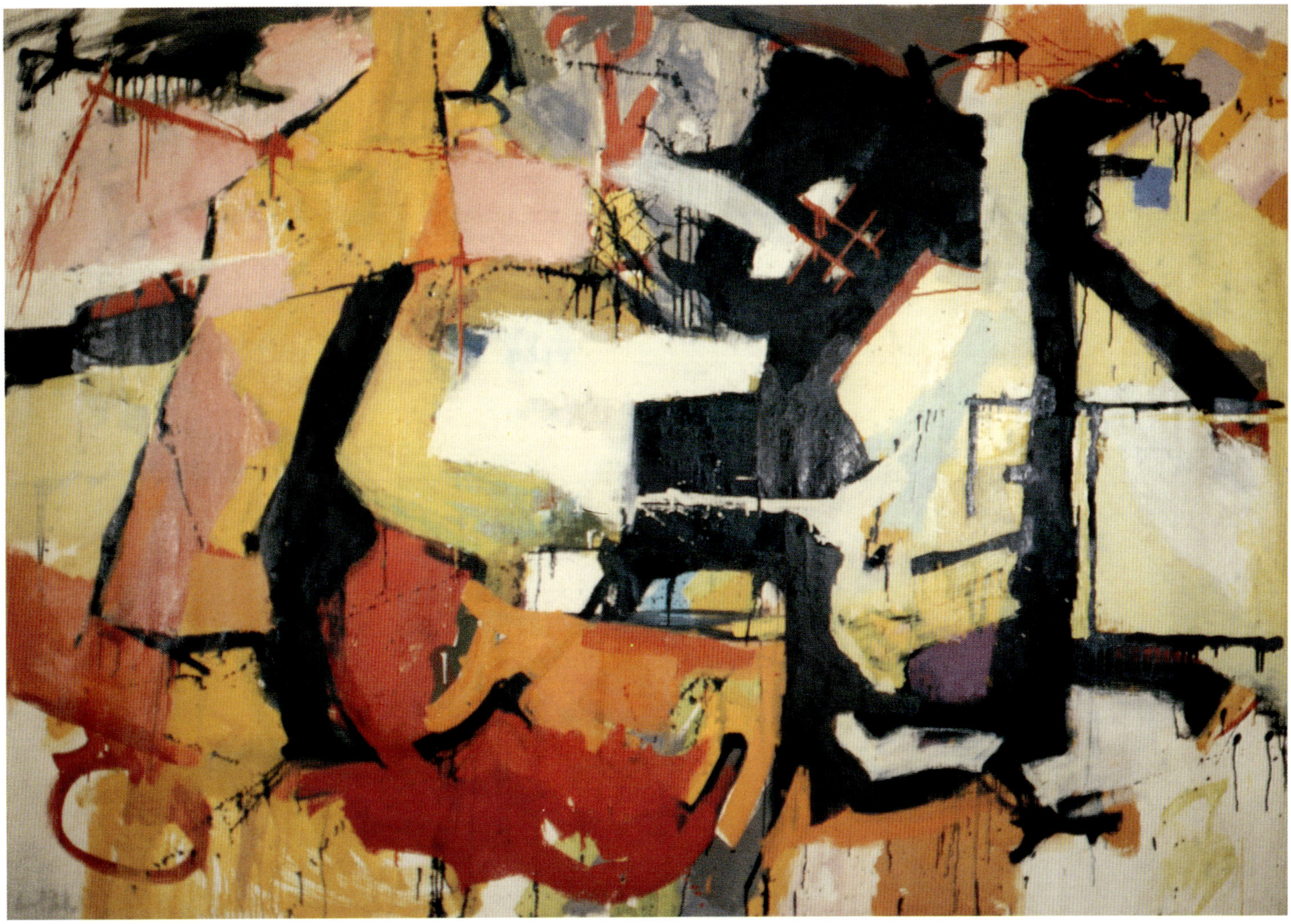

Abstract Force: Homage to Franz Kline. 1951–52
Oil on canvas, 49½ × 72″
Collection Norman and Sherry Bunin, New York

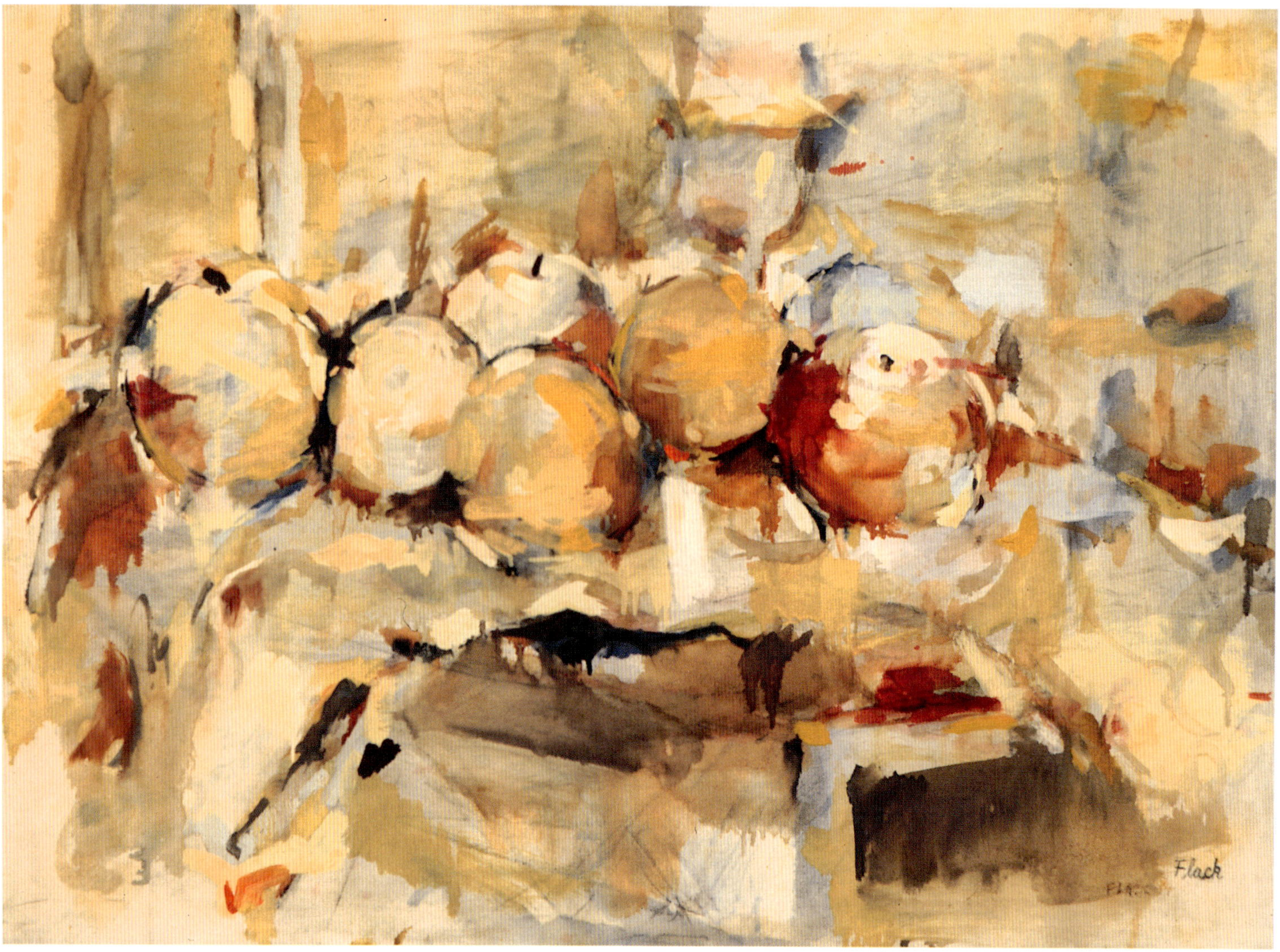

Still Life with
Apples and Orange. 1953
Oil on canvas, 26 × 36½″
Collection Beverly and
Hyman Dolinsky, New York

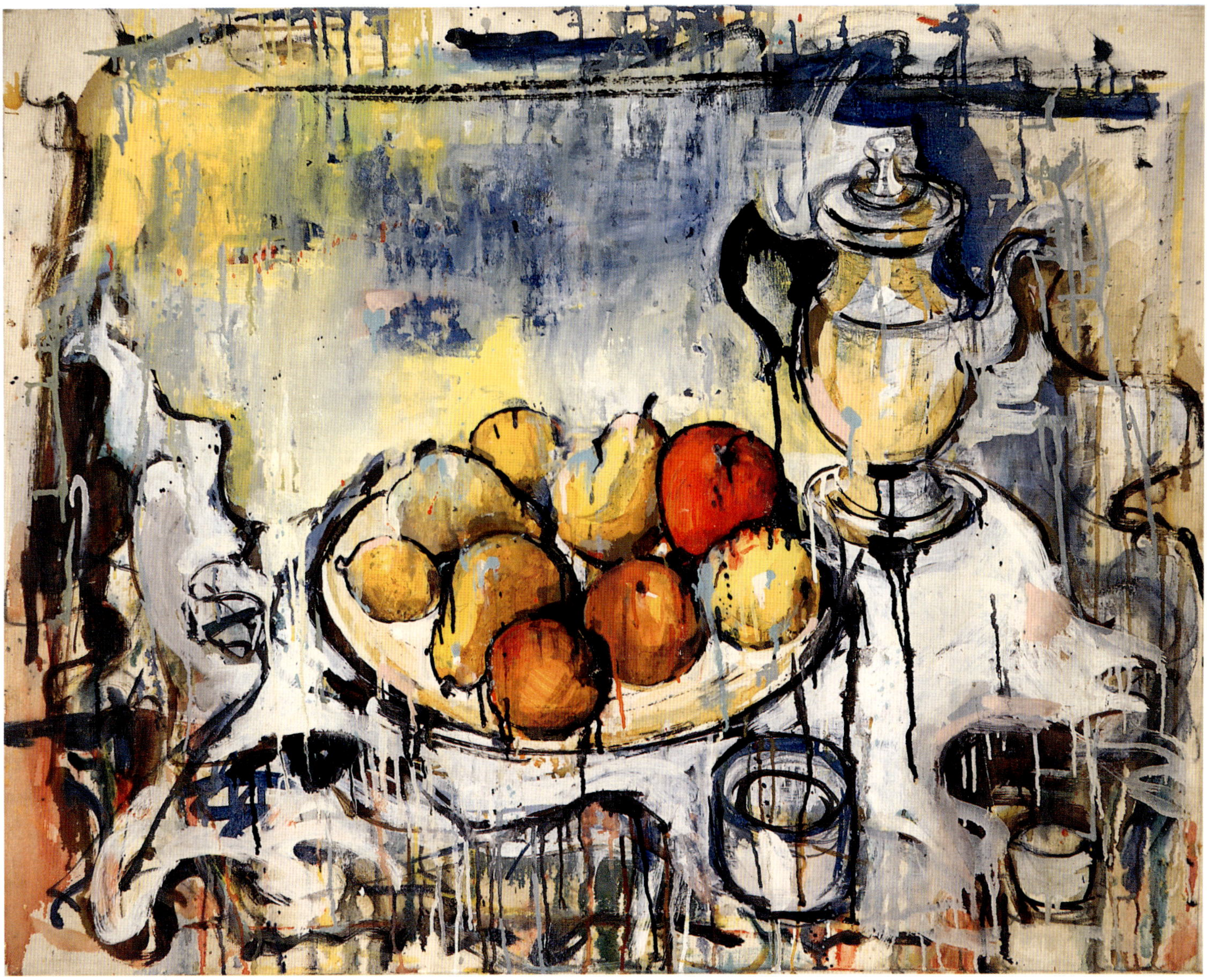

Still Life with Apples and Teapot. 1955
Oil on canvas, 28 × 36″
Private collection

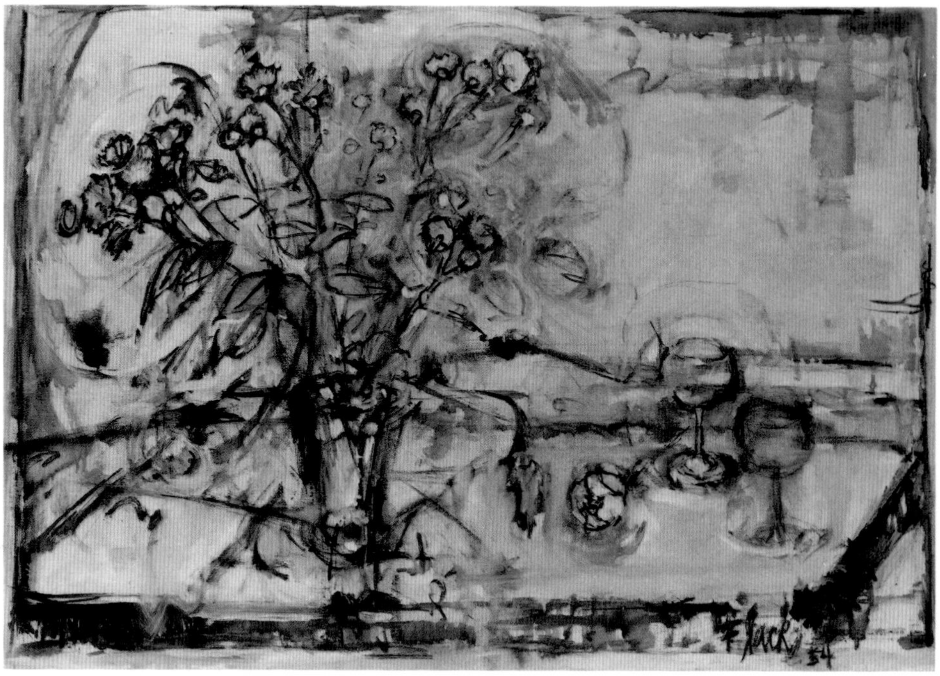

Black and White Still Life with Pompons, Chrysanthemums, and Wine Glass (For Franz Kline). 1954
Oil on canvas, 25×36″
Collection H. Robert Marcus

media photographs, for example, *Hitler,* 1963–64; *Teheran Conference,* 1964. Her *Kennedy Motorcade,* also of 1964, has been described as her first true Photorealist painting.[5] Painted in oil, these and subsequent works of the 1960s became more colorful, concluding in 1969–70 with the *Farb Family Portrait.* This work, of central importance in Flack's oeuvre, is the first of her paintings to be based on a Kodachrome transparency she herself had taken. Thereafter she increasingly worked from slides projected onto canvas. Focusing on color, light, and space, she eliminated line and transformed her blunt and painterly brush strokes into seamless and gleaming areas of color.

The discoveries made in painting the *Farb Family Portrait* led, in 1971–72, to a series of images of public and devotional monuments based on slides and postcards, beginning with the cathedrals of Siena and Amiens and the Pisa Camposanto and concluding with the *Macarena Esperanza* and *Dolores of Cordoba* group, inspired by the seventeenth-century Spanish sculptor Luisa Roldán. In this series Flack explored spiritual and feminist themes combining the female goddess and lamenting mother. These paintings of the early seventies, more than any other of her work, simulate photographic images and cross back and forth between photographic reproduction and painting. After 1973 she abandoned commercial slides and postcards and employed her own color transparencies. She set up a darkroom and printed her Cibachrome photographs, which she used as source material.

During the next five years (1973–77), her most prolific period of painting, Flack created two series of luminous still lifes based on compositions carefully set up in her studio: *Gray Border* and *Vanitas.* In these paintings, some of her most idiosyncratic and significant compositions, she began to airbrush acrylic paint, which she frequently combined with oils. In adopting the traditional still-life genre Flack gave it an innovative scale, a modern formal structure, and a rich iconography of personal symbolic meaning. Formally, the still lifes evolved from the multifocal, wide, and borderless compositions of 1973–74, such as *Solitaire* and *Chanel,* to the tightly knit and centrally focused paintings in the *Gray Border* series, which also are both visually and symbolically more complex. Flack's work reached a new level of intensity in the monumental

Vanitas series of 1976–77 (*World War II*, *Marilyn*, and *Wheel of Fortune*). In these very profuse and coloristically brilliant paintings, she created her most ambitious and modern versions of still life and pushed this ancient genre to new limits.

The years from 1978 to 1983 were ones of reflection and reassessment for Flack; during this time both the structure and the tone of her work changed. She returned to some of her earlier themes and motifs—fruit, artist's materials, skull (as in *Spaced Out Apple* and *Invocation*)—but the compositions became open and horizontal, the brush strokes more varied and painterly, and the tone calmer and more meditative. Concurrently Flack also did a series of private watercolors of landscapes and seascapes. These affected her larger paintings as is evident in *Baba* (1980–83), which is set in a monumental seascape. Also during this period Flack focused more on the human image in a series of iconic portraits and self-portraits (e.g., *Baba* and *We Are All Light and Energy*). The last paintings in this group, *Hannah* (1982) and *Isis* (1983), are personal interpretations of the eternal and the divine in the guise of female deities. *Isis* looks back to the *Macarena* images of 1971 and thematically anticipates Flack's goddess sculptures of the eighties and nineties.

Flack's sculpture, to which she has devoted herself almost exclusively since 1983, reflects her continued use of art historical precedents. Her sources are Graeco-Roman and Renaissance art and nineteenth-century sculptors such as Jean-Léon Gérôme and Alfred Gilbert. With her bronze goddesses such as *Islandia* and *American Athena*, Flack has attempted to do for the female nude what Giambologna did for the male, that is, to free the female body from its passive objectification and give it the vitality, energy, and independence associated in Western culture with the male.

Unlike other artists who have recently been identified with a revival of classical forms and more specifically the image of Venus,[6] Flack does not appropriate the fragmented and passive female body, nor is she interested in stereotypes of feminine beauty. Her *Islandia: Goddess of the Healing Waters* (1987), which clearly alludes to both the *Venus de Milo* (c. 120 B.C., Louvre) and the *Nike of Samothrace* (c. 200 B.C., Louvre), has become a modern goddess, empowered to action by an inner will. Muscular and athletic, she strides forward with assurance. In this and her other goddesses, Flack did not work from ancient fragments but rather from live, carefully posed female models, mostly dancers and athletes. Her goddesses confidently break through the mythic into the twentieth century. As symbolic reclamations of the female body, these figures are modern and personal interpretations of female power and divinity.

Audrey Flack's art consistently refuses to conform to conventional taste. Though her reputation is based on her Photorealist paintings, her work is neither cool nor detached—it is personal and self-revelatory. Historically conscious and emotionally charged, it is also passionate, involved, and unashamedly sentimental. Flack has turned away from easy success to face fresh challenges. Through much of her life she has been preoccupied with the marvelous, the miraculous, and the spiritual. *Breaking the Rules: Audrey Flack, A Retrospective 1950–1990* documents the artist's continuing ability to develop a structure, style, and technique to translate the marvelous into pictorial and sculptural form.

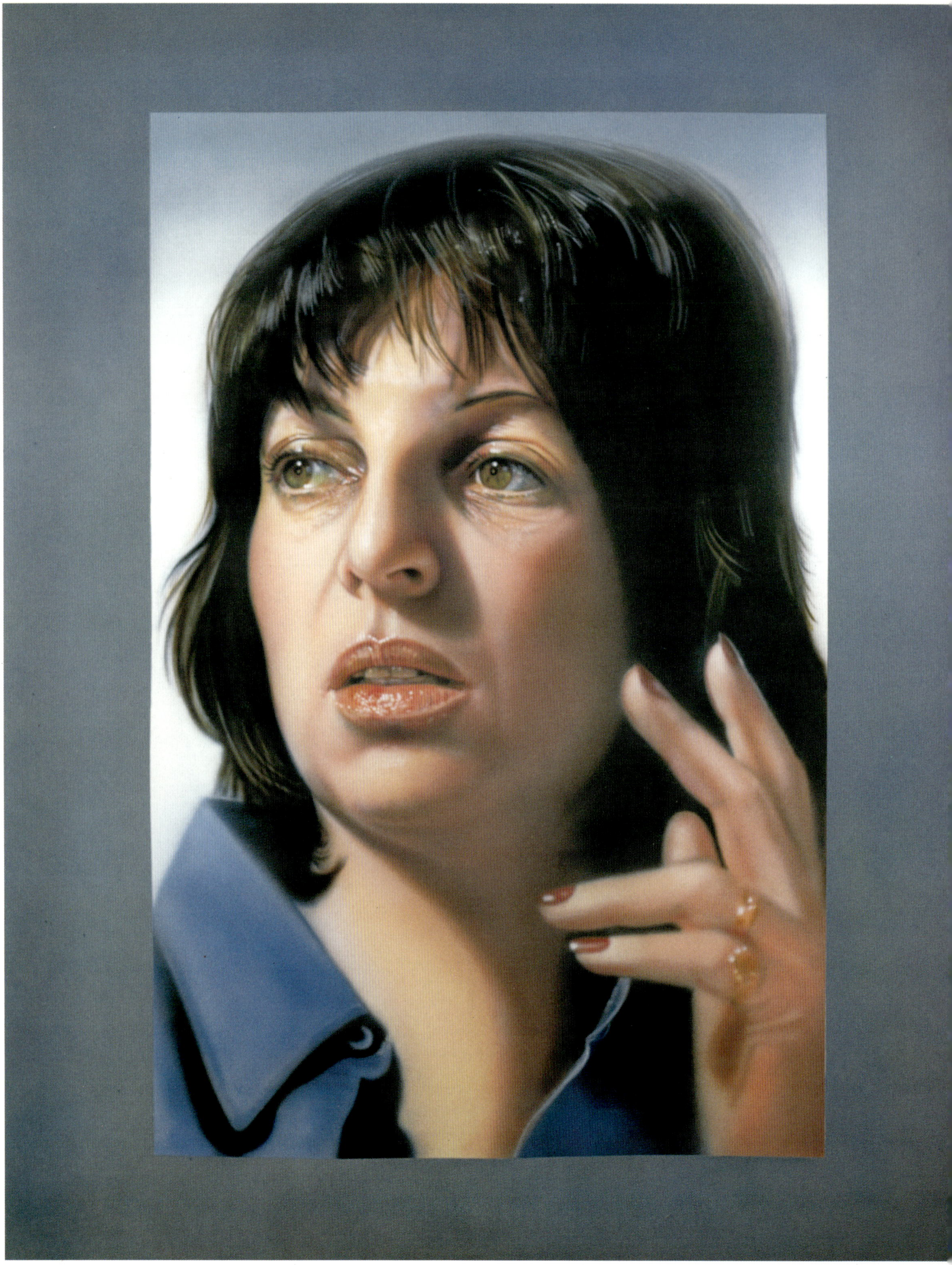

REFLECTIONS IN A MIRROR: THE SELF-PORTRAITS OF AUDREY FLACK: 1952–1982

Thalia Gouma-Peterson

"The self-portrait, the mirror of the self, becomes the mirror of the viewer as she sees herself, or at least aspects of her self, in the portrait."
—Audrey Flack, 1983[1]

The mirror image as an intensified reflection of and commentary upon reality has preoccupied Audrey Flack for years. In the 1970s she frequently dealt with this theme in her art, as in her two paintings of Marilyn Monroe, *Marilyn (Vanitas)* (p. 38) and *Marilyn: Golden Girl* (p. 94).[2] In both the ghostlike reflection of Monroe in the mirror belies the assurance and radiance of her public image. In *Golden Girl*, painted in 1978, one year after *Marilyn*, the mirror image is more intense and distorted. It also is threatened by a phallic, diagonally flying, lipstick and the red tip of a second lipstick within the mirror, weapons that ultimately destroyed the living goddess and effigy of American eroticism.

In these paintings the mirror reveals more about the realities of life than the original image does. That the image itself is based on a photograph, another kind of reflection, introduces a further complexity, as does the photograph of Flack and her brother between the two images of Monroe in *Marilyn*. Through this juxtaposition and in the emotional content the painting is a self-portrait, as Flack has acknowledged.[3] It is one of a number of works of the seventies in which she combines the still-life and self-portrait genres as a means of self investigation and commentary on issues central to her life.

These paintings also in several ways raise questions about the controlling and objectifying male gaze, introduced into feminist discourse by Laura Mulvey in 1975.[4] Mulvey's central thesis, the polarity of man as "bearer of the look" and of woman as its object in narrative cinema, was subsequently applied to images of women in other creative contexts, both visual and literary. In Flack's two paintings, the initial photograph of Monroe, taken by a man and a

Self-Portrait. 1974
Acrylic on canvas, 80 × 64″
Collection Marcus Kutter, Basel, Switzerland

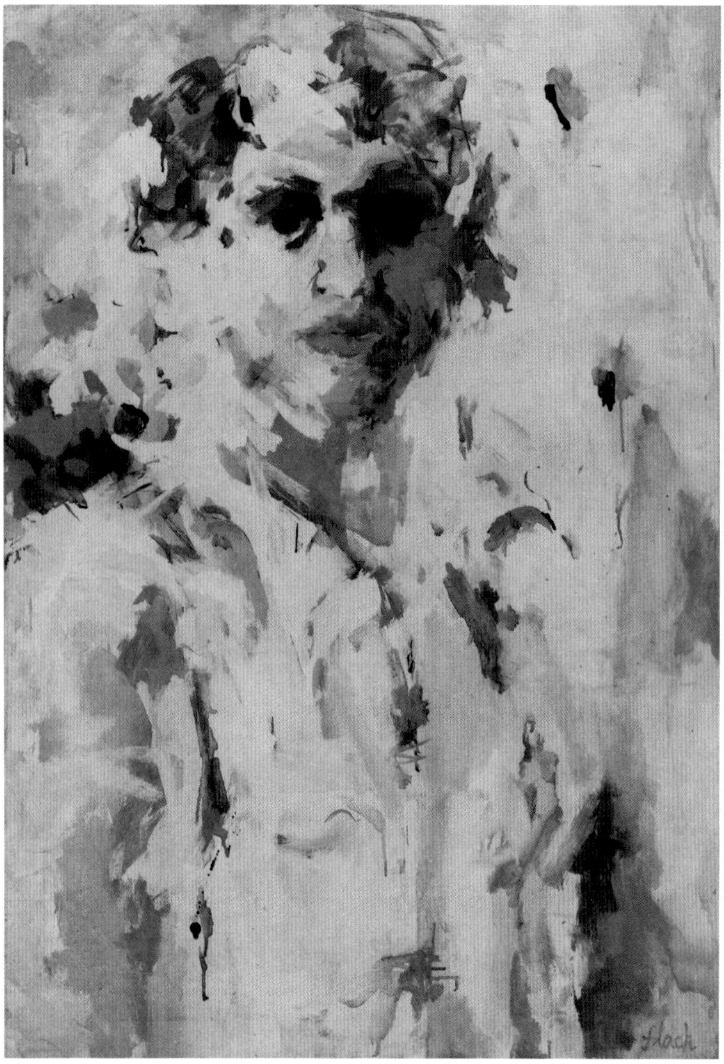

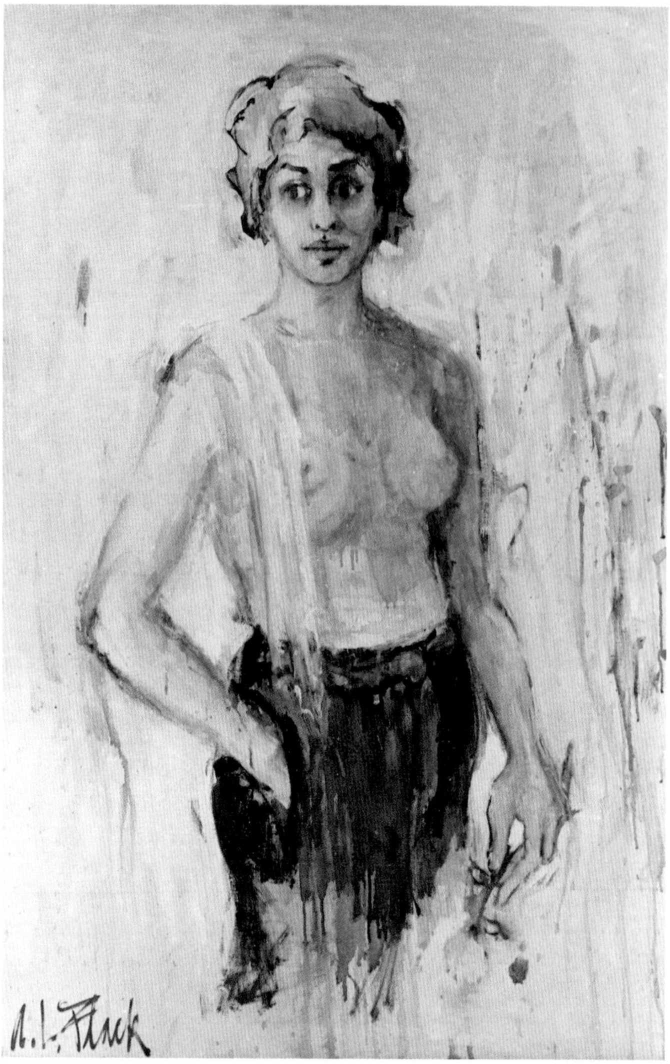

Abstract Expressionist Self-Portrait. 1952
Oil on canvas, 40 × 28″
Miami University
Art Museum, Oxford, Ohio

ABOVE, RIGHT:
Self-Portrait with Flower. 1953
Oil on canvas, 45½ × 29½″
Collection Beverly and
Hyman Dolinsky, New York

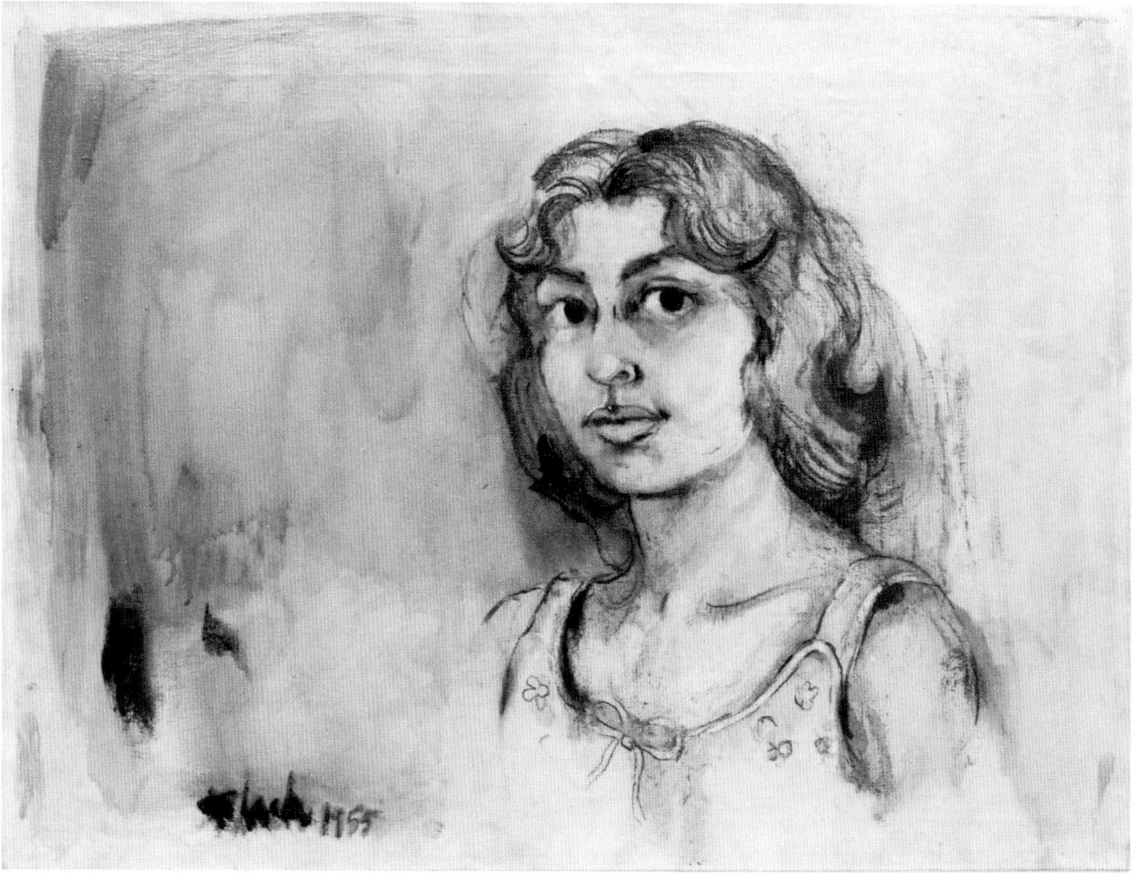

Self-Portrait in Gown with Bow. 1955
Oil on canvas, 18 × 24″
Miami University
Art Museum, Oxford, Ohio

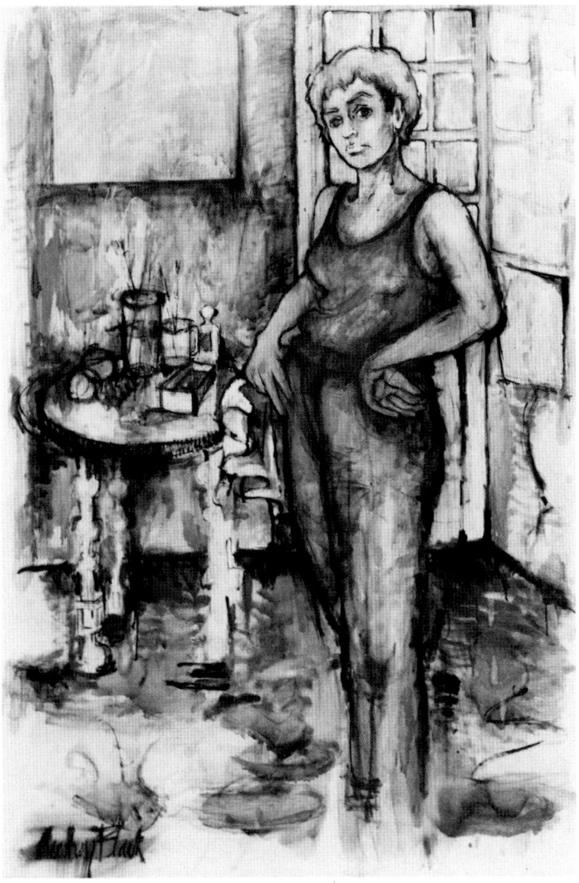

Self-Portrait in Tank Top. 1956–57
Oil on canvas, 70 × 48″
Miami University
Art Museum, Oxford, Ohio

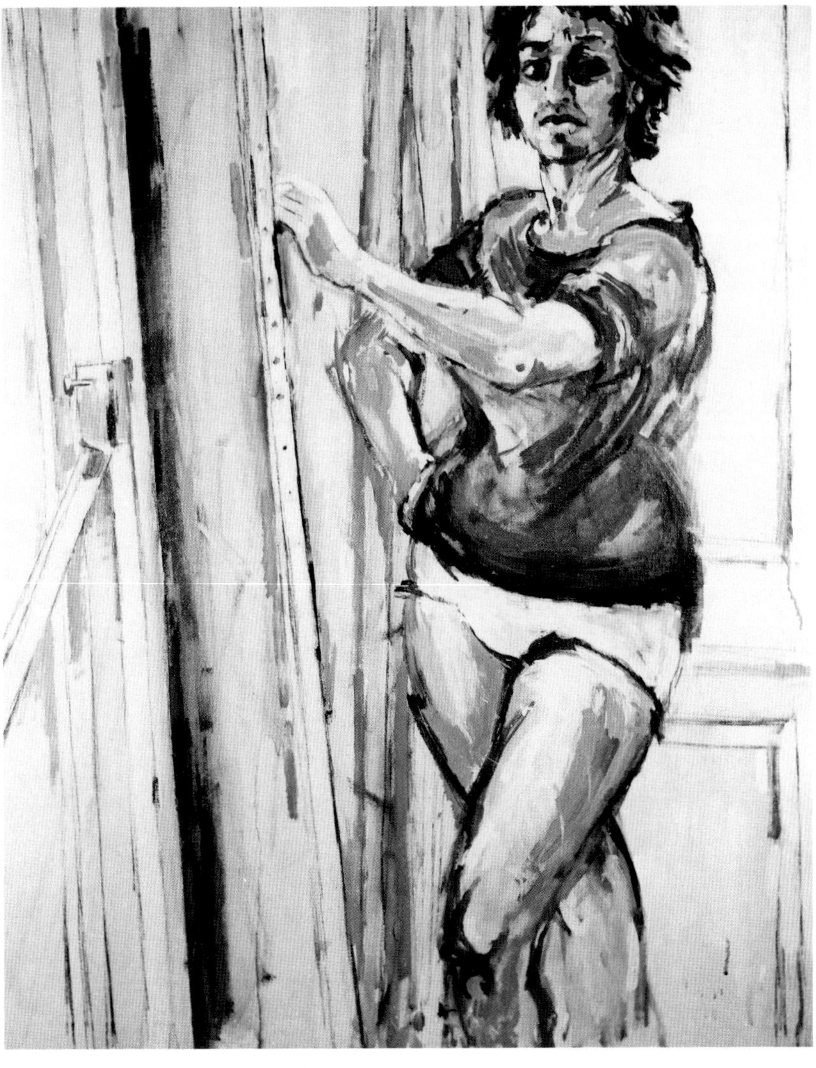

BELOW, LEFT:
Self-Portrait in Underpants. 1958
Oil on canvas, 52 × 48″
Miami University
Art Museum, Oxford, Ohio

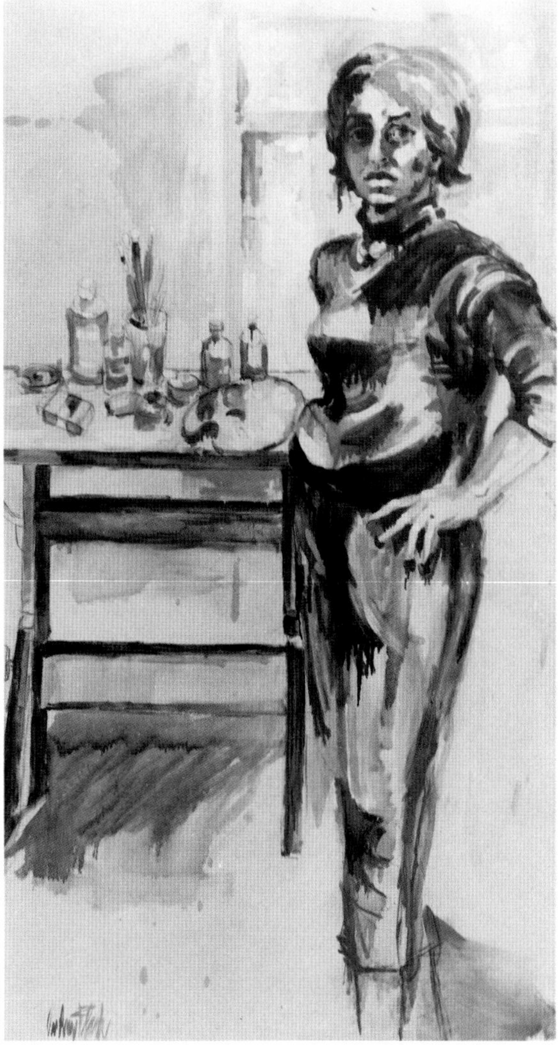

Self-Portrait with Drafting Table. 1958
Oil on canvas, 72 × 41″
Miami University
Art Museum, Oxford, Ohio

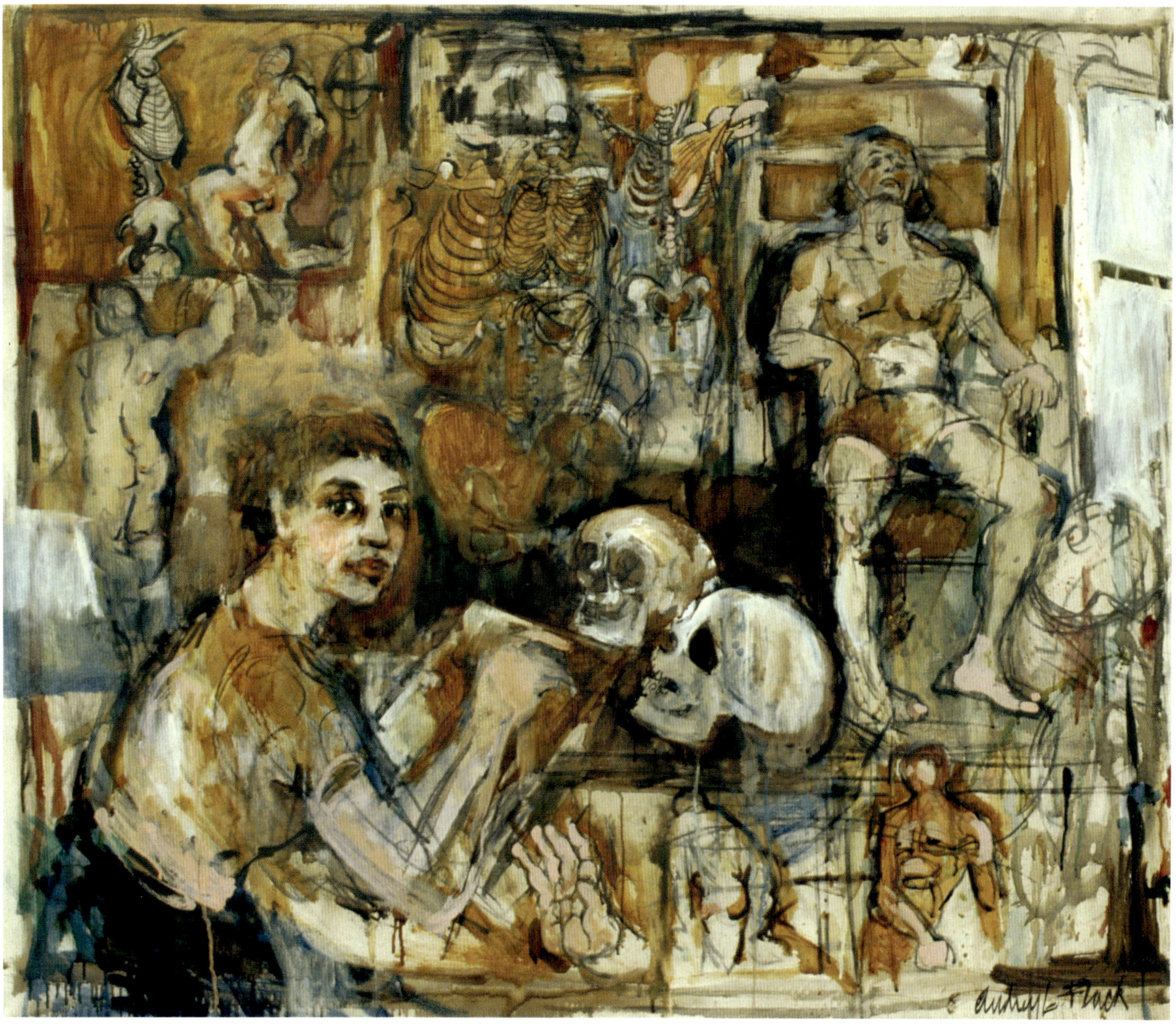

Anatomy Lesson. 1953
Oil on canvas, 42 × 50″
Miami University
Art Museum, Oxford, Ohio

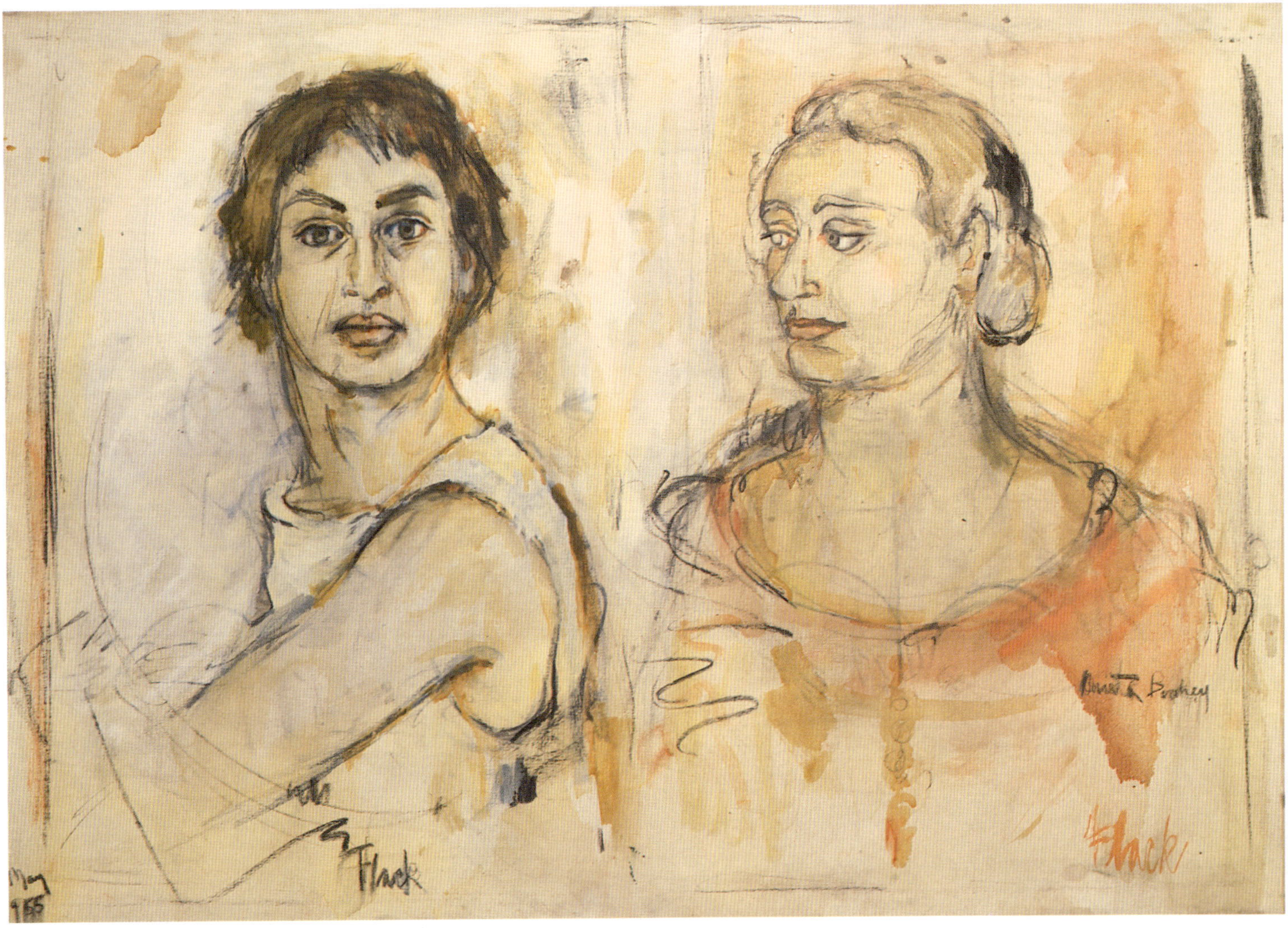

Self-Portrait with Anita. 1955
Oil on canvas, 25 × 36″
Collection Thalia Gouma-Peterson
and Carl A. Peterson,
Oberlin, Ohio

OVERLEAF, LEFT:
Self-Portrait Holding
Charcoal Stick. 1956
Oil on canvas, 40 × 28″
Miami University
Art Museum, Oxford, Ohio

OVERLEAF, RIGHT:
Self-Portrait (the Memory). 1958
Oil on canvas, 50 × 34″
Miami University
Art Museum, Oxford, Ohio

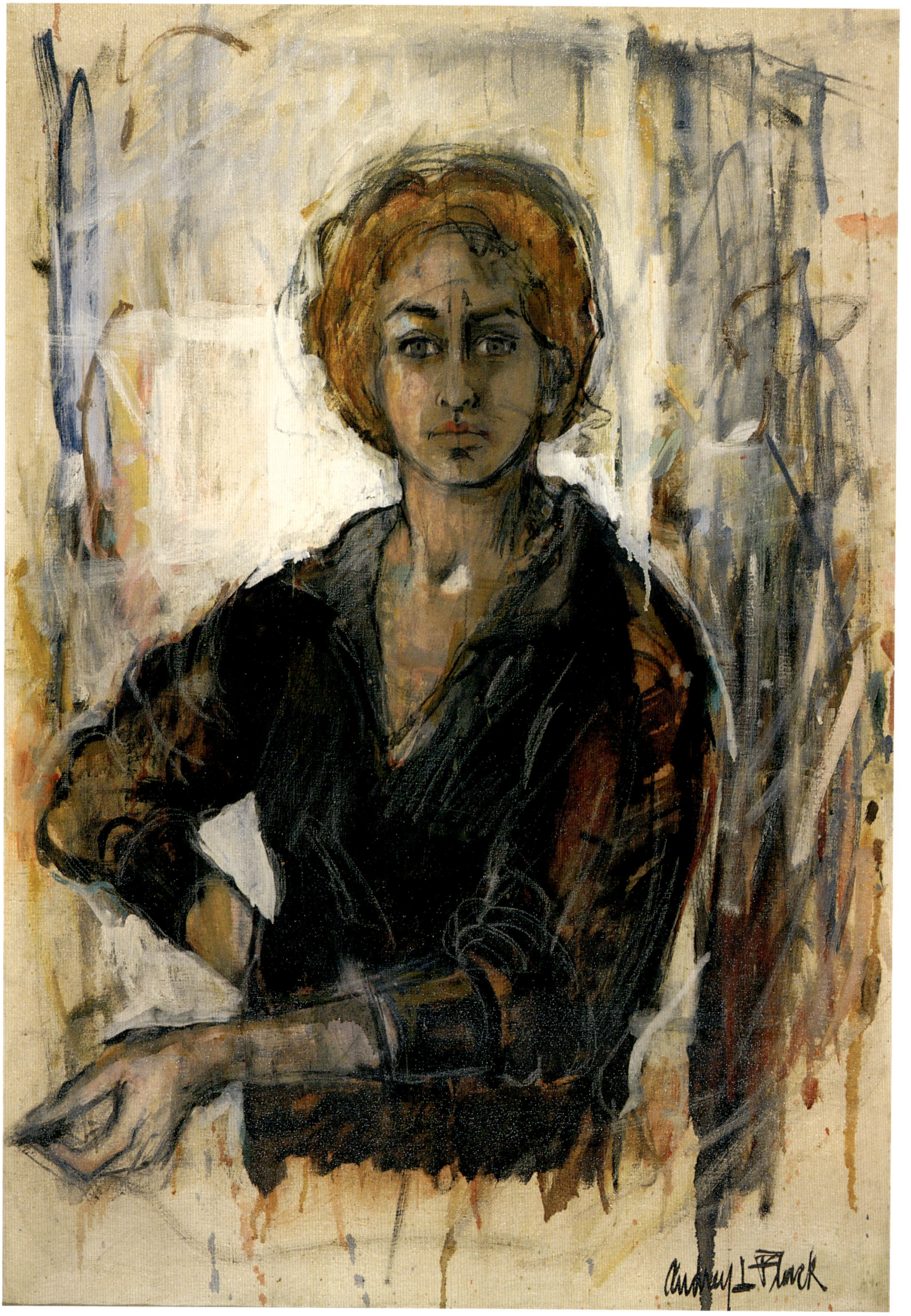
Audrey L Flack

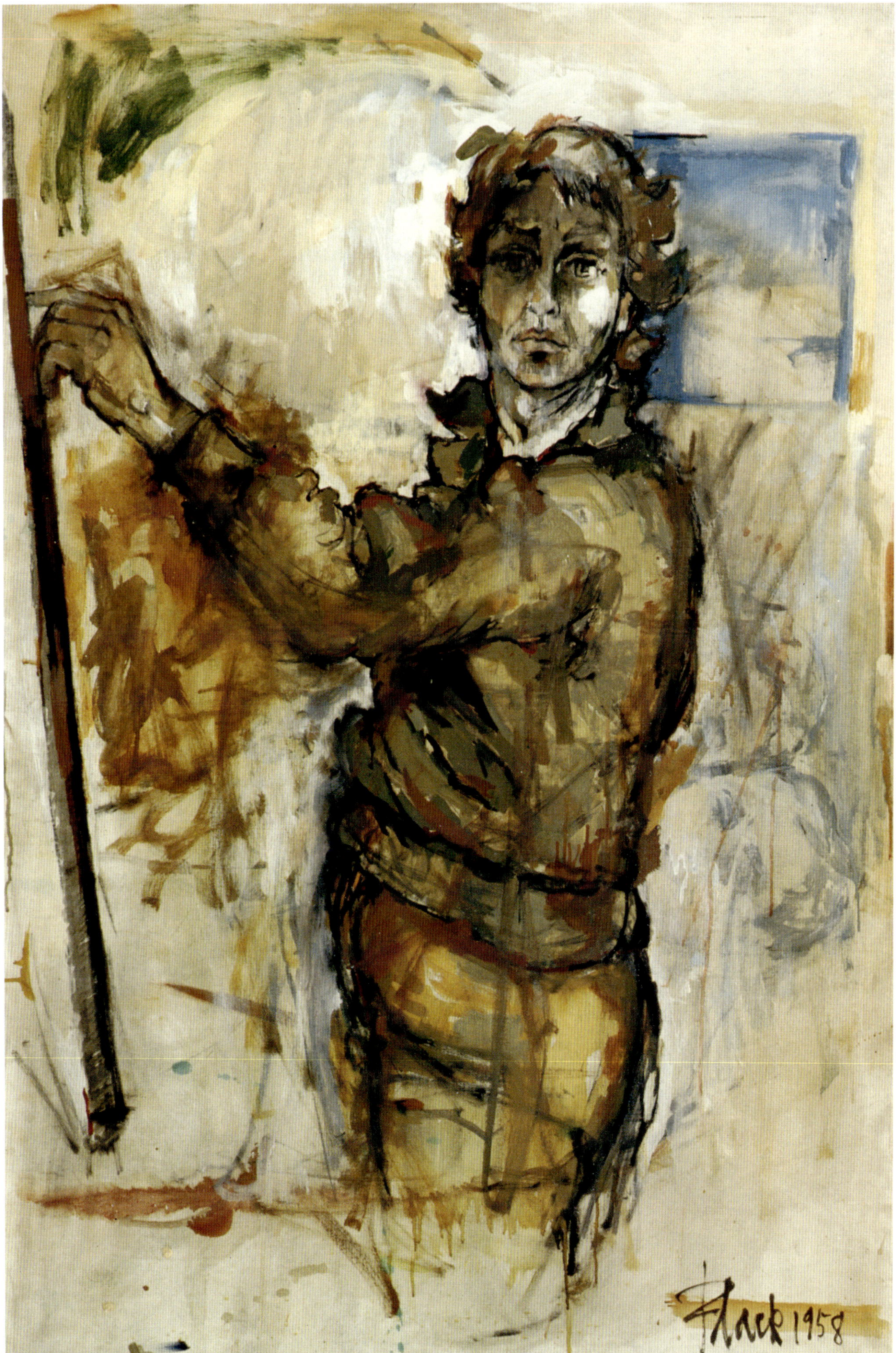
Flack 1958

pervasive sign in American popular culture, is put in quotation marks and re-contextualized. It is confronted by its reflection in the mirror and is surrounded by objects referring to a woman's life. The arrangement of these objects and the presence of the candle also suggest an altar. The celluloid illusion of Marilyn is reclaimed for women by a woman artist and given a new meaning. Significantly the text from Monroe's biography in the center of the composition concludes ". . . it gives a glimpse as the powder goes on and the mirror comes up of a future artist conceiving a grand scheme in the illumination of an instant—one could paint oneself into an instrument of one's will!"[5] These lines refer to Flack as much as they do to Monroe. It is Flack's dripping (or bleeding) brush, centrally placed in *Marilyn,* that allowed her to transform herself into an instrument of her own will, a creative artist.

These concerns first manifested themselves in a series of self-portraits painted in the 1950s, at a time when Flack was moving away from her large abstract compositions to smaller, more intimate figural paintings, primarily still lifes and portraits. The self-portraits move between two distinct referents: the creative artist who in Western culture is traditionally assumed to be masculine, and the young woman who is the "object of the male gaze" (Mulvey). Though painted in the fifties, before the rebirth of the feminist movement in the United States, it is clear in these paintings that Flack was conscious of the antithesis of traditional constructs of masculinity and femininity and was torn between the two. The self-portraits show the artist observing herself in the mirror and reflecting upon her identity and her relationship to others. These paintings span the years 1952 to 1960, from the completion of her Yale B.F.A. to the year when she learned that her first-born daughter, Melissa, was autistic. These crucial years of searching, questioning, doubting, and self-assertion were also years of self-definition. The portraits became means of investigation and reveal stages in this process. Through looking in the mirror and recording her observations Flack was able better to understand herself. These early self-portraits are essentially pieces of private meditation and were not exhibited.[6]

Flack's first step in this process of self-study was a painting she completed in 1952, at the age of twenty-one, *Abstract Expressionist Self-Portrait.* This work combines elements derived from Rembrandt's early self-portraits—the piercing eyes placed close together in the center of the face and the thick curly hair—with the broad, disengaged, and assertive brush strokes of abstract expressionism. Painted primarily in shades of ocher and white, this searching and powerful image belies the youth of the artist. It also shows her independence in the strong commitment to figuration at a time when the figure was unacceptable in official American art. The solid, immobile, and almost frontal image gazes intently and questioningly at herself and the viewer. The painting gives little information about the artist's gender and, as she frequently did in her early work, she signed with her last name only.

Flack reasserted her commitment to the figure a year later in *Anatomy Lesson,* a painting that is as much a statement of artistic intent as it is a self-portrait. She represented herself drawing, surrounded by images of skeletons, plaster casts, and a live model. It is not entirely clear whether some of these are sketches pinned on a wall or actual objects surrounding the artist. This ambiguity gives the composition the character of a mental construct: the images appear to be in the artist's mind as she proclaims her intent to abide by the figure as a compositional subject.

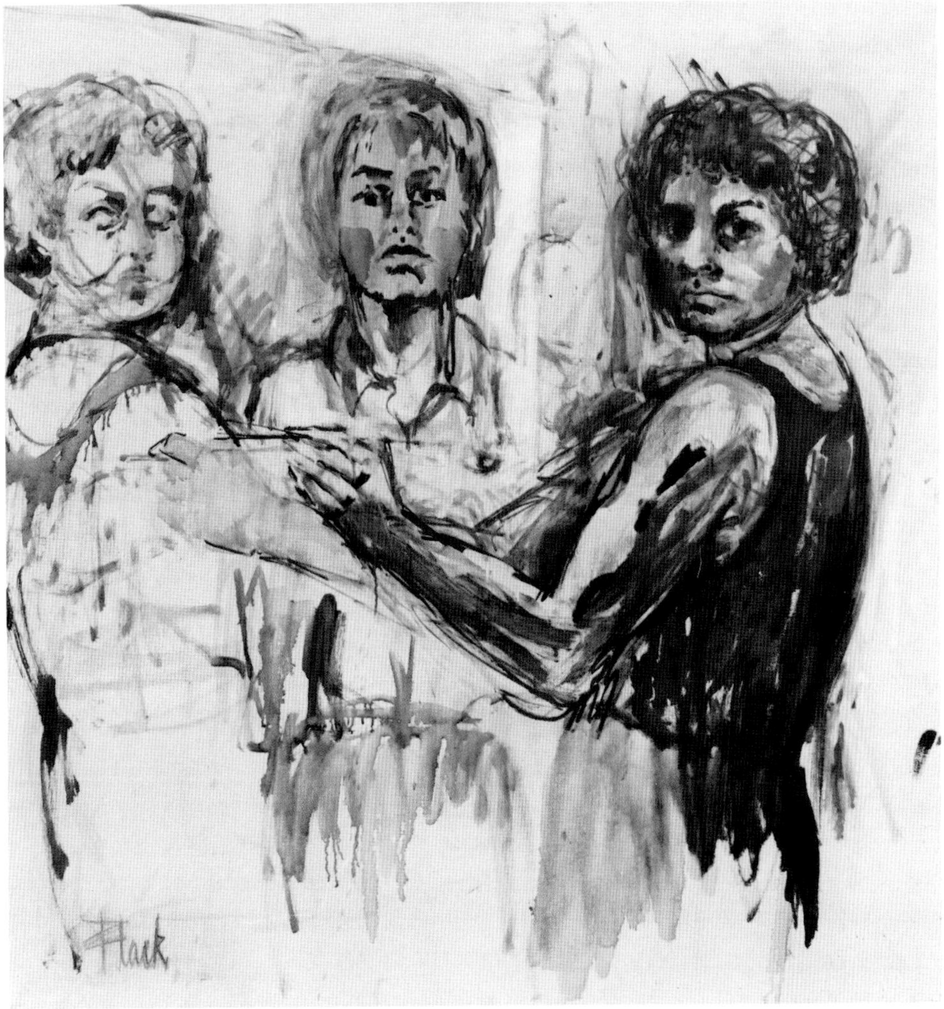

Triple Self-Portrait. 1958
Oil on canvas, 42 × 40″
Miami University
Art Museum, Oxford, Ohio

At the time, Flack was studying life drawing with Robert Beverly Hale at the Art Students League in New York. The images she combined in *Anatomy Lesson* were based on drawings done in that class. The central theme of the painting, whose focal point is two skulls, is the relation between art, life, and death, a theme she would return to in the late seventies and early eighties, in *Wheel of Fortune* and *Invocation.* The empty eye sockets of the skulls confront the artist as she looks at her reflection in the mirror and at the viewer. The sense of seriousness and self-assurance expressed in this youthful painting is emphasized by her full signature at the bottom right, "Audrey L. Flack."

Flack's study at the Art Students League resulted in a firmer and more solid figure style and in a more traditional, romantic, and idealized interpretation of the self. This is evident in both her 1953 *Self-Portrait with Flower* and her 1955 *Self-Portrait in Gown with Bow.* The more traditional character of these portraits is expressed in their iconography and style. *Self-Portrait with Flower,* the only self-portrait in which Flack represents herself nude to the waist, could be seen as a modern version of the Venus type. But, in fact, the painting questions the traditional passive interpretation of the female nude, as the frontally standing artist/model resolutely and confidently gazes at the viewer. The nudity of her torso contrasts with her black slacks, as does the rose held in her left hand with her right firmly placed in her pocket. This painting of contradictions the artist signed "A. L. Flack," in a way that would not reveal her gender and would, she hoped, ensure fair judgment. (A frequent comment at the time was, "That's a strong painting. It does not look like it was done by a woman.") The same is true of *Self-Portrait in Gown with Bow,* which she signed with only her last name. In this work the depth and steadfastness of

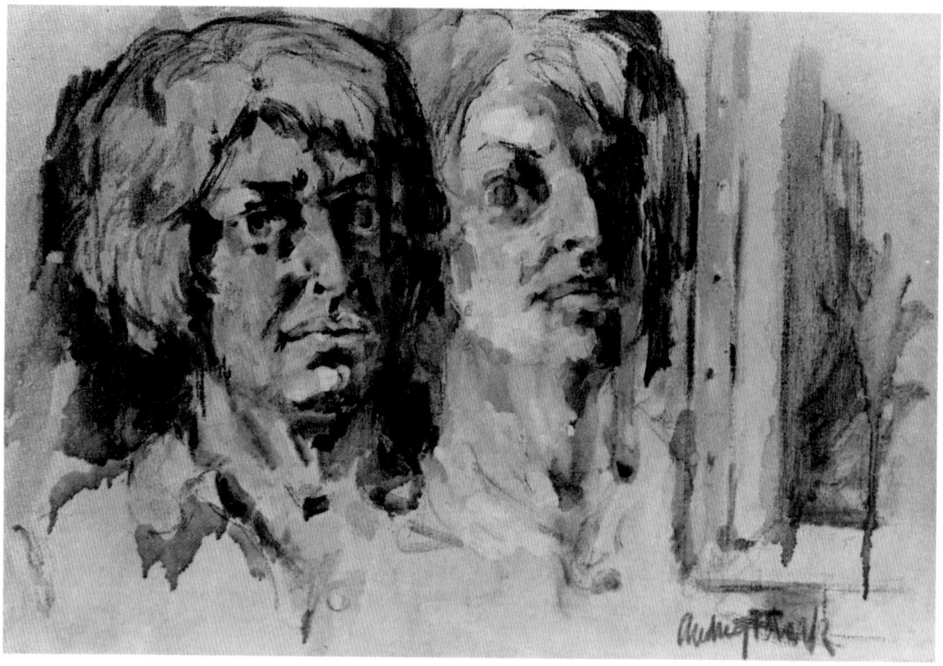

Double Self-Portrait. 1958
Oil on canvas, 15×22″
Miami University
Art Museum, Oxford, Ohio

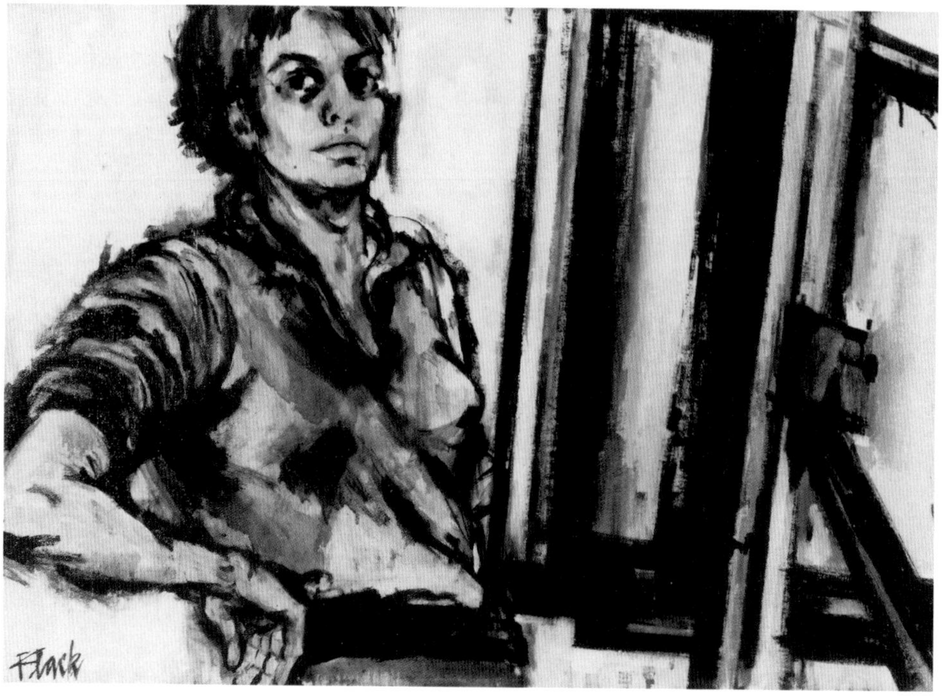

Self-Portrait at Easel:
For Franz Kline. 1958
Oil on canvas, 28×40″
Miami University
Art Museum, Oxford, Ohio

the gaze contrasts with the intimacy and pastel tonality of the paint. In both portraits Flack was dealing with her sexuality, which she had deliberately ignored in the two earlier portraits. This introduced a new complexity and, especially in *Self-Portrait with Flower,* raised the issue of woman's control over her body.

In 1955 Flack also painted *Self-Portrait with Anita,* the only early self-portrait to include a second figure. This very self-confident work, bristling with energy, includes Anita Bookey, a childhood friend whom Flack had admired and whose wedding portrait she had just completed. The lively definition of the figures, the richness of color, and the light and warm tonality express an active and positive view of the self. Also the varied levels of observation make this one of Flack's most complex early self-portraits: Anita observes Flack, as she observes herself in the mirror, and Flack looks at the viewer who is observing her and Anita. The portrait is full of youthful optimism and satisfaction. The impression that Flack, who had until then admired Anita, was in turn admired by her is not accidental. The painting is to a certain extent an act of appropriation as Flack's double signature, once on her own image and once on Anita, suggests. She represented herself at a moment of relative freedom, a young artist in control of her life.

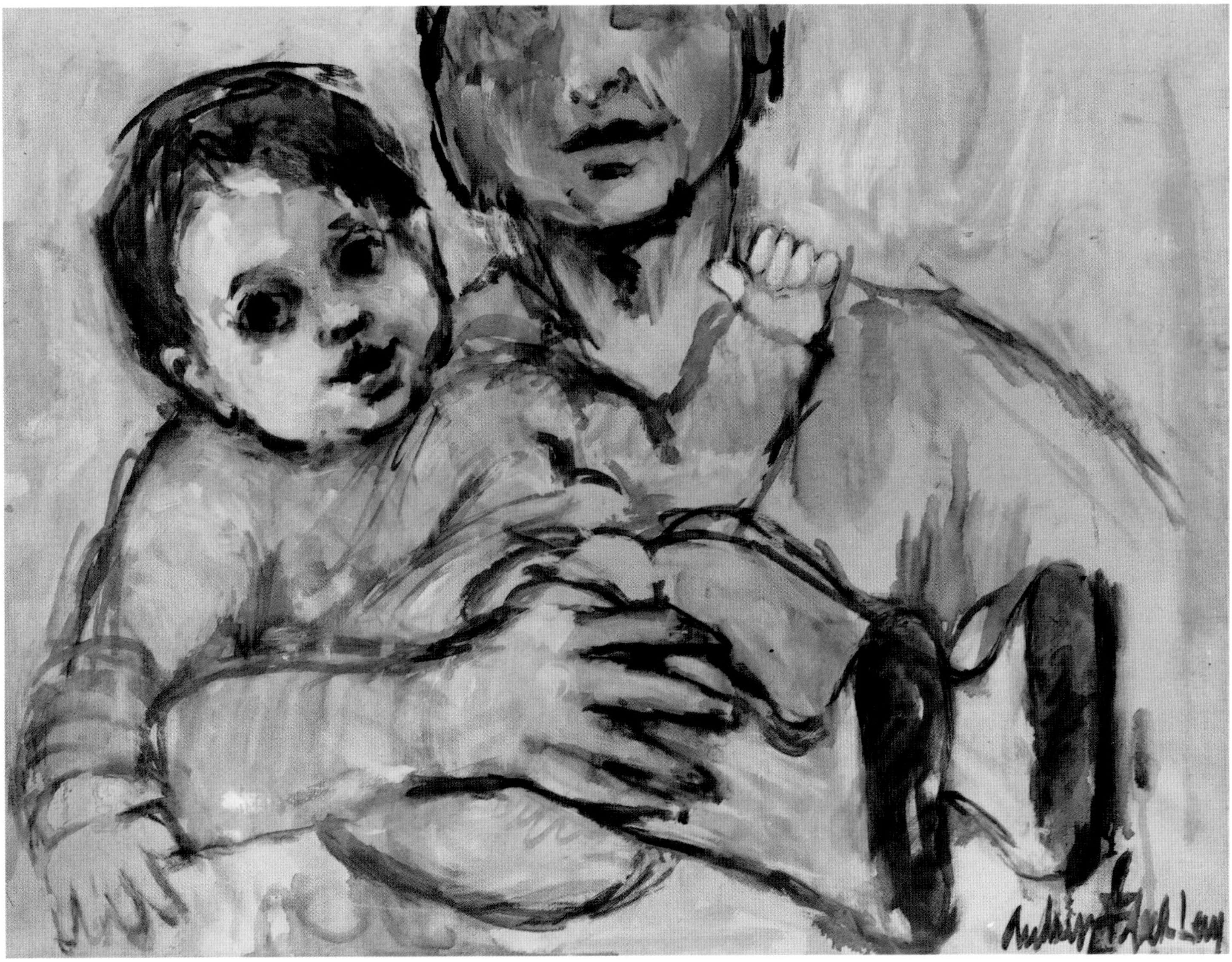

Melissa and Me. 1959
Oil on canvas, 19×26″
Miami University
Art Museum, Oxford, Ohio

The theme of the artist observing and recording herself painting her own image, suggested in *Anatomy Lesson* and clearly stated in *Self-Portrait with Anita,* was to preoccupy Flack from 1955 to 1959. Though the theme remained constant, the iconography, style, and mood varied significantly. From the restrained, quiet, well-behaved, and contemplative *Self-Portrait Holding Charcoal Stick* of 1956, Flack moved to the agitated, sorrowful, emotional, and dramatic *Self-Portrait (the Memory),* painted in 1958, after her father's death. That same year she painted the rebellious and unsentimental *Self-Portrait in Underpants,* the largest and most intense and explosive of these early self-portraits.

Both of these self-portraits reveal Flack's wish to assert herself as woman and artist, a wish intensified by current events in her life. The months from September 1957 to March 1958 had been crucial because, shortly after her father's death, Flack had entered an unhappy marriage. *Self-Portrait in*

Underpants expresses her refusal to give in. The irreverence of the title fits the mood of the painting. The dynamic composition of the active human figure framed by the strong verticals of easel and door bristles with energy and concentration. Clearly Flack had reached a new level of artistic self-definition. She showed herself to be in tune with the expressive emotion-laden art of the late fifties and, in the bold and dominant presence of the figure, to have a sense of the authority of her own experience. In this portrait she was intentionally not conforming to either social or artistic expectations and therefore was being intentionally subversive.

This is equally true of *Self-Portrait at Easel: For Franz Kline,* also dating from 1958. Here the energy is more controlled and the mood quieter, but more tense. The primary use of black and gray, the abrupt cropping of figure and easel, and the tension of body and face express force and conviction. Most significantly, as the title indicates, the painting is also an act of appropriation. The wide and dominant easel on which Flack paints her portrait looks like an abstraction by Franz Kline, whose work she admired. This homage, however, contains a subversive component: on the easel of contemporary American abstraction, a macho-style par excellence, she represents herself, denying the authority both of the style and of its great masters. Her belligerent stance and expression suggest that she was involved in a fierce struggle with abstraction —the authoritative language of the male art world—which she still admired but to which she was determined not to succumb.

The 1958 self-portraits challenge authority and proclaim the artist's refusal to accept "the perfect image of herself" historically imposed upon the creative woman.[7] This is intensified by the fact that in these paintings Flack emphasized her body and stressed her femaleness; that is, she combined her femaleness and sexual identity with her autonomy and authority as an artist. In *Self-Portrait at Easel: For Franz Kline* the viewer is very conscious of the tension introduced by the contrast between her full breasts and her short cropped hair and aggressive stance. The fierceness of the struggle against culturally imposed images of femininity evident in the 1958 paintings brings to mind the poem by Mary Elizabeth Coleridge and its vision of "a woman, wild with more than womanly despair" as she stood "in front of [her] glass one day."[8] The element of entrapment and despair is suggested by the closely cropped and tightly controlled compositions of the works. But, at the same time, the artist is painting herself into an instrument of her own will by representing both her physicality and her creativity.

The despair, only hinted at in the earlier 1958 portraits, became clearly expressed in *Triple Self-Portrait* and *Double Self-Portrait,* both painted later in 1958. These are among her most introspective and psychologically complex paintings. In *Triple Self-Portrait* the artist looks at herself painting a ghostly mirror image, while with a second hand she paints another image, a bust that looks beyond the viewer. This triple Janus portrait looking at her reflections in the mirror is deeply disturbing. The multiplicity and fragmentation of the images, their varied articulation, and the relentless, almost hypnotic brush strokes convey a profound turmoil and conflict. The viewer is both amazed and disturbed by the artist's capacity to speak with a triple voice while examining her experience and feelings.

Self-Portrait: Dark Face. 1960
Oil on canvas, 18 × 14″
Miami University
Art Museum, Oxford, Ohio

Double Self-Portrait goes one step further. Flack eliminated herself as an active participant and retained only two spectral reflections of her head—one with intensely furrowed brow ready to break down, the other distant and

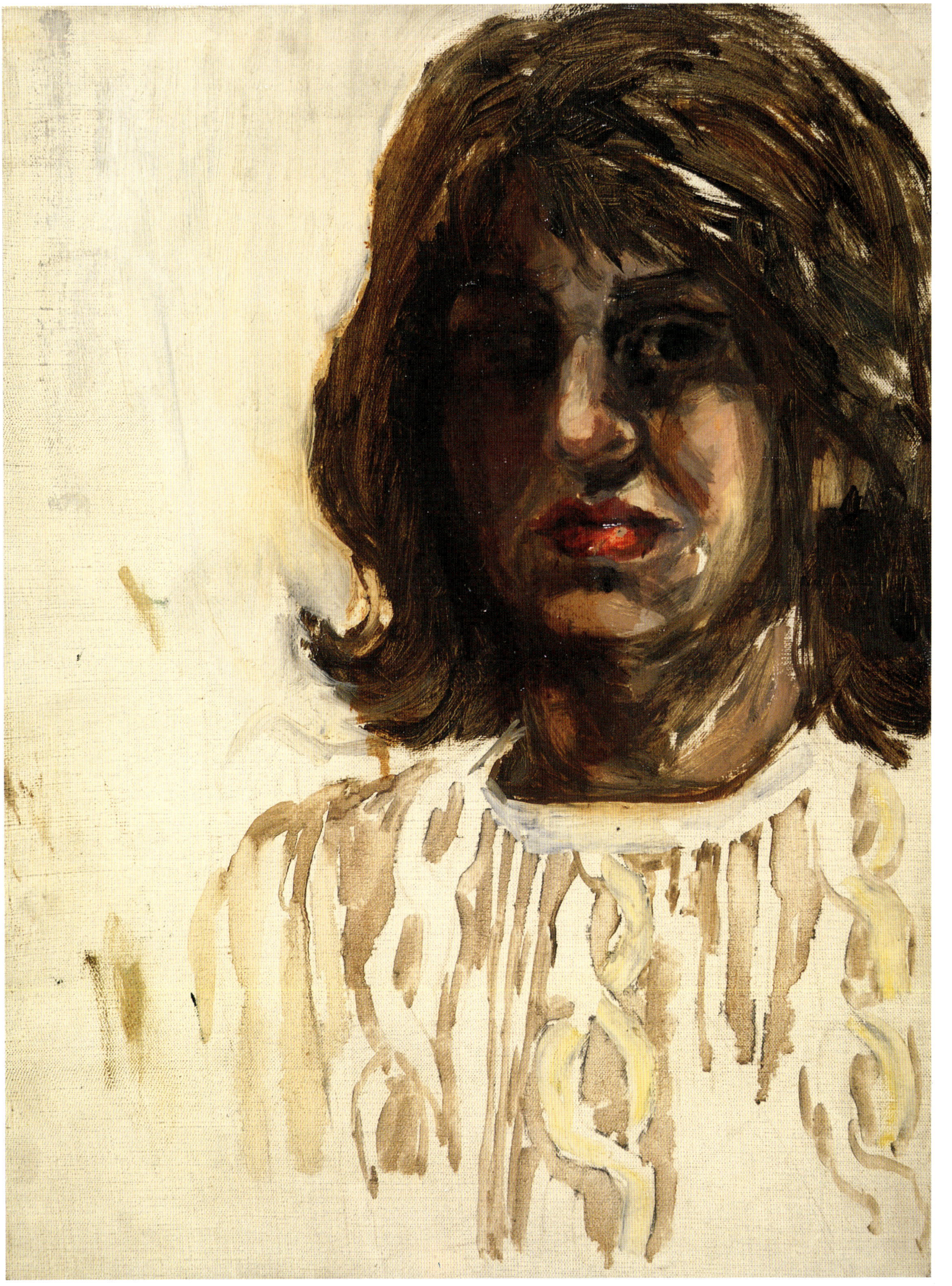

terrified. With this portrait Flack had gone as far as possible in analyzing and commenting upon her reflections in the mirror. "The vision of a woman wild" became too painful. In her next self-portrait, titled *Melissa and Me* and painted some months after her daughter's birth in 1959, she almost obliterated herself. Flack was no longer looking at herself in the mirror. Instead she looked at her "strangely beautiful child that cried a lot and never slept." Though she sensed there was something wrong with Melissa, this did not diminish her love for and attachment to the child. This love brought some hope into Flack's life. Both love and hope are expressed in this small painting, so full of feeling and tenderness in its combination of pinks and light blues, in spite of the tragic mask of the mother in the background. This was the only painting Flack signed "Audrey Flack Levy," adding the name of the child's father, to whom she was then married.

The final stage in this personal drama was recorded in *Self-Portrait: Dark Face,* of 1960. Flack had just learned that Melissa was autistic, and as the artist looked in the mirror she saw nothing but darkness and despair. This very small painting is Flack's most static, inactive, and withdrawn self-portrait. Her eyes, which had been the focal point in all her self-portraits, are here masked in shadow. She did not sign the painting. "She had no voice to speak her dread" (Mary Elizabeth Coleridge). The four self-portraits of 1959–60 are autobiographical fragments that record the making of the maternal feminine. The resolute and independent young artist of 1955 (*Self-Portrait with Anita*) had become the grieving mother, a characteristically female role in Western culture and the antithesis of the masculine creative artist.

In the self-portraits of the 1950s Audrey Flack claimed the right and capacity to speak in her own voice, an equivalent of what literary critics have identified as the narrative "I."[9] She did not paint another self-portrait for fourteen years. She could not bear to look into the mirror. Instead, during the 1960s, she turned to family members, Mexican workers, public personages, and world events as recorded in newspapers as subjects.[10] She also began, in 1962, to use the photograph as the initial step for her painting. During this period of deep personal unhappiness she looked at others to find aspects of herself and evidence for the meaning of life. The majority of these others were women: her daughters, aunt, and grandmother; actresses; Truman's teachers; black women grieving over Kennedy's assassination; Mexican orange sellers, beggars, potters, and weavers; and marching nuns (pp. 54–59). This assembly of images of women, painted from 1962 to 1968, is strikingly diverse and unsentimental—a collection of fragments of women's lives that refuse to lapse into pleasurable passivity.

In the early 1970s, a period of new stability and happiness in her life, Flack painted a series of monuments and icons of public devotion, which culminated in her 1971 *Macarena Esperanza* and *Dolores of Cordoba* series (pp. 63–65), archetypal images of the grieving mother and extensions of Flack's own state of being. Inspired by works of the seventeenth-century Spanish sculptor Luisa Roldán, these images hold a pivotal position in Flack's oeuvre. Representing effigies/goddesses created by a woman, they are means for Flack to bring together the opposing referents of creative artist and grieving mother. These paintings of sculptures that are still worshiped today are the first of the goddess images that were to surface intermittently in Flack's paintings of the late seventies and eighties and, with renewed concentration and fervor, in her sculptures of the eighties and nineties.[11]

The *Macarena* and *Dolores* paintings were followed by a series of still lifes that became the major focus of Flack's art during the seventies and for which she is best known.[12] During this decade she also evolved the visually accurate style of photographic exactitude characteristic of Photorealism. After 1972 the still lifes began to include objects she owned and used. As a result, the paintings acquired an increasingly personal significance and became extensions of herself, as for example *Jolie Madame, Chanel,* and *Solitaire* (pp. 70–71). *Solitaire,* of 1974, includes a hand that could be the artist's own, placing the card on the table, surrounded by self-referential objects. It creates a solitary mood of introspection and suggests that after years of evasion Flack had started again to look inward.

In *Self-Portrait* (p. 18), painted the same year, Flack did not look into the mirror. This was the first self-portrait Flack had painted since 1960 and the first to be based on a slide or photograph. And, unlike her portraits of the fifties, it was a public piece. Through the gesture of speech and the open mouth the artist is addressing us—asking us to look at her and listen to what she has to say as a public person. On one level the painting expresses a new self-confidence—the artist consciously addressing her audience through the artifact—while on another it suggests a shielding of the inner self from scrutiny. Flack is not letting the viewer into her heart and mind, and this psychological distancing prevents us from identifying with her, unlike the self-portraits of the fifties. The effect of remoteness is intensified by the large size of the painting and its precise technique, which creates the effect of a poster or billboard.

The changes in Flack's approach to self-portraiture that occurred between 1960 and 1974 were the result of both a different intent and a different method. The 1974 portrait was based on a Kodachrome transparency of a subject composed by the artist but photographed by someone else. The double distancing introduced by this process—the person taking the photograph and the artist looking at herself in the projected slide—removed the spontaneity and immediacy of the mirror reflection. Idealized and to a certain degree depersonalized, the portrait asks to be observed from a distance. Through this self-distancing Flack gained a new control over the image and the viewer. She presented herself as a real—in fact, superreal—figure of authority. Her large gesturing image addresses the viewer and asks to be taken seriously as a thinking subject. The gesture of speech asserts the vocal presence of woman, as opposed to her usual silent bodily presence in representation.[13] This work is the complete antithesis of her 1960 self-portrait, *Dark Face.*

The 1974 *Self-Portrait* was consonant with American art of the late sixties and early seventies, a remote art of impersonal execution, machinelike precision, and inhuman perfection. Yet in this picture the artist did retain elements of personal expression. Unlike the frontal and detached over-life-size busts of Chuck Close, which are about painting and not about people, Flack wants to engage the observer whom she addresses. After this public and authoritative self-portrait, Flack created her two most meditated and carefully worked out groups of still lifes: the *Gray Border* series (1974–75), to which the *Self-Portrait* belongs, and the *Vanitas* (1976–77). In a number of these works, most of which are overtly autobiographical, she combined still life with self-portraiture.

The last three paintings in the *Gray Border* series—*Leonardo's Lady* (1975), *Grand Rosé* (1975), and *Queen* (1975–76)—are visually and symbolically the

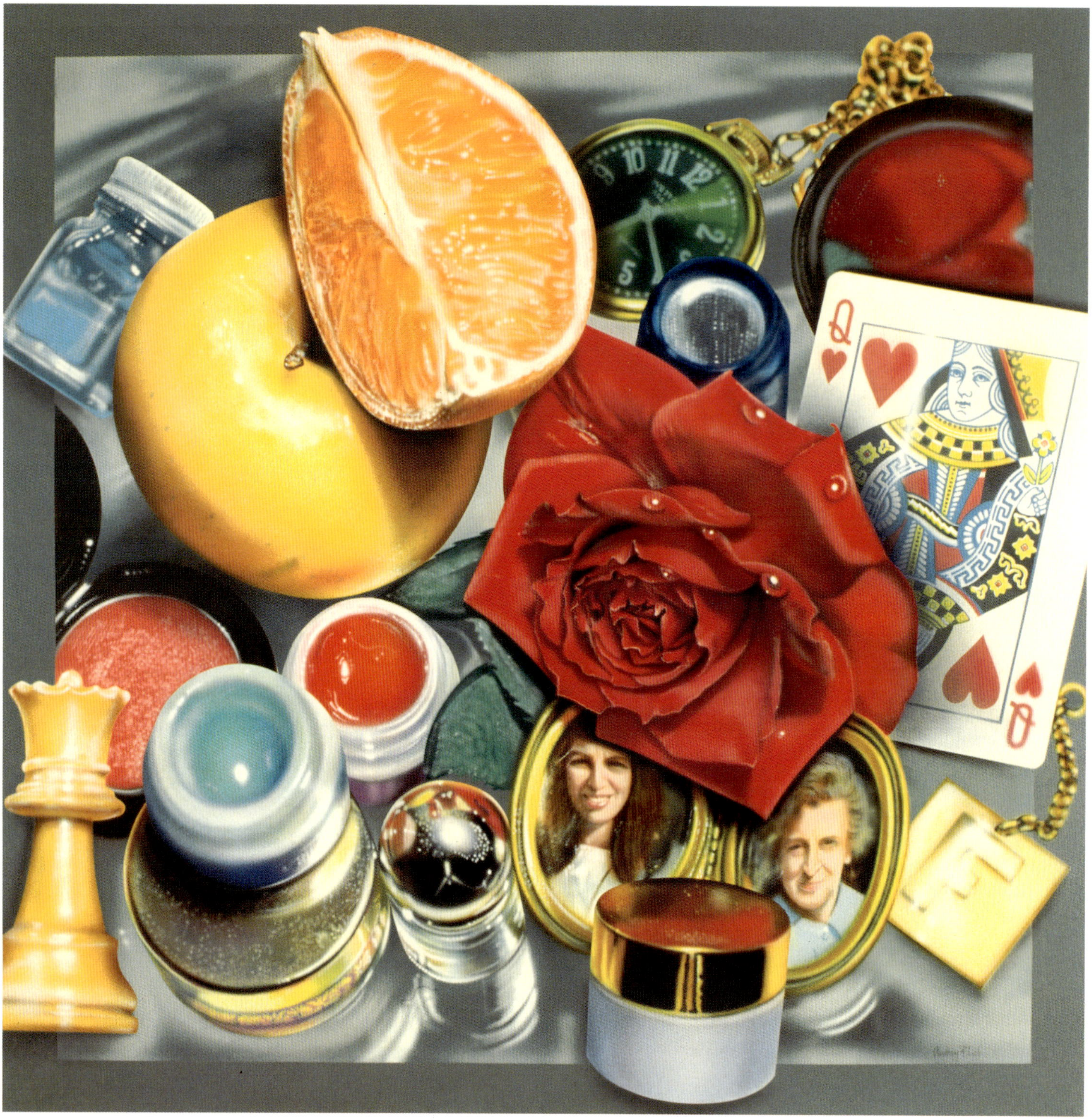

Queen. 1975–76
Acrylic on wet sanded canvas, 80 × 80″
Collection Louis K. Meisel Gallery,
New York

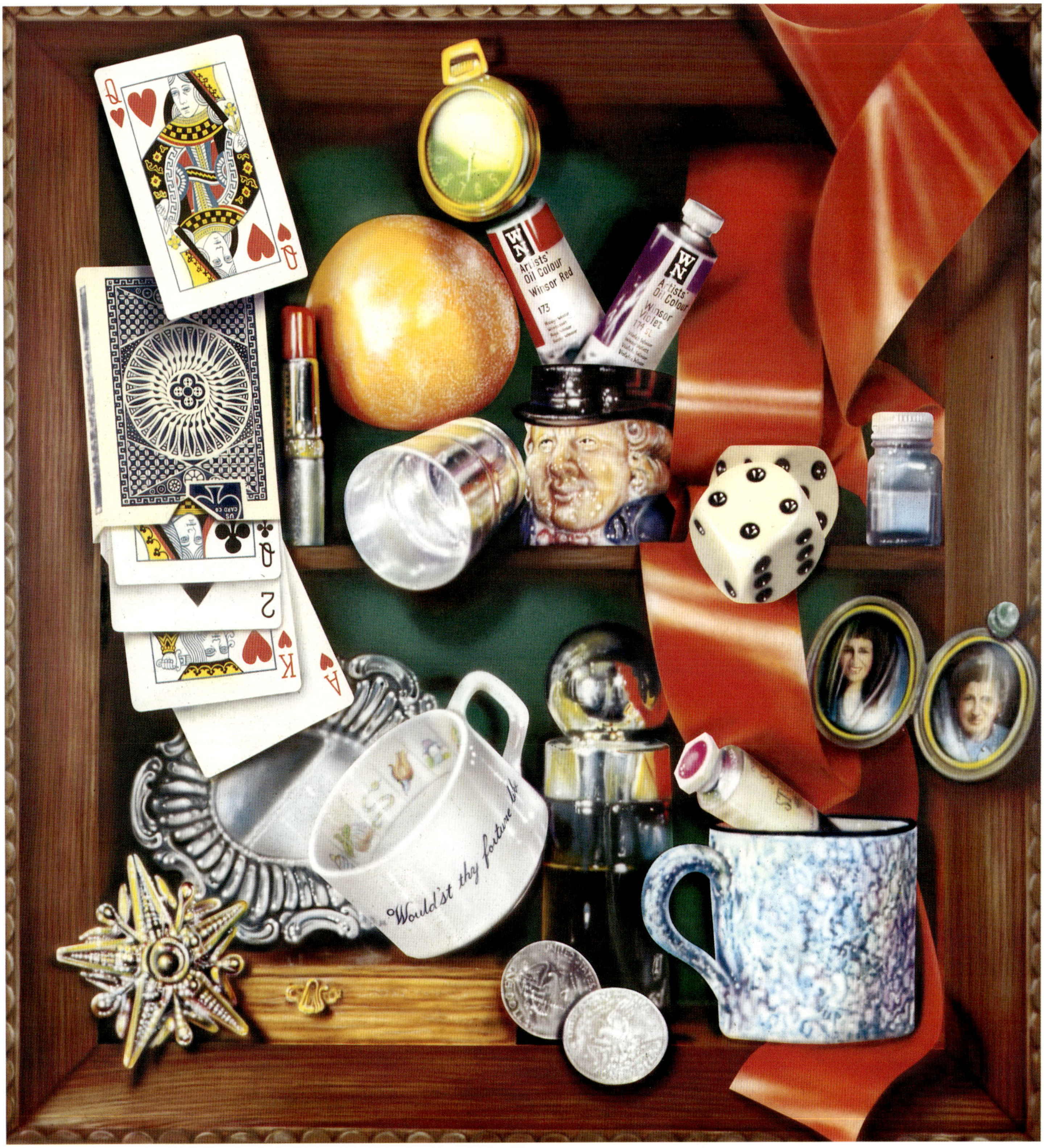

Gambler's Cabinet. 1976
Oil over acrylic on canvas, 83 × 78″
Collection Louis, Susan,
and Ari Meisel, New York

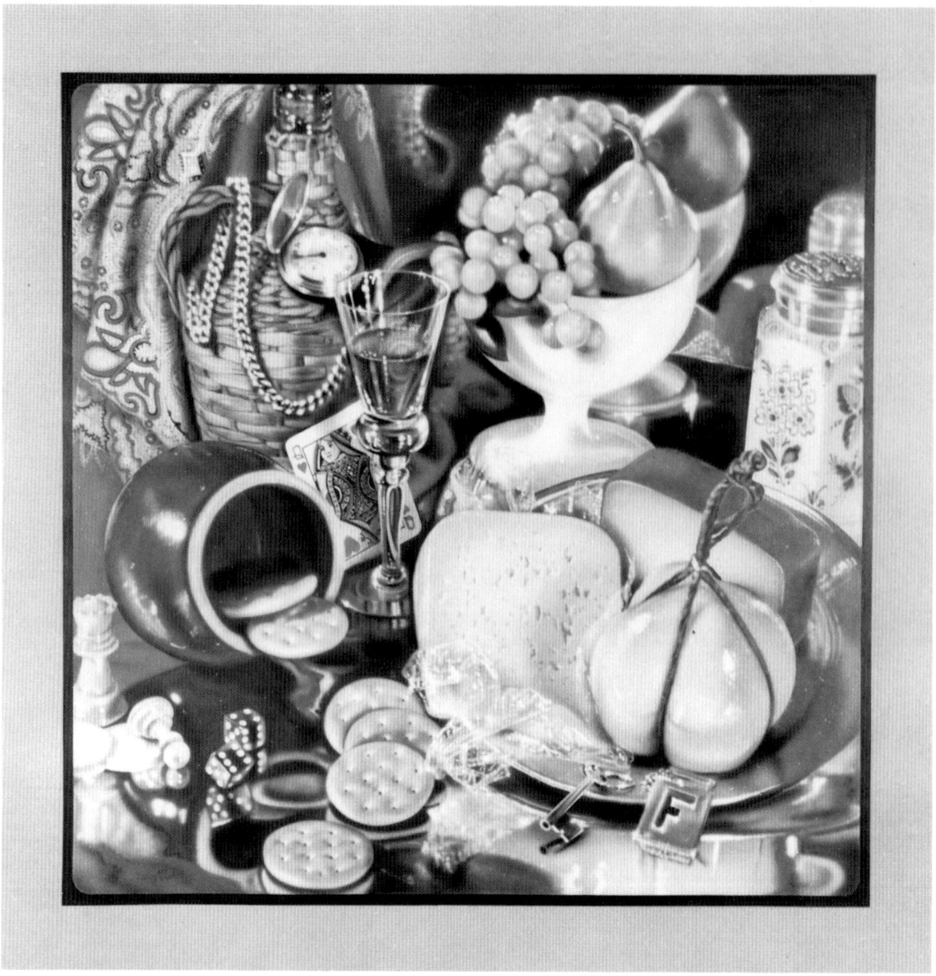

Grand Rosé. 1975
Oil over acrylic on wet sanded canvas, 90 × 90″
Private collection, California

most complex. They all contain objects of private use and images of or allusions to a female presence and are overtly self-referential. In *Grand Rosé* Flack combined the queen of hearts and chess queen with her own key and key chain engraved with her initial. This covert allusion to herself became explicit in *Queen*, which in addition to the queen of hearts, chess queen, and engraved key chain includes a double portrait of Flack and her mother. These paired images of photographs in a gold locket look intently at the viewer. The mother, a proper gray-haired lady, is smiling; the daughter's smile, however, has become painfully distorted.

Queen is as much a self-portrait as it is a still life. The large rose, in full bloom, that crowns both mother and daughter, will soon wither. The transitoriness of both the rose and the fruit above it belies the calm assurance of the queen of hearts as does the scratched surface of the two photographs. The passage of time is continuous and inevitable. The painting is both about a daughter's relation to her mother—the making of the maternal feminine—and about the process of aging, on which the daughter/artist reflects. It also comments on femininity: encased in gold lockets, passively blossoming, ripening, and withering away. Like the queen, the most powerful piece on the chessboard, women's fate ultimately is controlled by the male king. His absence from the painting creates an illusory world exclusively occupied by women. The artist puts in quotation marks the trappings and cycles of the feminine and actively encourages the viewer to meditate on these and to see aspects of herself in the painting.

Flack returned to this theme in 1976 in *Gambler's Cabinet*. Here, too, she included the queen of hearts, the clock, the fruit, and the double portrait in the golden locket. But the allusions to gambling and fate or fortune are more extensive—a pack of cards, a pair of dice, and a cup with the signs of the zodiac and a wish for good fortune. To the references of female beautification—lipstick and perfume bottle—which predominate in *Queen*, Flack added references to the creative artist: three tubes of Artists' Oil Color. The centrally placed pair of tubes, Winsor Red and Winsor Violet, become the focal points in the composition and relegate the paired images of daughter and mother to the periphery. These images, which through their placement and intensity dominated the composition in *Queen*, here are seen through a muting and blurring glass. They become ghostlike memories of the past displaced by present realities—the creative artist seeking her fortune and painting herself into an instrument of her own will. *Gambler's Cabinet* suggests that the passage of time can also lead to a renewed creative freedom and can give the woman artist some control over her life.

Flack further pursued the self-portrait/still life combination in her *Vanitas*, in both *Marilyn* (1977) and *Wheel of Fortune* (1977–78). *Marilyn* was her homage to the American goddess of female sexuality. The powder puff, perfume bottle, lipstick, mascara, eye shadow, and string of beads refer to Marilyn but belong to Flack, as does the dripping paintbrush. Unlike Marilyn, who literally painted herself into a sign of femininity, Flack painted a work of art to comment on femininity and its relation to creativity. The complex and layered references in this work are expanded through Marilyn's distorted mirror reflection ("the mirror of the viewer as she sees herself") and the childhood photograph of Flack and her brother, flanked by Marilyn's two effigies. The passage of time recorded by the clock and hourglass and implied in the ripe and drying fruit and burning candle applies as much to the artist's growth from childhood to maturity as to Marilyn's growth and death.

In *Wheel of Fortune* death becomes the focus. Here, the reflection in the mirror no longer conveys a human being but a skull, and even though Flack included a rainbow in the mirror as a symbol of transcendence, the skull remains the dominant image. Over the fortune-telling tarot card is a photograph of a young girl whom the viewer might identify as an image of the artist. It is, however, an image of Flack's autistic daughter, Melissa, the baby whom she held in her 1959 self-portrait. In *Wheel of Fortune*, as in the 1959 painting, Melissa's reality almost obliterates her mother's. Flack is present only as a reflection in the silver crystal-gazing ball, in the upper right-hand corner. Here, as in *Queen* and *Gambler's Cabinet*, there is a mother/daughter parallelism, but here the daughter has become the mother. She also is the creative artist who conceived and created the work of art. In her reflection she is, with camera and tripod, taking the photograph that served as the basis for the painting. The painting then, in spite of the central presence of death, also provides hope through the continuity of life and the mastery of fate through creative energy.

Two years later Flack briefly returned to traditional self-portraiture in a small painting on paper. This 1980 *Self-Portrait*, based on a time exposure that she herself had taken, comes closer to her early self-portraits than any other work since 1960. Unposed, Flack looks at the camera directly and anxiously. Her colorful necklaces, the brilliant and thick color pigments, and the brush strokes of reflective paint contrast with the worried eyes surrounded by dark circles and the strong facial lines of the mature woman. The face "conjures up

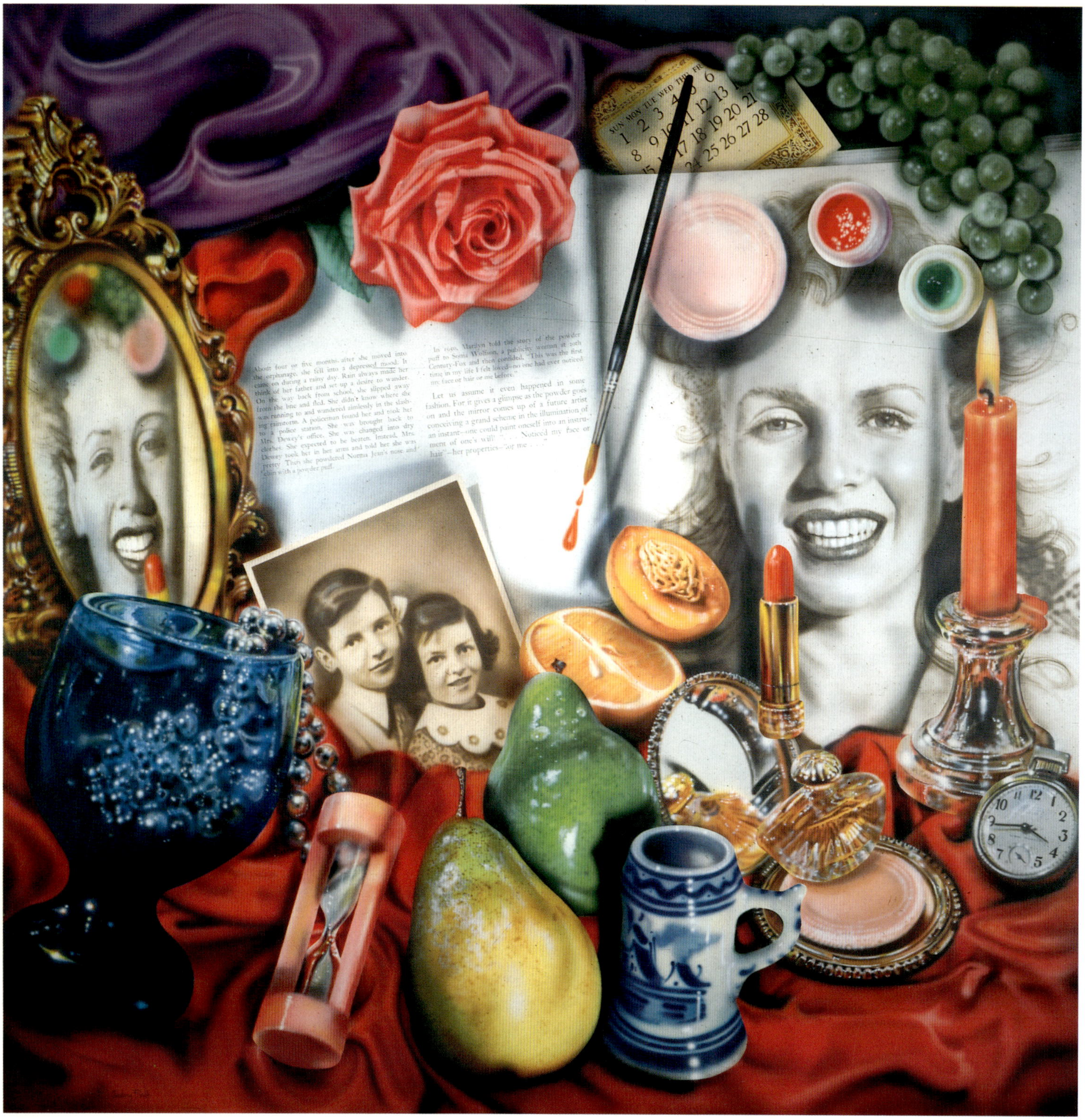

Marilyn (Vanitas). 1977
Oil over acrylic on canvas, 96×96″
University of Arizona Art
Museum, Tucson

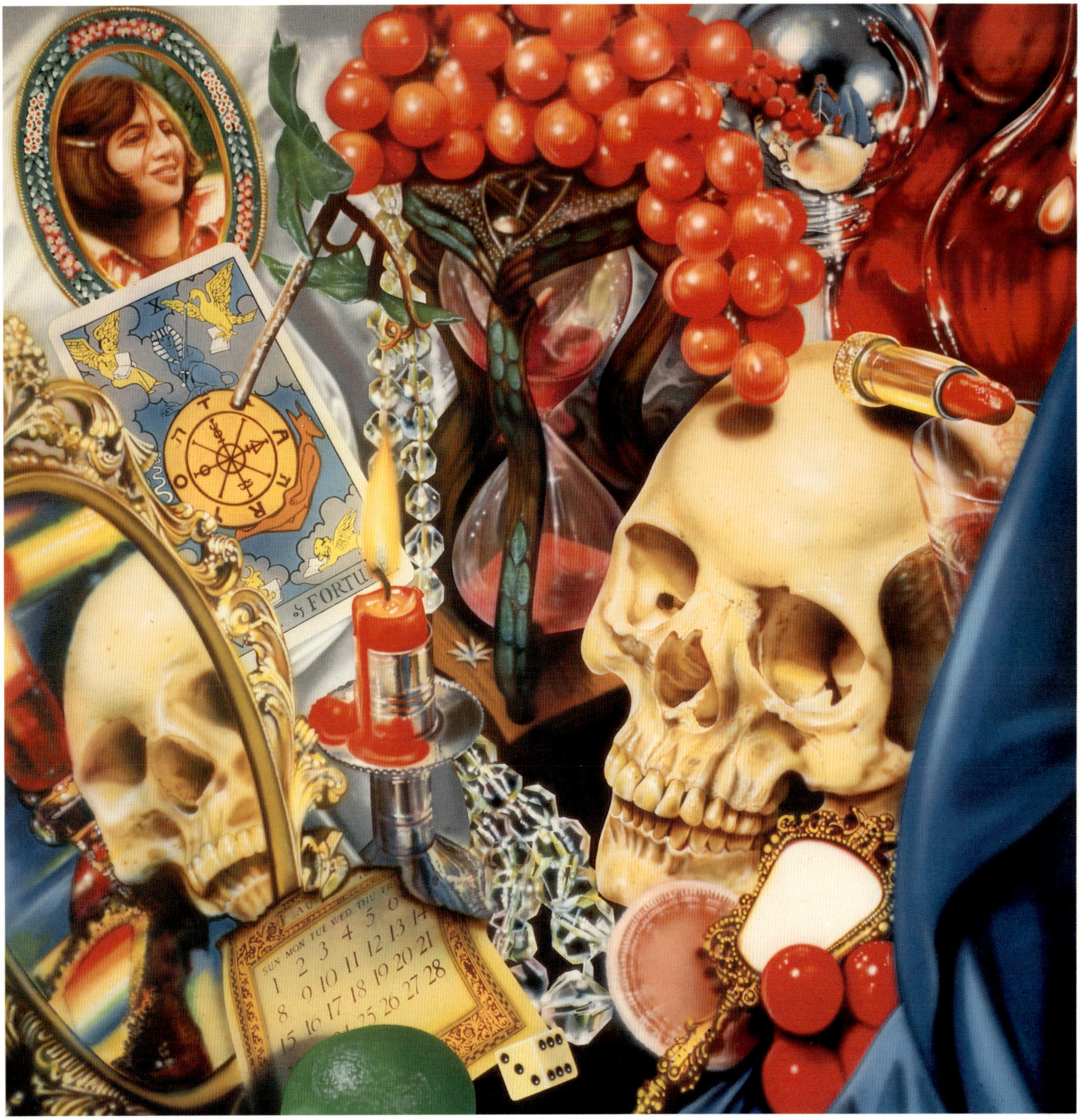

Wheel of Fortune (Vanitas). 1977–78
Oil over acrylic on canvas, 96×96″
Collection Louis K. Meisel Gallery,
New York

a vision bare" (Mary Elizabeth Coleridge) and lets us look into the artist's heart. We occupy the position of the camera into which she looked directly and in that sense become her reflector. This portrait was too private and vulnerable to be transformed into a larger and more public painting.

For the painting that followed in 1981, Flack, as in her 1974 *Self-Portrait,* used a slide taken by someone else and went through a process of self-distancing to gain control over her image. Titled *We Are All Light and Energy,* this self-portrait is about half the size of the 1974 portrait. Here, again, Flack addresses the viewer, but the message, which in the 1974 painting had remained enigmatic, is clearly stated in the inscription "we are all light and energy" that runs across the top like a flash of light and becomes the title of the painting. This was the first of several of her paintings of the early eighties where inscriptions, written in script directly on the canvas or frame, elaborate on the meaning of the work.[14] The element of directness and personal expression introduced by the inscription is present also in the dynamic brushwork and painterly modulation that hark back to Flack's early self-portraits. This portrait, however, with its intentional spatial ambiguity and its iconic symmetry and frontality is unlike the emotional and expressive early portraits. The iconic element is further emphasized by the halolike, short yellow strokes around the face. Like a medieval saint, the artist holds her attribute, the parrot, as a symbol of longevity. In spite of its specificity the portrait remains strangely ambiguous and depersonalized. In creating an iconic image that incorporates elements of her individualized presence and asking the viewer to perceive her as a generic human type, Flack, as she had done in *Marilyn,* attempted to transform the feminine into a universal archetype.

One year later, in *Invocation,* her last still life/self-portrait, Flack again addressed the double theme of mortality and transcendence. As in *Wheel of Fortune* the composition is centered around a skull; but unlike *Wheel* all the other objects refer to the artist as creator—tubes and jars of paint, paintbrush, and watercolors. The strangely beautiful skull is crowned with flowers and framed by a rainbow, and next to it a lone candle burns in a silver vase. The artist taking the initial photograph is reflected in that vase. The painting, like the much earlier *Anatomy Lesson,* is a dialogue between death and the creative act; and, like *Anatomy Lesson,* it is strangely peaceful and serene. The symbols on the frame, the Lord Krishna blessing, a wreath or crown of thorns with a skeleton behind it, and Native American and Indian emblems of renewal, allude to the relation between the human being and the universe, as do the inscriptions from Yajur Veda and Shree Avadhuta Stotram with their references to the cosmic and eternal.[15] As the artist comments on life and death so the painting comments on itself as an artifact. The various levels of illusion culminate in the thick paint spilling over the outer frame, an overt allusion to the creative act.

Audrey Flack's observations of and reflections upon her image in the mirror expand over the years to an investigation of the self in relation to others. They also become assertions of female creative power and comments on traditional femininity and the roles assigned to women. Struggling with the contradictions between creativity and femininity, her self-portraits stress the authoritative and vocal presence of woman denying her traditionally passive definition. In their increasing complexity and in dealing with universal issues these paintings have come to reflect upon reality and upon themselves. They become Flack's metaphor for the transcendent power of art.

Self-Portrait. 1980
Oil and crayon on paper, 32½ × 20″
Collection R. Wesley Mutchler, Jr., Oakland, California

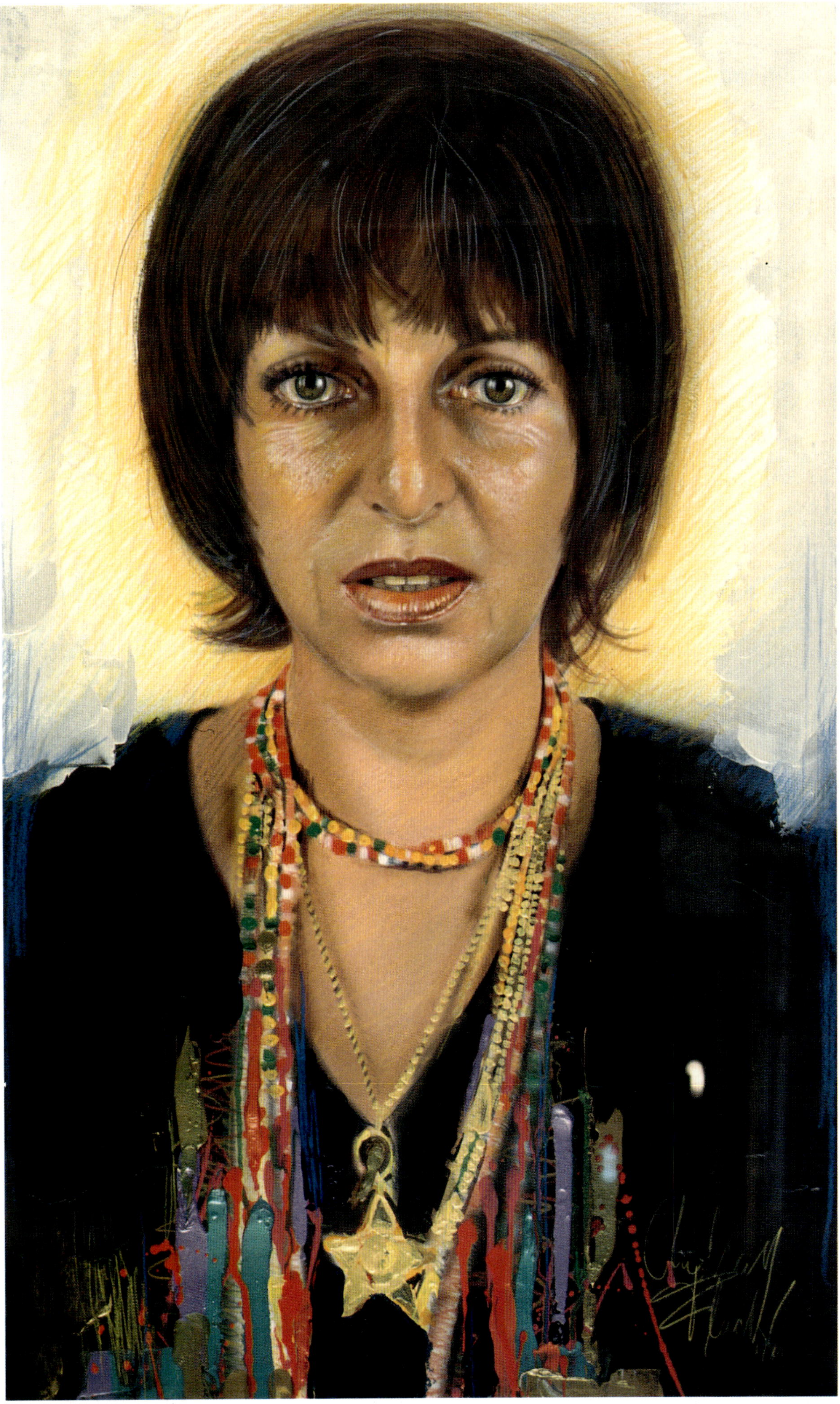

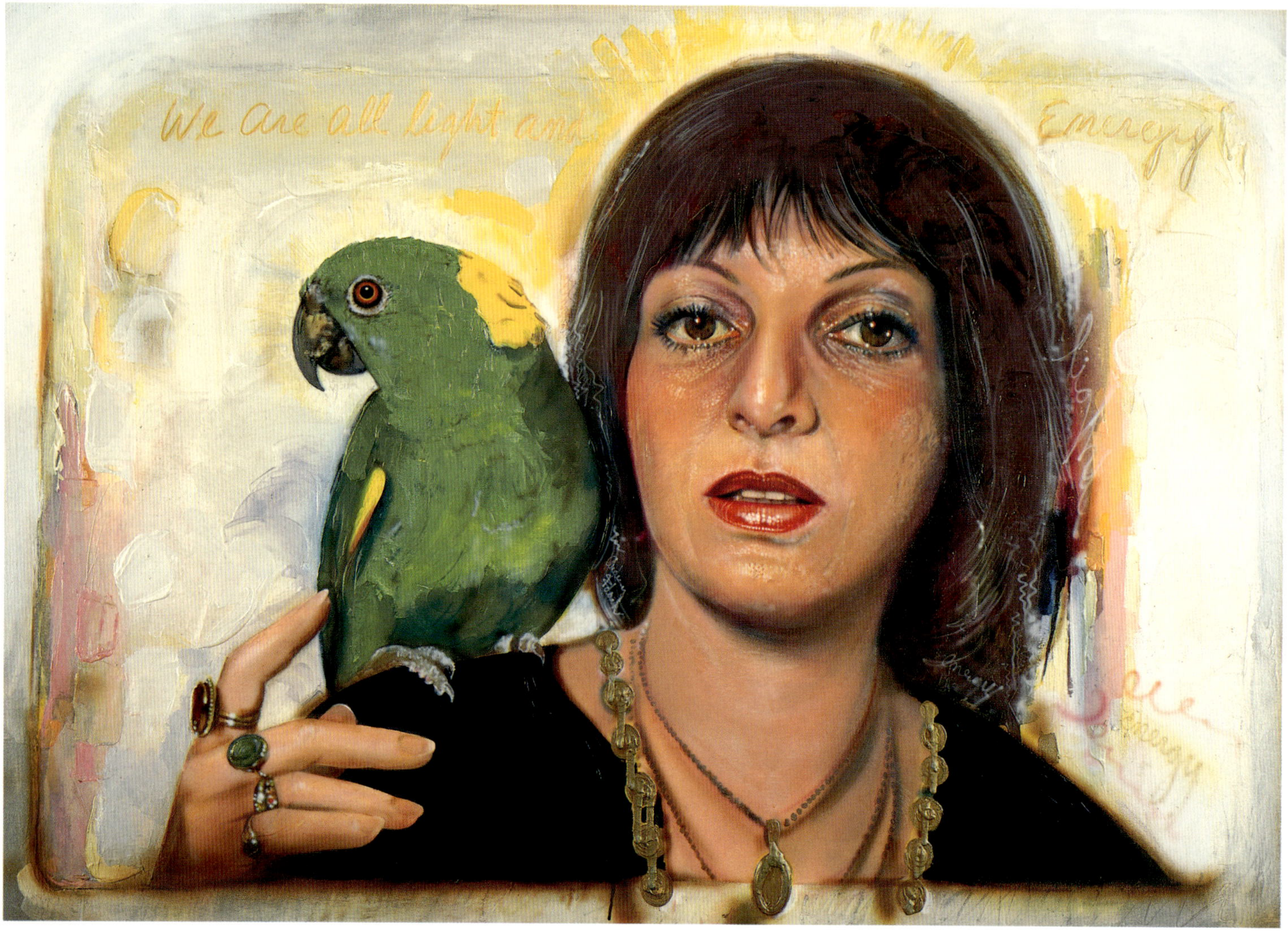

We Are All Light and Energy. 1981
Acrylic and oil on canvas, 46 × 66″
Private collection, Switzerland

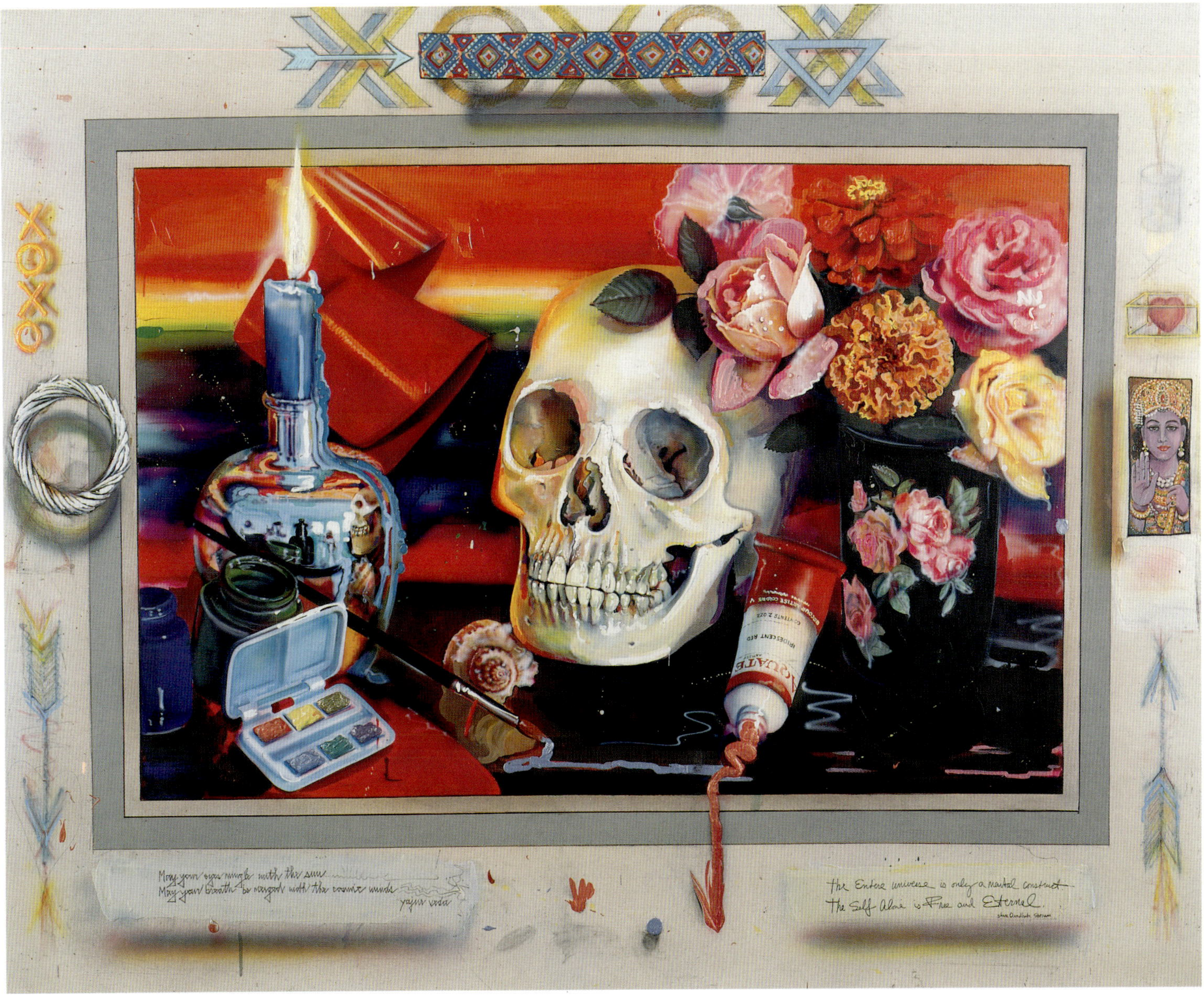

Invocation. 1982
Acrylic and oil on canvas, 64 × 80″
Collection Louis K. Meisel Gallery,
New York

THE PERSON, THE STUDIO, THE WORLD: AUDREY FLACK IN THE 1960s

Patricia Hills

In 1960 Audrey Flack confronted a crucial decade. She had been painting for over ten years and living the life of an artist. Both Jackson Pollock and her Yale teacher Josef Albers had inspired her to believe in the integrity of painting and the worth of an artistic calling, yet she was determined to break with their styles of art. She wanted to clarify her own future as an artist not just in the art world of power and glitzy celebrity but in the everyday world of compassion and very human ordinariness and extraordinariness.[1]

Her personal circumstances mattered a great deal: her role as a mother could not be subordinated to her life as an artist. And it was no ordinary motherhood, for she faced the irreversible disability of her autistic first child, Melissa, born in 1959, and she strove to hold together a home for the healthy second daughter, Hannah, born in 1961. For Flack there was no set routine to structure her day; no stalwart mate to tend the children, keep house, screen visitors, and answer calls; and no nurturing art dealer to provide her with a regular stipend, even though she was showing her work in exhibitions. Instead, there were the disruptions of doctors' visits, the coping with a spouse then attempting to launch his own all-absorbing career as a classical composer and free-lance cellist, and the travel out to Brooklyn to teach part-time at Pratt Institute in the mornings and to NYU in the afternoons. With her studio in the living room of a six-room Upper West Side Manhattan apartment, where she moved in the early 1960s, it could hardly be said that painting to her was a retreat into an ivory tower of aesthetic contemplation or tortured self-analysis. Life intervened too often, and her responsibilities drove out the compulsive narcissism that characterizes so many young artists. With her own realities ever present, she turned to representation in order to gain the sober self-knowledge she found missing in the art and ethos of the Abstract Expressionist generation.

It is in this 1960s decade that we see Flack coming to artistic maturity—moving from an expressionist figure style relying for subject matter on her own body, on her family, and on studio props, to a realist social commentary that explored the public images of the politicians and movie stars offered up by *Life* magazine, the press services, and the archives of photojournalism. In the middle years of the decade, aided by her camera, she brought a heroic naturalism to the faces of Mexican peasants and social protest marchers. And, finally, by 1970, having mastered the ways the camera could serve painting, she began to define a new style—Photorealism. She was by then part of a movement, and in control, with a world of objects submissive to her brush.

Surrounded by non–art-world people, she wanted most of all to communicate with them through her art. The choice always had to be one of the variations on realism—ranging from expressionist realism to Photorealism. Years later, in 1974, she told Cindy Nemser:

Hannah (Golden Head). 1963
Oil on canvas, 12 × 9″
Collection Hannah Flack Marcus, San Francisco

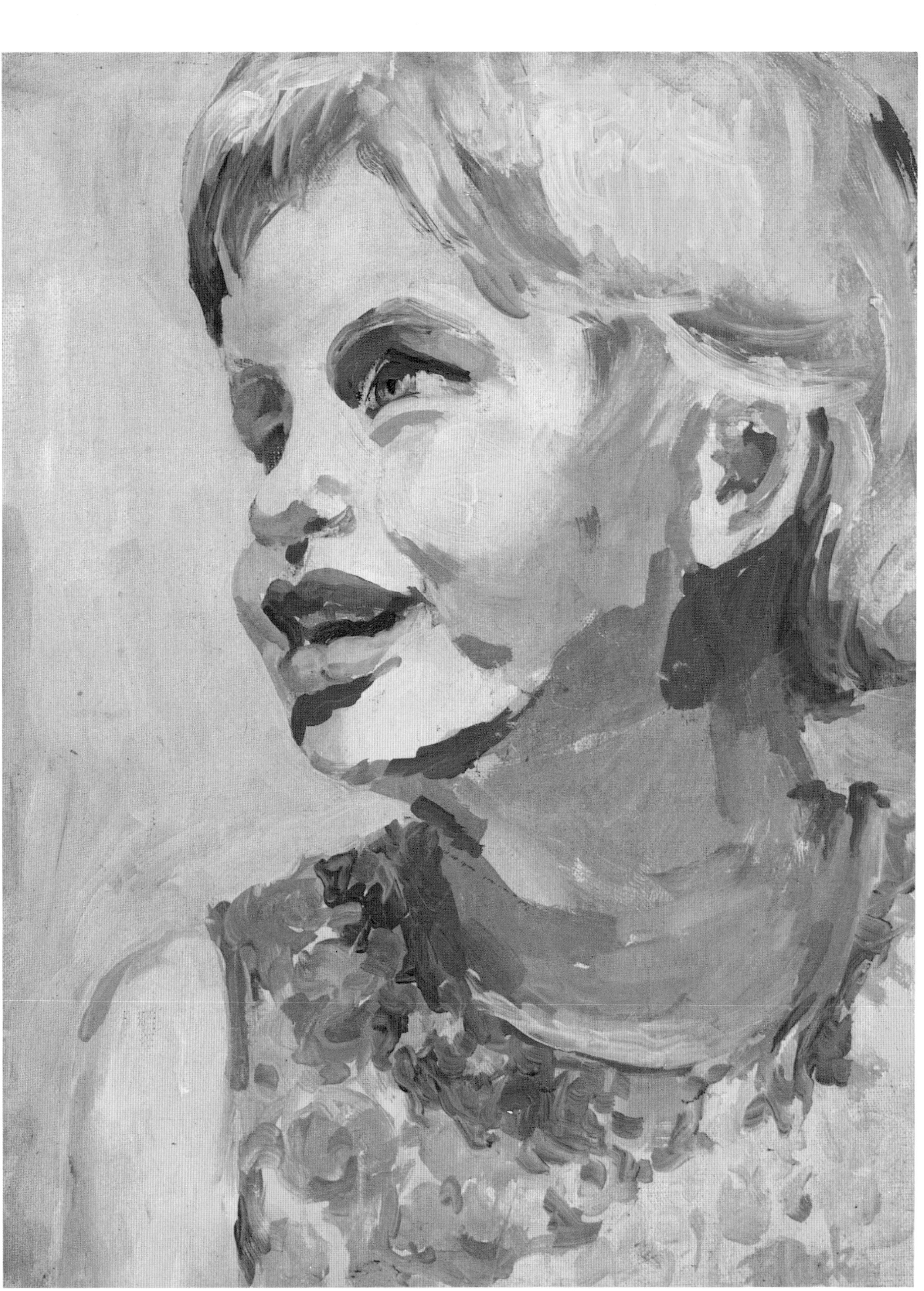

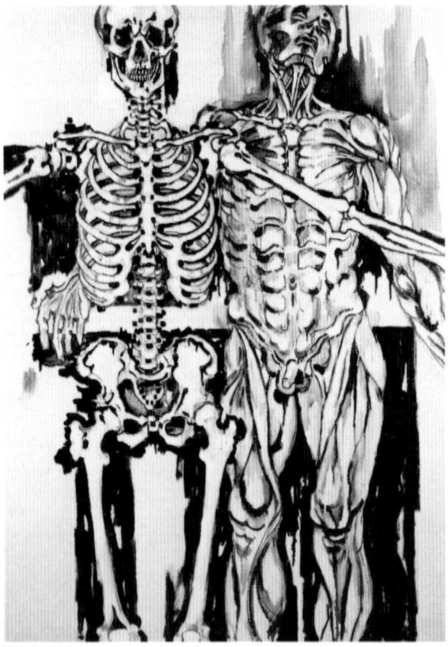

Vesalius Study (Anatomy). 1958
Oil on canvas, 50×36″
Private collection

> I always wanted to draw realistically. For me art is a continuous discovery into reality, an exploration of visual data which has been going on for centuries, each artist contributing to the next generation's advancement. I wanted to go a step further and extend the boundaries. I also believe people have a deep need to understand their world and that art clarifies reality for them.[2]

Indeed, it was Flack's own deep need that brought her from academic expressionism and pushed her through the discoveries of the 1960s to her mature style of the 1970s.

Flack's independent quest began in 1952 when she returned to New York from study at Yale. Since she still felt the need to bring discipline to her art and to explore the figure, she enrolled in an anatomy class with Robert Beverly Hale, then teaching at the Art Students League. During these years of the mid-1950s she turned to her own self, reflected in the mirror, as a handy model to paint and produced a number of scrutinized reflections, such as *Anatomy Lesson* of 1953 and several 1958 self-portraits—*Self-Portrait (the Memory), Self-Portrait with Drafting Table, Self-Portrait in Underpants, Triple Self-Portrait,* and *Double Self-Portrait.* As a group these often merciless representations chart the range of emotional responses to herself as an artist in the context of the home studio.

The skull and the skeleton as studio props and teaching tools link art-making with a contemplative philosophical reflection on the nature of human existence. On the one hand, to master the perspective of the skull and the skeleton was to learn about the structure and movements of the human body. It was to get inside the human form. But as the palpable flesh of the material world rests on muscle, cartilage, fat and sinew, which in turn rest on the rigidity of skeletal bone, so, too, is the content of painting revealed through the artist's control of the inert substance of pigment and the creative deployment of imagery. Learned techniques in dialogue with experimentation, tradition ameliorated by innovation, guide the artist toward the possibilities for meaning. Thus, while *Anatomy Lesson* (p. 22) provided the occasion for learning, it also heralded through its imagery—the skull and the skeleton—the

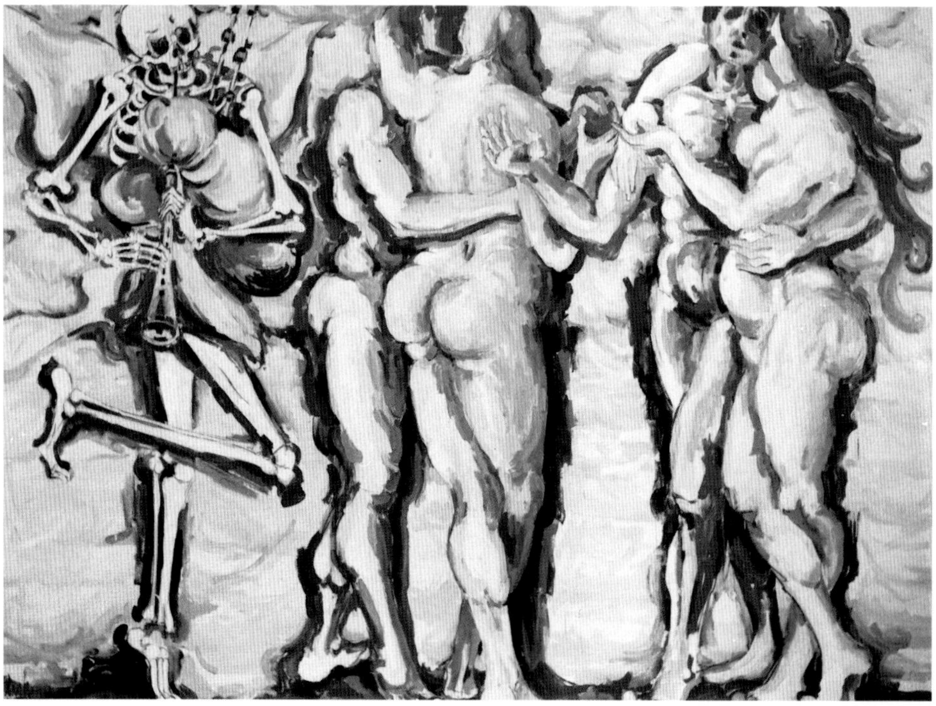

Dance of Death. 1959
Oil on canvas, 6×8′
Collection the artist

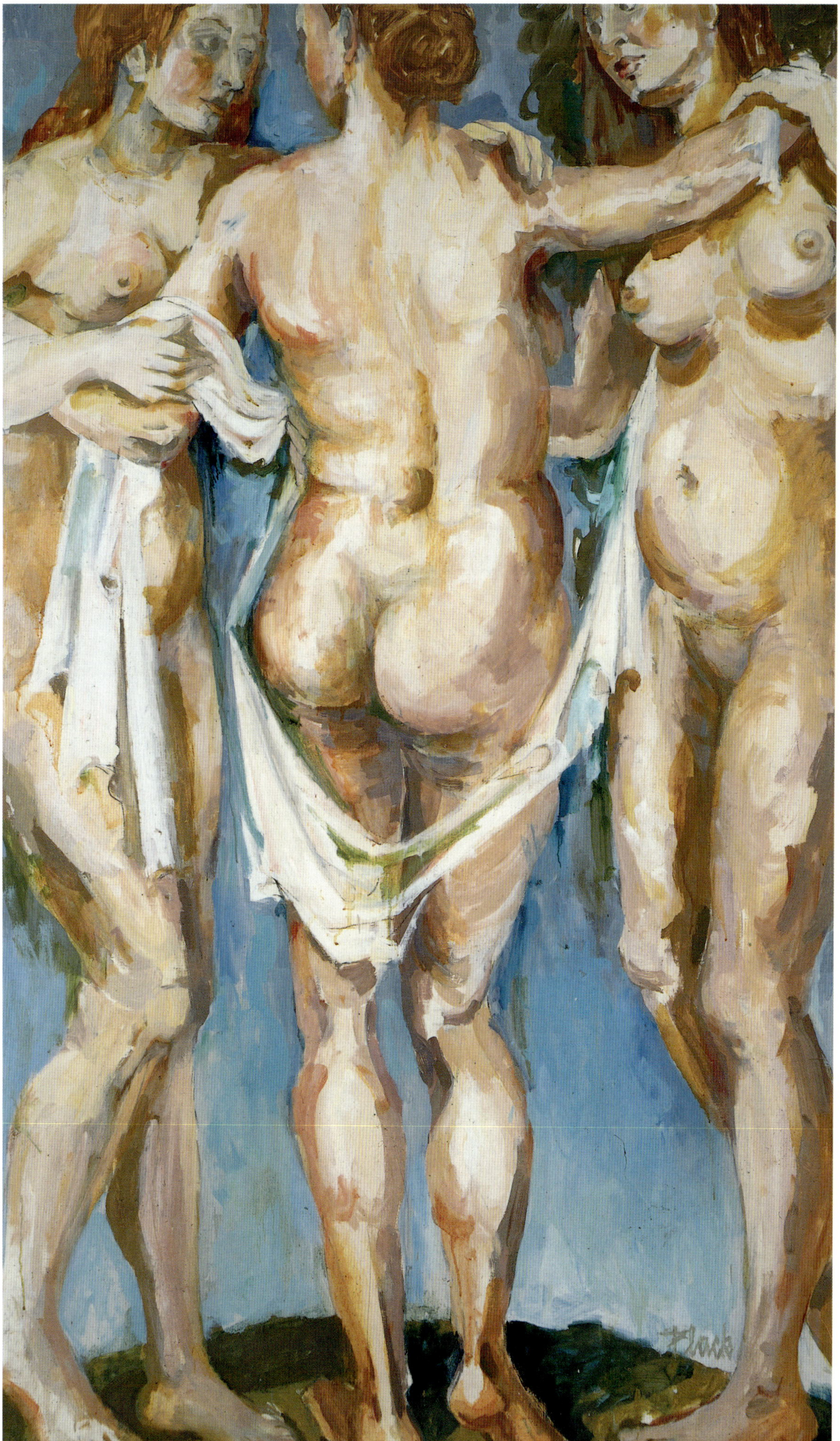

The Three Graces. 1962
Oil on canvas, 67×40″
Private collection

major themes of her oeuvre: the tension between transitory illusionism and timeless signifying images, art as the mediation between life and death, and confrontation as the essence of life.

Description helps to isolate the images: the artist Flack sits at a table in the left lower quadrant of the picture. While she sketches, she looks out at us. In the center of the canvas are two skulls and in the upper right is a seated male model with his head thrown back and forearms lying on the armrests of his chair. To the left of him and above the artist's head is a grid of figure sketches and quick studies of écorché figures and skeletons. A similar set of sketches spreads along the bottom right of the canvas, while closest to her is a disembodied hand held up as if to calm her. These images—skulls, seated figures, hanging skeletons, écorché figures—have an ambiguous three-dimensionality. On the one hand we sense the materiality of rounded nude torsos and curving rib cages of studio skeletons, but the sketchiness of the lines and the way color floats outside the perimeters of the forms sabotage the illusionistic imagery. Moreover, we are unsure whether we are looking at a montage of sketches pinned to her wall, or real events and objects in the background. But does it matter? This is, obviously, not a work of realism where mimetic concerns assert a primacy and the unities of space and time keep their integrity.

Ultimately we come to the realization that the real substance of these images is their power to signify as words do. They communicate as signs for the art process: artist (the artist's self-portrait), the medium of drawing, the objects (props and the model), the sketched results, and ourselves, the audience—toward whom the artist looks and who at the moment returns that gaze.

Anatomy Lesson montages the artist's memory of the teaching studio as a moment of process, of making art. And what most rivets our attention are the face of the artist and the two rounded skulls set against a vertical rectangle of black paint—skulls with a pitiless presence, a memento mori to remind us of our own mortality. Those same skulls also physically intercede between the activist female artist at the lower left and the passive male model sitting at the upper right. In no other earlier work has Flack brought the polarities of image and process, male and female, passive and active, and death and life into such a complex harmony.

Flack's *Dance of Death* of 1959 underscores her essential, life-affirming attitude and carries her explorations further. The skeleton is no longer a static prop but an engaged actor of the drama. Dancing and playing the bagpipes, he looks to control the four figures to the right. This male figure (and Flack always portrays death as a male figure) perches precariously on the tips of his toes and aligns himself along the edge of the canvas. In contrast, the four solid, voluptuous forms, firmly standing along the baseline of the painting, ignore him. These two intertwined couples link together with outstretched arms and affirm their material presence. The full bellies and buttocks of the female figures suggest a fecundity or maternal presence as well. Perhaps, too, Flack had in mind her own pregnancy, a time when stretching flesh and the quickening of the unborn child would have reminded her of the life forces that irresistibly conquer death.

She brought life into the world on March 2, 1959, with her beautiful Melissa, but this child was to live in an autistic netherworld of neither joy nor sorrow, neither achievement nor disappointment. However, the paintings of Melissa can deceive us. The early *Melissa and Me* of 1959 shows a smiling child and a

OPPOSITE, CLOCKWISE FROM TOP LEFT:

Hannah in Sunsuit. 1962
Oil on canvas, 21½ × 18″
Collection Hannah Flack Marcus, San Francisco

Hannah and Annie. 1962
Oil on canvas, 16 × 20″
Collection Hannah Flack Marcus, San Francisco

Hannah Marie (Mickey Mouse Hat). 1965
Oil on canvas, 10 × 8″
Collection Hannah Flack Marcus, San Francisco

Portrait of Melissa. 1964
Oil on canvas, 15 × 10″
Collection the artist

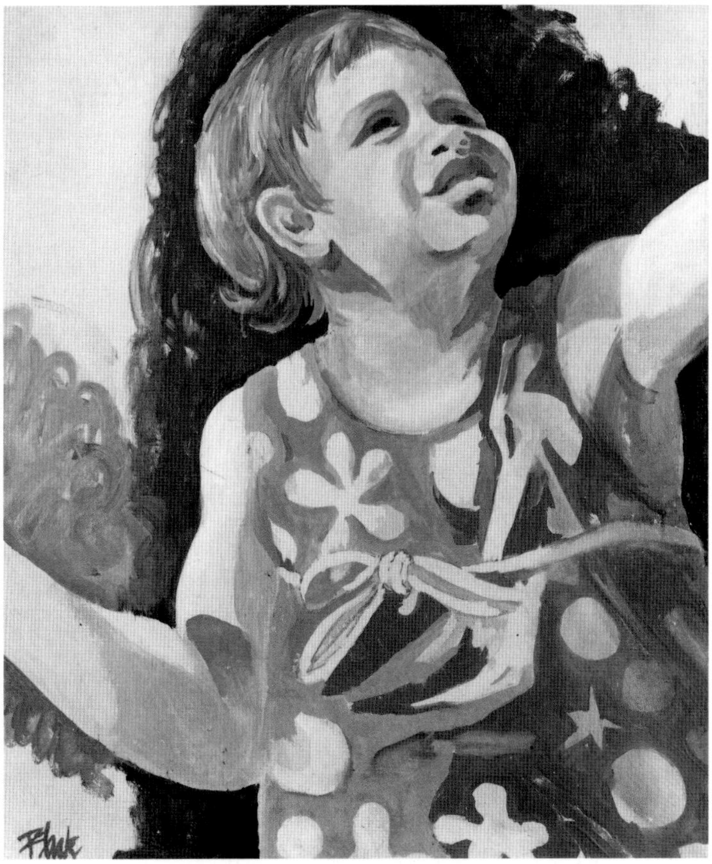
Flack

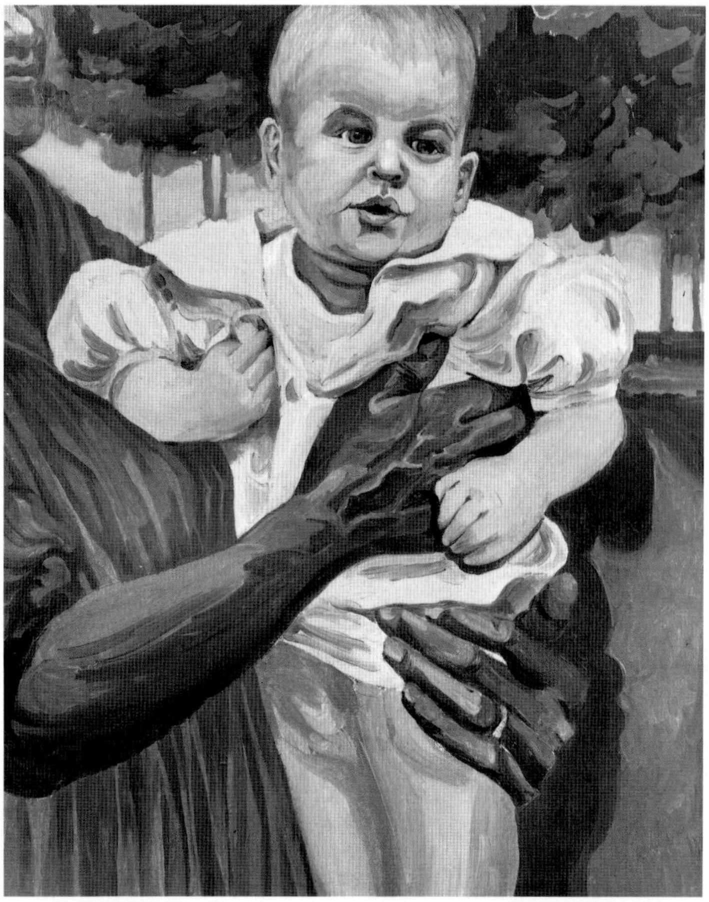

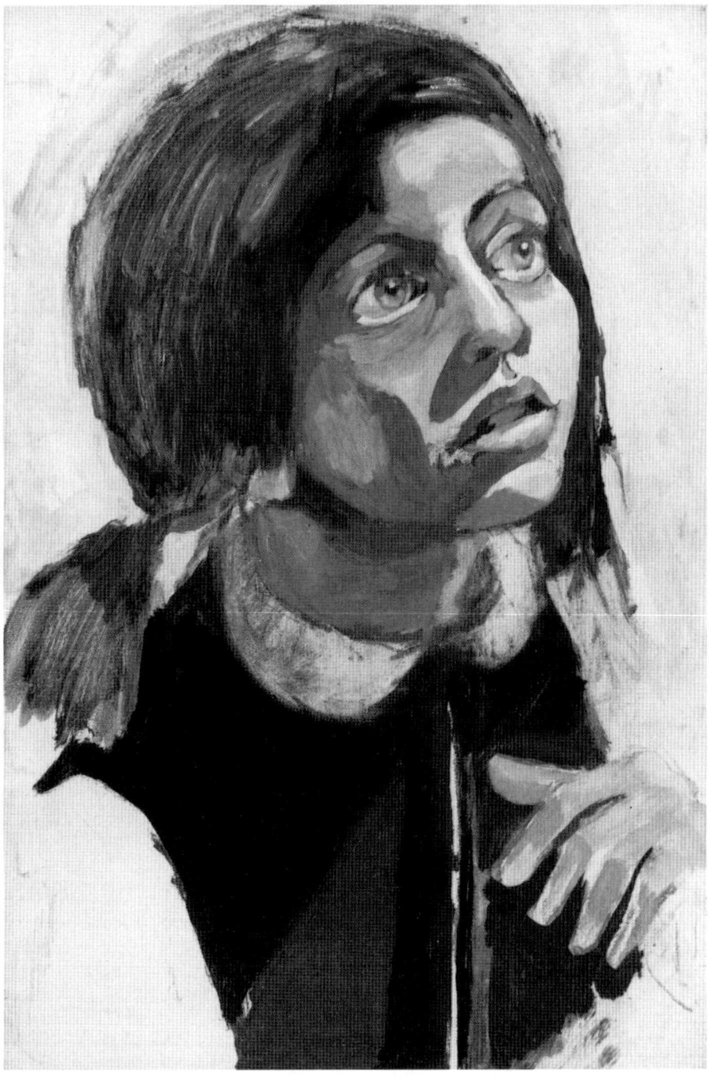

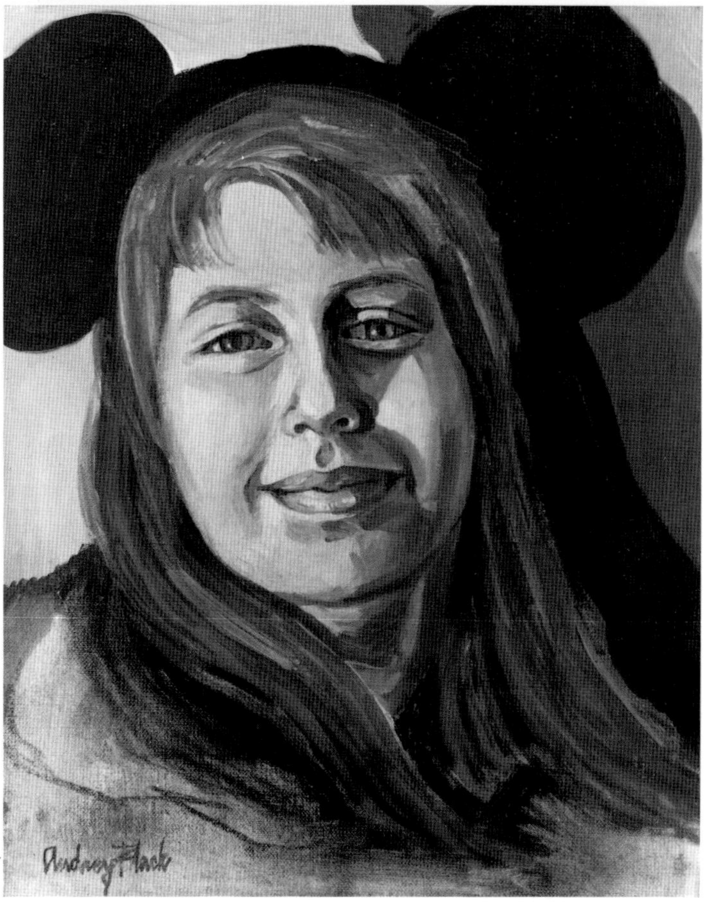
Audrey Flack

mother whose face is cut off at a line running through the eyes. Flack does not want us to see her own facial expression, only to sense the nurturing maternal presence of loving arms. Yet, her *Portrait of Melissa* of 1964 hints at the clinical reality of her daughter's condition. Here we see an imploring child supplicating the world to care for her. It would be Flack, the mother, who would set aside the needs of self to meet Melissa's claims of total dependency. These were exhausting years for Flack.

Her second girl child, lusty and happy Hannah, born in 1961, brought her some measure of unmitigated joy. She painted Hannah in the arms of her Jamaican housekeeper (*Hannah and Annie* of 1962); another of Hannah at two years old reaching up toward the world; Hannah in a sun suit; and Hannah in a Mickey Mouse hat—a very ordinary child delighting in the world of make-believe. Both daughters reappear in later paintings, and it is relevant to speak of these pictures here because the story of her children is a continuously unfolding one. Later Melissa was to make a cameo entrance in Flack's *Wheel of Fortune* of 1977–78 as a photographic image in a pocket-sized frame tucked behind a fortune card. As part of a catalogue of memento mori, she reminds us again of the fragility of life and of health. In a decided contrast, Flack reincarnates her younger daughter in 1982 as the monumental *Hannah: Who She Is,* a self-composed larger-than-life deity symbolizing the possibilities of human potential. The interpenetration of art and life, the good fortune of some to live and flourish and of others to endure a life arrested or unfulfilled, have been continual themes throughout Flack's career.

In 1962 and 1963 Flack began to paint subjects from the world of documentary news. She wanted to move away from the confines of her Upper West Side apartment—with the noises of Broadway buses, the neon lights of liquor stores and cheap residence hotels flashing across the street, and the smells of the city—out into the space of the world, even if only vicariously through photojournalism. Using photographs published in magazines and pictorial albums, she scrutinized the public demeanor of political leaders as a way to understand the workings of the world: Hitler, Roosevelt, Stalin, Churchill, Rockefeller, Kennedy—men who need no first names to identify them. *Hitler,* painted in 1963–64, is a skull with a wrap of flesh, like an Aztec stone head whose frozen smile can strike terror in his intended victims. More elaborate, and somewhat more confidently painted, is *Rockefeller* of 1963 representing the Republican party politician pumping the hand of a welcoming Oregon local official. Behind, a crowd leans over the chain link fence separating incoming passengers at the airport terminal. They grimace in the western sun, cameras hanging from their necks, waiting for a "photo opportunity." Both *Hitler* and *Rockefeller* are based on snapshots taken of political leaders moving among the crowds, smiling, and projecting themselves as men of the people.

Teheran Conference of 1964, on the other hand, is based on a posed "state" photograph of Franklin Roosevelt flanked by Joseph Stalin and Winston Churchill. The Teheran photograph portrayed statesmen concluding an agreement with global implications: during those meetings of November 28 to December 1, 1943, the three leaders planned the invasion of Europe, Stalin committed Soviet forces to the war against Japan, and they put in place postwar plans for peace. In their presentation of themselves—their public masks and assured poses (recall Roosevelt was a cripple and thus always sat for his portrait)—Flack sees a kind of social realism: not a social realism representing the oppressed or class struggle but one depicting the powerful (no

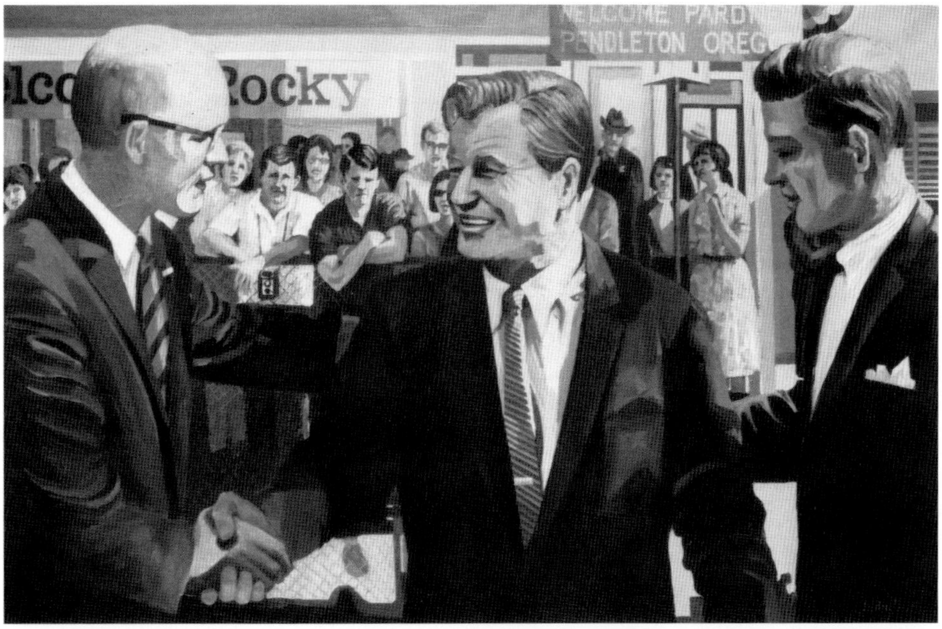

Rockefeller. 1963
Oil on canvas, 30 × 40″
Greater Lafayette Museum
of Art, Indiana

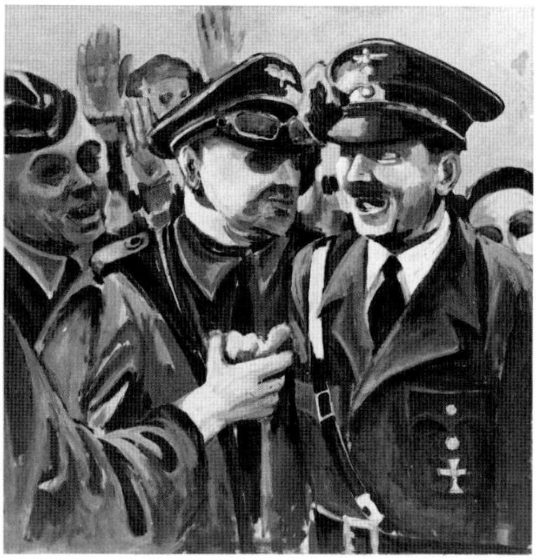

Hitler. 1963–64
Oil on canvas, 28 × 28″
Collection the artist

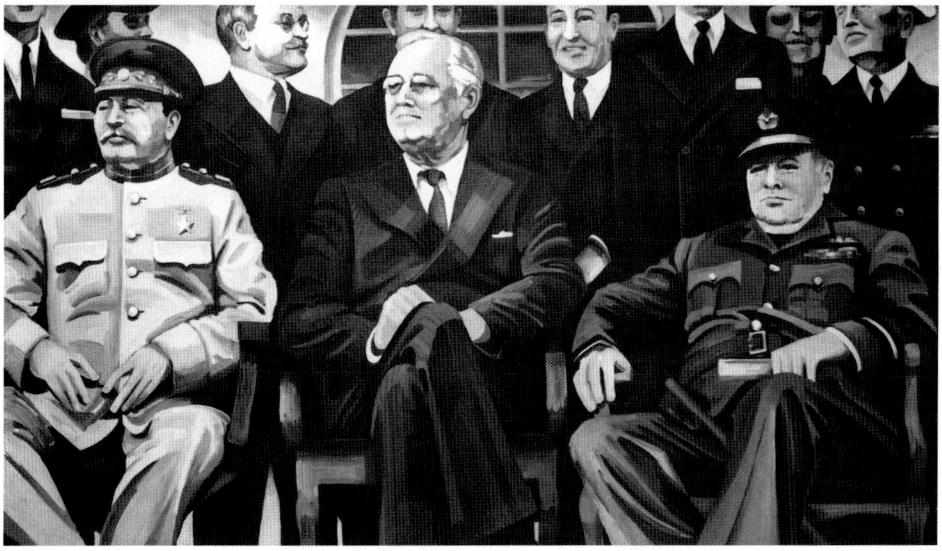

Teheran Conference. 1964
Oil on canvas, 41 × 72″
Jimmy Carter Library

matter what their political ideology) as they seek to steer the course of world events for their own national interests. These are history paintings seen through Flack's prism of social conscience.

And then there are the superficially powerful men such as the boxer Davey Moore, painted in 1964. Moore was unknown in the art world when he died. His tragedy had none of the scent of scandal, he was not married to a famous person, there were no rumors of glamorous lovers, and yet his story touched Flack. She painted his picture as "a kind of social protest realism." She told Cindy Nemser that: "He was sitting in the back of Madison Square Garden after a match, talking to *Life* reporters, when he dropped dead. Ironically his boxing trunks said 'Everlast,' which is what is printed on all boxing trunks. I saw his pose as Christlike."[3] Seeing the news photo of Moore taken immediately after the fight, with his outstretched arms, Flack recalled Edouard Manet's *Dead Christ.* Although Moore collapsed in the locker room, he actually died seventy-eight hours after his fight with Sugar Ramos in Los Angeles on March 22, 1963. The injury, a panel of doctors decided, did not come from any boxing blow, but from a snapping ring-rope that hit him at the back of the skull. Flack's preoccupation with the quirks of fortune led her to pick Davey Moore as a subject: a working-class African-American who might have achieved a larger measure of fame had not that split second occurred when his skull would come in contact with the snapping rope.

But the death that jolted the nation in the 1960s was the assassination of President John F. Kennedy. The man who seemed to live a charmed life—war hero, dynamic speaker, energetic leader, glamorous husband, seemingly doting father—was suddenly dead. His beautiful and stylish wife became a statesmanlike widow. Like other artists of the time, Flack felt compelled to express an incident from the event. For her own homage, *Kennedy Motorcade* of 1964, she selected a color news photograph of John and Jackie Kennedy sitting in the convertible as they wait to begin the parade route that took them from their plane to downtown Dallas. Ten years later Flack recalled:

> President Kennedy's assassination had a great effect on me. I wanted to make a statement about it. . . . [The painting] got the most incredible reviews. People were horrified at the subject matter. Now it looks like such a mild painting. It was just a picture of Kennedy riding in the Dallas motorcade with Jackie at his side holding a bunch of roses and Connally riding in the front. Everybody is smiling, and, of course, you know that one moment later Kennedy is going to get shot. This event solidified and confirmed the direction in which my art was going to go in terms of subject matter and style.[4]

By "style" Flack meant that she would begin to focus on the qualities of color as real light, a shift inspired by the use of the color news photograph.

By subject matter she meant a narrative that could be read by the spectator not only for its unfolding story line but for the metaphoric import of the images. In the distant background sits the presidential jet airplane on the runway. The couple sit in the back seat of the motorcade convertible in the bright November Texas sun. Between them are a bouquet of flowers, and in front of them sits Texas Governor John Connally. Fanning out behind the convertible are airplane pilots, mechanics, and security men, standing on the road as the convertible readies to leave. A hatless Kennedy looks off to the right toward the crowd, while Jackie, in her jaunty pink suit and pillbox hat, gestures in the same direction with her hand sheathed in a one-button white glove. (Millions of American women would have noticed such details, for the President's wife was the leading role model in terms of fashionable chic.) Connally, in the front, begins to insert his left hand into the inside of his dark jacket—a gesture that Flack saw as sinister. An ominous shadow, to Flack a portent of future events, falls across the arm and breast of Kennedy as he smiles absently. But precise description merely records the context—the background, the props, and the actors before they begin to play out their parts. The real action comes from us, the viewers, who fill in the story: we know that Kennedy on that late fall day will be shot in circumstances never satisfactorily explained. When that convertible rolls directly into the firing range of the assassin his life violently ends, whereas Jackie and Connally survive. Jackie's outfit will be bloodstained and soon exchanged for widow's weeds. She would publicly grieve, and Lyndon Baines Johnson would be sworn in as the thirty-sixth president. Flack presents us with not just an instantly recognizable scene but one in which we fill in the tragic denouement and fateful conclusion. And the fleeting, admiring smiles on the faces of the pilots and mechanics played off against Kennedy's frozen smile give a piquancy to our memory of events.

From the faces and masks of our public officials Flack turned her attention to women in public spaces, women given identity by their contexts, by their

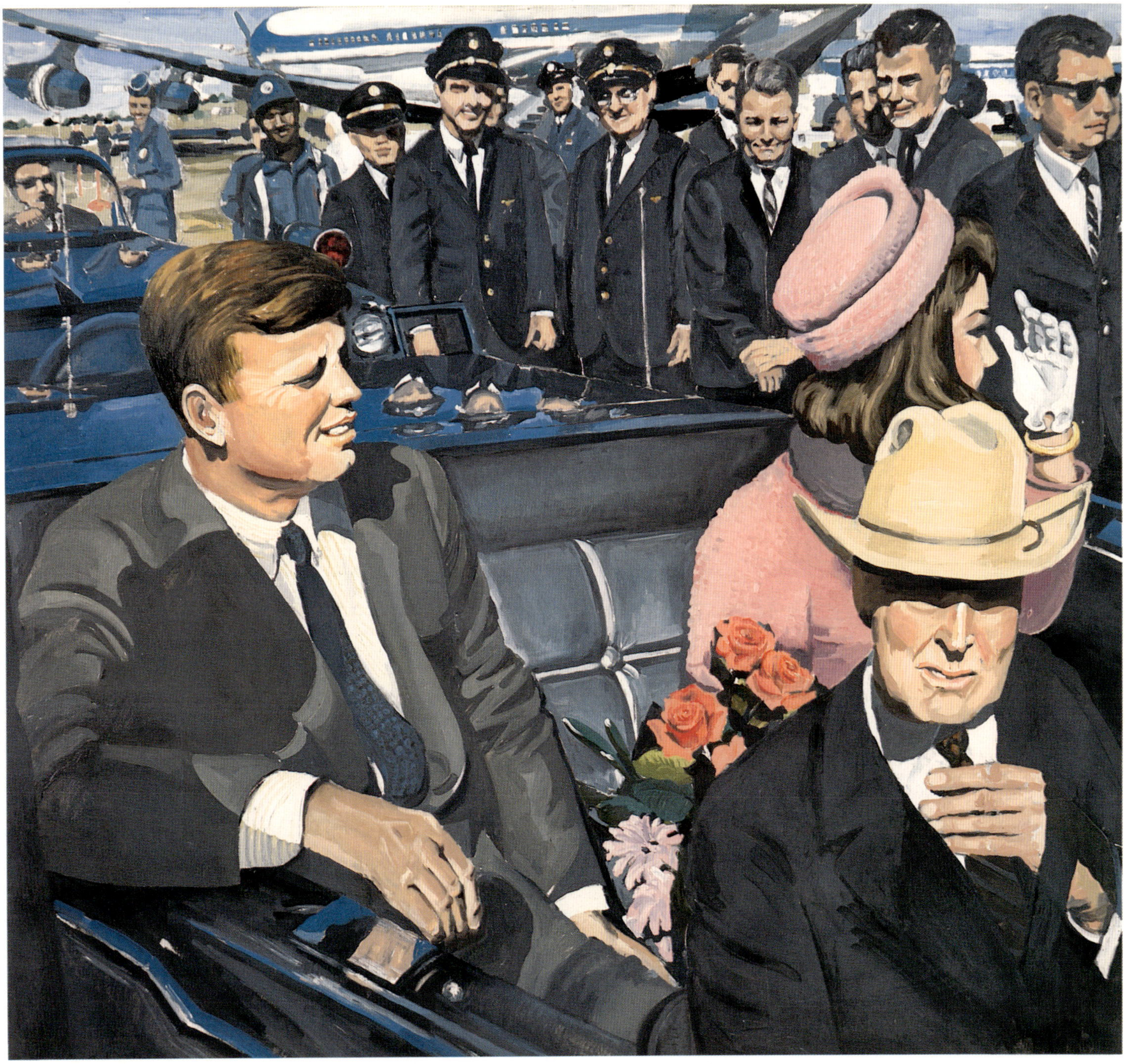

Kennedy Motorcade. 1964
Oil on canvas, 38×42″
Private collection

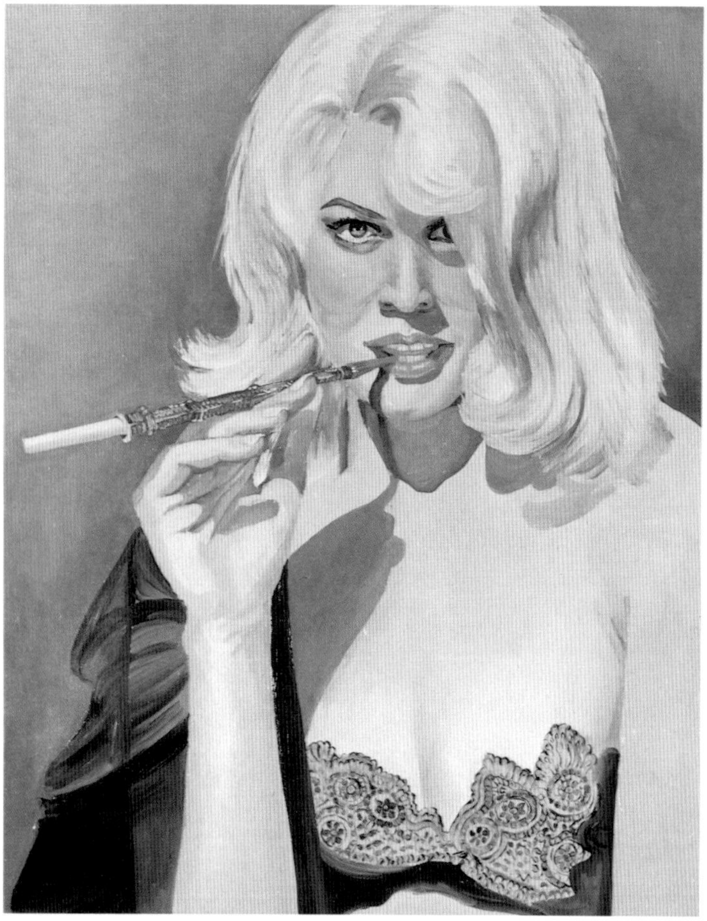

Carroll Baker. 1964
Oil on canvas, 20 × 16″
Private collection

Truman's Teachers. 1964
Oil on canvas, 20 × 30″
Collection Beverly and
Hyman Dolinsky, New York

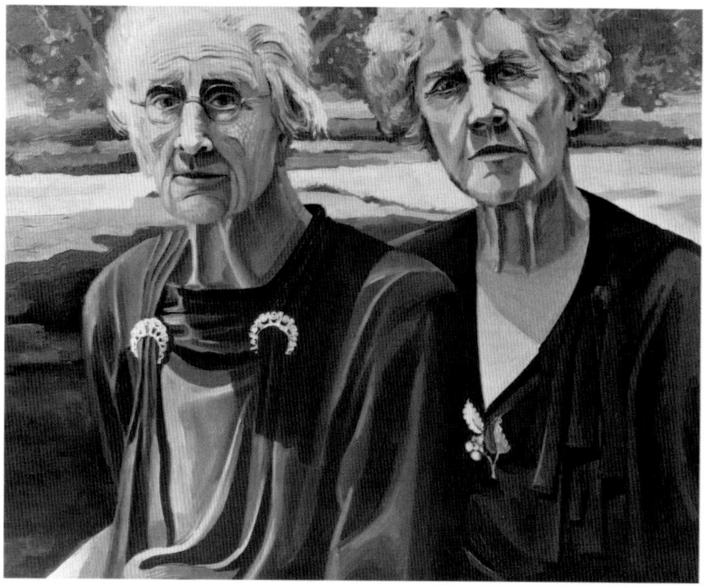

Sisters of the Immaculate Conception
Marching for Freedom. 1965
Oil on canvas, 38 × 70″
New York University, New York

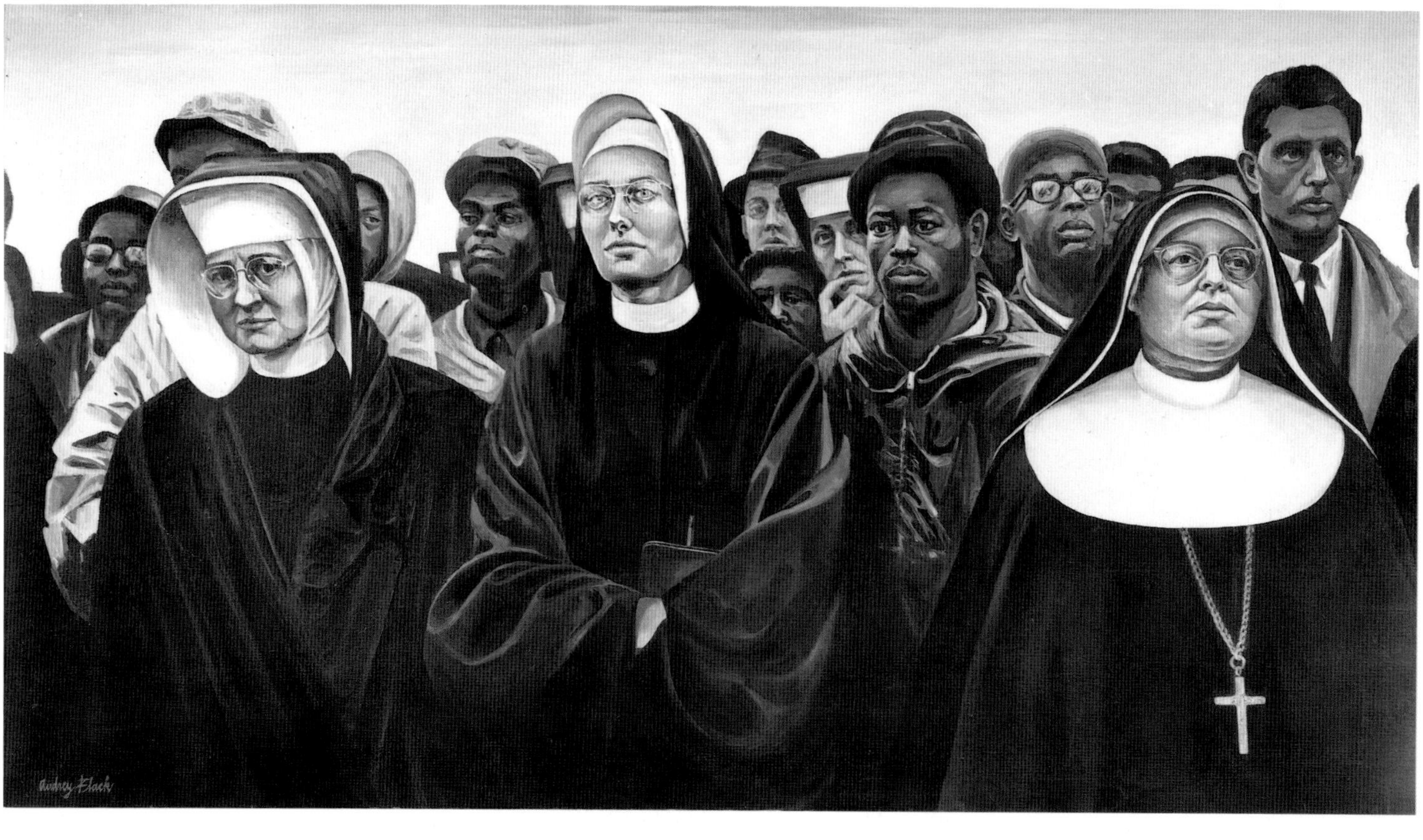

participation in events, such as *Two Women Grieving over Kennedy Outside a Dallas Hospital*. Again, Flack chose a news photo—a UPI telephoto, one of the first to hit the newspapers. *Newsday* of Long Island, New York, captioned it "Two Women of Dallas. Two unidentified women standing outside Parkland Hospital in Dallas yesterday weep upon learning of President Kennedy's death." The subtext should read: a leader who has captured the love of the people is being publicly and spontaneously grieved. Rejecting the often-reproduced, stately image of the mourning Jackie (that Andy Warhol later appropriated), Flack chose two anonymous black women stunned at the moment when the news became public: a strong woman with set lips and the furrowed brow of stoic control comforts her weeping companion with a tender but firm hand. The long arms of the other direct our gaze to her face whose composure has been shattered.

In 1964 Flack painted a range of representations of women. *Two Women Grieving* was one—of women in compassionate solidarity. Other images included a kittenish *Marilyn Monroe* and a seductive *Carroll Baker*, followed by the stalwart figures in *Truman's Teachers* and the determined *Sisters of the Immaculate Conception Marching for Freedom*. This turning point in America's social history—civil rights protests, riots in Harlem, the election of Johnson, and the secret escalation of the Vietnam War—was a propitious time to explore the image of women.

The paintings of the sex goddesses Monroe and Baker do not have the kind of authority enjoyed by the grieving women, the teachers, and the nuns. This is not because of the subjects themselves, but because Flack does not seem to have had the commitment to persuade us of their sexual power. The paintings are flat, the shadows have little claim to realism, the props seem arbitrary, and their pawlike hands are clumsily articulated. These works were experiments, failing, I believe, because they contradicted Flack's inner convictions about the possibilities for women. This series of blond actresses, brief as it was, ended with *Party Laugh* of 1965. With her head thrown back and bangs hanging into the corners of her eyes, the Greek star Melina Mercouri abandons herself to peels of laughter as her neck muscles strain to sustain the intensity. Flack did not know the particular circumstances of Mercouri's laugh, nor of the intentions of the photographer who snapped the picture, but she interpreted the laugh as one containing "tremendous pain."

The coy smile, the fatuous grin, the theatrical laugh preoccupied Flack then because of her own life circumstances. Dwelling on Mercuri's laugh, Flack recalled it was a period when "I had to keep some semblance of sanity, so I tried to smile through my tears. My father used to say: 'You are a Flack, so don't let anybody see you cry.'"

Truman's Teachers, drawn from a much earlier news photo, sympathetically portrays two elderly women who once taught Harry S Truman in Independence, Missouri. Flack found them appealing: "These tough old birds made Truman what he was," she will say of them. Unpretentious, solid, worn, intelligent, shrewd, simply dressed, they are posing for their photographs, outside, under the trees, and the sharp glare of the sun reveals the care lines and wrinkles, the evidence of years teaching young stubborn boys the ways of books and the values of citizenship. Being "tough" was another virtue to Flack.

Flack painted *Sisters of the Immaculate Conception Marching for Freedom* using a contemporary news photograph. In the forefront of the crowd are three nuns in habit, the avant-garde of the march, both leading and protecting the

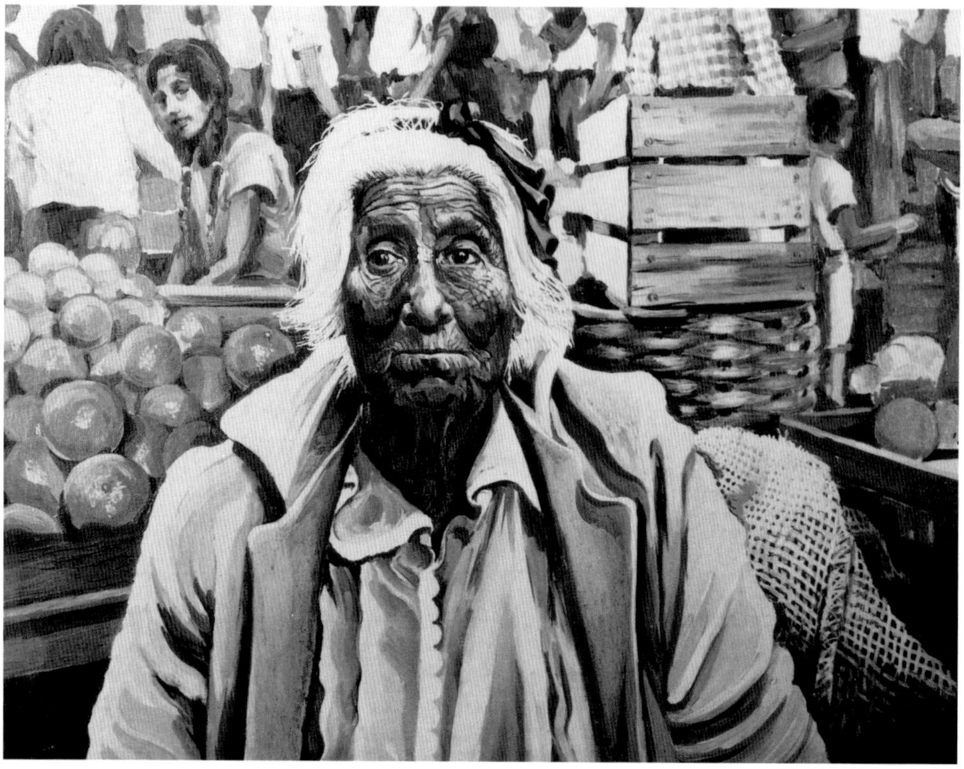

Old Mexican Orange Seller. 1967
Oil on canvas, 20×26″
Collection Jerome Spiller, New York

men who have joined the ranks behind. Such assertion of determined belief, of the merging of personal self with idealism, of religiously devout people committed to social change, drew Flack's deep respect. Flack's willingness to make art out of social protest recalls the 1930s, when paintings of protestors received the unqualified support of most artists and critics. But in the mid-1960s such pictures were painted by only a few artists. Nevertheless, Flack brings a modern sensibility to the image through intensifying the immediacy of the participants. They seem about to burst through the picture plane, displaying a range of depicted emotion as each struggles to overcome individual fears for a common cause.

In the winter of 1967–68 Flack went with her husband for a ten-day vacation in Mexico without the children. In Oaxaca, Flack photographed old market women peddling oranges and other fruits and vegetables. It was the first time Flack took photographs with the express purpose of using them for later paintings. When she returned she painted *Two Weavers from Oaxaca*, *Old Mexican Orange Seller*, and *Orange Seller Laughing*. Like the figures in *Truman's Teachers*, the weavers in *Two Weavers from Oaxaca* stand shoulder to shoulder, facing the photographer and radiating a sense of self-worth and wisdom. When Flack looked at the scene in *Old Mexican Orange Seller*, her gaze was arrested by the young girl looking out from above the bin of oranges at the left. The image of the girl balances the form of an empty crate at the upper right. The nubility of the young girl, the fullness and fecundity of the oranges, and an empty box bracketing the figure of the older, wizened woman symbolize the stages of her life—youth, ripeness, and eventual loss. Flack's humility in the presence of such women is further revealed in *Orange Seller Laughing*, also painted from Flack's own snapshots. Here the subject controls Flack's representation by good-humoredly laughing at the artist and making us aware of Flack's own self-conscious but empathetic confrontation with her subjects.

Finally, the most ambitious painting to result from that trip to Oaxaca is

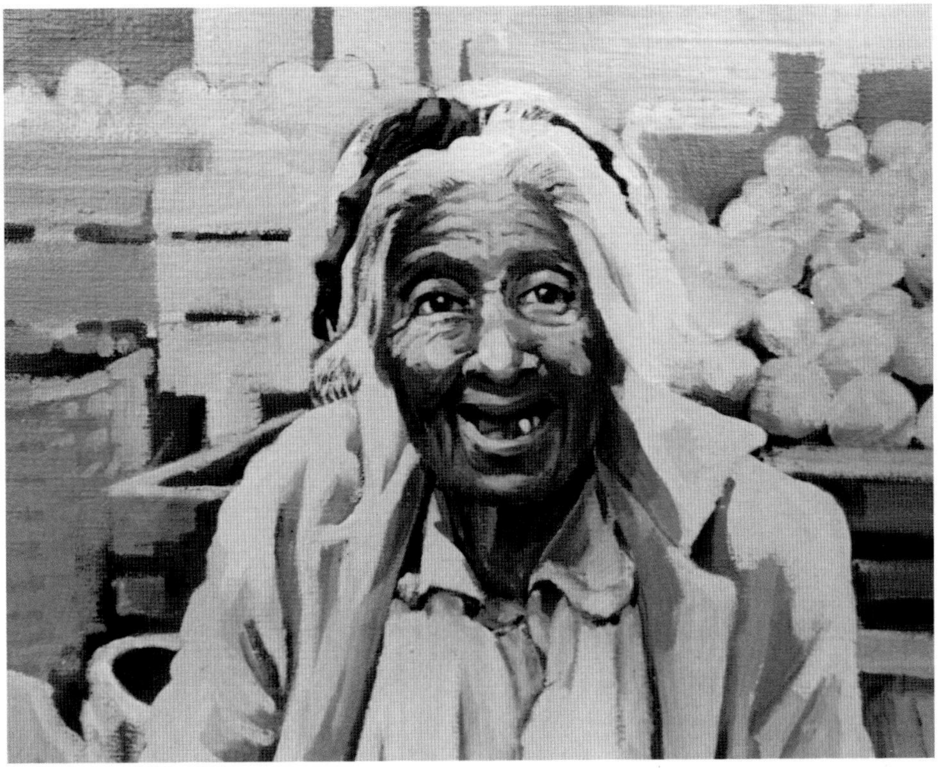

Orange Seller Laughing at Me for Taking Her Picture. 1967
Oil on canvas, 8×10″
Collection Steve Weil,
Washington, D.C.

Young Mexican Farmer in Oaxaca Market, finished in 1968. The painting recalls a pencil and watercolor drawing, *Striking Workers, Florence*, that Flack made on a trip to Italy in 1956; in that earlier work picketers sit at the base of Renaissance statuary enjoying a lunch break. Although somewhat sketchy, one worker turns to look at the artist. What Flack remembered as notable about that scene was "the blend of high art and poor Italian workers" and how much at home the workers were with their artistic heritage that they even "would strike their matches on the base" of the sculpture.

As with the earlier sketch, we view *Young Mexican Farmer* at ground level, and we witness his and his friends' viewing us. But here Flack gives us much more information about the situation than in *Striking Workers*. The sunlight, open sky, bright blues, shadows, and reflected lights create a vivid spectacle for this artist/tourist with her camera. Unlike painters who view as curious and quaint the local people of the lands through which they travel, Flack captures the intelligence, the sense of humor, and the steady imperturbability of these Mexican people; they are the subjects, not the objects, of her art. Their strong gaze toward her subverts their "otherness." To them *she* is the other, the exotic—rootless and searching for an identity. But, more than likely, they do not care. They tolerate her picture-taking like gnats flying about, merely pesky at times.

She returned to the theme of social protest when she painted *War Protest March* in 1968, after the assassination of Martin Luther King, Jr., whose face appears on the button of the young man marching at the left. She had gone to a demonstration and taken photographs of the crowd with their placards reading "Support our GI's/Withdraw all U.S. troops from Vietnam Now!" and "Stop the Bombing." The photograph she chose for her painting clearly showed the seriousness and multiracial quality of the march. By bringing the demonstrators right up to the picture plane—even cutting off the face of one figure at the left—Flack persuades her viewer to join in and to embrace the social and political goals of these marchers.

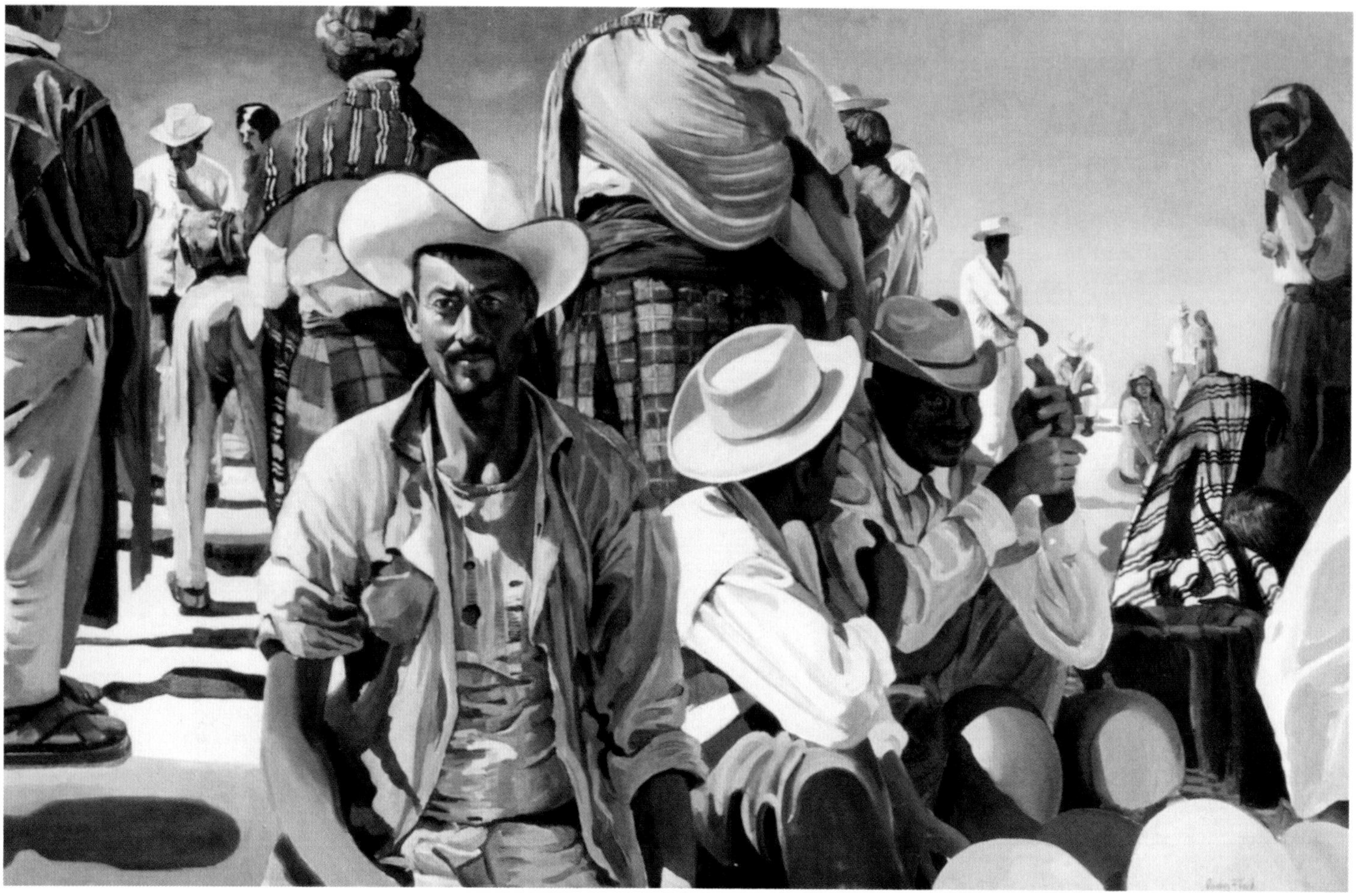

Young Mexican Farmer in Oaxaca Market. 1967–68
Oil on canvas, 40 × 62″
Collection Sidney Singer

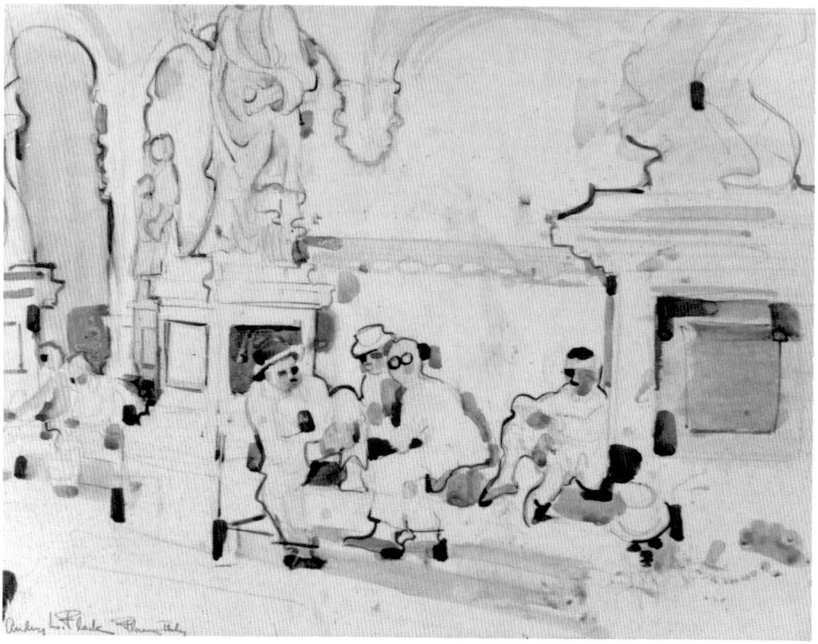

Striking Workers, Florence. 1956
Pencil and watercolor on paper, 11¾ × 15½″
Private collection, Cambridge, Massachusetts

In 1969 Flack was commissioned by Oriole Farb to paint her family's group portrait, *Farb Family Portrait.* Oriole Farb then ran the Riverside Museum, which contained her family's collection of Tibetan paintings of various stages in the life of Buddha. One of these we see hanging behind the group. The four figures, Peter and Oriole Farb and their two sons, formally face us; no smiles linger on their faces, merely four penetrating gazes. They pose not for the painter Flack, but for the photographer Flack, whose camera at the moment

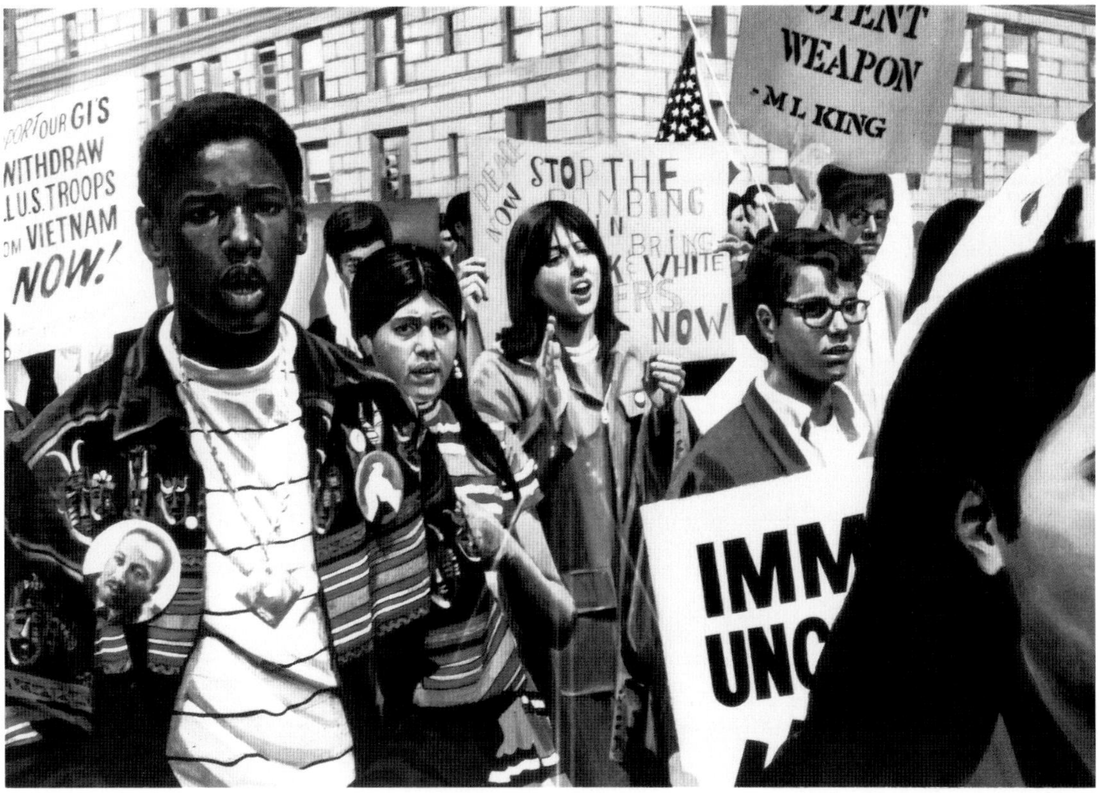

War Protest March. 1968
Oil on canvas, 20 × 30″
Collection Phil Desind,
The Capricorn Gallery,
Bethesda, Maryland

Two Women Grieving over Kennedy Outside a Dallas Hospital. 1964
Oil on canvas, 36 × 28″
Collection Edward Lamb,
Toledo, Ohio

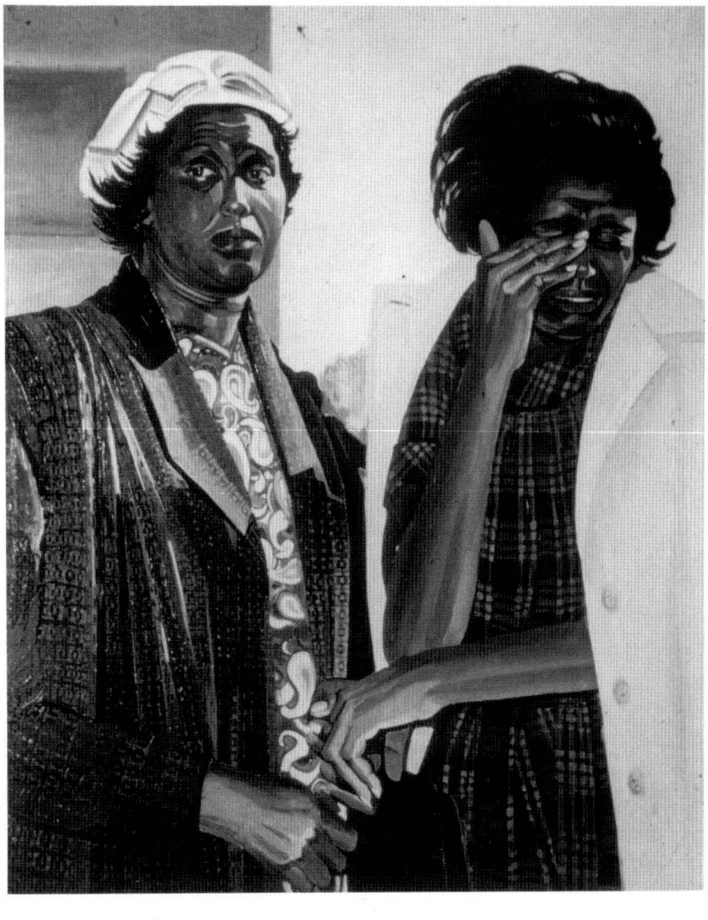

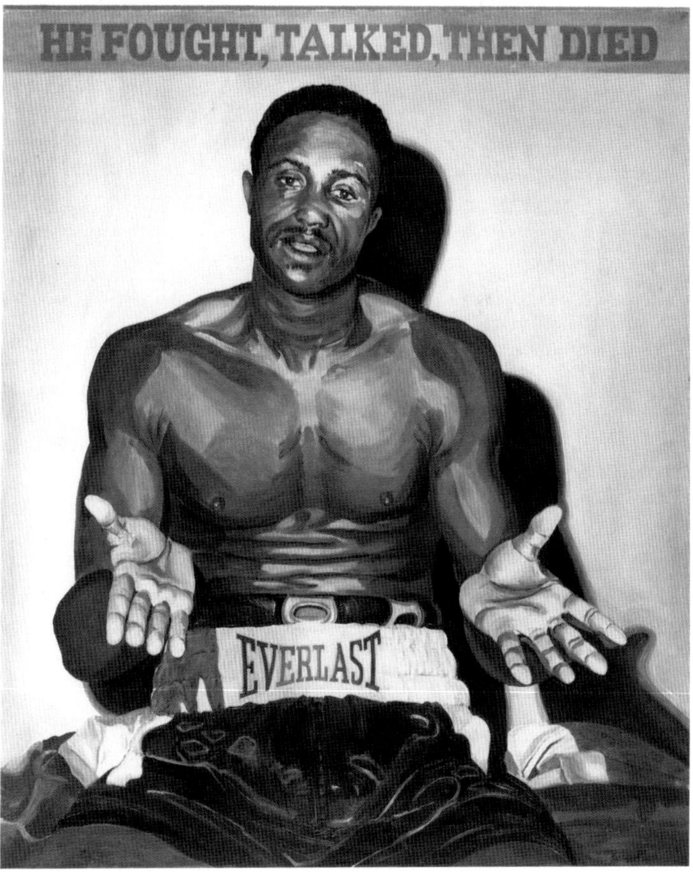

Davey Moore. 1964
Oil on canvas, 36 × 30″
Private collection

exposes the slide film later used when Flack worked up the portrait in her studio.

Within the painted trompe l'oeil frame, each figure quietly asserts his or her individuality. The handsome older boy with bold tie projects the image of assured intelligence. His father, standing behind, commands the center of the canvas; he wears a tie adapted from Native American regalia. The younger son almost mocks the artist with his finger poised on the shutter of his camera. Oriole, the only woman, stands tall and firm, bathed in the light from the left side of the canvas.

With this painting Flack moved into her mature style, Photorealism. She developed the technique of taking a slide of the subject, then projecting the developed slide right onto the canvas and painting over the projected image. The shift of technique happened spontaneously. Flack later recalled:

> I photographed the family, posing them in what I felt was the family balance. I started by drawing on canvas with charcoal, as was my usual practice. When I had completed three of the four figures, I became impatient, wanting to get beyond this stage and on with the painting. It also seemed a waste, since all of the charcoal lines would eventually be eliminated by being painted over. It was late at night and I suddenly had the idea of projecting an image onto the canvas. In this way I could place the figures rapidly and proceed with the painting. To this point I had only been working with the live models and with photographs. I owned no projector but was so excited by the idea that I called a friend who immediately responded to the urgency of my request. . . . This was the beginning. It opened up a new way of seeing and working. I started to paint directly with no preliminary drawing, thinking in terms of mass, volume, silhouette, and edge. It took a while for me to drop line altogether, but when it finally happened it allowed me a greater freedom and a direct contact with the canvas.[5]

The light image from the slide then became the basis for the alternations and intensity of color she would bring to painting. In works of the early 1970s, following *Farb Family Portrait,* she would begin to use an airbrush and select only the red, yellow, and blue found in the gels of the color slides. The result would be an increasing intensity of color and light.

Although using slides as the basis of her painting in a more direct way than ever before, Flack declares *Farb Family Portrait* to be a painting within the tradition of painting when she surrounds the image with the painstakingly painted trompe l'oeil frame. That frame removes the Farbs from us and asserts their place in the high art of painting. (After all, when does a subject in a photograph come surrounded by a frame?) Moreover, she asserts her own crucial role as artist by giving her name prominence: the trompe l'oeil brass plate on the frame announces:

FAMILY PORTRAIT
1969–70
AUDREY FLACK

Subject—date—artist. Time bridges the space between the subject and the artist, between the static objects of painting and the process itself.

Behind the Farbs sits the all-knowing Buddha, sightless in Flack's painting, but he reminds us of a long-past epoch of spirituality. In her art of the 1980s Flack would yearn for such calming and transcendent presences, no matter how much she immersed herself in present-day realities.

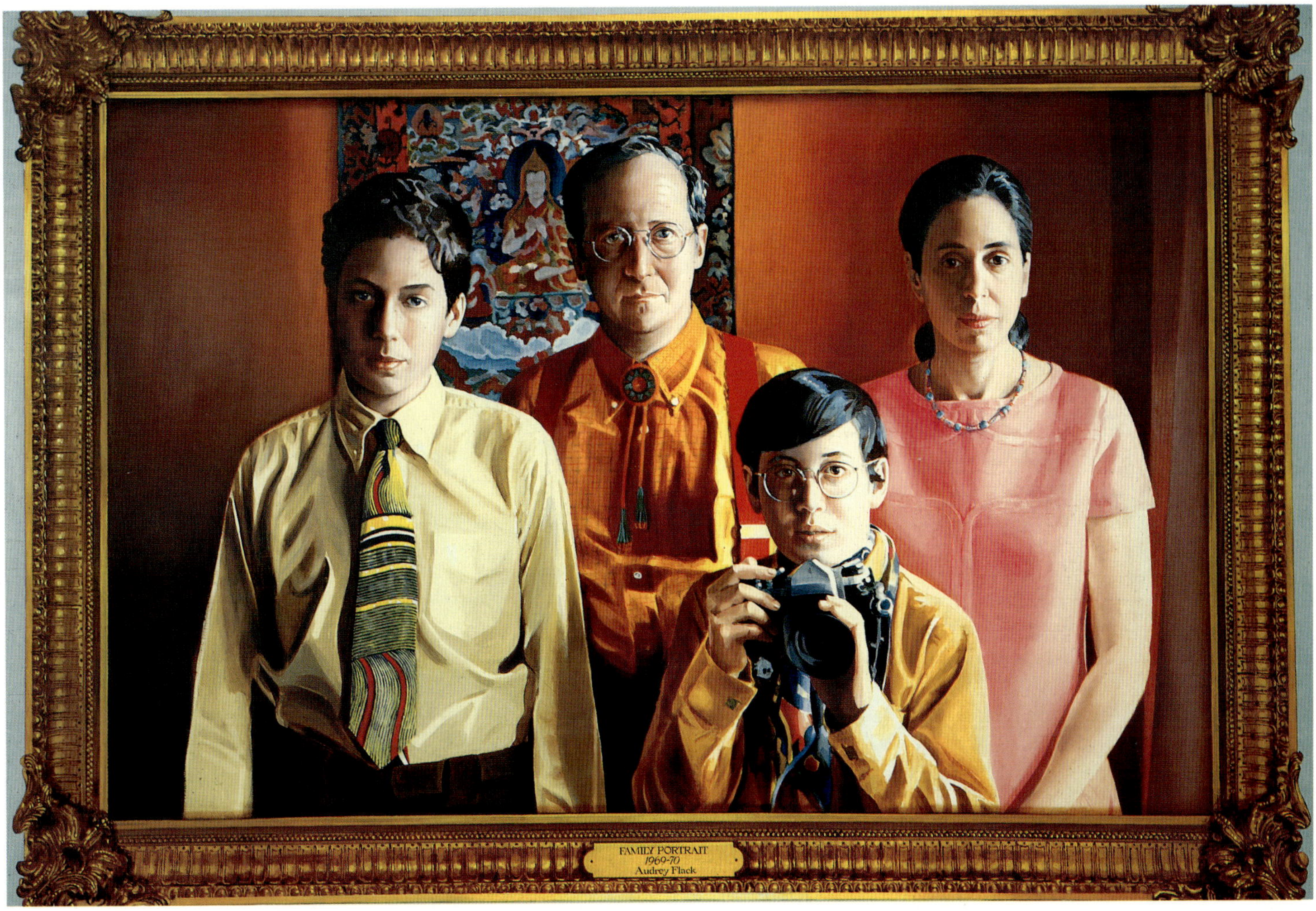

Farb Family Portrait. 1969–70
Oil on canvas, 40 × 60″
Rose Art Museum, Brandeis University
Waltham, Massachusetts

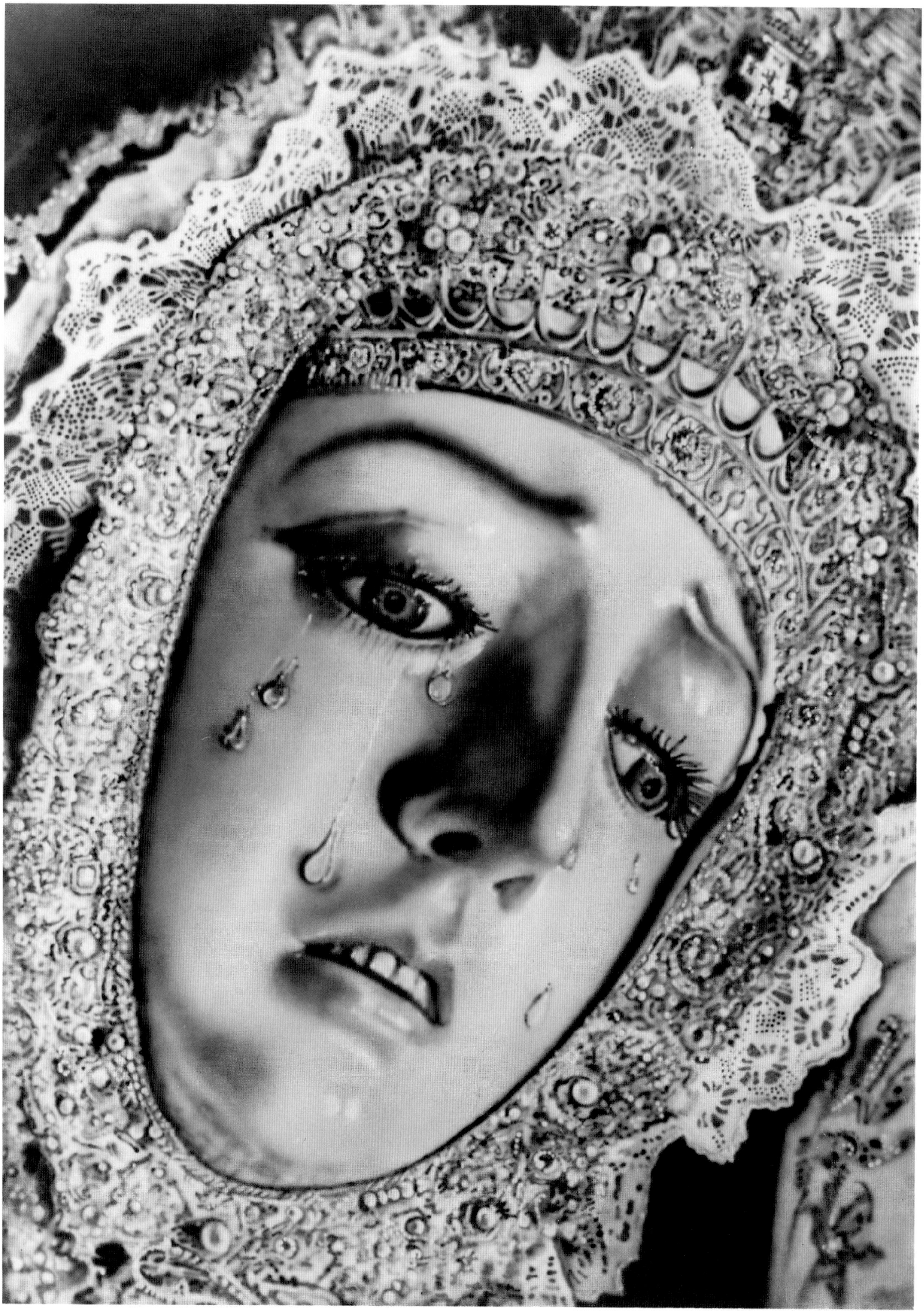

AUDREY FLACK'S STILL-LIFE PAINTINGS IN THE 1970s

Lawrence Alloway

The 1970s is a remarkable decade for Audrey Flack's still-life painting, beginning with her paintings of sculpture and architecture. In effect she took the Dada view of existing objects and known monuments and made them the subject of immaculate illusionist paintings. She combined touristlike views of cities and articles, such as *Siena Cathedral* and *Michelangelo's David*, both of 1971. They are like Marcel Duchamp's *Bicycle Wheel* or *Bottle-Rack* in the age of tourism and color reproduction. Instead of anonymously designed, mass-produced objects, of which a sample functions as sculpture, she presents celebrated manufactured objects as the subject of painting. In them, fidelity to reproduced images is linked to art history. She made it clear that Photorealism could cope with historical reality no less than with the current highway and its furniture. She stresses, too, the role of talent and patience compared to Duchampian all-at-once gestures of choice.[1]

The works that gave Flack a sudden and intense fame at the start of the decade combine an ideal Madonna-image with implications of self-portraiture. These works lead to an actual *Self-Portrait*, 1974, which Flack linked to the sculpture of Luisa Roldán. Taking Spanish Baroque sculpture as her point of reference, she painted *Macarena Esperanza*, *Macarena of Miracles*, and *Dolores of Cordoba*, all of 1971, and *Lady Madonna*, 1972. These combined the grandeur of her slightly earlier figure painting with minute, still-life detail. Malcolm Morley had occasionally demonstrated this possibility, but not in consistent, hallucinatory form.

Flack's sculpture-paintings of 1971–72 (*Macarena* and *Dolores*), superbly female, came at a time when manifestations of the "Great Goddess" were sought by feminists and by any woman dissatisfied with available mythologies, male-centered, or at least male-oriented. Without expressing open dissatisfaction with the tradition in which she worked, Flack nonetheless coined female images, sensual, uncanny, intimate. Roldán could be seen in Spain and Flack did so, but a piece could also be seen at the Hispanic Institute in New York, and the general type of Spanish Baroque existed in the Southwest of the United States, and in varying density in Central and Latin America. Flack's historical sense had a factual basis in American museums and vernacular churches as well as in tourism.

After the Madonna-image group, an imaginative reconciliation of the ecstatic and the immobile, Flack considered the effect of borders in the *Gray Border* group, 1974–76. These, however, were preceeded by several paintings, in 1972–73, without the border containment and in which she expanded her space and subjects (*Crayola*, *Rich Art*, and *Spitfire*). Several of these deal with artist's

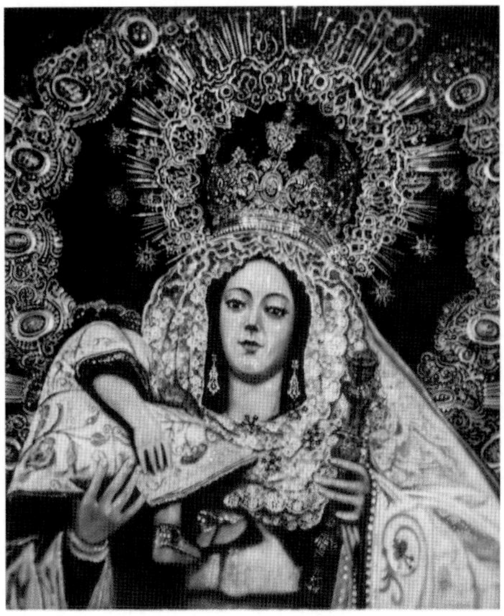

Lady Madonna. 1972
Oil on canvas, 78×69″
The Whitney Museum of American Art,
New York (gift of Martin J. Zimet)

OVERLEAF, LEFT:
Macarena of Miracles. 1971
Oil on canvas, 66×46″
The Metropolitan Museum of Art,
New York (gift of Paul F. Walters)

OVERLEAF, RIGHT:
Macarena Esperanza. 1971
Oil on canvas, 66×46″
Collection Paul and Camille Hoffmann,
Naperville, Illinois

OPPOSITE:
Dolores of Cordoba. 1971
Oil on canvas, 70×50″
Collection Jane Rubin, New York

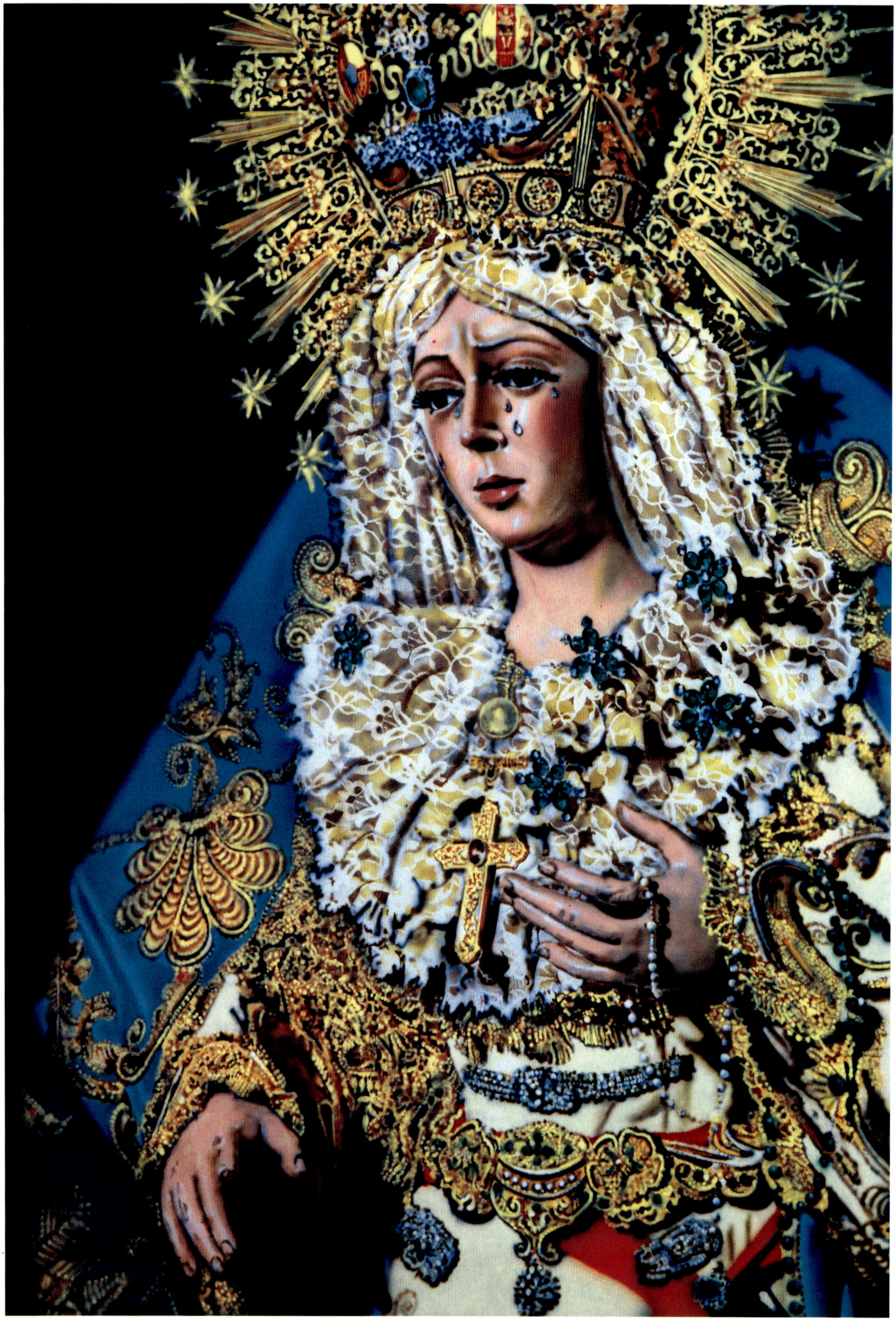

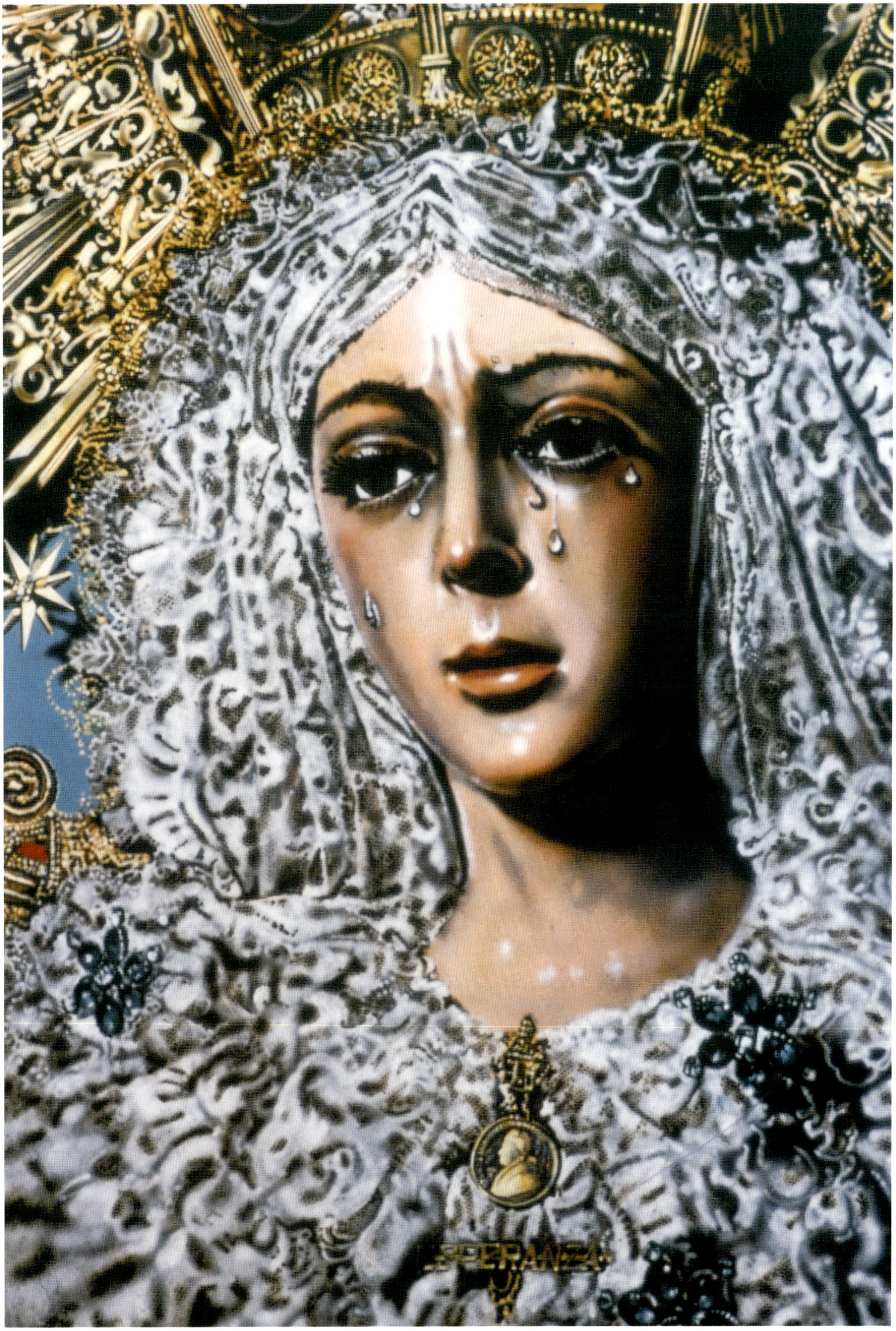

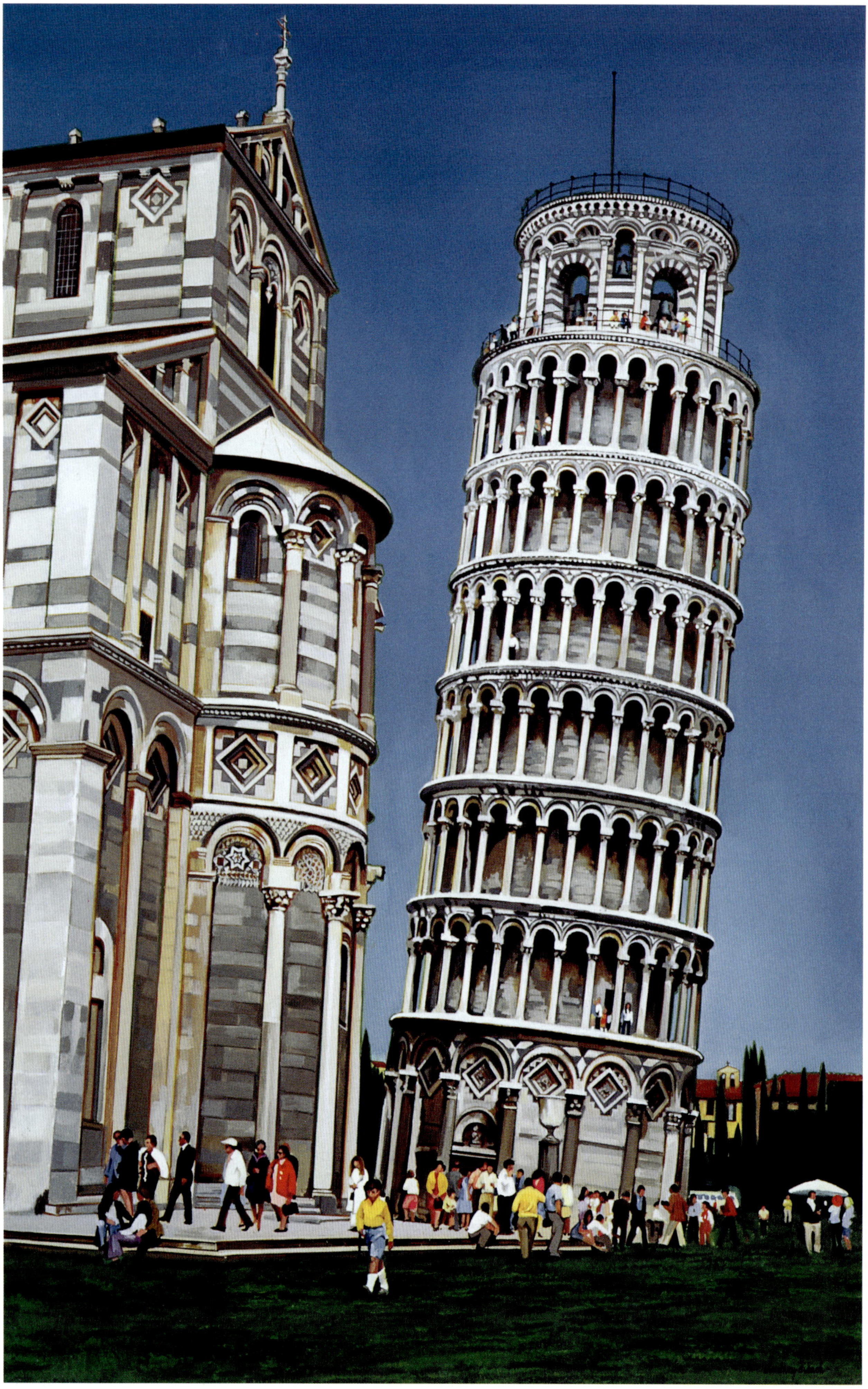

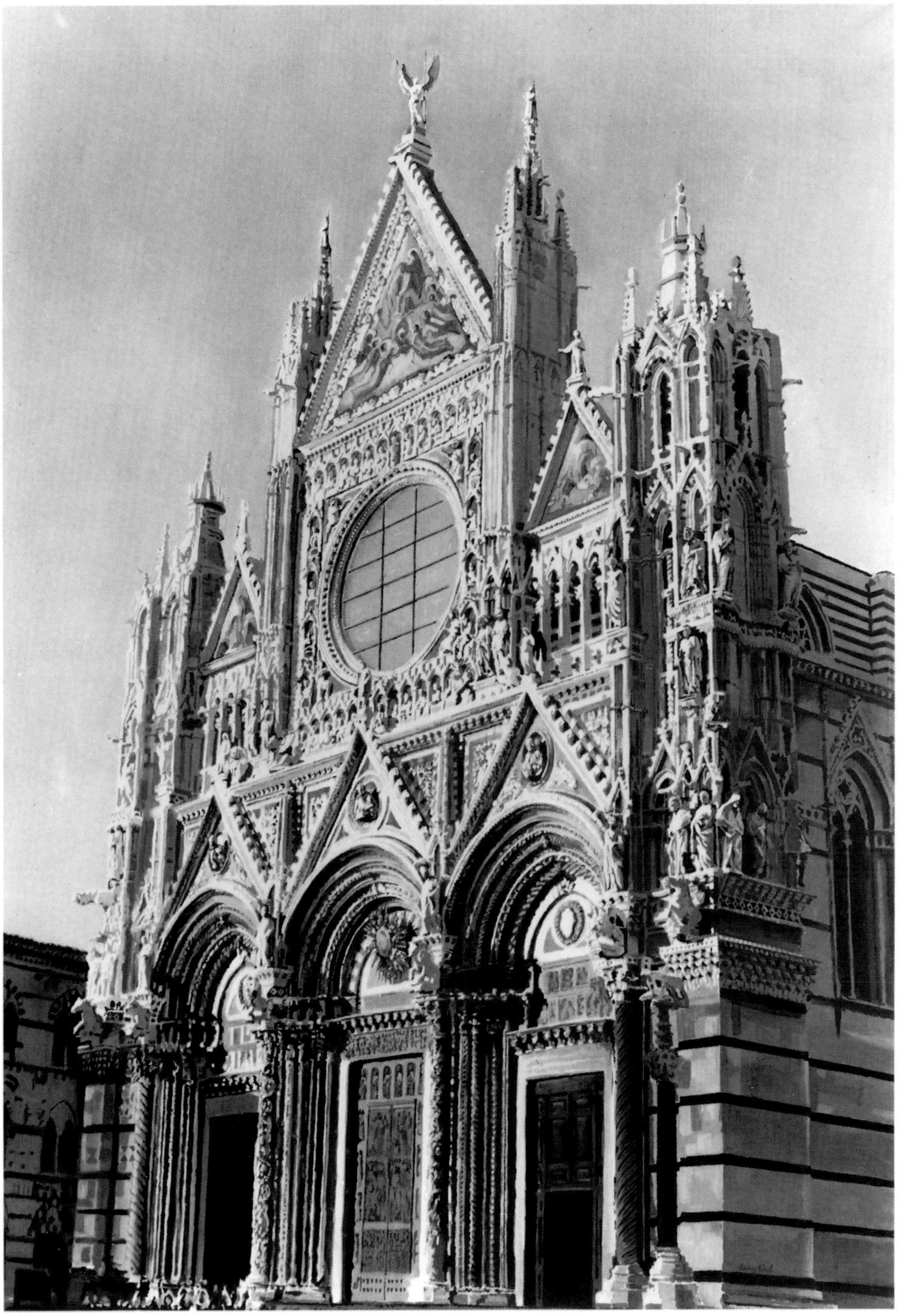

Siena Cathedral. 1971
Oil on canvas, 66 × 46″
Collection Louis K.
and Susan Pear Meisel,
New York

OPPOSITE:
Tower of Pisa. 1971
Oil on canvas, 72 × 48″
National Museum of American Art,
Smithsonian Institution,
Washington, D.C.

Michelangelo's David. 1971
Oil on canvas, 66 × 46″
Private collection

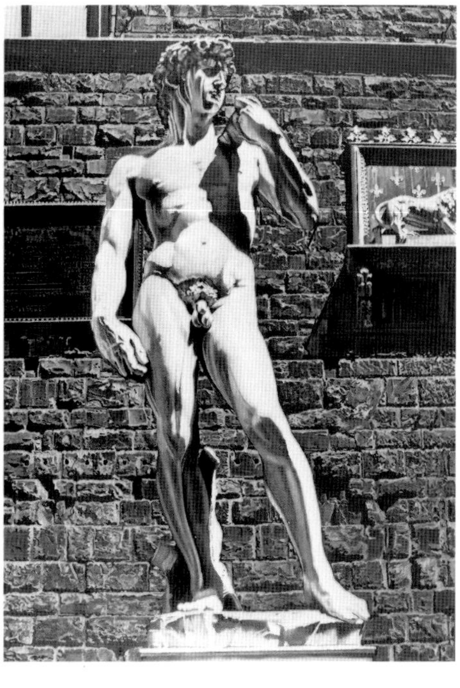

materials and have in common the apparently random distribution of similar objects. These were certainly in Flack's mind when she painted several larger works with more personally allusive meanings (*Royal Flush*, 1973; *Solitaire*, and *Chanel*, both of 1974), which also do not have painted borders. The result is an immediate effect of participation; one looks at the scene precipitously, without delay. This applies especially to the two green baize table pictures devoted to games in progress. The cards in the foreground of *Royal Flush* wipe out the other fan shown (two queens and three eights); in addition the winning hand is associated with two dice that show lucky 7. This and other details represent the game as a climax of good luck for the imagined foreground player. *Solitaire* has a similar vantage point, in and up. The *Gray Border* pictures, however, approach another possibility of Flack's theme. In this group of seven paintings, all but one of them still life, the border is part of the painted surface. The gray borders are fairly broad and tend to be dark, so

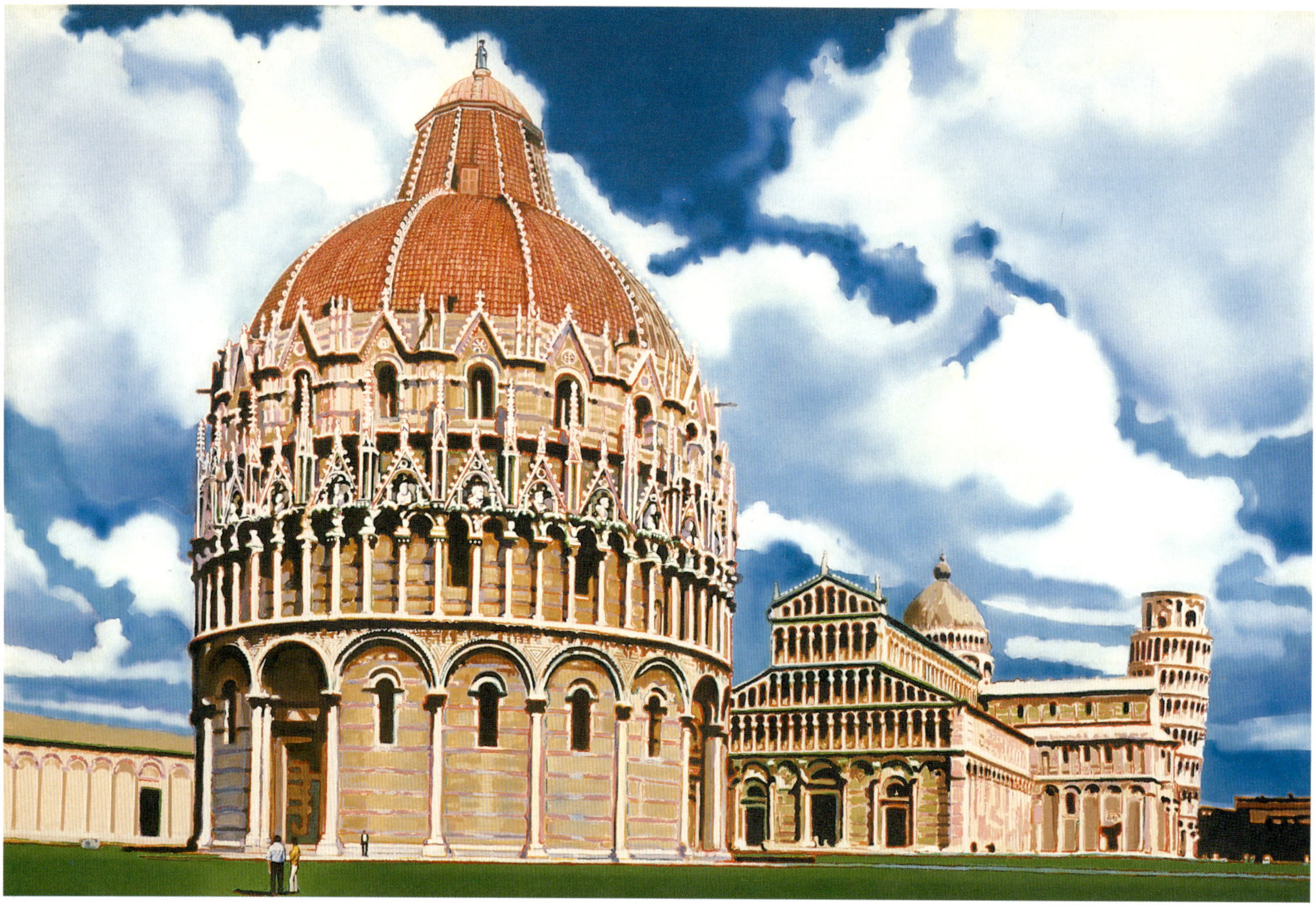

Piazza of Miracles. 1971
Oil on canvas, 48×72″
Collection H. Robert Marcus

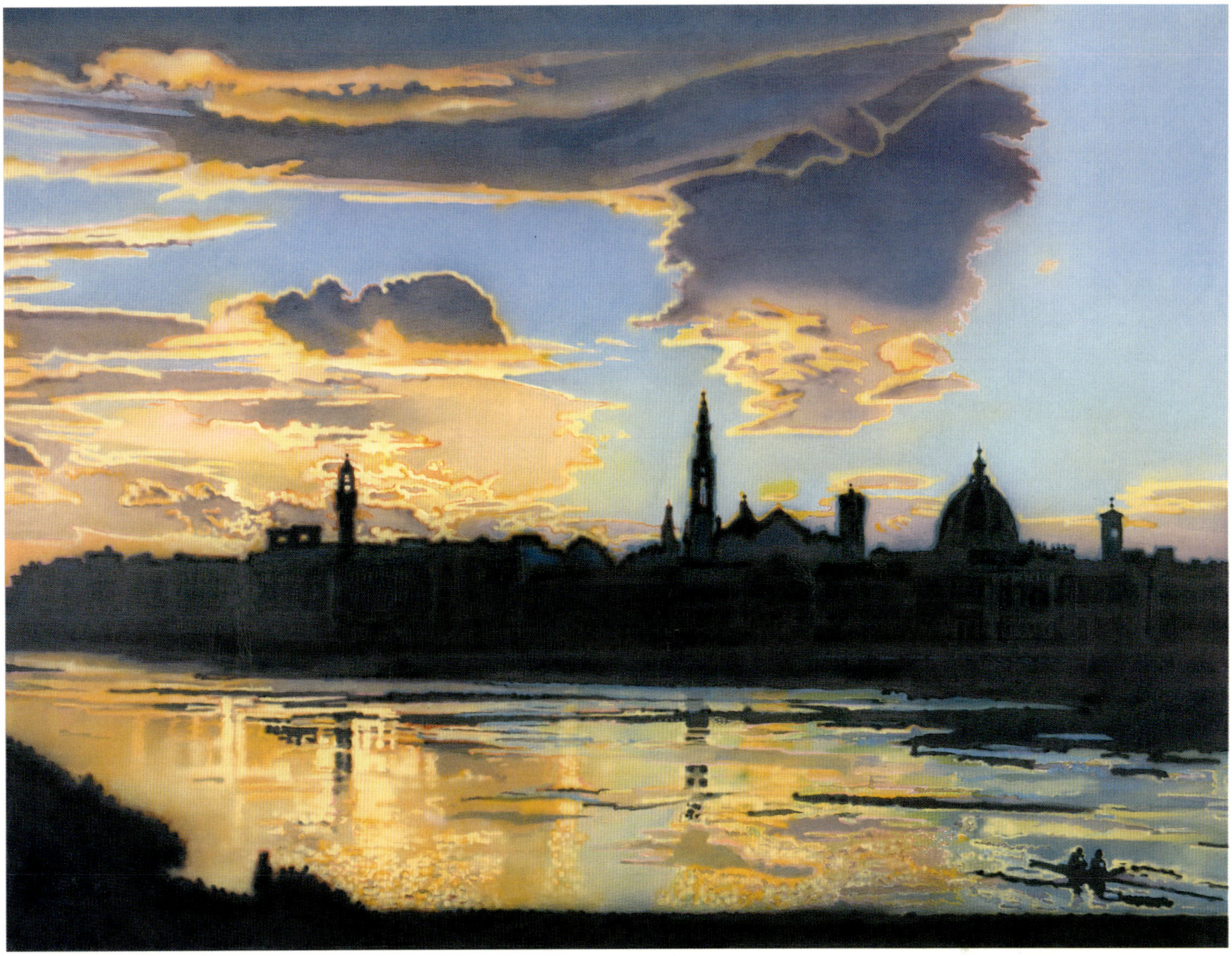

Sunset over Florence. 1971
Oil on canvas, 46 × 66″
Collection H. Robert Marcus

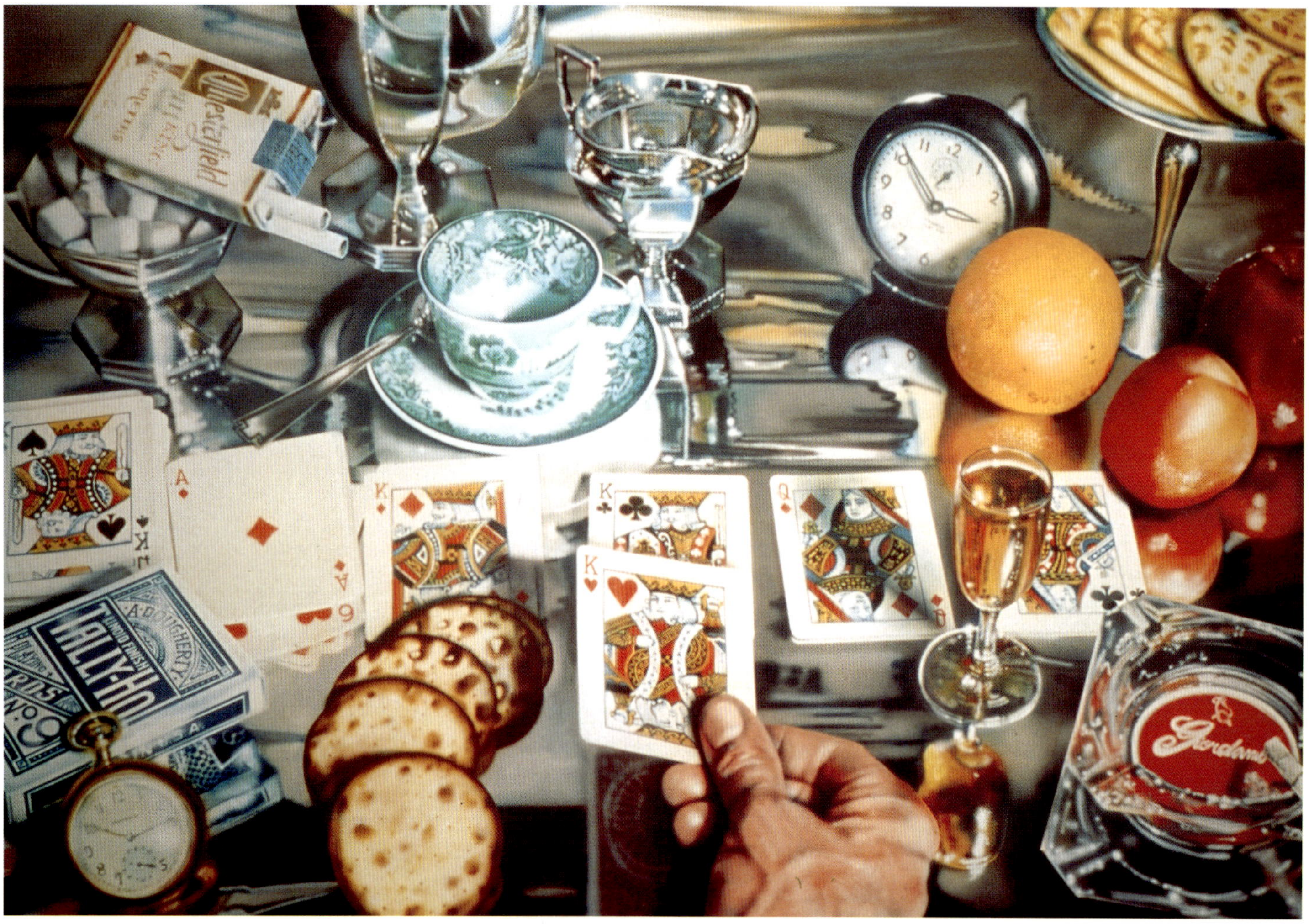

Solitaire. 1974
Acrylic on canvas, 60 × 84″
Collection Joan and Barrie Damson,
New York

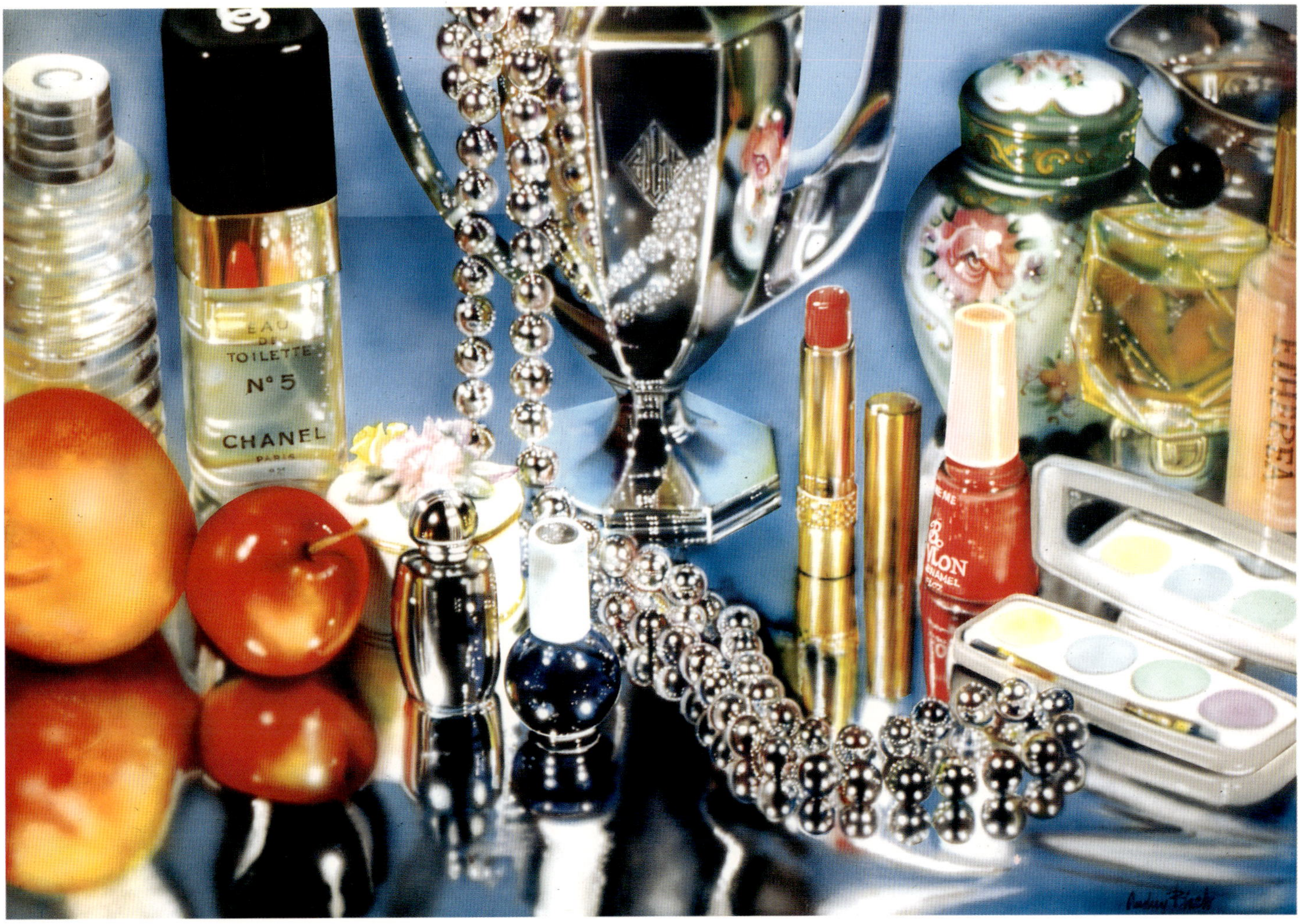

Chanel. 1974
Acrylic on canvas, 56 × 82″
Collection Mrs. Morton G. Neumann,
Chicago

their culmination in two pictures with black borders in 1975–76, *Dutch Still Life* and *World War II*, seems a logical step. The first of the three *Vanitas*, *World War II*, whose focal point is a photograph, has a black border containing a tight spectrum.[2] Prints, drawings, and photographs, that is to say works on paper, were often displayed with extensive borders and layered surrounds. A comparable ambiguity seems to exist in Morley's slightly earlier white borders, derived from photographic prints but used by him to surround crisp, painterly brushwork. Flack was interested in framing problems at this time: in *Queen*, 1975–76, objects overlap the painted gray surround and in *Gambler's Cabinet*, 1976, narrow carpentry forms outline the picture-area itself.

The *Gray Borders* as a whole represent Flack's expansion of her color controls as she expanded her iconography. Take a work like *Buddha*, 1975: on one side a *green* china, bald, belly-sporting effigy of Buddha (the mysterious East); on the other side *white*, spiky porcelain putti (the mysterious West). Both mythologies are enclosed by a wide dark tonal border that retards the snap of participation that marks, say, *Royal Flush*, and which stress a greater elaboration of local color (which is, I take it, the delimiting property of objects). The blue ribbon and sparkling pearls that lead forward out of the picture zone and over the border of *Buddha* function as color intensification and diffusion.

At the midpoint of the decade, Flack apparently decided to pull the camera back, as it were, presenting in most of her paintings more extensive views of numerous objects, with less use of enlargement to achieve close-up or cropping. *Spaced Out Apple* and *Strawberry Tart Supreme*, both of 1974, present edibles in close-up, as if Flack were to challenge urban Photorealism on its own ground of timeless contemporaneity (specifically she may have had Ben Schonzeit in mind). Subsequent *Gray Border* paintings depend less on inversion and enlargement and more on an aesthetic of profuse array. By that I mean a scatter of more and smaller objects. In *Grand Rosé* and *Leonardo's Lady*, for example, the authority of the tabletop is asserted as the natural site of clutter. Flack handles multiplicity in a way that enlargement had certainly

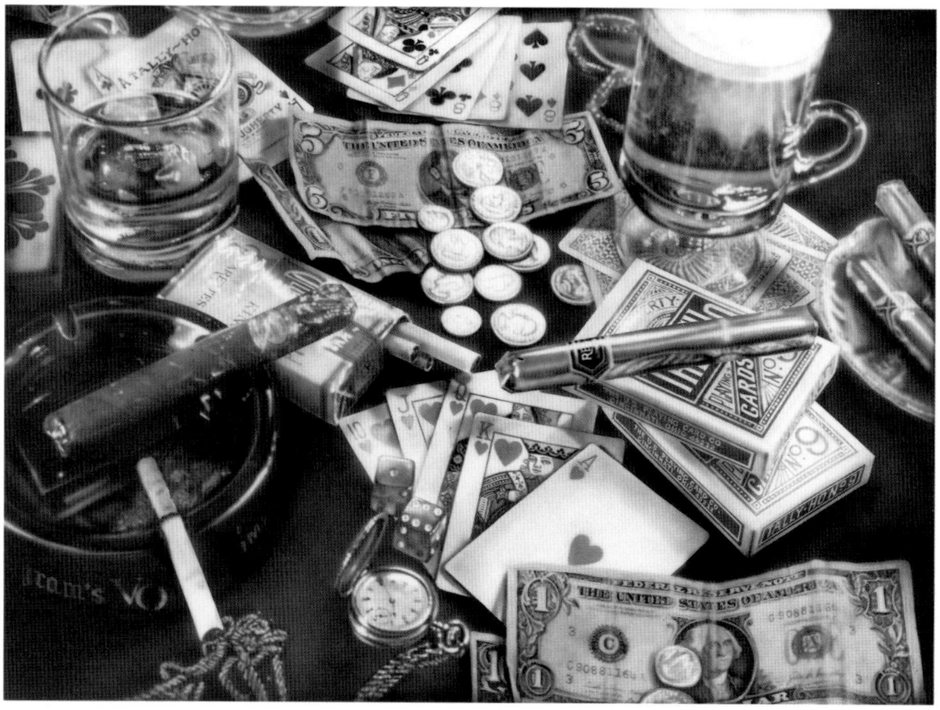

Royal Flush. 1973
Oil over acrylic on canvas, 70 × 96″
Private collection

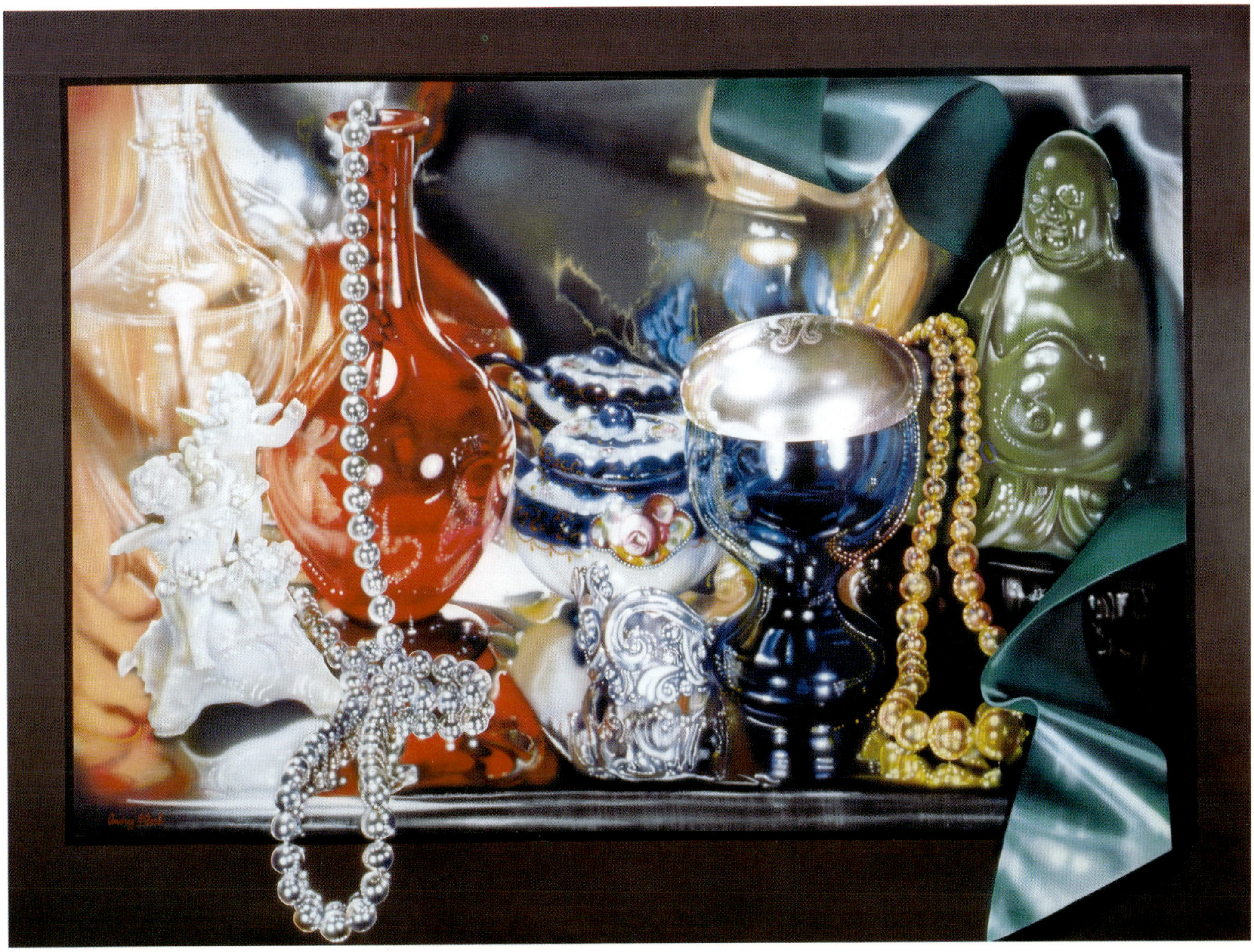

Buddha. 1975
Oil over acrylic on wet
sanded canvas, 70 × 96″
Saint Louis Art Museum
(Purchase and Contemporary Art
Society Fund)

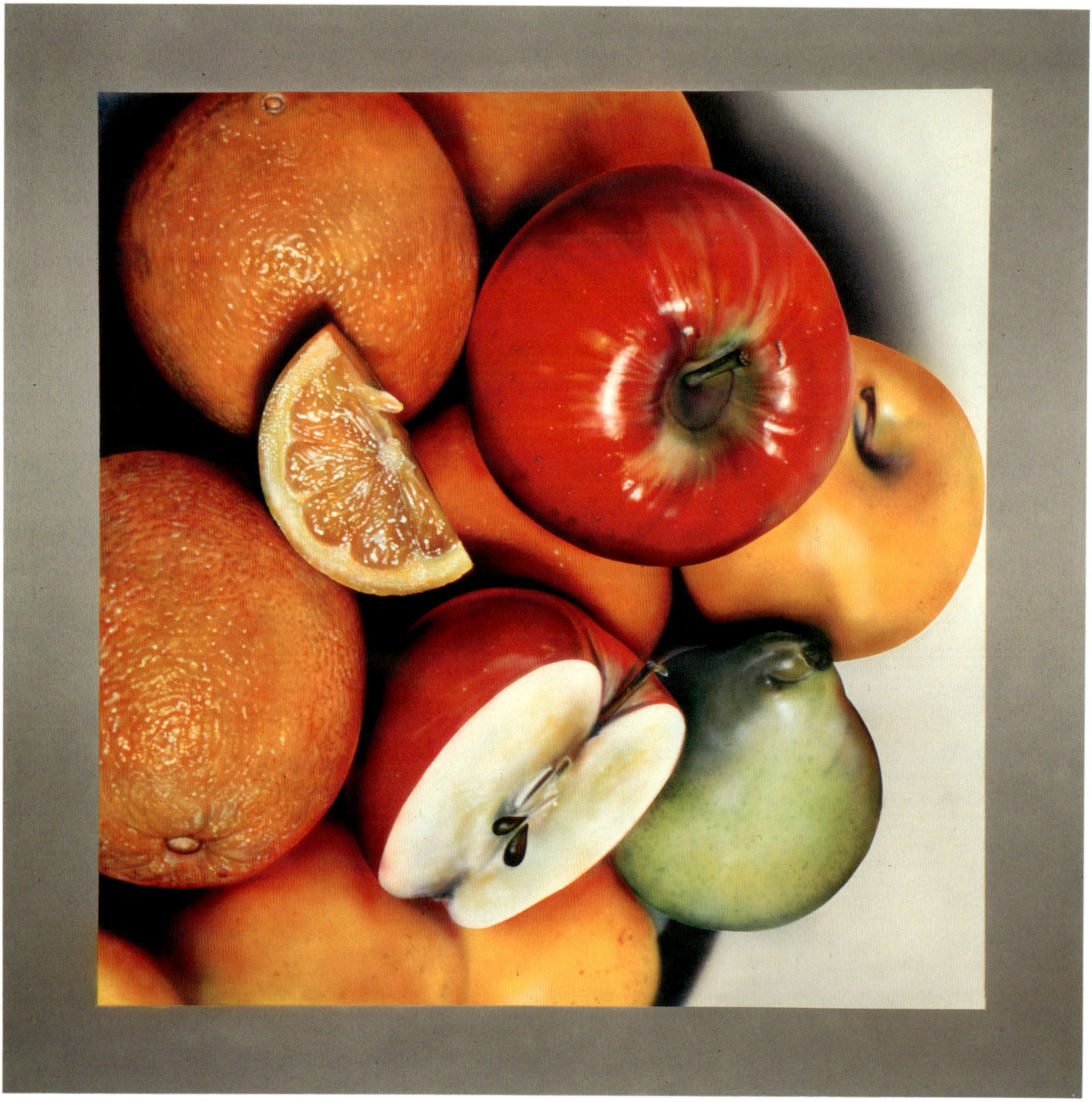

Spaced Out Apple. 1974
Acrylic on wet sanded canvas, 58 × 60¼″
Collection Mr. and Mrs. Jerome Westheimer,
Ardmore, Oklahoma

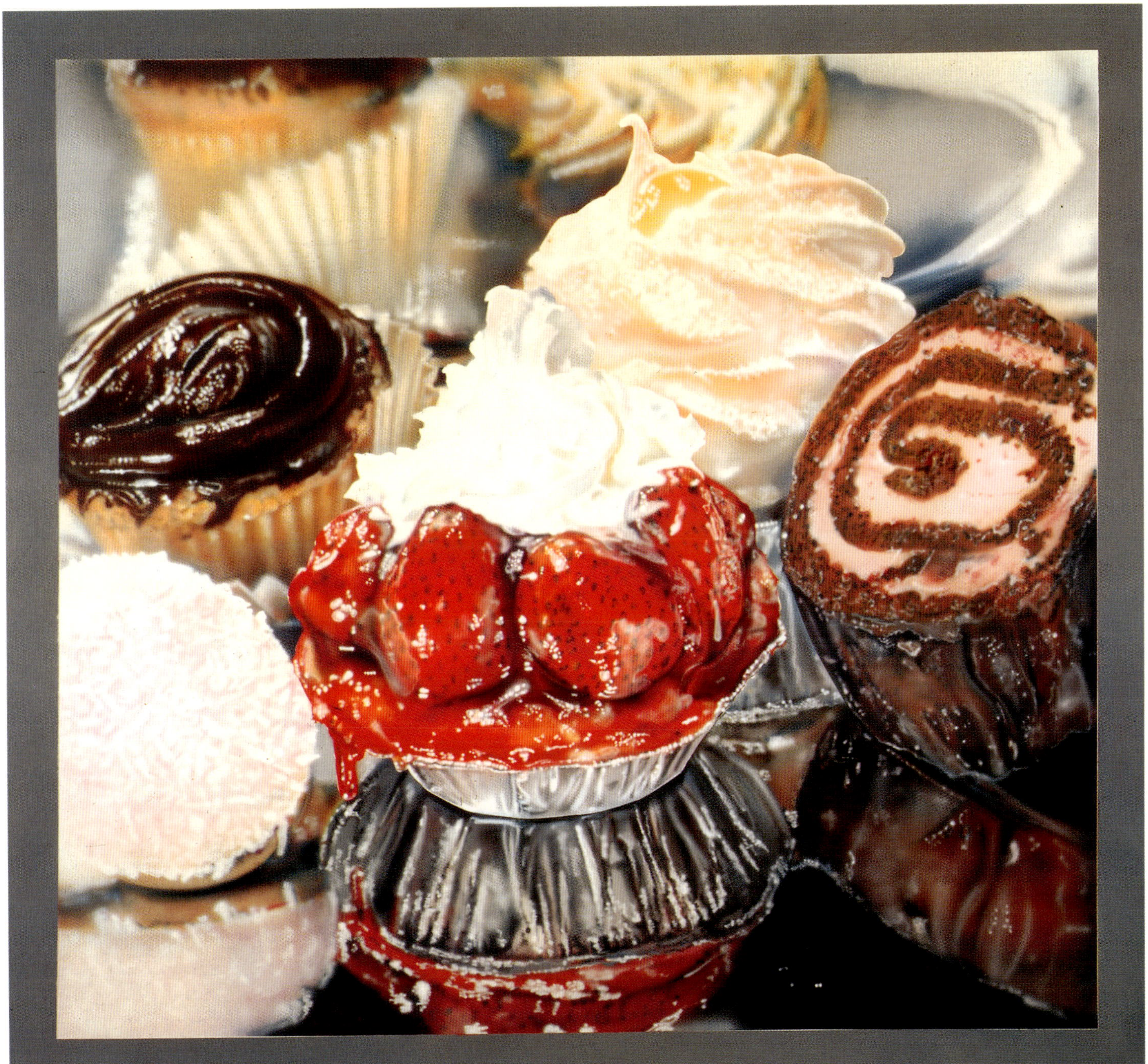

Strawberry Tart Supreme. 1974
Oil over acrylic on canvas, 54 × 60¼″
Allen Memorial Art Museum,
Oberlin, Ohio (National Endowment
for the Arts Museum Purchase Plan)

reduced (less is larger). She includes both the copious enumeration of objects and the echoes of prior images, such as *La Belle Ferronnière* (Louvre) in *Leonardo's Lady,* a picture in a picture. The sense of the world as a place full of objects is brilliantly stated, but this is not the same as authentication. The Leonardo reproduction is of a work the authorship of which is still disputed or is, at best, an early work. The *Vanitas* group, as we shall see, depends on this sense of a zone of inanimate but expressive artifacts; public and personal images, prior images and unanticipated clusters of objects jostle one another constantly, usually contributing to a single theme, often that of time. A picture like *Gambler's Cabinet,* of 1976, is a compilation of game pieces associated by the artist not with pleasure but with destructive obsession, relatable to the *Vanitas* theme.

The first phase of the *Gray Border* pictures represents the closest Flack came to traditional Photorealism: the turned image of *Spaced Out Apple,* the fly's eye view of *Alpine* confectionery in *Strawberry Tart Supreme,* and Roman emperor–head scale of the artist's *Self-Portrait,* all 1974. In the following year, in *Buddha, Leonardo's Lady,* and *Grand Rosé,* she affirmed traditional still life, using numerous articles to indicate recession in depth as well as the surprise and impact of each crafted object. As a rule still life offers the spectator a scenic space, fairly narrow but defined precisely. The second group of *Gray Borders* is of this sort, with numerous objects so that space is phased and complex, like the start of a chess game rather than the end of a Ludo game.

Photorealism ranges from paintings by artists who emphasize the photo or photographic reproduction to others that are object-oriented. Flack has expressly denied the label of Photorealist, but she is an artist who is at ease with a battery of mechanical fictions even as she remains object-oriented. Jeanne Hamilton has described her photographic work with Flack, stressing the active presence of the artist.[3] When Flack and Hamilton worked on the *Vanitas* photos, for instance, the heat of the lights affected the candle. Flack "exclaimed to Jeanne, 'My God, the candle is bleeding.' The tilt we had given the candle made the red wax drip all over the book and it looked very much like flowing blood."[4] The point is that Flack's process as a painter incorporates the information of photography, not as a generator of quotable imagery with mass media undercurrents but as a source of painterly definition. She does not need her preferred term "Super Realism," which has a prior history in the twentieth century: she is a Photorealist with an object-oriented art.

Earlier in the twentieth century still life was regarded as the realm of dumb objects: familiarity of use or shape was identified with the silence of things. In fact, objects have voices, and Flack is one of the artists who set herself to release them. The voice can be transmitted by the imminence of objects (inherent characteristics scrupulously realized in painting and drawing) or by their iconography (compounded of associative and historical meanings). For example, the notion of visual poetry in seventeenth-century Dutch art has been gradually subverted: allegorical and emblematic meaning has been discovered in works that had been supposed to celebrate the passing show. In fact the pleasure of deception and of concealed meaning are by no means incompatible.

There are scattered precedents for the renewal of interest in the iconography of still life. Alfred H. Barr, Jr.'s, majestic chronology of Picasso includes Jean Cocteau's reading of Cubist images of woman and bottle as implicative of

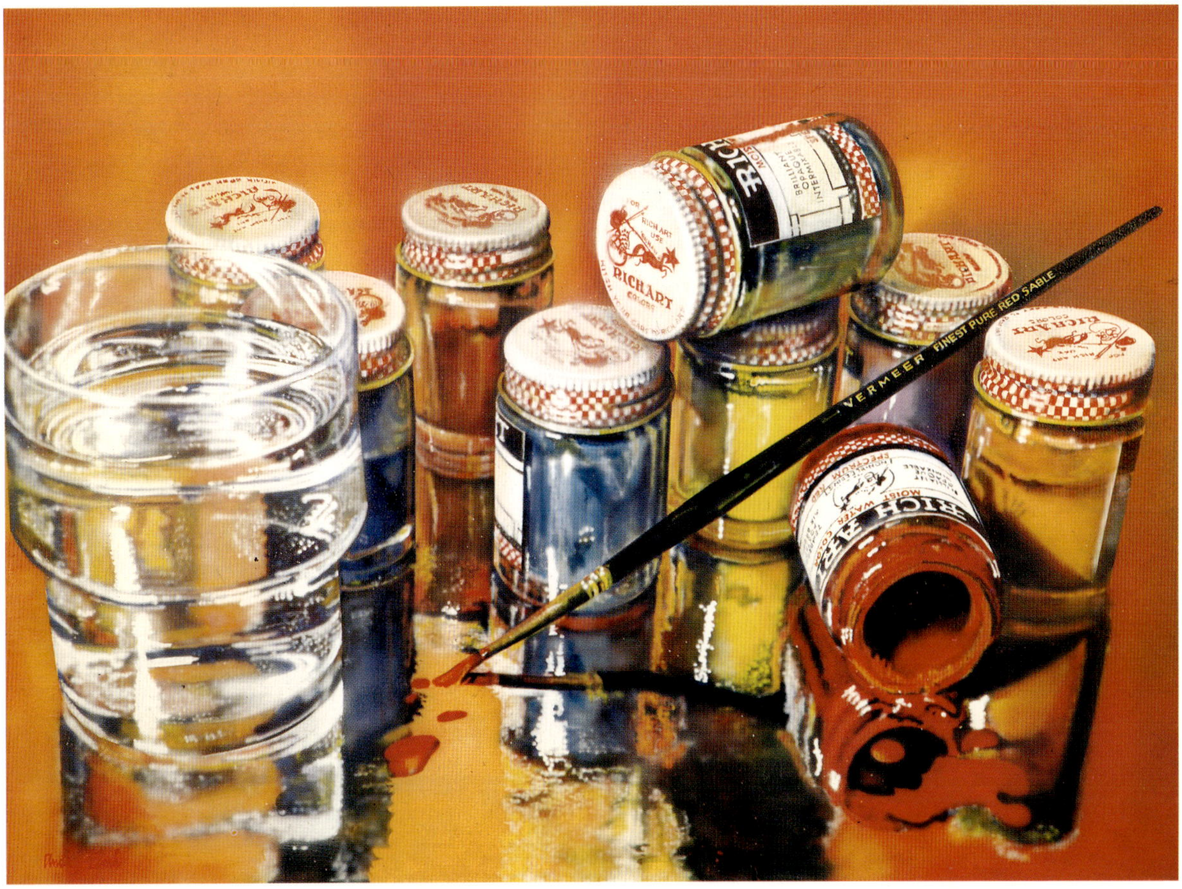

Rich Art. 1972–73
Oil over acrylic on canvas, 36 × 50″
Private collection

Crayola. 1972–73
Oil over acrylic on canvas, 28 × 40″
Private collection, Switzerland

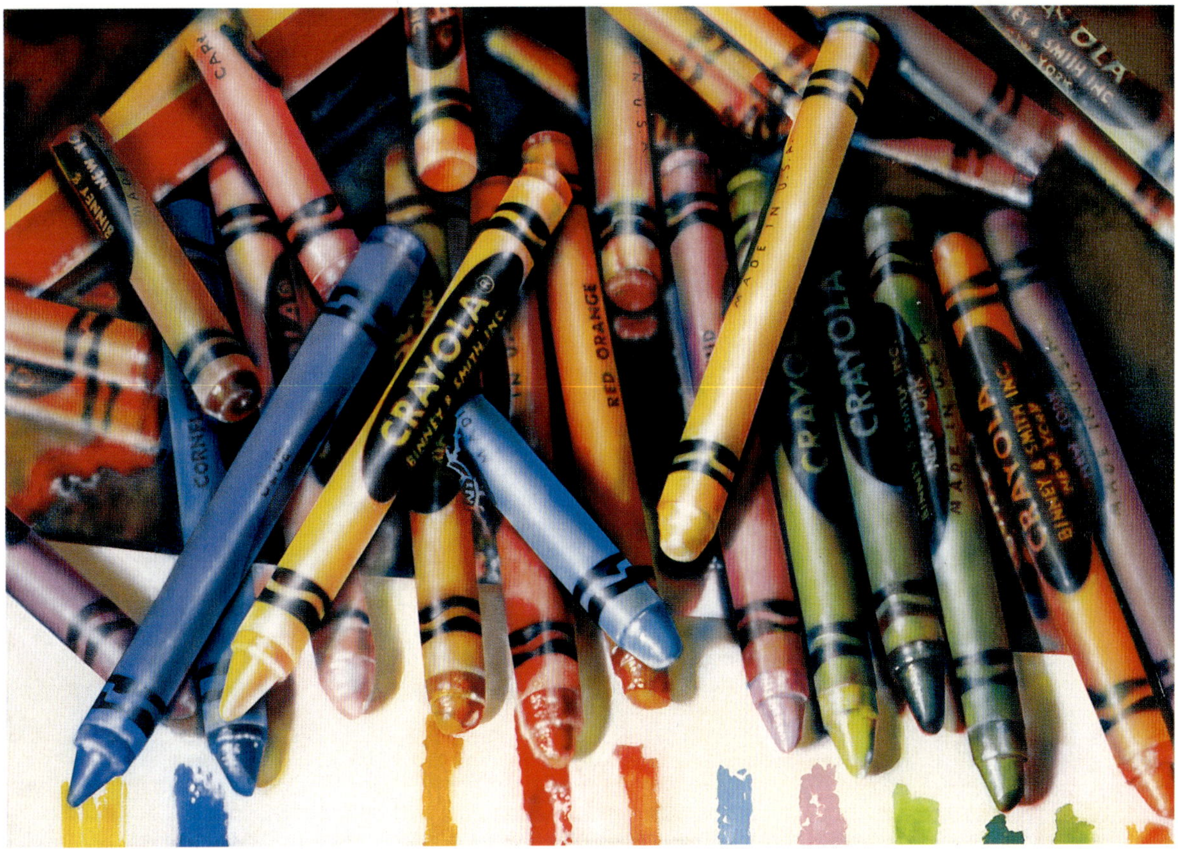

scaffolding.[5] Another factor is the tendency of women artists to equate their lives with objects and images. This was sufficiently widespread to lead to an exhibition in 1976, "Close to Home."[6] Here were shown, among related works, Lucy Sallick's studio-floor paintings, Marion Lerner Levine's shelf or table pictures, Mimi Weisbord's dollhouse images (suggested by her analyst), and Susanna Shatkin's views of indoor/outdoor thresholds eloquently juxtaposed. Flack was in "Close to Home" with an early still life of kitchen ingredients: *Royal Jello* of 1962. The coexistence of an articulate Cubism, symbolic Baroque painting, and speaking women's art gave Flack's still lifes, starting with *Jolie Madame* of 1972, a congenial setting.

"Couldn't one imagine some kind of writing (brand new) which, placing itself more or less between the two (definition and description), would borrow from the former its infallibility, its indubitability, and its brevity; and from the latter, its respect for the sensory aspect of things. . . ."[7] The author of these speculations is Francis Ponge, author of an earlier book *Le Parti Pris des Choses.* His *choses* usually refer to the products of geological, botanical, evolutionary process, whereas Flack's artifacts are mostly the result of other people's industry. However, sufficient parallels exist to emphasize that we are in an era of speaking things, not dumb objects. "Definition and description" are not left by Flack to writers, but her painted articles certainly possess "indubitability" and a relish for the "sensory aspect of things."

This may be the point at which one should point to the reemergence of the genres in later twentieth-century art. It is a sign of the reduced authority of abstract art in which the different genres were effectively homogenized and indeed of skepticism concerning visualist theory at large. The genres were a way of classifying art by subject matter and neither abstract art theory nor judgment by eye alone needed such systems. With the return of the image in later twentieth-century art, classification by subject again became a relevant critical method. Initially genre-theory became firmly attached to a notion of hierarchy (history painting and portraiture first, landscape and still life lower on the scale). Genre painting was also understood to be a kind of secular and contemporary form of figure painting, but as it depicted daily life it was below the hierarchic preference bestowed on classics and the Bible in history painting. Flack is skilled at fusing history painting and genre in the second sense and in the infusion of ennobling themes into still-life subjects.

In the group of three paintings called *Vanitas,* all the articles, spatially speaking, occupy the foreground, but the artist differentiates scrupulously between objects, images, symbols. There are the candle and candlestick, sweetcakes and discolored fruit, and a necklace; Flack stresses their object-status. In *Marilyn* (p. 38), the second *Vanitas* picture, Flack made a point of reproductions and reflections, including an early photo of Marilyn on the right, reflected on the left side with an intrusive vertical lipstick (signifying age and experience). The calendar page of August denotes the month of Marilyn's death. (Symbols include the butterfly, the rose, and the clock.) In *Wheel of Fortune* (p. 39) a skull on the right is reflected in a mirror on the left, a parallelism to the *Marilyn.* In all three paintings Flack wants the freedom to show images and objects at unexpected angles and orbits. Clarity and surprise are fused. The total inventory is of forms at rest, and each one is given the greatest facticity. She clearly varied the convention of still life to release things from single-point perspective and the attendant sense of gravity. Some of the objects therefore appear in *orbit,* to repeat the word used

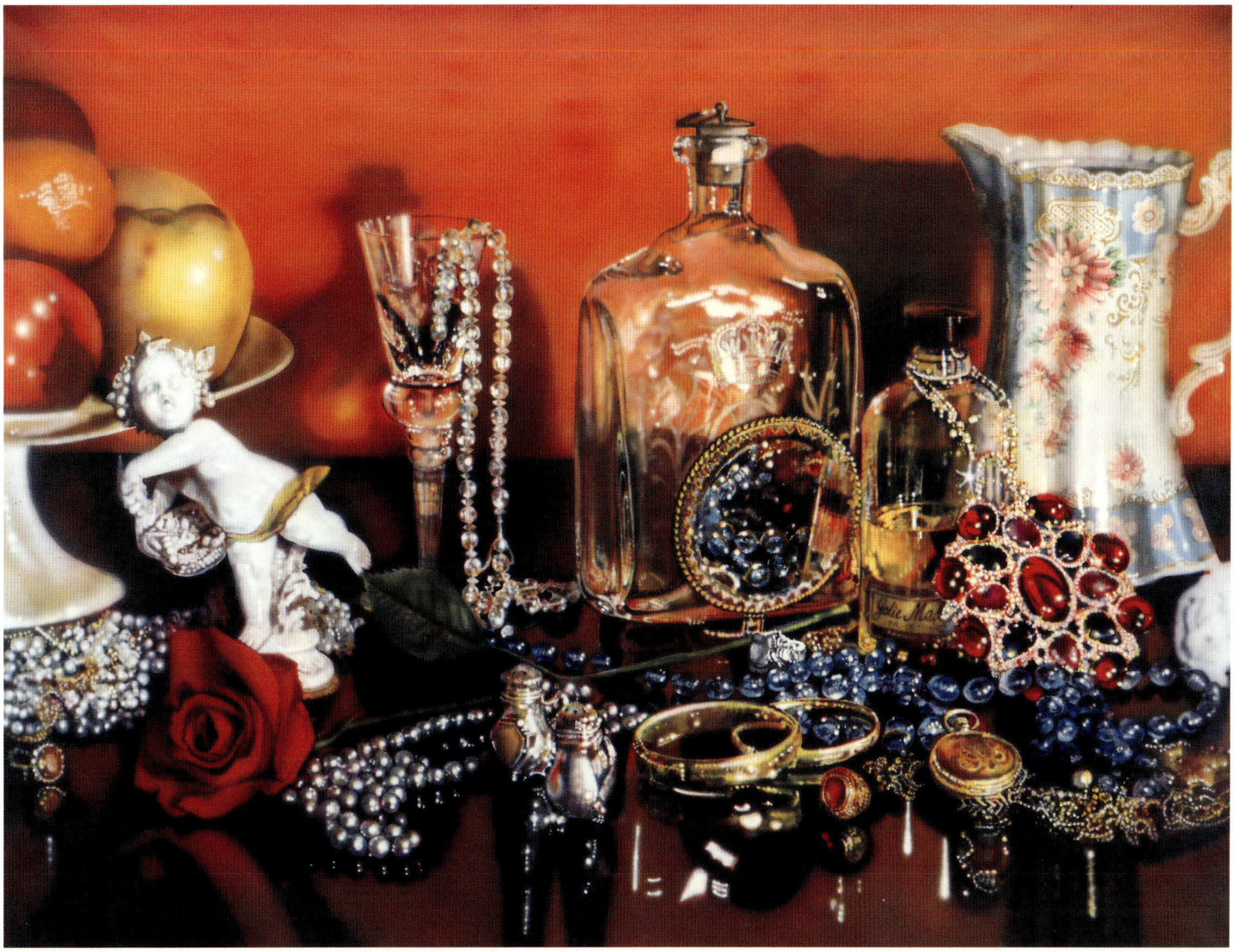

Jolie Madame. 1972
Oil on canvas, 71 × 96″
National Gallery Australia,
Canberra

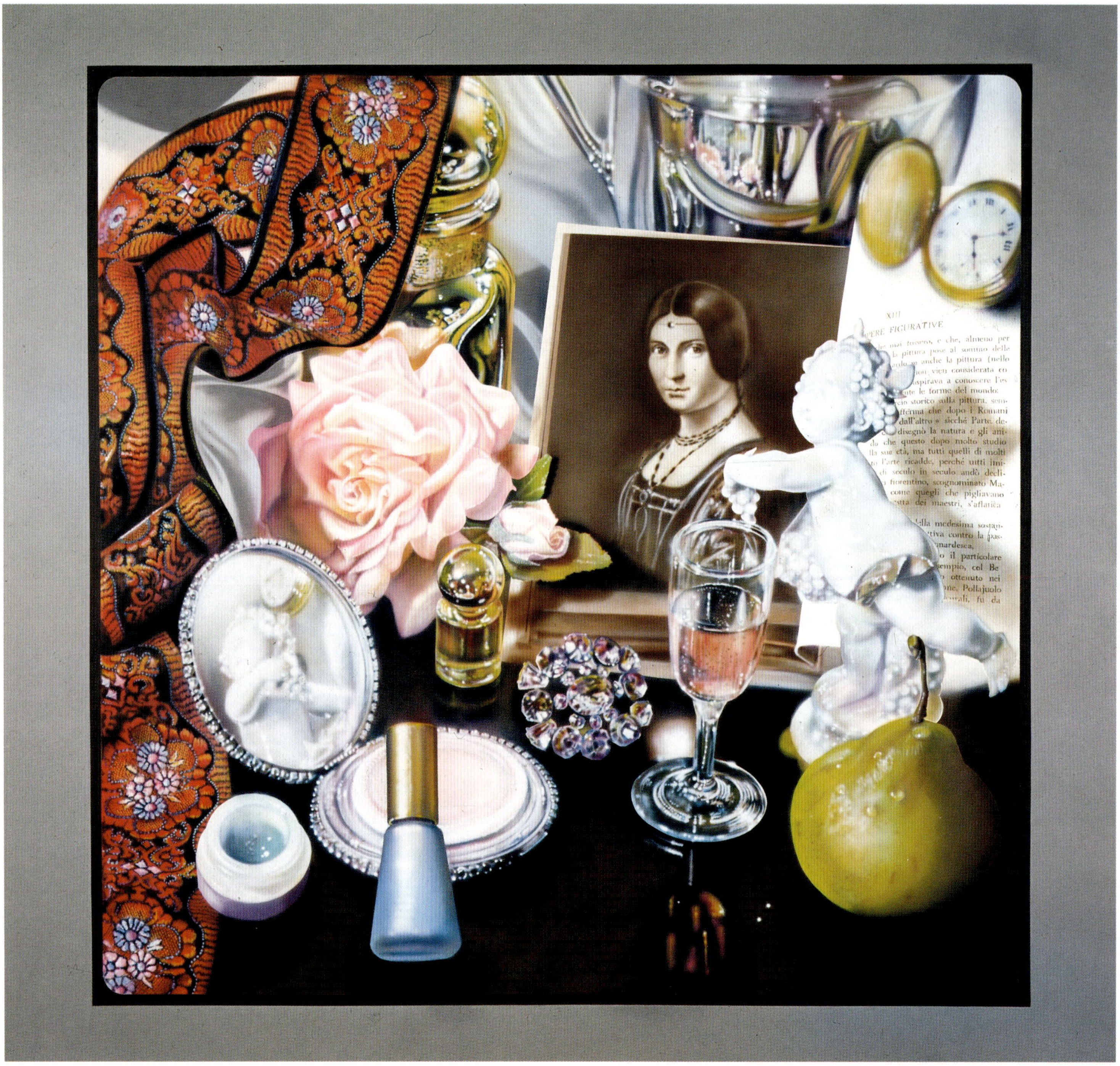

Leonardo's Lady. 1975
Oil over acrylic on wet
sanded canvas, 74 × 80″
Collection, The Museum
of Modern Art, New York
(Purchased with funds
from the National Endowment
for the Arts and
an anonymous donor)

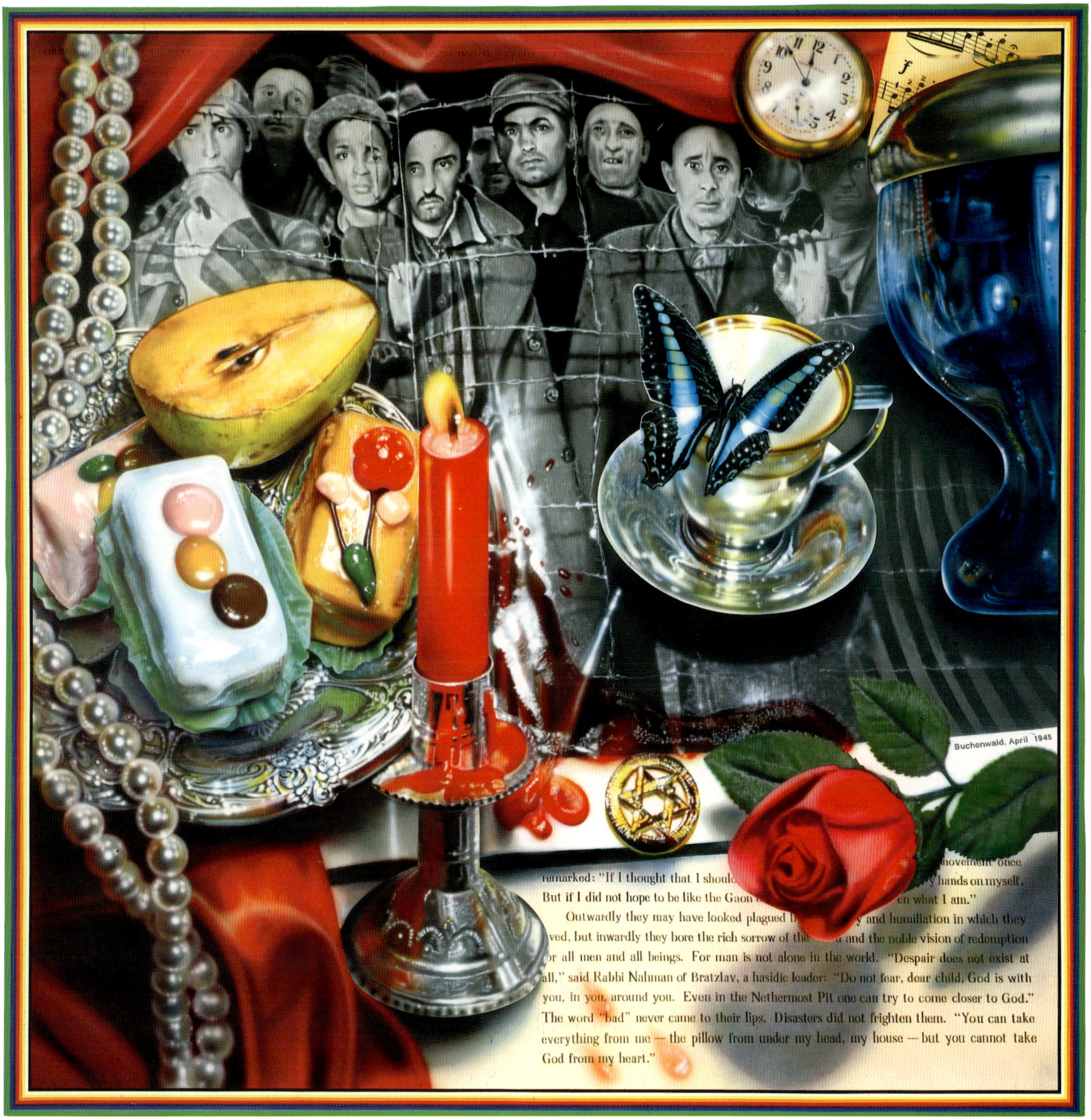

World War II (Vanitas). 1976–77
Oil over acrylic on canvas, 96 × 96″
Collection Mr. and Mrs. David Pincus,
Philadelphia

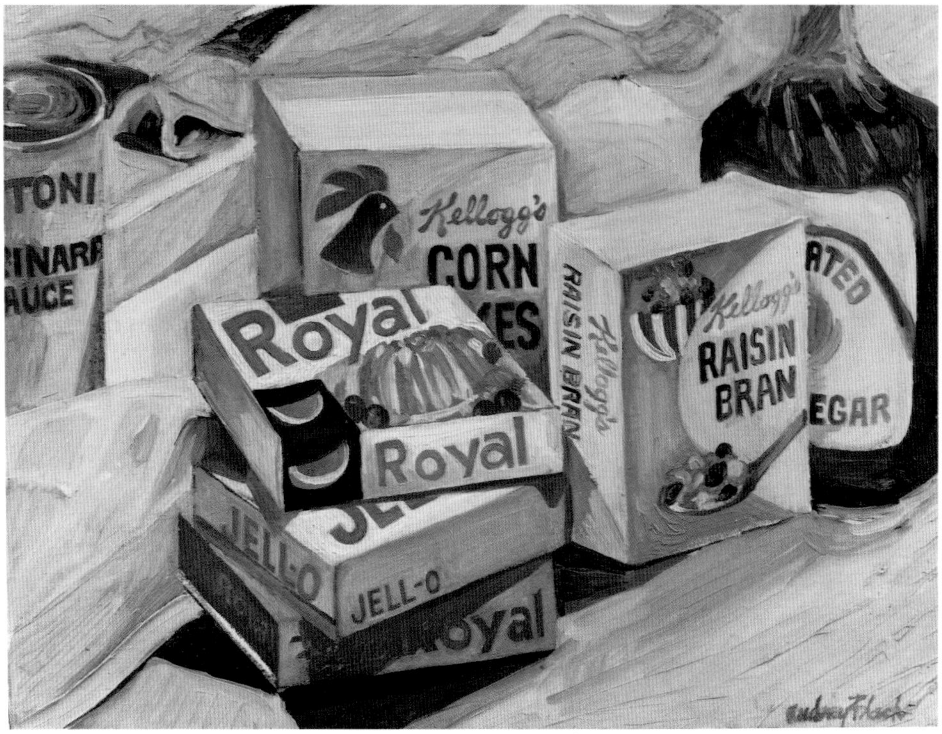

Royal Jello. 1962
Oil on canvas, 9×12″
Collection the artist

lustrous and full. The themes are didactic and miniatory, but the messages are above. The first art gallery to show the three *Vanitas* put them in a huge New York loft space. It was Flack's original notion to include drapery and mementi mori along with the paintings, rather as W. E. Henley's poem "Invictus" was inscribed on one of the frames. Her final decision left us free of environmental drama, however, and stressed the sufficiency of pictorial intricacy. It was enough to show that thin air is as solid a surface as tabletop or floor space; this is the lesson of our crowded space, the upper atmosphere, and needs no further justification.

The first *Vanitas* picture, *World War II*, has a black border and a tight spectrum of colors. The second *Vanitas* painting has no border but is contained in an essentially circular composition, with the photograph of Marilyn on one side and its reflection on the other. The photo is head-on (later than Norma Jean but earlier than a full Marilyn image), but the reflection is shown at right angles to the book page. There is a bed of foreground things and an upper arch. The hovering paintbrush, that of the "future painter" invoked in the text behind it (?), releases a drop of red paint, implying blood, even though the emission rhymes in shape with the water drops on the pear or the pip in the orange half. The grapes behind the photographed head (like a garland) and the small pots of makeup color, pink and green, recur blurrily. The open lipstick that hovers before the photos is repeated in the reflected head as if it were being applied. The repetition therefore animates and celebrates the star. Flack's Marilyn exists in the trappings of elegy with which she is frequently associated. Indeed her appearance in a trilogy of *Vanitas* states that this is so. The youthful portrait of Monroe may permit elaborate references, but it carries a sense of Flack responding to the star's later status as a media-victim.

One factor of Flack's still life should be emphasized: her persistent enlargement based on the Pop Art generation after Abstract Expressionism and before Photorealism. The big forms of her still life deliver vast fruit and missile-sized lipstick, but dilation never reveals any of the pores and creases that make the skin an excretory surface. It is, so to say, a non-destructive enlargement that affirms the wholeness and survival of the integrity of objects, carried by objects in which Flack's confidence never wavers.

Flack saw Maria van Oosterwyck's painting *Vanitas*, 1668 (Vienna, Kunsthistorisches Museum), in the important survey show "Women Artists, 1550–1950" [as she was completing her own *Vanitas* series]. The exhibition was a revision of art history demonstrating the presence of women artists in European and North American art since Sofonisba Anguissola and hence by implication the reality of women's art. Though 1950 was taken as the cutoff date to avoid arguments with living women in the arts,[8] the show acted as a manifesto of female identity. Flack was challenged by the handling of detail in Oosterwyck's paintings, stirred by its symbolism, and moved by its authorship. As Ann Sutherland Harris, organizer (with Linda Nochlin) of the show, has written: "The genre of still life known as a 'Vanitas' first developed in Leyden in the 1620's" represents "the most intellectual and literary form of still life and the only kind that always has a social message."[9] For Flack the "Vanitas" concept seems to have justified her desire to combine the exalted themes from figure painting and the full realization of three-dimensional form.

Van Oosterwyck's painting does not approach the squarish format that attracted Flack.[10] The plane of vision is horizontal as it tends to be owing to our possession of two eyes. They are usually linked to stereoscopic vision, but in fact the consequence of paired eyes is a side-to-side, east-west preference, a relational rather than definitional stress. The *Vanitas* paintings of Flack are each eight feet square, thus turning the dualistic aspect of van Oosterwyck into a rotational rhythm but retaining the moral contrast of skull and globe.

It will have been noticed that Flack tends to paint systematically in logically sequent runs: one thing leads to another. There are different reasons for painting in sets: some sets originate with art dealers who prefer a recognizable multiple project to a work in awkward singleness; others with artists who have a recurrent obsession or a visual problem that exceeds single resolution. Flack's groups appear to be of the latter sort, a sophisticated reading of art's partial and provisional status, not a cynical acknowledgment of its commodity status. More than one example may be needed to approach a theme in depth. One such set can be clustered around the Luisa Roldán, for instance. Also a kind of cross-indexing occurs among ostensibly different periods which authenticates persisting ideas. Her sets and sequences are the consequence of problem-solving and the pursuit of intelligent solutions. The square format of her *Vanitas* picks up the earlier idea of equal composition. The color intensity of the *Gray Border* series extends the small-scale sparkle of early work to a larger scale and dismisses lingering monochrome habits. The angles and optional bases of the objects in the *Vanitas* group posit a profusion like that of our crowded planetary space, a domain of slanted planes and crisscross vectors.

There is an important point to be made concerning Flack's use of scale. The dilation of objects does not lead to a sight of the flaws and fissures below the level of formal vision. Hers is a non-destructive enlargement that celebrates the pleasures of survival by the integrity of the objects. They may be emblematic of death but they preserve the unified surface, the completeness, which is our normal experience in the sight and handling of such objects. Thus Flack's amplification of objects does not lose their wondrous sense of specific identity. In this sense the artist's meditation on the emblems of death becomes a victory over mortality as she exemplifies the objects of the world as whole, lustrous, and full.

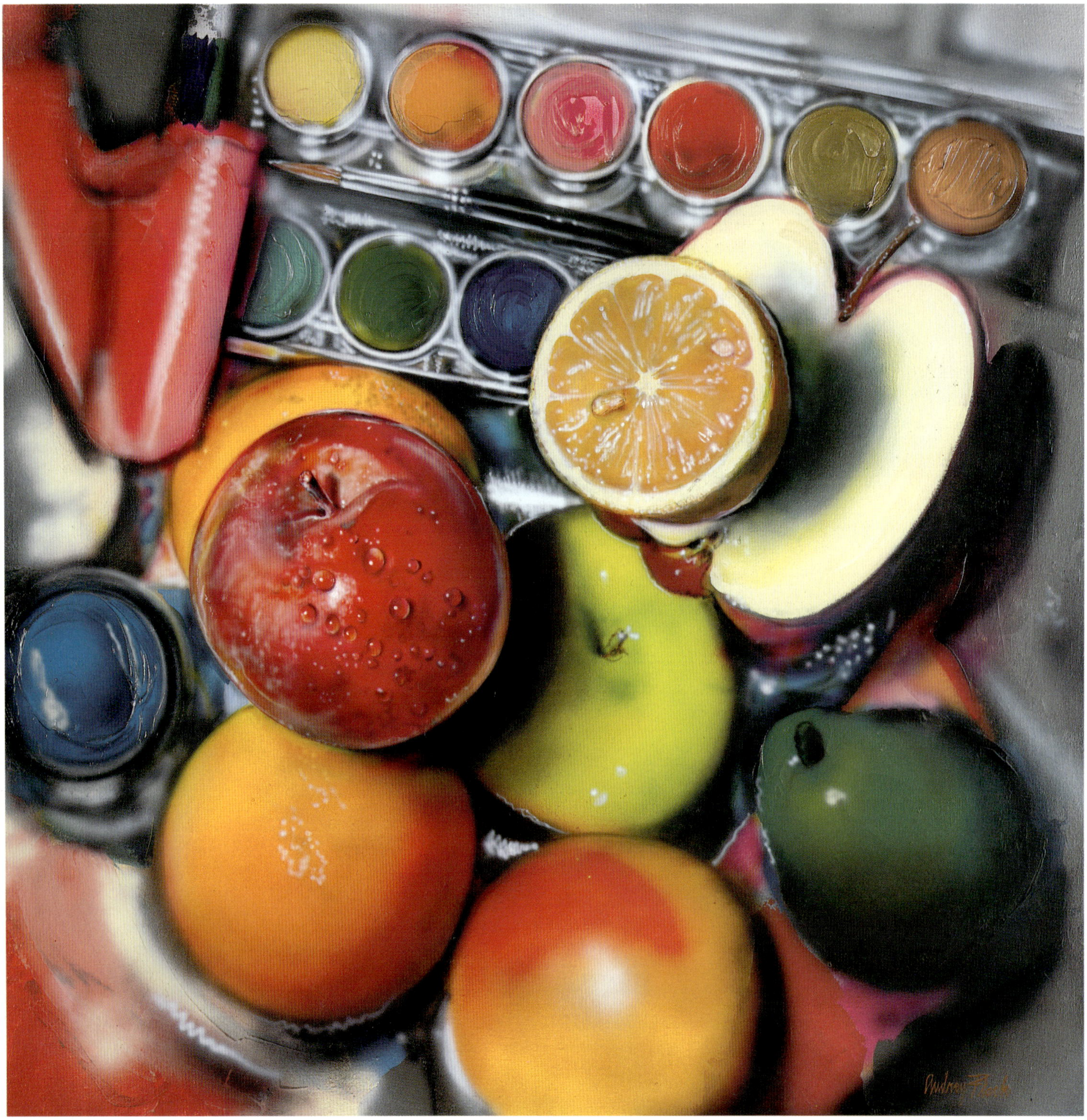

Energy Apples. 1980
Acrylic and oil on canvas, 47¾ × 48¼″
Collection Susan Pear Meisel,
New York

ICONIC IMAGES FOR A SECULARIZED AGE: 1980–83

Thalia Gouma-Peterson

In a 1983 interview Audrey Flack stated categorically: "My intention now is completely clear in my mind: I want to create healing energy."[1] She said this, knowing full well that in the context of a secularized age and of today's art world paintings with an overtly religious content would most likely be adversely criticized. Her *Macarena of Miracles* (p. 65), which had been in the 1972 Whitney Museum Annual Exhibition of Contemporary Painting and Sculpture, had been praised when it was thought to be camp. But when in an interview the artist earnestly explained that she admired the seventeenth-century Spanish sculpture on which her painting is based and considered it a great work of art, the painting and by extension the artist herself were accused by some critics of being sentimental and vulgar.[2] In spite of this and in spite of similar accusations leveled at her 1976–77 *Vanitas* series (*World War II*, *Marilyn*, and *Wheel of Fortune*), Flack was determined in the body of work that she completed in 1980–83 to create contemporary icons that would, like Byzantine icons, convey to the viewer a sense of the spiritual.

In this body of work Flack continued her search for the fusion of the real with the spiritual that had preoccupied her in the *Vanitas*. In that series, related to the Baroque *Vanitas* genre and more specifically to the paintings of Maria van Oosterwyck, Flack had explored the capacity of still life "for ethical commentary."[3] She had used the Jewish survivors of the Holocaust (*World War II*, 1976–77) and Marilyn Monroe (*Marilyn*, 1977), and her own daughter Melissa (*Wheel of Fortune*, 1977–78) as universal symbols of human survival. In these paintings, which are a protest against death, the human figure, a main subject in Flack's work of the fifties and sixties, reemerged with new force and meaning. Symbolic objects surrounding the human images reinforce the themes of survival and the transitoriness of life. The paintings are poetic statements about the beauty and evil of human existence, about its tragedy and hope. By means of scale, contrast, profusion, Photorealist style, and overt and contemporary content, Flack had pushed the boundaries of still life to new limits.

Flack's passionate investment in the *Vanitas* drained her emotionally. In 1979–80, a period of reassessment and spiritual search, she wrote an article on Carlo Crivelli, the fifteenth-century Venetian artist from whom, she believes, history has unfairly withheld a place equal to that of Giovanni Bellini or

Andrea Mantegna.[4] In her appreciation and defense of Crivelli, whom she had admired since her years as an aspiring art student, Flack revealed her own state of mind. She recognized Crivelli as a kindred spirit and defended him as the loner "who breaks the rules, the eccentric, the maverick," who "does not fit into the mainstream of a movement," a position she herself had been in for much of her life. She praised him for his technical skill, his illusion of dimension, his meticulous modeling, and his obsessive attention to detail, qualities also found in contemporary American Photorealism and in her own work.[5] But she also praised him for his humanity and passion, which she considered key attributes of his painting and for which she had been searching in her own art. She also was attracted by the mystical and devotional quality of Crivelli's work and the elements of late Gothic religiosity within a formal Renaissance framework. In his paintings she perceived the fusion of the real and the spiritual that she had been working toward.

That same year Flack met Baba, an Indian philanthropist who is descended from a line of spiritual masters and who in 1955 took a vow of silence that he has not broken (he communicates only in sign language). Baba impressed her with his powerful spiritual presence and humanity, and she resolved to paint his portrait. Having spent a considerable amount of time preparing herself and an even longer time shooting photographs (in the hundreds) and selecting the final image, Flack painted Baba's face on a seven-by-thirteen-foot canvas in three days in 1980.[6] That image looked at her from the unfinished canvas for three years while she worked on nine other paintings in which she progressively searched for images of the goddess. A year and a half later, again in a short time, she painted the roses next to Baba's face. She did not complete the landscape, or more precisely the skyscape and seascape, until late in the summer of 1983.

Baba was the first of Flack's paintings intended to transform a contemporary living person into an icon of spiritual significance—a modern equivalent of a Byzantine icon. Her awareness of the iconic power of art had been manifested in her 1971 series of monuments that cross the boundary between tourist attraction and object of popular devotion—e.g., *Michelangelo's David, Siena Cathedral, Tower of Pisa,* and *Piazza of Miracles.* In these relatively small paintings, Flack reduced large public monuments into intimate and, potentially, private images. Concurrently, by using photographic images as her sources (picture postcards and commercial slides), she enlarged the small tourist memento and gave it a new validity and meaning as a work of art. In these Photorealist paintings it became evident that Flack, unlike many of the other Photorealists, was not interested in impersonal images of the American urban scene. She chose instead subjects rich in history and with a continuing life. These monuments have both a past and a future, which Flack admires and respects.

In the *Macarena Esperanza* and *Dolores of Cordoba* series, also completed in 1971, Flack pushed the technique of Photorealism to a higher degree of visual sophistication. She successfully crossed the boundaries between two kinds of illusion: that of the original polychromed sculpture, which appears to shed tears, and that of the Kodachrome slide and its diverse levels of focus. Concurrently the content of her work became more pointed and intense and the religious/devotional nature of the image more explicit. With these iconic images, based on the work of the seventeenth-century Spanish sculptor Luisa Roldán, whom she discovered during a trip to Spain in 1970, Flack firmly established her own version of Photorealism: expressive, symbolic, and highly personal. The antithesis of the potential neutrality of the photographic source and precise technique and the highly charged content with which Flack personally identified remained characteristic of her painting through the seventies.

In spite of thematic continuity, Flack's work of the early eighties departs from her more strictly Photorealist paintings of the seventies. Her technique became more diversified and her brush strokes looser and more expressive. Also, in a number of the paintings she introduced portraits of living persons and self-portraits, returning to aspects of her figural work of the fifties and sixties.

Her first act in painting *Energy Apples*, completed in 1980, was to write "energy" diagonally across the canvas. This word, not visible to the viewer, became part of the title and expressed her intent that "energy should emanate from the painting." *Energy Apples* can be compared to earlier still lifes in the *Gray Border* series, especially *Spaced Out Apple* of 1974 with which it shares both the dominant fruit motifs and the contradictory relationship of objects to border.[7] However, the complete elimination of ground plane, the closure of the back plane, and the almost total denial of depth recession pushes the whole still life farther out of the picture into the sphere of the viewer. The emphatic projection and crowding of the three-dimensional objects, the dominant use of primary colors, and the reflection of light all intensify the impact. Also, *Energy Apples*, unlike the earlier work, contains the brush and paint box that assert the artist's presence. Smaller in size and more expressive in execution, *Energy Apples* is a more personal work.

This is true also of Flack's 1981 self-portrait, *We Are All Light and Energy* (p. 42), which is much smaller than the 1974 portrait and in which the intent to generate visual and spiritual energy is clearly stated in the inscription "we are all light and energy" that runs across the top like a flash of light and becomes the title of the painting. The word "energy" also is inscribed in the lower right corner. This was the first of several paintings in which the artist wrote inscriptions directly on the canvas, in script, to elaborate and complement the meaning. The directness and personal tone introduced by the inscription is present also in the dynamic brushwork and painterly color modulation that is derived from her abstract and figural paintings of the fifties. But the frontal figure with halolike yellow strokes around the head also creates an iconic effect. Like a medieval saint, she holds her attribute, the parrot, as a symbol of longevity.[8] The contrast between the physically asserted painterly back plane, which can also be read as a lighted spatial ambience, and Flack's emphatically projecting figure, with illusionistically painted necklaces hanging over the border, creates a lively tension in both form and content. The photographic illusion of hand and necklace is negated by the thickly painted impasto of the face. The viewer cannot determine the picture plane with any certainty as various planes are established and then denied by bordering shapes. This ambiguity created through modernist, illusionist, and expressionist formal means is similar to late medieval art as it survives in, among others, the work of Carlo Crivelli. Flack in a modern idiom recreated the "special eccentricities" of Crivelli's art which she found "magical."[9]

In 1980–81, at the time she was painting the self-portrait, Flack started doing watercolors. She felt an urgent need to leave the studio and to break with the carefully controlled working habits that she had developed. Through working outdoors in nature, with the speed and freedom necessary to capture the shifting illusion of color, weather, and light she achieved a new "discovery into reality." She allowed herself to become impulsive and even uncontrolled. Pulling out her watercolors and "just painting" was both a pleasure and an urgent need.[10]

In the tradition of landscape painter John Constable, whose work she admires, Flack's main concern was to capture the time of the day, the reflection of light on water, the weather conditions, the atmosphere, and the specificity of the place. These she often recorded in the titles—for example, *Little Albert's Landing, East Hampton, July 21, 1982, 5:30 p.m.* She worked rapidly to capture time and weather and in the process she drew on the immediacy and emotional brushwork of her Abstract Expressionist training, which she combined with the solidity and luminosity of her more recent work. This combination and her treatment of the watercolors as a record of perception makes her landscapes akin to those of a group of contemporary American landscape painters whose style has recently been identified as Painterly Realism. They are reflections made visible, "the artist's meditations on nature embodied on canvas."[11]

The watercolors gave Flack the license to do things "one is not supposed to do." They also renewed her faith in her ability to paint in a style other than the one she had worked in during the previous fourteen years.[12] Inevitably, too, they affected her paintings, though often in ways which are not immediately evident.

In 1982–83, within a time span of six months, Flack completed two major still lifes, *Invocation*, and *A Pear to Heade and Heal*, which, in different ways, were departures from her still lifes of the seventies. Both have a horizontal format, and in both there is an element of reduction and focus combined with a strong illusion of spatial recession and of projection in front of the space of the painting into the viewer's sphere. The new elements in these still lifes become evident in comparing *Invocation* with *Wheel of Fortune*, completed in 1977, which also is centered on a skull (pp. 39, 43). The open, horizontal format in *Invocation* and the luminous treatment of the glowing rainbowlike background (the rainbow in *Wheel of Fortune* is reflected in the mirror) create a spaciousness and calm that differs from the intense crowding in the earlier still life. Equally striking is the painterly treatment of the still life objects in *Invocation*, which contrasts with the trompe l' oeil illusion of the outer frame surrounding the flat gray double border.

The border had been an important element in Flack's work since the midseventies, when in the *Gray Border* series she introduced it as a two-dimensional and neutral framing device, establishing the flatness of the picture plane against which the projecting and receding colored objects were defined. In *Invocation* the contrast of the flat border and the painterly objects surrounded by colored space is intensified and complicated by the semi-iridescent pearl-gray outer frame, which can be read either as an outer space or as a smooth lacquered wood surface with objects and signs floating on it and casting shadows. The different levels of illusion established through texture, color, and spatial organization are visually bound by the tipped tube of red iridescent paint spilling over the frame. The complexity and freedom of the

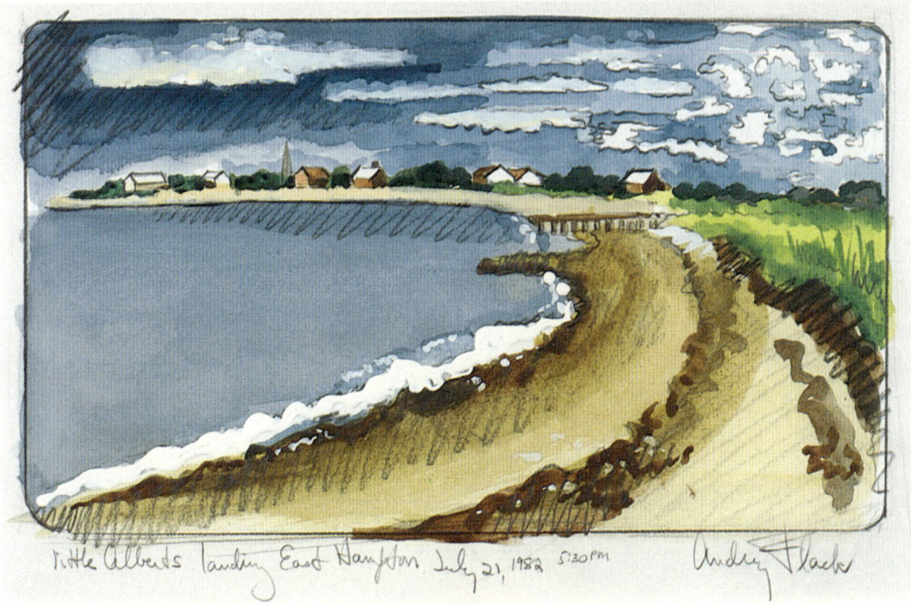

Little Albert's Landing, East Hampton, July 21, 1982, 5:30 p.m. 1982
Watercolor on paper, 5¾ × 9″
Collection Thalia Gouma-Peterson and Carl A. Peterson, Oberlin, Ohio

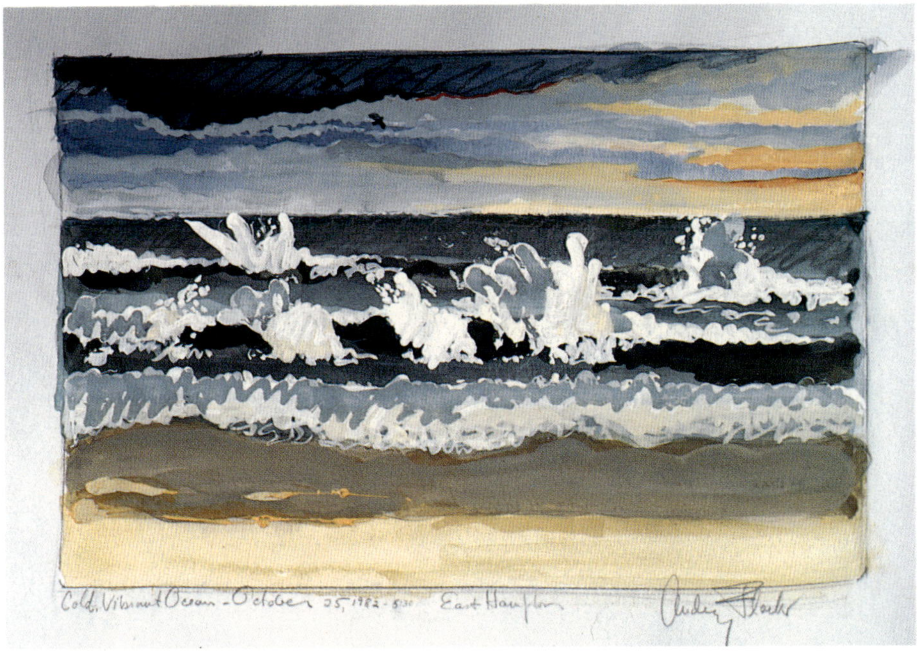

Cold, Vibrant Ocean—October 25, 1982—5:30 East Hampton. 1982
Watercolor on Arches paper, 8¼ × 11¾″
Private collection

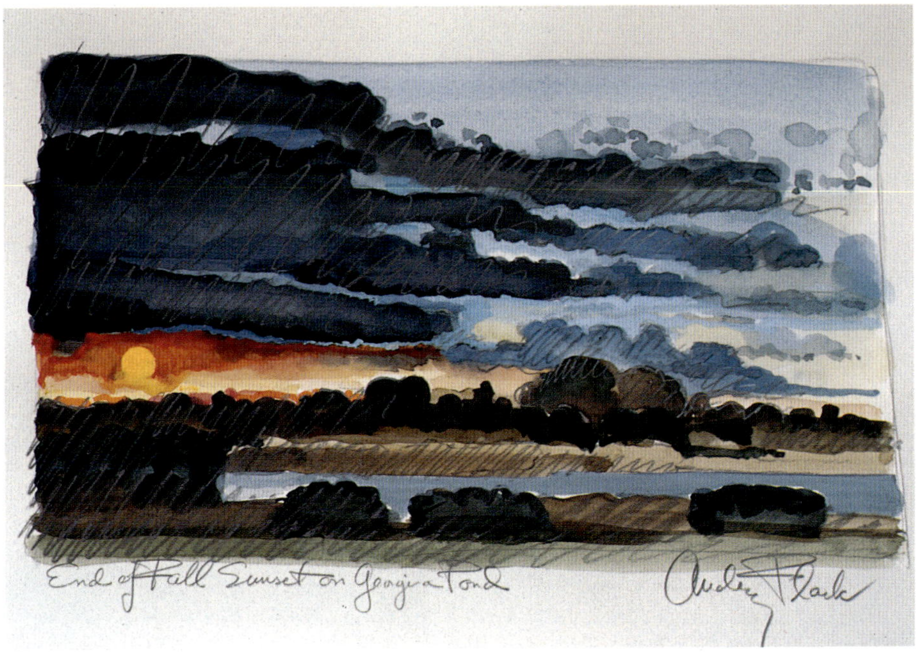

End of Fall Sunset on Georgia Pond. 1982
Watercolor on Arches paper, 5¾ × 8½″
Private collection

formal treatment in *Invocation*, which moves away from the photographic vision of Photorealism and combines divergent and even opposite ways of painting, parallels an equally complex symbolism. To the familiar symbols of skull, burning candle, and flowers in full bloom Flack added on the frame (completed last) an image of the Lord Krishna blessing the viewer, a wreath (crown of thorns) with a skeleton walking behind it, and Native American and Indian emblems of renewal.[13] The meaning of the painting is clarified by ancient Hindu texts inscribed in the lower strip of the frame on two thickly painted areas that differ from the rest of the surface. The texts appear to have been written in pencil in two kinds of very personal cursive script, a formal and old fashioned hand (left) and a more modern and casual one (right), intended to identify the two authors, Yajur Veda and Shree Avadhuta Stotram. Both inscriptions allude to the relation of the self to the universe and complete the painting. (Veda, at left, "May your eyes mingle with the sun / May your breath be merged with the cosmic winds." Stotram, at right, "The entire universe is only a mental construct. / The self alone is free and eternal."[14])

Invocation, like most of Flack's paintings since 1975, is an expression of her search for universal significance and hope for human transcendence. And as in other recent still lifes, she includes in it self-referential objects: a miniature set of watercolors given to her by her daughter Hannah, a brush with dripping paint, and a tube of red iridescent Aquatec, which is used in the painting and also spills into the viewer's plane. Both brush and paint tube allude to the act of painting, which in *Invocation*, unlike in earlier more precisely painted still lifes, we are allowed to witness. As the artist comments on life and death so the painting comments on itself as an artifact. This it does both in its iconography (watercolor, jars of paint, paintbrush, spilling tube of paint) and its various levels of formal illusion culminating in the actual thick paint spilling over the outer frame. A further complexity is introduced by the reflection, in the silver vase that holds the candle, of the artist herself taking the initial photograph that inspired the painting. Flack here deals with issues of reflexivity.

In this work, Flack also juxtaposes formal means, images, and symbols not normally associated with one another. Unlike the *Vanitas* series—especially *World War II* (p. 81), which shocks through juxtaposition—*Invocation* harmoniously correlates and unites disparate elements. The open tube of paint is an important agent in this correlation. It states that the act of painting can achieve what is impossible in life. To reach the viewer with this message, the painting spills out of its frame into another plane, a mental plane which extends beyond the outer border.

A Pear to Heade and Heal, though visually different from *Invocation*, shares many elements with it. The title, an integral part of the painting, has a double meaning: it signifies that the painting is an homage to "the little heeded" nineteenth-century American still-life painter Martin Johnson Heade; it also refers to "the mystical, magical effect of healing," here achieved primarily through color.[15] The purple glow of the still-life setting, the green of the fruit, and purplish-gray of the outer border, are colors Flack associates with peaceful meditation. Through the use of color and spatial illusion, the background, the still life, and the space of the border are harmoniously juxtaposed and fused. The lighter space of the border surrounds the inner darker space, and the two are divided only by a thin red line. These unified ambients extend into the space of the viewer—an illusion intensified by the monumental fruit, which

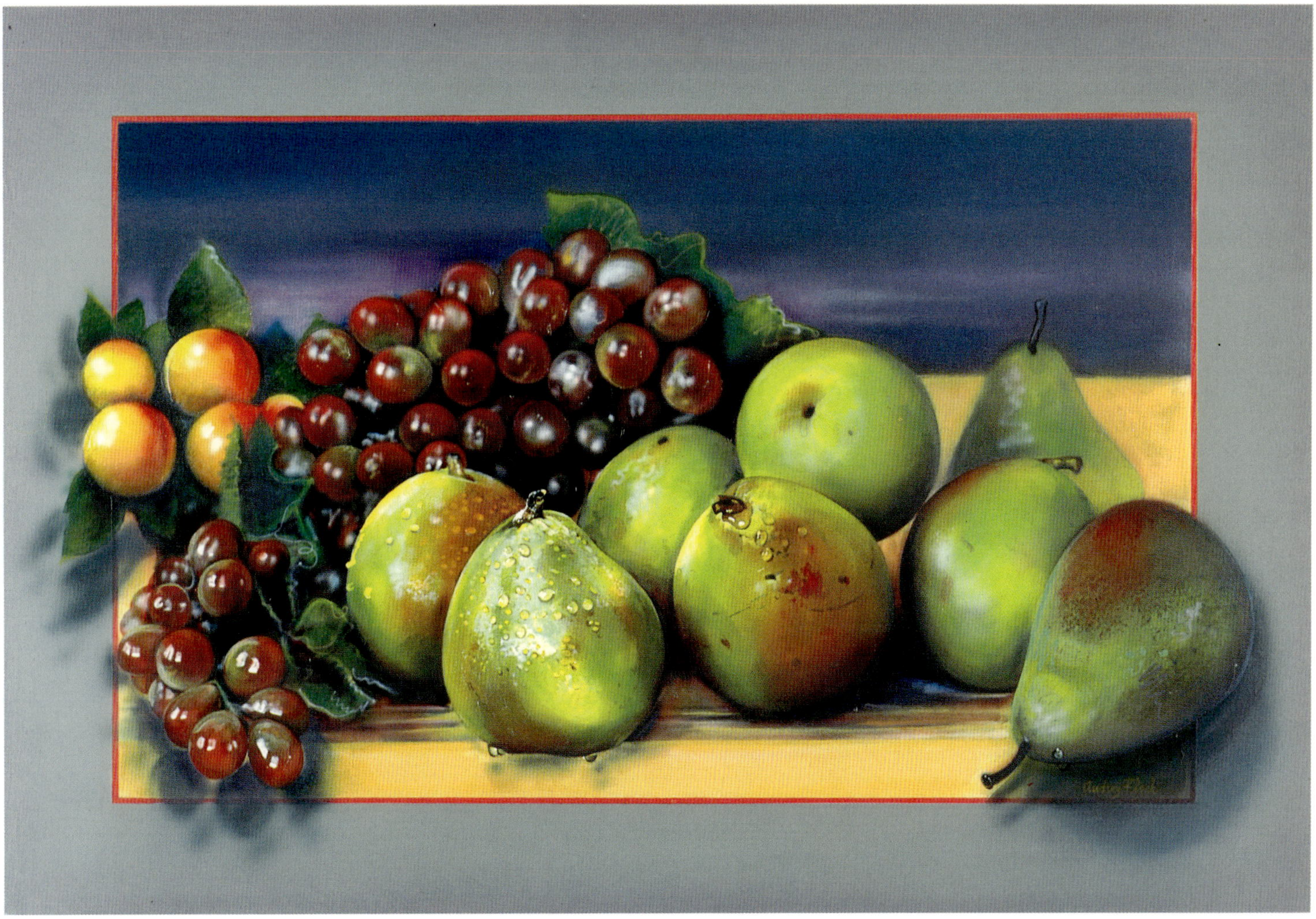

A Pear to Heade and Heal. 1983
Acrylic and oil on canvas, 38×56″
Collection Mr. Glenn Golenberg,
Los Angeles

freely curves in and out of the picture space and casts a shadow on the border. The placement of the fruit against a generalized landscape setting (the first such combination in Flack's oeuvre) enhances its monumentality and otherworldliness. It was partly inspired by Heade's use of landscape settings for his luscious tropical fruit and flowers and partly the result of Flack's own landscape watercolors. In the painting, however, nature is transformed into an ambient of colored light, a visualization of "the mystical light of meditation."[16]

During 1981–82 *Baba* continued to preoccupy Flack. She set up a series of still lifes incorporating the original photograph and took a large number of shots. She titled these *A Course in Miracles* from the title of a book on meditation she had been reading and which she included in a number of the compositions. The setups and photographs, though varied, included certain basic components: the fruit, flowers, paint, and brushes (the same miniature set of watercolors as *Invocation*), the burning candle and large butterflies familiar from Flack's still lifes of the 1970s. To these she added a photograph of Albert Einstein, a small devotional statue of Christ, a candlestick with the star of David, and a silver devotional diptych. The composition was intended to unify the major and often conflicting religions of Judaism, Christianity, and Hinduism. Baba (a living human being of great spiritual substance), Einstein (recently deceased and through his scientific and philosophical thought a "connection with the universe"), and an effigy of Christ ("the healer who sacrificed himself for humanity"), set in a rainbow of spiritual light, were to achieve the unity never achieved in this world and show "that God can be in each of us."

In the summer of 1982 Flack added the iridescent red, pink, and orange roses to the painting in thick impasto. On reconsidering, wanting a painting "with a physically vibrational healing effect that would not be read as a story," she decided to reduce the number of objects and to simplify the color scheme in order to achieve an effect of quietude. Baba's face was to dominate. Like the human images in *World War II* and *Marilyn*, Baba was to function as an archetype and symbol for all humanity. As her conception of the painting evolved, Baba's face, as a reflection of human spirituality, overwhelmed everything else in importance and she settled on *Baba* for the title of the painting (a word that in Hindu also means "father"). As she continued to struggle with the composition Baba himself observed "you need a woman in it."

The image of the woman goddess materialized in Flack's mind in 1982, as an independent image, in the monumental portrait of her daughter *Hannah*. The painting's subtitle, "Who She Is," is from the title of a poem by Joe Pintauro and is inscribed in longhand under the image.[17] As in *Invocation* the text of the poem becomes an integral part of the painting in both content and form: "She is stars in the sunrise / Lightning on a sunny day / Rain on the ocean / She is flown, so very far above us now / Over our politics of love / Over the limits of consciousness."

Flack understood the poem to be about a goddess and chose her daughter to embody that concept.[18] In addition to her 1981 self-portrait, she had dealt with the human goddess effigy in her 1977 *Marilyn* (*Vanitas*) and in a smaller version of the same subject, completed in 1978 and titled *Marilyn: Golden Girl*. In this smaller version the two images of Marilyn Monroe and the text in the book are similar to those in the earlier *Marilyn*, but the image of Monroe becomes freer, larger, and more heroic. All still-life elements are eliminated,

Hannah: Who She Is. 1982
Acrylic and oil on canvas, 84 × 60″
National Museum of Women in the Arts, Washington, D.C.

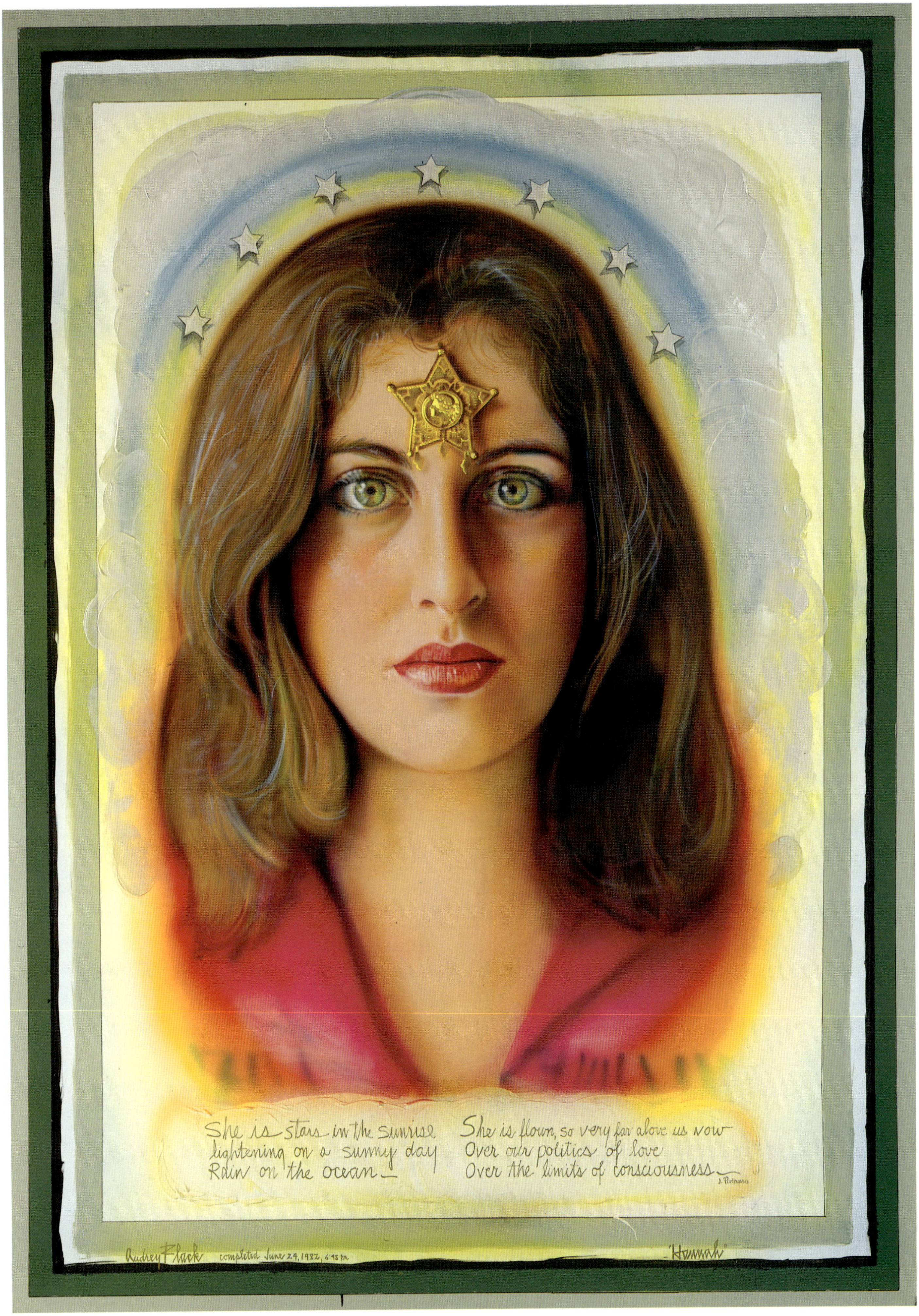
She is stars in the sunrise
lightening on a sunny day
Rain on the ocean—
She is flown, so very far above us now
Over our politics of love
Over the limits of consciousness—
Audrey Flack
completed June 24, 1982, 6:48 pm.
"Hannah"

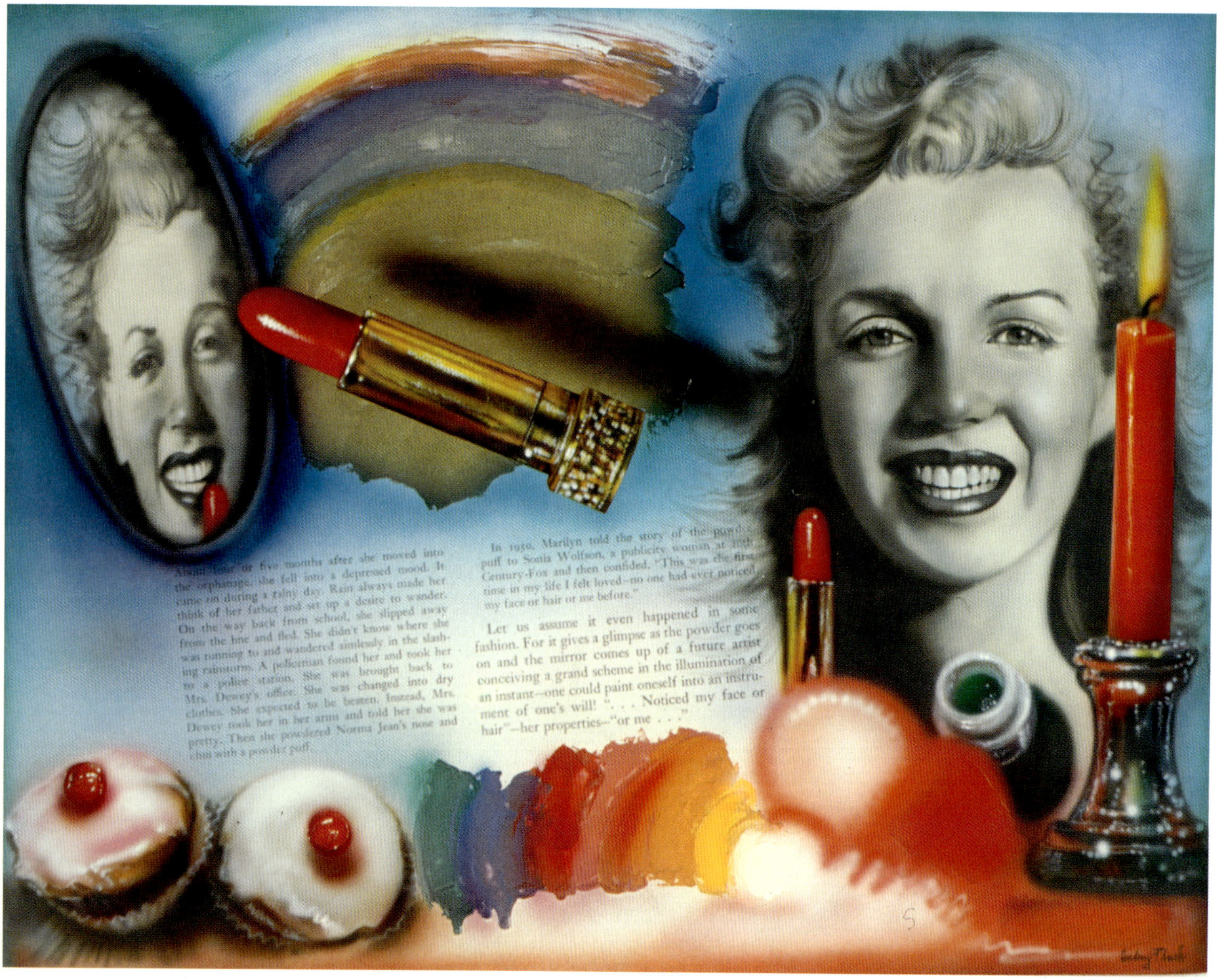

Marilyn: Golden Girl. 1978
Oil over acrylic on canvas, 48×60″
Private collection

except for the burning candle and lipstick flanking the goddess, a second phallic lipstick diagonally flying at the image in the mirror, and two breastlike frosted cupcakes under the mirror. The two images of Monroe are framed by a blue atmosphere and are connected by a painterly rainbowlike shape. The starkness, monumentality, and overtly sacramental qualities of this painting express Flack's attempt to capture aspects of divinity in a woman who, in her lifetime, became an effigy of worship.

In *Hannah* a living young woman who is not a public figure was transformed into a goddess. Taken out of any specific context, reduced to a monumental bust, surrounded by light, stars, and a halo of blue celestial atmosphere, the goddess no longer smiles. Frontal, immobile, and serene, with an almost symmetrical face, she acquires qualities of ancient female effigies. The neutral strips of flat, unevenly painted borders contrast with the perfection of the image and provide a reference to the physical existence of the painted surface, as do the films of thinly applied background color. The tangibly visible paint and the sheer size of the painting help to separate the image from any real physical context. In trying to create an effect of permanence, Flack, like artists in Late Antiquity and the Middle Ages, relied on frontality, symmetry, size, and an assertion of the eyes through emphatic delineation. Upon finishing the painting she dated it to its exact moment of completion (June 24, 1982, 6:48 p.m.). "It was like giving Hannah a second birth."

The next and perhaps inevitable step in Flack's search for a spiritual and eternal female image was a direct turn to Late Antiquity. The result was *Isis*, completed in the summer of 1983, shortly before *Baba*. Flack had had for years a slide of the mummy (c. 100 A.D., Metropolitan Museum). She chanced upon it in 1982 and it answered her need for an image of "an eternally living goddess." The idea of continuity and eternal life is central to the painting and is in harmony with the Egyptian style of the prototype. It is restated in the quotes from the *Bhagavad-Gita* on the frame, on the left: "That which exists / shall never cease to be / That which was not / shall never come in to being." And on the right: "From non existence / Nothing comes / There is always preexistence / There is always continuity of existence." The meaning of the texts is close to those in *Invocation* and expresses Flack's continuing search for universals. While part of the painting, they also act as a commentary on and elaboration of the meaning. As in *Hannah*, the female image is a bejeweled frontal bust in red robe (though *Isis* also includes the hands of the mummy and more jewelry). Surrounded by a blue firmament and an uneven border of stars and painted in thick oil pigment, the female image in *Isis* acquires a relieflike character and hovers in front of the turquoise blue background from which she emerges.

Unlike *Hannah*, *Isis* is based on an ancient and schematic portrait of a woman, placed over a once living face after death. Flack's effigy of the woman, irregularly painted and defined by schematic lines, looks strangely unreal. The wide and heavily encrusted frame, more dominant than the frame in *Invocation* and painted in iridescent acrylic paints, shimmers and reflects light. It visually and symbolically alludes to past, present, and future. The gold Egyptian seals with symbols of eternal life, the Indian signs, and the inscriptions allude to continuity, as does the translucency. The present is introduced in sketchily drawn lines, splotches of color, and blobs of paint that assert both the physical presence of the artifact and the act of painting. It is confirmed in the precise dating of the painting to its time of completion (1983 7:2: 12:00 A.M.).

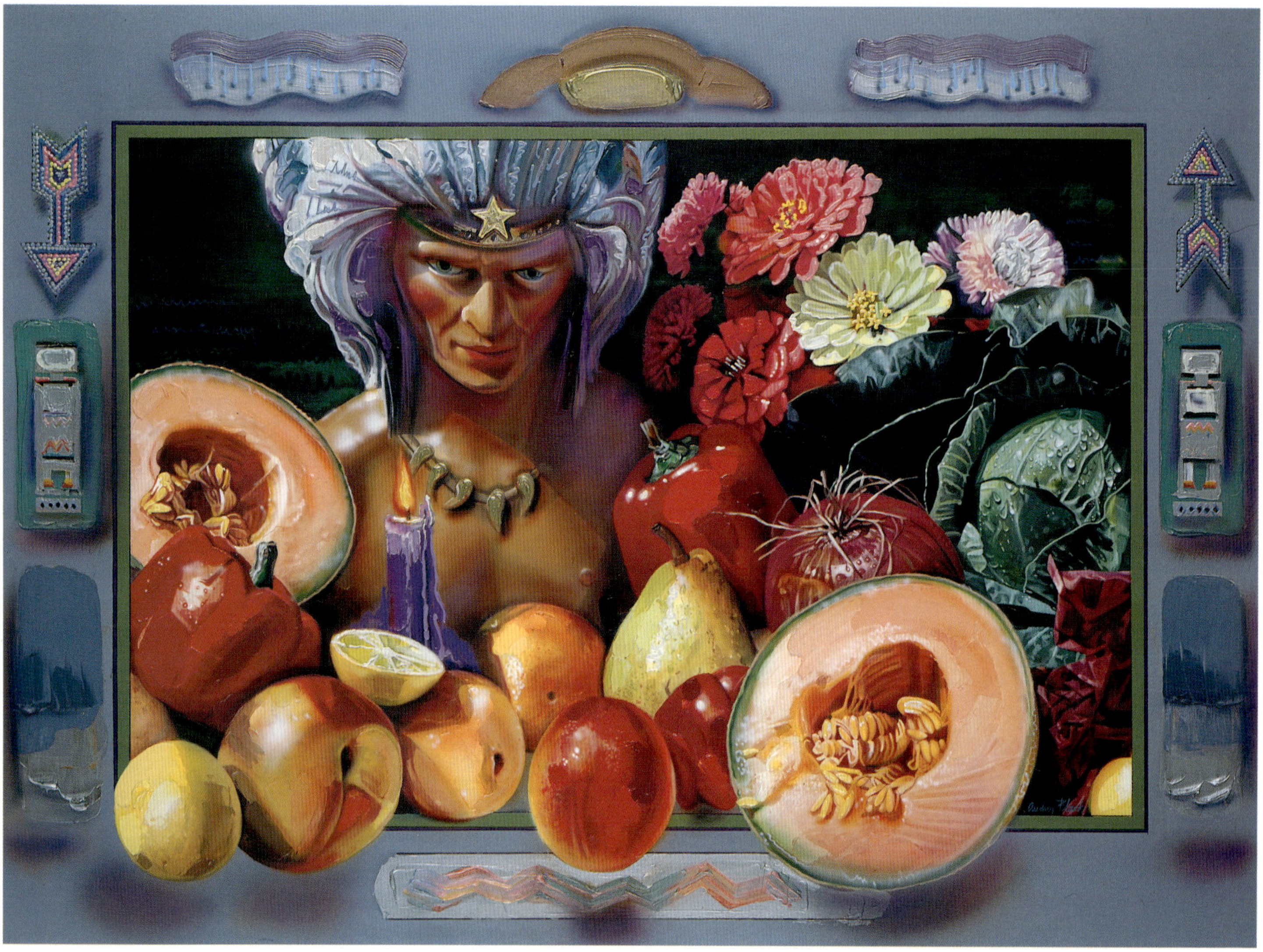

Fruits of the Earth. 1983
Acrylic and oil on canvas, 54 × 74″
Private collection

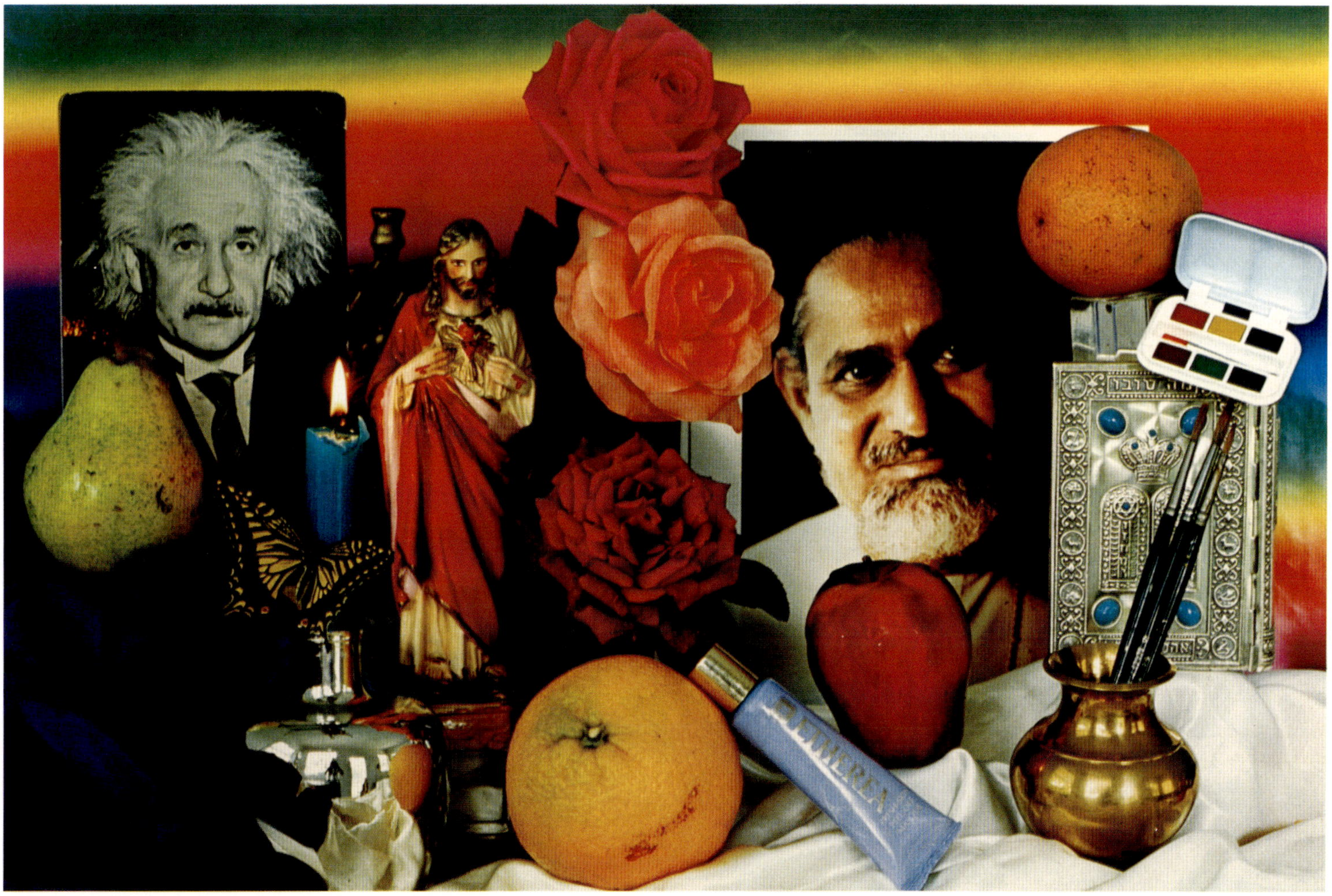

A Course in Miracles. 1983
Photograph, 14¾ × 22¼″
Collection Linnea S. Dietrich

OVERLEAF:
Baba. 1980–83
Acrylic and oil on canvas, 7½ × 13′
Collection Mr. and Mrs. Barry Hirschfeld, Denver

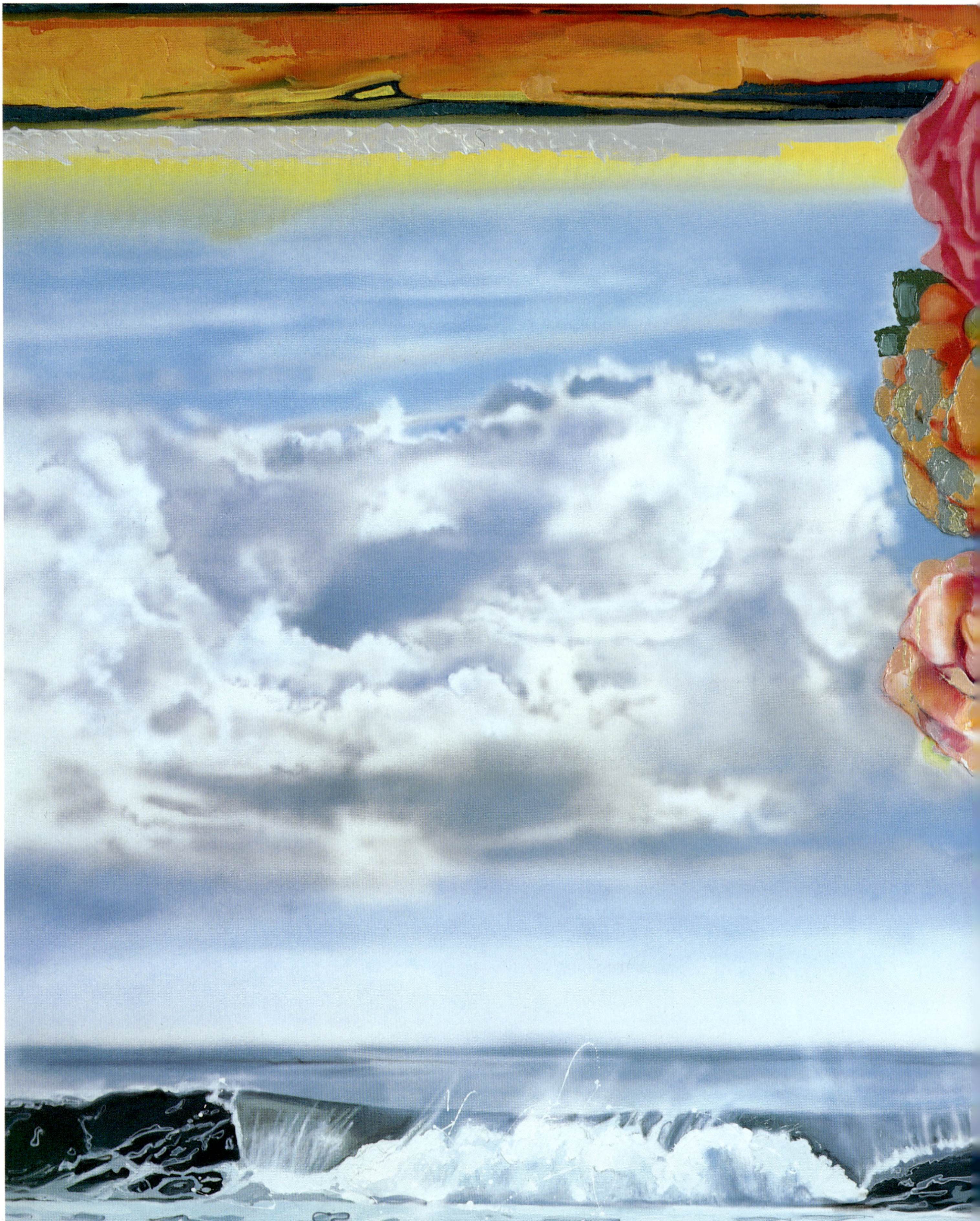

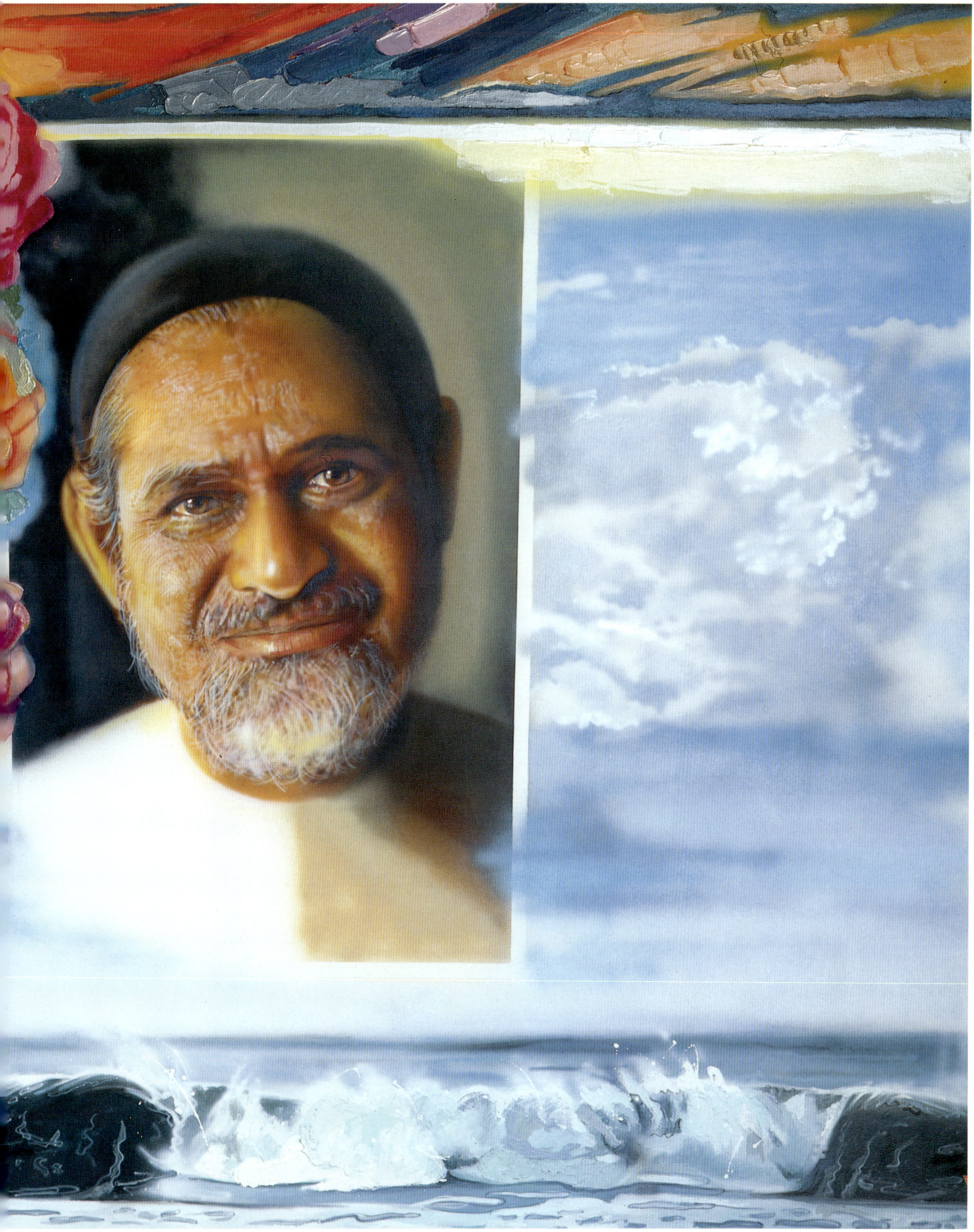

The image of *Isis* creates the effect of a brightly painted devotional statue reminiscent of the *Dolores* and *Macarena* paintings of 1971. But *Isis* is more remote and does not express emotion; she also remains strangely untransformed. The artistic goals Flack set for herself in *Hannah* and *Isis* were exact opposites. In the former she wished to make a living woman permanent by disassociating her from any temporal specifics. In the latter she wished to bring the schematic image of a dead woman out of the past and into the present. One has the sense that Isis was unwilling to leave the past. But, concurrently with the completion of *Isis*, Flack began modeling in clay. Having dealt with the image of the goddess at various times during the last two decades in her paintings (*Macarena* and *Dolores*, *Marilyn* and *Golden Girl*, *Hannah* and *Isis*), she felt that she needed to embody the goddess in three dimensions.[20] Her goddess sculptures of the eighties acquire strong and active bodies, looking back to her full-length self-portraits of the fifties, and literally step out of the past into the present.

Late in the summer of 1983, having had the painting in her mind for four years, Flack completed *Baba* in one week. She retained Baba's face and the roses and floated them in a wide expanse of sky and sea, introducing the female element in the guise of nature. Predominant blues and whites establish an atmosphere of peace and calm, and the lack of vertical border suggests eternal expansion. The horizontal edges are defined by an intense sunset (in reverse, as seen from an airplane) and by waves splashing upwards toward the clouds, both painted in thick impasto in almost relieflike, emphatic, abstract brush strokes. This expansive, elemental, and mystical setting is Flack's most monumental seascape. It was the result of her direct involvement with nature and pays homage to the early American landscape tradition of large vistas and untamed nature. The painting is a modern combination of the human and the sublime.

In her paintings of the early eighties Flack had wanted to recreate the sacramental and contemplative relation of viewer to icon characteristic of late medieval spirituality. She commented: "I want the viewer's mind to get absorbed in the reverie of the painting and, through the act of looking, calm and heal itself. I would like people to be able to sit in the gallery. I would like to have candles. I would like that whole process of the viewer's relationship to the painting to take place." Her desire to recreate aspects of an active devotional and spiritual communion between image and viewer and to resurrect what she considers "the true meaning of art"[21] is both passionate and romantic. That this would be adversely criticized in the context of a secularized age and a commercial art world did not deter her.

At a time when much contemporary art dwells upon the anxiety-ridden conditions of modern life, and survival seems possible only through overt criticism and ironic detachment, Flack's affirmation of piety, sentiment, and nostalgia as positive may seem utopian. But, then, Flack's symbolic realism has always been one of affirmation, and her preoccupation with the marvelous, the miraculous, and the astounding has informed much of her art. It reflects her belief that "art makes life more livable, more beautiful, more comprehensible" and that "it helps us deal with the basic fact of our physical mortality."[22] Her art is the active voice of a woman who has refused to accept the given truths of patriarchal culture and has looked into herself and at the presences of other women for a different kind of reality.

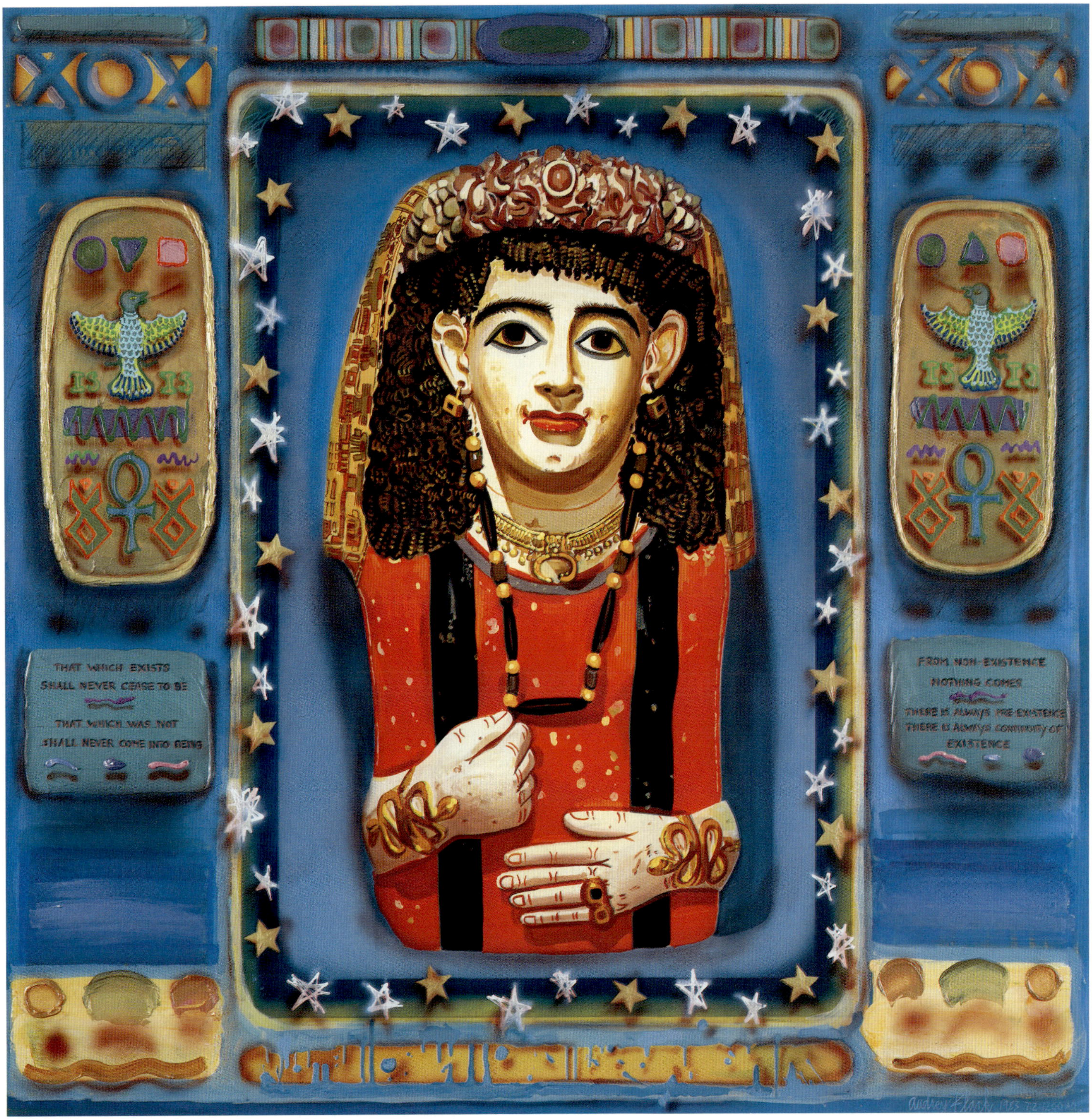

Isis. 1983
Acrylic and oil on canvas, 60 × 60″
Private collection

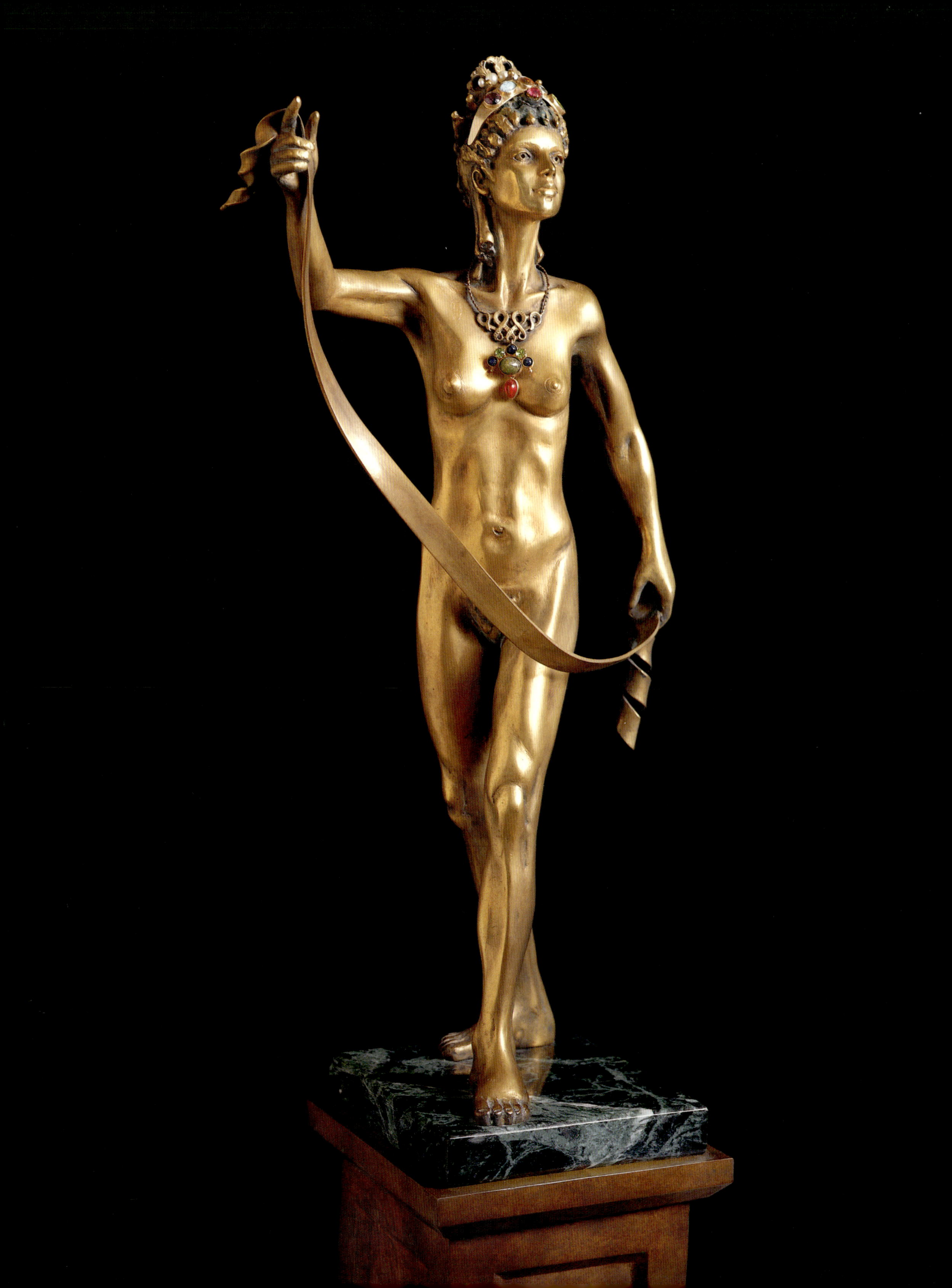

BREAKING THE MOLD: AUDREY FLACK'S SCULPTURES

Susan P. Casteras

In the early 1980s Audrey Flack began to sculpt in earnest, shifting focus from her pioneering Photorealistic paintings to another area of visual inquiry. This renewed involvement in sculpture simultaneously encompassed the artist's interest and knowledge of anatomy and reflected her love of nineteenth-century painting and sculpture, including works she had absorbed into her consciousness as a daily passerby in her student years, among these Gertrude Vanderbilt Whitney's sculpture at 168th Street.[1] In explaining her decision to devote herself almost exclusively to sculpture (although she still produces some watercolor paintings), Flack has described the act of sculpting as "a life and art-affirming act and a source of solidity on many levels" for her, something she must do out of a sense of creative urgency, dissatisfaction with the art world, and even political necessity.[2] As she has previously explicated in her writings,

> And why sculpture after a lifetime of painting? . . . The art world and the world outside of it seems to be going haywire—out of control, structureless, oversized, and temporary. I need the substance of sculpture, the compactness of scale reduction in the form of a recognizable human figure—something solid, real, tangible. Something to hold and to hold on to. Something that won't fly away or disintegrate. Bronze, heavyweighted, yet portable. I want people to be able to own these pieces as well as exchange them. My fantasy is to be able to produce them in great numbers, large editions, inexpensive, affordable—votive figures, some to be left as markers, some to be kept and carried off with their owners.[3]

Various aspects of Flack's career as a painter anticipate her work in a three-dimensional medium after 1981, particularly if one recalls that her famous image of the *Macarena Esperanza* of 1971 was rooted in a sculpture she had actually made years before painting the Spanish Madonna.[4] In this and other works the spiritual and the material, the real and the elusive, coexist and challenge viewers, and such is the case with her sculptural pieces, too. Nor is the projected colossal scale of some of the sculptures a surprise in the artist's oeuvre, given her earlier enlargements of objects in order to magnify aesthetic experience of them in her often densely packed canvases. Similarly, the emergence of an all-female pantheon is a natural extension, above all of Flack's strands of female-related imagery, beginning with her portraits of strong women in *Truman's Teachers* and *Two Women Grieving over Kennedy Outside a Dallas Hospital* of 1964, *Tante Feige* of 1967, and including the astonishing, feminized still lifes *Jolie Madame* of 1972, *Chanel* of 1974, *Leonardo's Lady* of 1975, and *Marilyn* (*Vanitas*) of 1977. In all these, Flack was constantly manipulating stereotypes and pushing them to their limits, reinventing the subjects and objects in a daring way that riveted viewers with their multivalent layers of personal and public iconography.

The Art Muse. 1988
Gold-plated bronze with jewels, height 16½″ (without base)
Private collection

In Flack's recent sculptures as well, myriad resonances are generated and intensified. Like her powerful paintings, these sculptures also have a strong presence and are never neutral in meaning or impact. Like the Victorian and nineteenth-century academic artists whom she admires (and collects—including works by William Etty, Francis D. Millet, Adolphe-William Bouguereau, and John Everett Millais), Flack's art is about image making, about representing familiar objects or subjects in particular as real and unreal, literal and symbolic, all at once. Like these earlier artists, she imbues her art with narrative, emotion, politics, and personal meanings. Nostalgia and sentiment, modernist bugaboos, are not an anathema to Flack, who incorporates these taboos into her own vocabulary and ideology of representation.

In a sculptural context, thus far Flack has dedicated herself almost exclusively to inventing a repertoire of ancient, thus far entirely female deities, named and unnamed, imaginary and classical. This "return of the goddess," as she has described this phenomenon, however, was not a conscious or preconceived undertaking. This series of goddesses and personifications "just happened—I started posing the female model, and all of them seemed to be heroic, special individuals who just naturally enacted and embodied mythology in modern times and across the ages. These women are real yet idealized, creative, the 'goddess in everywoman' in some ways. Each one has materialized in my sculptures as woman to be met as an equal, if not more than that."

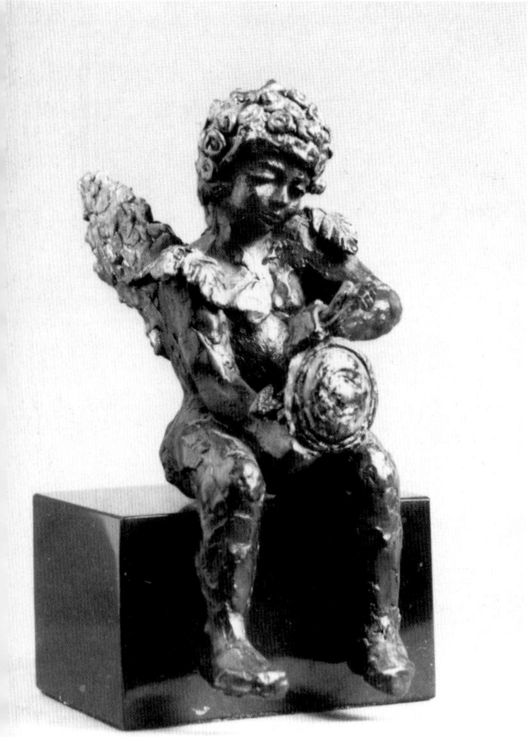

Angel with Heart Shield. 1981
Bronze, height 9″ (with base)
Collection Ari Ron Meisel,
New York

Flack's first sculptural work of the 1980s was *Angel with Heart Shield* of 1981, a small bronze seated putto/child, seemingly related somewhat in spirit to *Pluto with a Torch* (1880s, private collection, England) and kindred works by a Victorian sculptor, Alfred Gilbert, whom the artist also admires. While vaguely mythological in its Eros/Cupid implications, *Angel* thematically has little in common with the succession of female personifications who evolved in the following decade. Although the chronology of Flack's works is not always easily established (she works on numerous pieces simultaneously, as well as over long periods of time, that is, a great many have been produced since 1985), *Black Medicine* of 1981–82 was the first in this unofficial series. Although Flack originally planned to use a different kind of model, a seventy-five-year-old black woman posed for this piece. The artist, as is typical of her approach with all her sculptures, asked the model to assume a natural pose that was right for that individual, here one that is "as slow, ponderous, and powerful as the woman herself was." The result is a figure that seems partly bowed down, swaying slightly off axis like an aging dancer burdened by heavy weights from above and within. A priestess of sorts (and an homage perhaps to African sculpture), this figure does not embody traditionally youthful standards of appeal, thus challenging stereotypes of feminine beauty and power. The very title may be a pun, referring to "black medicine" or magic and more generally to the the arts and beliefs of non-Western cultures, past and present, that empower women in the ways of healing, wisdom, and foretelling the future. Significantly, virtually every object worn by the figure on the belt around her waist presages motifs or themes that reappear in later works by Flack—a bullet, shell, stars, turtle, owl, tiny Pegasus, and eagle.

OPPOSITE:
Black Medicine. 1981–82
Clay, height 17¾″ (without base)
Collection Pamela Roseneau,
New York

Another woman with healing powers is personified in *Medicine Woman,* whose body was "like a rock" and whose legs in particular seem boyishly strong. Flack, who is sensitive to the plight of the Native American (and has imagined herself in the role of chieftain in a sepia photograph of her in ceremonial headdress), portrays a shamanistic priestess in a healing trance, a

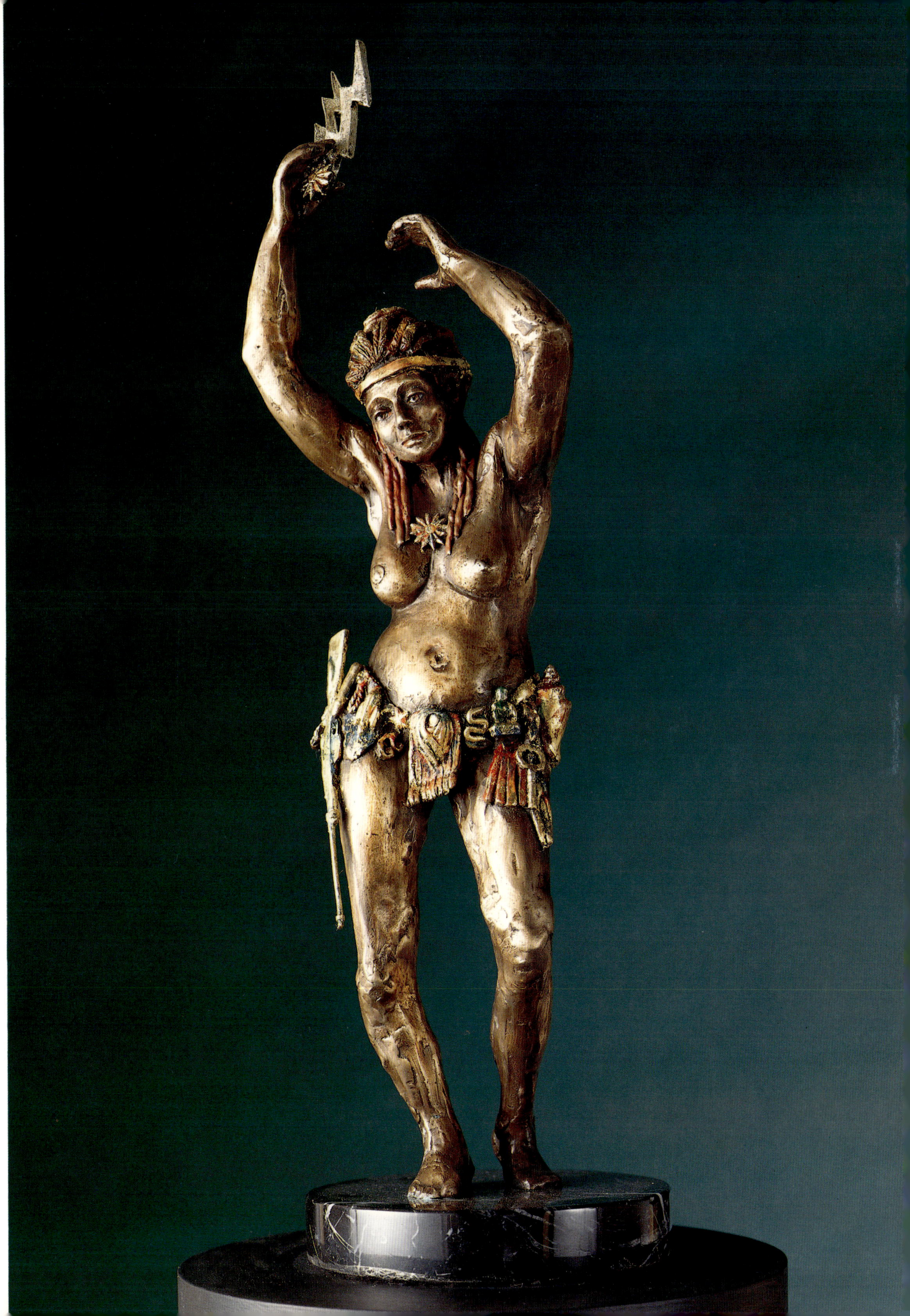

female who is simultaneously "tribal, yet universal, ancient, yet timeless." Her transfigured expression is both privately internalized yet visible to viewers, and like other sculptures, this figure belongs to her own realm of inner knowledge and wisdom. Besides curing illnesses, medicine men/women would help escort the souls of the dead to other worlds, perform meteorological magic, and in a state of ecstatic trance could serve as a medium for the spirits. In some North American tribes shamans also served as guardians and creators of tribal lore, as artists who preserve culture and become poetic sages for their people. An artist and prophetess, this figure is also a kindred spirit in some respects to Flack's *Medusa*, especially in her electrifying hair, which consists of lightning bolts, and in the snakes that entwine her arms and feet. While the serpent has largely feminine connotations, lightning bolts have both procreative and destructive ones, since their zigzag forms are derived from the priapic scepters of male sky gods who fertilized the female earth. Like *Black Medicine*, the figure in *Medicine Woman* wears a medicinal arsenal around her waist and carries a bag of feathers as part of her means of asserting power over the universe. The bolts and slagbursts on her head, like the objects adorning her—feathers, box with cures, elk horn, and animal skull on her head—allude partly to creation myths and also to the great energy over the elements that she can summon and channel as a healer. The stars and moon on her headdress also ally her with other cultures' mythological figures, such as Diana. In one hand *Medicine Woman* holds a ball of fire, suggesting, like the lightning bolts, the power and energy she can harness and use for healing.

Permutations of Medusa resurface not only in *Medicine Woman*'s hair but also in *Receiver of the Sun* (*Sun Goddess*), who has little phalluslike snakes radiating from her pubic hair in quasi-erections. Like the previous figures this one wears a belt with symbolic motifs (skulls, stars, and sunbursts) and is associated with Native American culture by the bracelet on one hand and feathers on the other. Like *Medicine Woman*, she is in a trance (ironically evocative of the agony/ecstasy of the transfiguration of a Christian saint), her eyes closed in a symbolic state of rapture and strength, self-containment and empowerment. Despite her rather small breasts, this figure, too, seems androgynous to some extent, the disruptive ambivalence of her body parts combined with the masculinity of her pose, basically the assertive stance of a Colossus of Rhodes capable of striding across the Hudson River or another site. Even more than some of the other female figures, she seems to be gathering power into her, personifying her role of inhaler of the sun, drawing in solar warmth for sustenance and regeneration. Although traditionally the sun is considered a male principle, archaic solar images in North America, Siberia, Japan, and among the Celts celebrated the sun as a female deity, and in pre-Islamic times the sun was also gendered as female.[5]

Another forceful prophetess/shaman emerges in *Egyptian Rocket Goddess*, completed in 1990, whose model was a woman who naturally assumed this empowering, outstretched pose and who in private life broke through a bad marriage into a new world of autonomy and assertiveness. This personal aspect became a hieroglyph or emblem for the entire piece, in which the Egyptian figure (with the contemporary face of a modern Queen Nefertiti) "breaks through the time barrier to our time . . . and exists in all temporal periods simultaneously."[6] On the base are emblems of transcendence—footprints of the American eagle (allying her with the *American Athena*), discarded missiles, mechanical and toy parts, coins, prehistoric fossils, a turtle, and part of a

Receiver of the Sun (Sun Goddess). 1989–90
Polychromed resin with objects, height 33½″ (with base)
Collection Janet Lehr

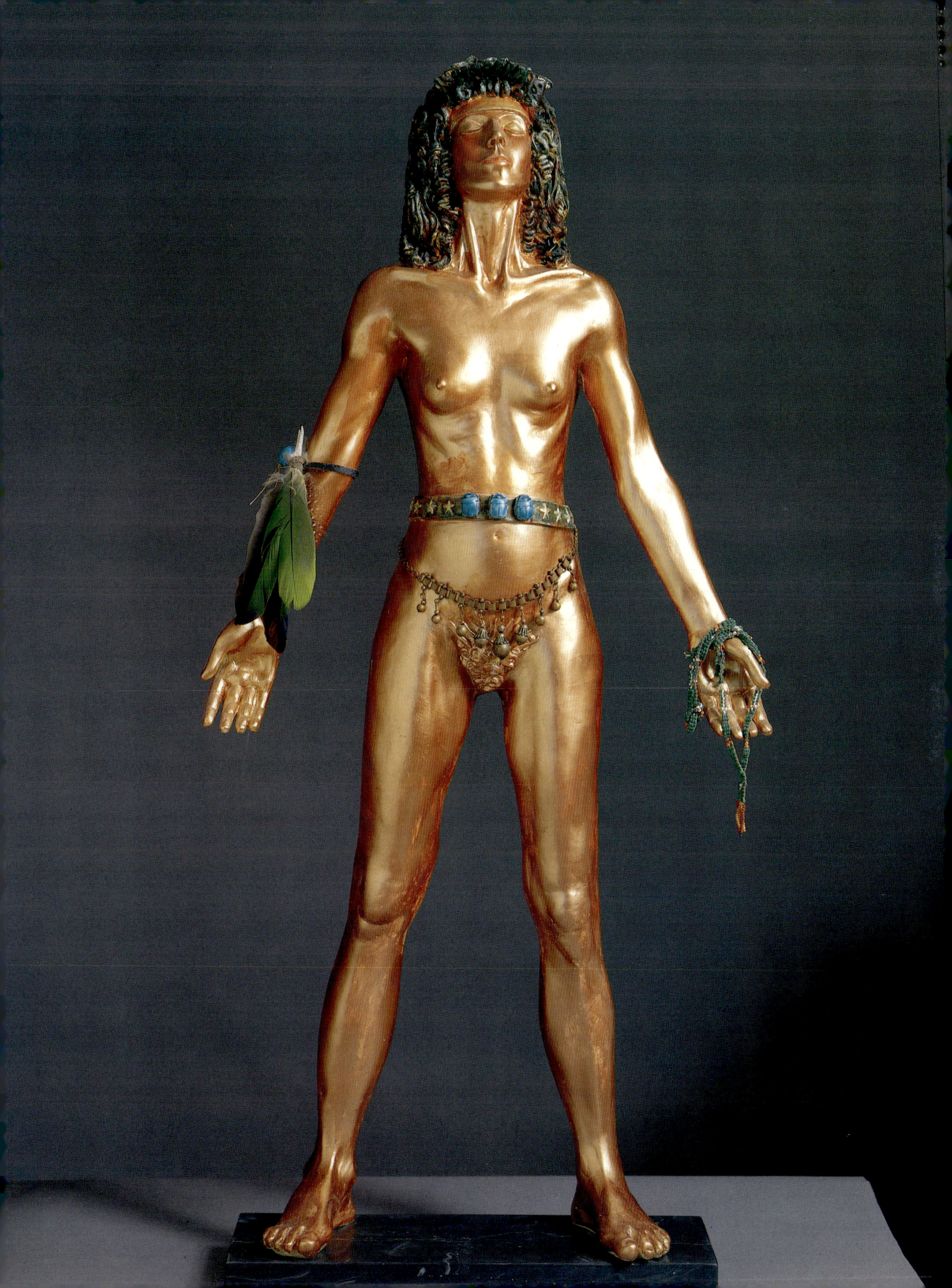

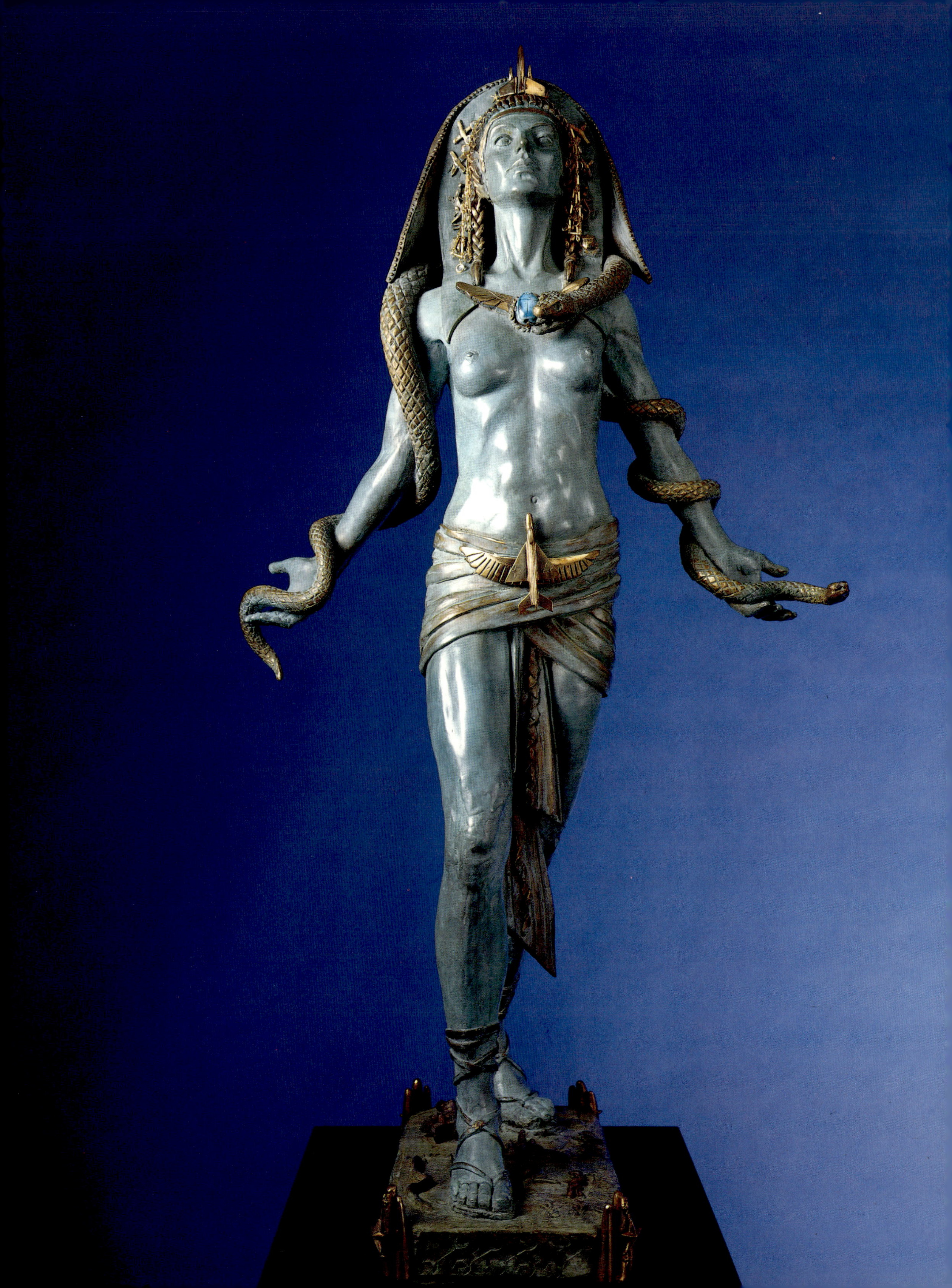

rocket ship. On the sides of the base are impressions from the artist's airbrush wrench, which connote the literal imprint of art and industry in a personalized hieroglyphic design. Flack has also played with scale by putting a tiny jet and creatures in dwarfed proportion to the colossal striding figure. Other shapes on the base and elsewhere—*x*'s, stars, circles, and serpentine lengths—are reminiscent of *Isis,* a 1983 painting by the artist with an Egyptian goddess and theme. Along the bottom corners are four tripartite phallic forms with stars that recall World War II bombs and blend sexual with machine motifs, the natural with the unnatural and warlike, in a contemporary pictorial cuneiform.

Related extraordinary details have been integrated into other parts of the *Egyptian Rocket Goddess.* Her headdress (an adornment worn by some of Flack's female figures seemingly as an affirmation of their special powers and status) is emblazoned with tiny sphinxes, reptilian forms of prehistoric life, and a phallic rocket at the apex, which is reminiscent of the configuration of the Empire State Building. On her chest an ancient Egyptian scarab (symbolic of eternal life) is centered over a pair of wings and echoed by a phallic eagle with a rocket "erection" above her genital area. Like the birds whose parts she displays, this figure is in a visionary state rather like that of a shaman. In Egyptian art the hawk represented the *ba* part of the soul that was free to fly, and in this respect the figure may be construed as one of the many shamans who were givers of omens, priestesses of the occult and secret, and soul carriers whose trance symbolized a ritualistic possession or ecstatic flight "initiating death and rebirth."[7] She communes as well with other creatures, the snakes on her arms, which evoke primarily ominous associations with female mythology and remind viewers as well of earlier cult figures portrayed in sculptures such as the Minoan *Snake Goddess* (Museum of Fine Arts, Boston) or a painted terra-cotta snake goddess (Herakleion, Crete).

Another kind of figure that transcends time and space is represented by *Islandia: Goddess of the Healing Waters,* also called *The New Winged Victory* by the artist. Indebted to the famous winged Hellenistic prototype of the *Nike of Samothrace* (Musée du Louvre) for its fluttering drapery—and yet a quantum leap beyond—this beautiful and young figure with gilt iridescent wings projects an air of both fragility and strength. As in other examples, the female body goes beyond the striding Egyptian precedents and Greek kouroi to step out of her immediate plane of existence and, in her dramatic flight from confinement transcends spatial and temporal boundaries to break into those occupied by contemporary spectators. Here and in other works Flack "absorbs, reaffirms, honors, values" past art and artists as she forges her own imagery. Besides the *Nike of Samothrace* and even the *Venus de Milo* in the Louvre, the artist seems to pay some visual acknowledgment to Luisa Roldán's *Death of St. Mary Magdalene,* 1686–87 (Hispanic Society of America, New York), for example, to the wings of the angels, and to other polychromed works by this Spanish Baroque artist. In addition, Alfred Gilbert's *Victory* of c. 1887, may have provided other visual grounding for Flack's interpretation, especially since she knows of and admires some of his extraordinary sculptures. In her dual identity and in multiple sizes, colors, and permutations, this sculpture is charged with various meanings. Flack has indicated that she invented the name *Islandia,* yet perhaps this goddess is subconsciously a personification of the pagan legends of a matriarchal paradise island ruled by a royal virgin and blessed with the presence of the tree of life.[8] In one of two bronze versions,

Egyptian Rocket Goddess. 1990
Patinated bronze, height 42″
(with base)
Private collection, Ontario

OPPOSITE:
Islandia: Goddess of the Healing Waters. 1987
Polychromed and gilded plaster, height 5′ (without base)
Samuel P. Harn Museum of Art, University of Florida, Gainesville

Sir Alfred Gilbert. *Victory*. c. 1887
Bronze, white onyx, and ebonized wood, height 19″ (with base)
Ashmolean Museum, Oxford

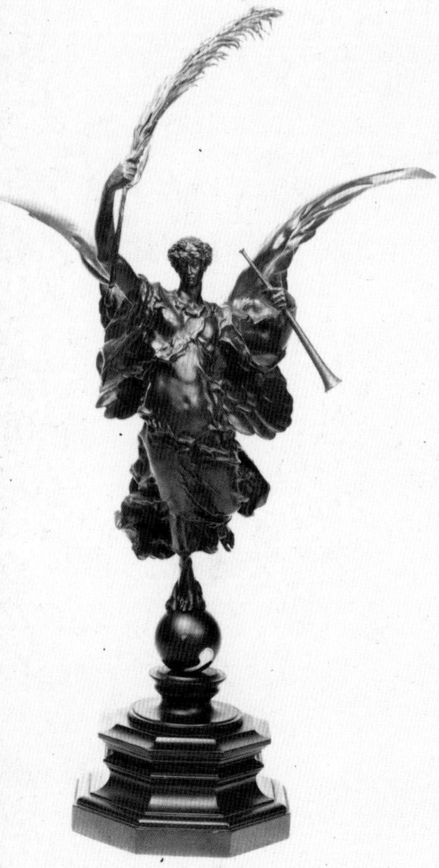

Islandia's face shines like gold, her wings are streaked like those of a seraph, and her torso drapery is colored a deep Aegean blue. Another variation (plaster painted in ivory and gold hues) is subtly decorated in a consciously Jackson Pollock "drip" style, an allusion to Flack's early exposure to Abstract Expressionism in her student days. In this 1988 sculpture, the figure's golden hair and creamy skin evoke comparisons with a Botticellian Venus or even John Gibson's Victorian masterpiece, *The Tinted Venus* (c. 1850, Walker Art Gallery, Liverpool). The dynamic drapery is at least partly indebted to the *Venus de Milo*, although its sinuous convolutions may also mutely acknowledge Victorian neoclassicizing visions of draped females, among them Edward Burne-Jones' *The Beguiling of Merlin* (Lady Lever Art Gallery, Port Sunlight) of 1874. Indeed, Flack's indebtedness to British nineteenth-century sculpture is subtle and transformational, inspired by numerous painters and sculptors and yet very different in mood and meaning.

Visually this goddess with latent healing powers also shares some affinities with Flack's image of the polychromed Madonna Esperanza in the glittering crown of roses she wears (making her a pagan goddess as well as a Virgin Mary or angelic messenger) and the similarly garish "carnival" hues in both. The *Macarena Esperanza*, in return, invites comparison with the extraordinary surface embellishment in Alfred Gilbert's bronze figure of the *Virgin Mary* from the Clarence Tomb of c. 1894–96, Kippen Parish Church, Stirlingshire, England. These same carnival and gold tonalities resurface in the drapery, while the wings look as if they were wrought from submerged gold, bejeweled treasure that is an alloy of ethereal hues with those of the sea. Moreover, the mood Islandia sustains is one of beneficence and generosity. She is both receiving and giving in her gesture, confidently extending one hand while raising the other with some sense of triumph, a pose that seems to conflate both Christian and Greek traditions. The entire body is in motion, with the thrust of Islandia's knee and left arm counteracted by the contrasting direction of her wings and animated drapery; in her restless yet stationary stance both movement and self-confidence are conveyed.

Islandia was made somewhat smaller than life-size (in emulation of rather Victorian ideals of proportion), and Flack feels this scale is easier to take, clarifying that the figure was not "simply taken as a body cast in resin from a real person—she was sculpted and deliberately made that way." *Islandia* was created actual size, but in terms of process, Flack usually works at first in small scale, creating a Plasticine sculpture of tabletop size and then enlarging it considerably. For commissioned pieces (for example, *Rock Hill Gateway*), she has rough enlargements of the entire figure or its head made at the foundry. She then spends months at the foundry, refining and recarving the enlargements. In one version *Islandia* holds a conch shell and wears one earring and a coral necklace (coral being associated with feminine blood and the tree of life). Intended to personify gentleness, she was conceived by the artist to have a calming effect and has already achieved this iconic significance in one public setting. A version of *Islandia* has been permanently installed in the New York City Technical College in Brooklyn, where, according to Flack, students rub the figure's knee for good luck and bring her small offerings. *Islandia* arguably symbolizes the covert psychological effect of Flack's sculptures, intended to empower, heal, and calm audiences rather than threaten viewers or the space they occupy. These reactions further reinforce her role as Nike, the goddess of success, who brought gifts to winners and athletes, a so-called "pure

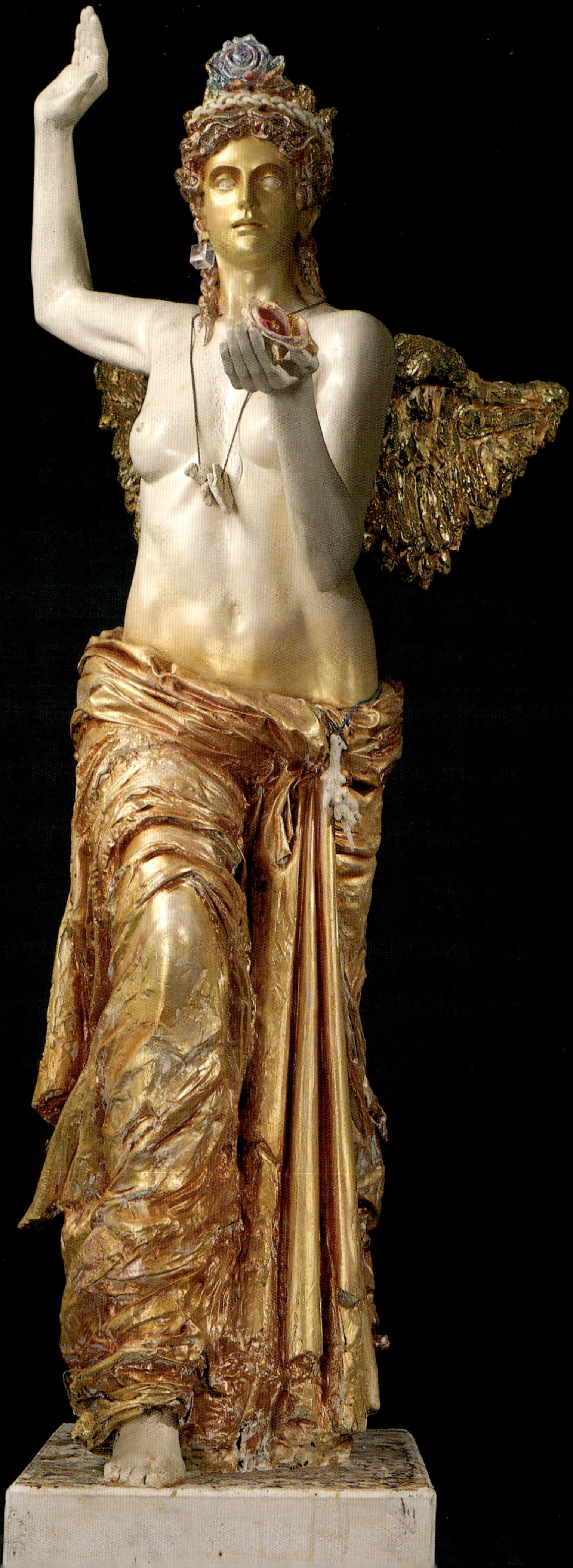

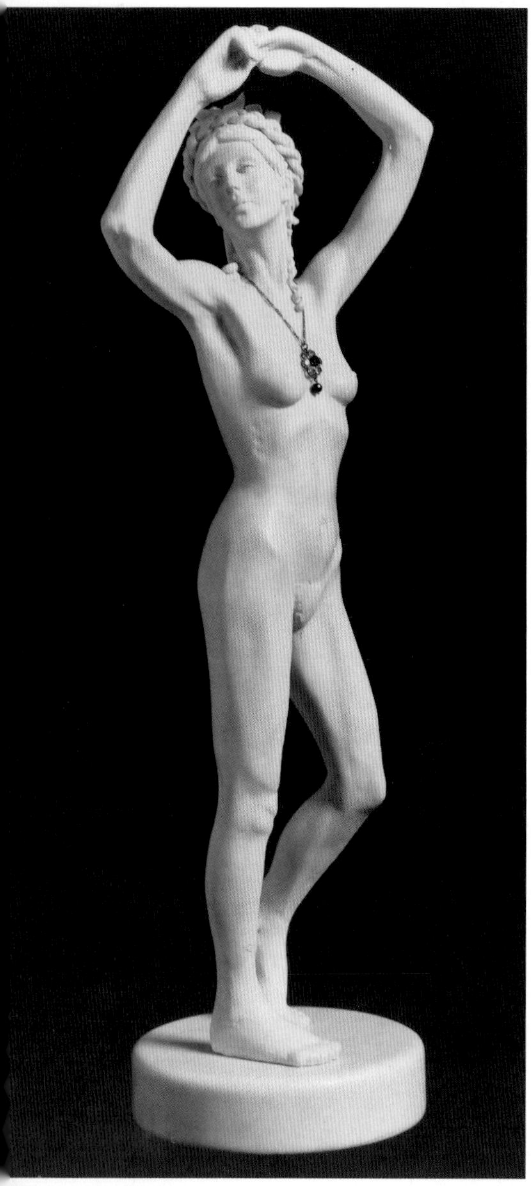

Diana. 1988
Cast marble with jewels,
height 23⅛″ (with base)
Collection Mr. and Mrs. Marvin Padover

OPPOSITE:
Diana. 1988
Gold-plated bronze with jewels,
height 21⅝″ (without base)
Private collection

personification" without story or myth who was ultimately transformed into the archangel of Christian glory, a messenger of good tidings.[9]

These healing figures—*Black Medicine, Medicine Woman, Receiver of the Sun* (*Sun Goddess*), *Egyptian Rocket Goddess*, and *Islandia*—all accrue the characteristics of surrogate artists, guardians of secret imagery and lore who have the power to transcend the ages and to heal and comfort. Indeed, Flack has written about the artist's role in precisely these terms. To her great art is restorative, its energy able to transfer revelations and meanings to others and to "mend and heal." The act of creation is akin to entering a dream state, because "the act of painting is a spiritual covenant between the maker and the higher powers."[10] The shaman can "hold the spirit" in a work of art because s/he "is someone who has been through the fire, who has been ill and healed himself. The shaman can then return and heal others."[11] To Flack, even late-twentieth-century artists can become shamans possessed and empowered by magical forces. In tracing the collapse of classical techniques of art to the demise of the shamanic culture, she has written that "the shaman cures not only the individual but the entire community as well, by bringing it together and extending perimeters and boundaries. All rules are suspended during the ritual act, and a balance is created between this world and the supernatural one."[12]

But there are other kinds of figures besides artists/healers in a state of trancelike intensity in Flack's pantheon of female achievement and potential.[13] Among these is *Diana*, who recaptures the independent feminine spirit of the goddess of the moon and hunt. Tall and willowy, she typically bore either torches or a bow as she roamed the wilderness. Moreover, as a virgin goddess, she was an ideal embodiment of self-reliance, achievement, and competence, although she was also a mother goddess linked to the Madonna.[14] In Flack's 1988 bronze statuette (also in a plaster version), she endows Diana with a body that is both feminine (adolescent) and yet boyish, a tendency to androgyny perhaps linking her to her twin brother, Apollo. Diana wears no coy drapery—only some jewelry and an emblematic crescent moon in her hair—and her pose suggests that of a lithe young athlete (or artist) honing her bodily strength and agility, her natural competitive edge, to even greater heights of perfection and performance. (The model, according to the artist, was a "tall, silent dancer with a kind of mannerist elegance and poise to her body and movements.") Nor does this goddess look out at, move, or reach toward viewers; instead she seems autonomous, absorbed in orchestrating her arms, body, and mind to achieve even more coordinated performances and victories over man and nature alike, rather like a female body builder with beautiful male and female body parts and proportions—akin in some respects to Lisa Lyons, whom Robert Mapplethorpe photographed in some famous images. Tautly attenuated and streamlined, she seems beautifully narcissistic. In actuality, Flack has said that she sought to use very strong female models "with muscular bodies, not soft, boneless, gorgeous 'French' types. I wanted definition of the biceps, triceps, ribs, breasts, and every part of anatomy, in part to emphasize the anatomy, in part to emphasize inner strength. I did not want to emulate Edouard Manet's *Olympia* or odalisques and create merely beautiful bodies waiting to be admired and ravaged."

Like *Islandia* in particular, *American Athena* of 1989 harks back to sculptural archetypes struggling to break out of the blocks of stone and space that impede them. Standing on a little pedestal "island," this figure wears a

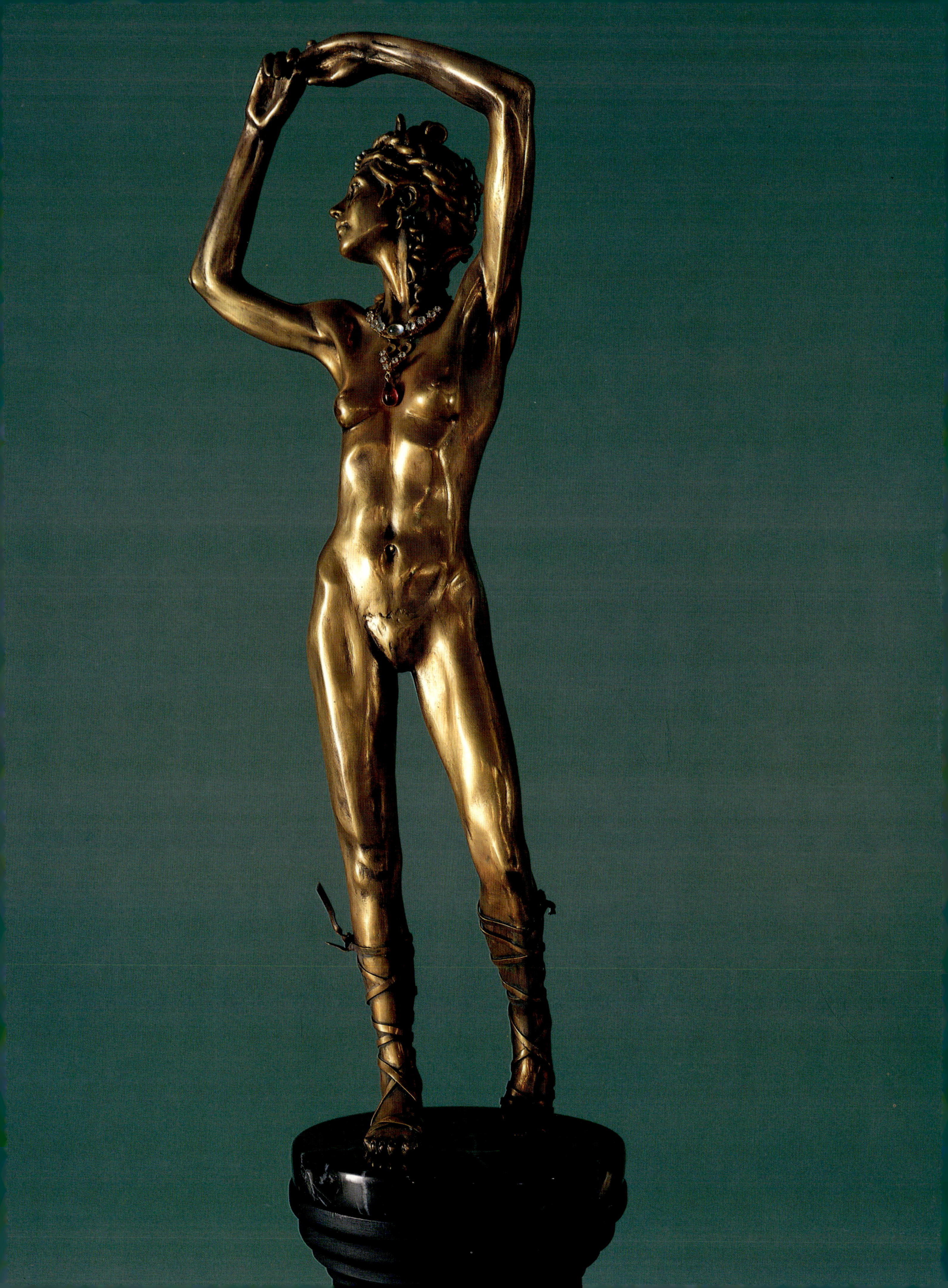

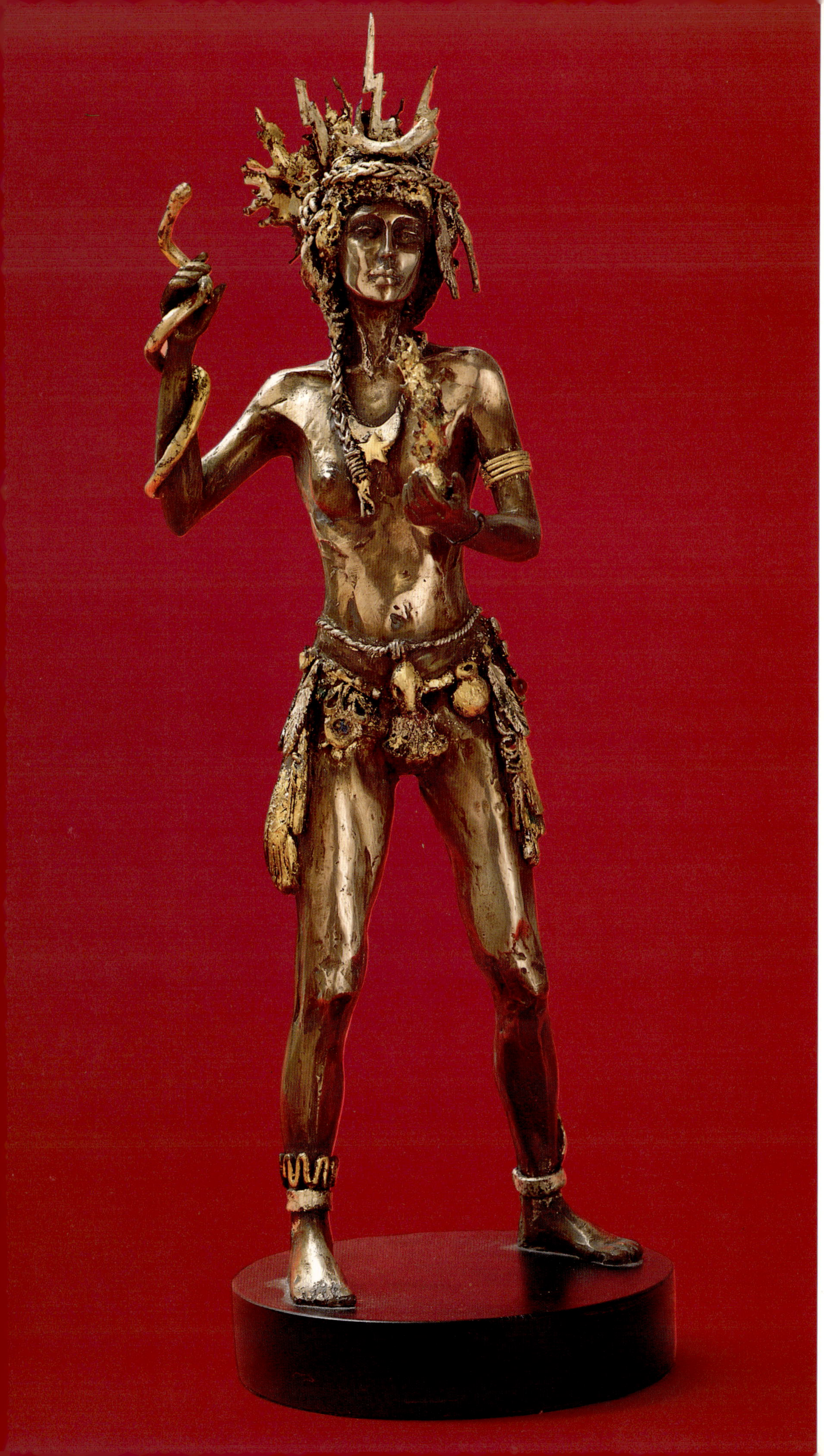

Medicine Woman. 1989
Patinated and gilded bronze,
height 19″ (with base)
Collection Sophie Burnham

OPPOSITE:
American Athena. 1989
Patinated bronze with
gilded ornament
and mother-of-pearl inlay,
height 37″ (with base)
Collection Donna and
Neil Weisman, New Jersey

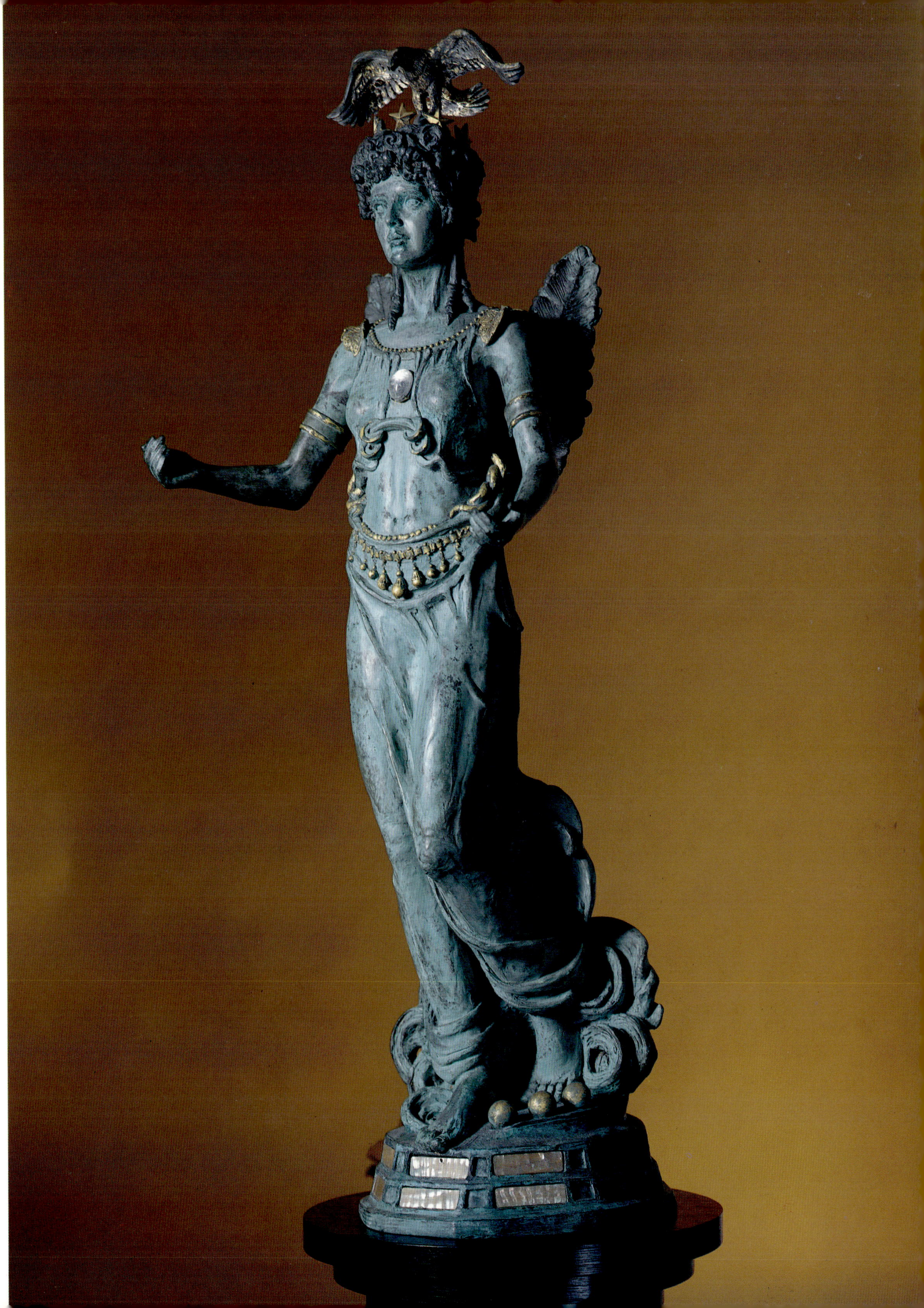

snaky necklace that allies her with Medusa (and with pre-Greek female deities) as well as a crystal scarab and stars that make her "sister" to the *Egyptian Rocket Goddess* and the *Civitas* prototype in particular. Projecting an air of unwavering self-sufficiency and supremacy, *American Athena* gestures outward, as if to utter something, and the balance suggested by her supportive arms is in counterpoint to the gentle billowing of drapery at her feet, as if sea breezes have produced these undulating waves. This sculpture transcends the boundaries of time and nationality, although she is firmly linked to traditional American iconography by the presence atop her head of an American eagle, a bird totemic of imperial power in general and of predicting the future as well.[15] The artist has mentioned that she was partly inspired in this piece by the nineteenth-century sculpture of Stirling Calder and also by the work of Charles Grafly, a friend of Thomas Eakins. The choice of nomenclature is significant, for Athena was the virginal patron "saint" of Athens and protector of many heroes. Her association with birds, especially owls, is reflected here in the inclusion of a national emblem that is also a Christian symbol of resurrection. Athena was the object of worship in citadels and among cults, and as mother goddess of Athens she was worshiped as holy virgin. Besides her well-known role as the goddess of war, she was also venerated as a patroness of the arts and crafts, a connotation that is especially apt for Flack's vision of the goddess and a possible site for her in the nation's capital.[16]

Originally this sculpture evolved from another idea called *Emissary,* and Flack has described how this new figure came about:

> I have been changing the contours of the face, draperies, headdress, and title of a new sculpture that I have been refining and reworking for well over a year now. She has carried projections of ancient mythological figures—Greek, Far Eastern, Indian, Tibetan, Chinese, and Japanese, as well as American Indian. What seems to be happening, in spite of myself, is a composite figure, a complement of all of them. I can't seem to help what's coming out. . . . Sometimes the artist is not the final control. She absorbs the basic tenets of the age in which she lives, creating an assemblage. This subconscious assimilation of the flavor of the age, combined with archetypal concepts, is poured out in the form of art.[17]

A literal coming together of these potent figures and forces occurs in Flack's commission for the *Gateway,* a colossal sculptural undertaking that dominates a section of parkway and land in Rock Hill, South Carolina. Collaborating with architect Michael Gallis, Flack has designed an incredible monument. Four huge figures, each cast from one basic prototype and standing at a height of twenty-two feet (thirteen feet figural, nine feet for the pedestal), bear different attributes and zodiac signs. Each faces inward at a different corner, with an intersecting "magic" square and circle shared in the central, overlapping space at the intersection. One might wonder, however, whether or not the final impact is too overpowering—e.g., a site of confrontation between huge personifications and anxious drivers—, a speculation that will be confirmed or negated only after the passage of time.

Each of these four quintessential figures is individually named a *Vision;* collectively, they form a grouping called *Civitas,* a word that aptly connotes the shared responsibility and common purpose of serving the community and citizenry. They interact as part of the gateway with some huge sixty-foot pillars (supposedly replicas of those from King Solomon's temple), which were paradoxically rescued and refurbished from a bastion of male secrecy, a

Civitas: Four Visions (Gateway to the City of Rock Hill). 1989
Patinated and gilded bronze maquette, with cast glass flame and marble orb, height 54″ (with orb)
Collection Donna and Neil Weisman, New Jersey

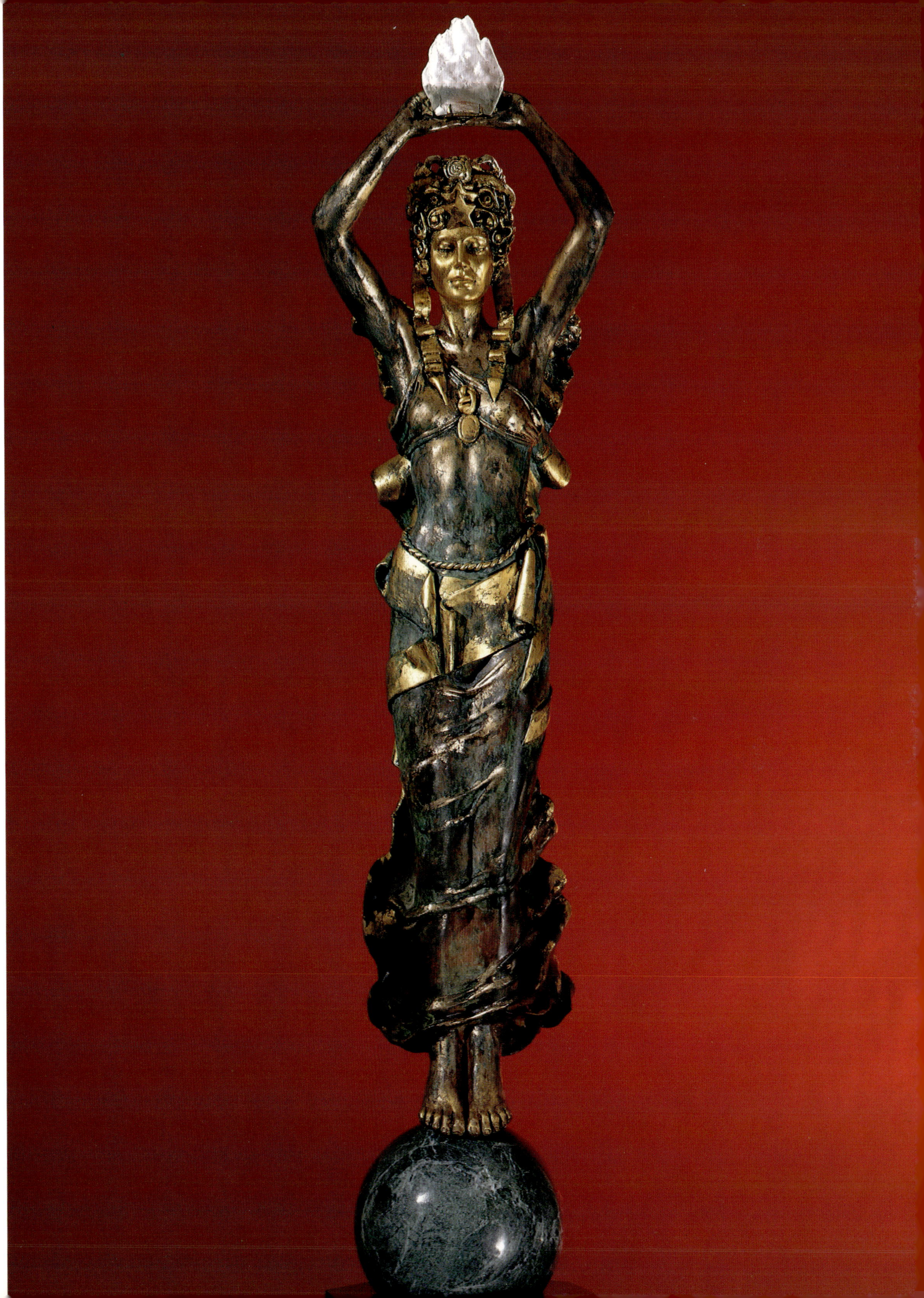

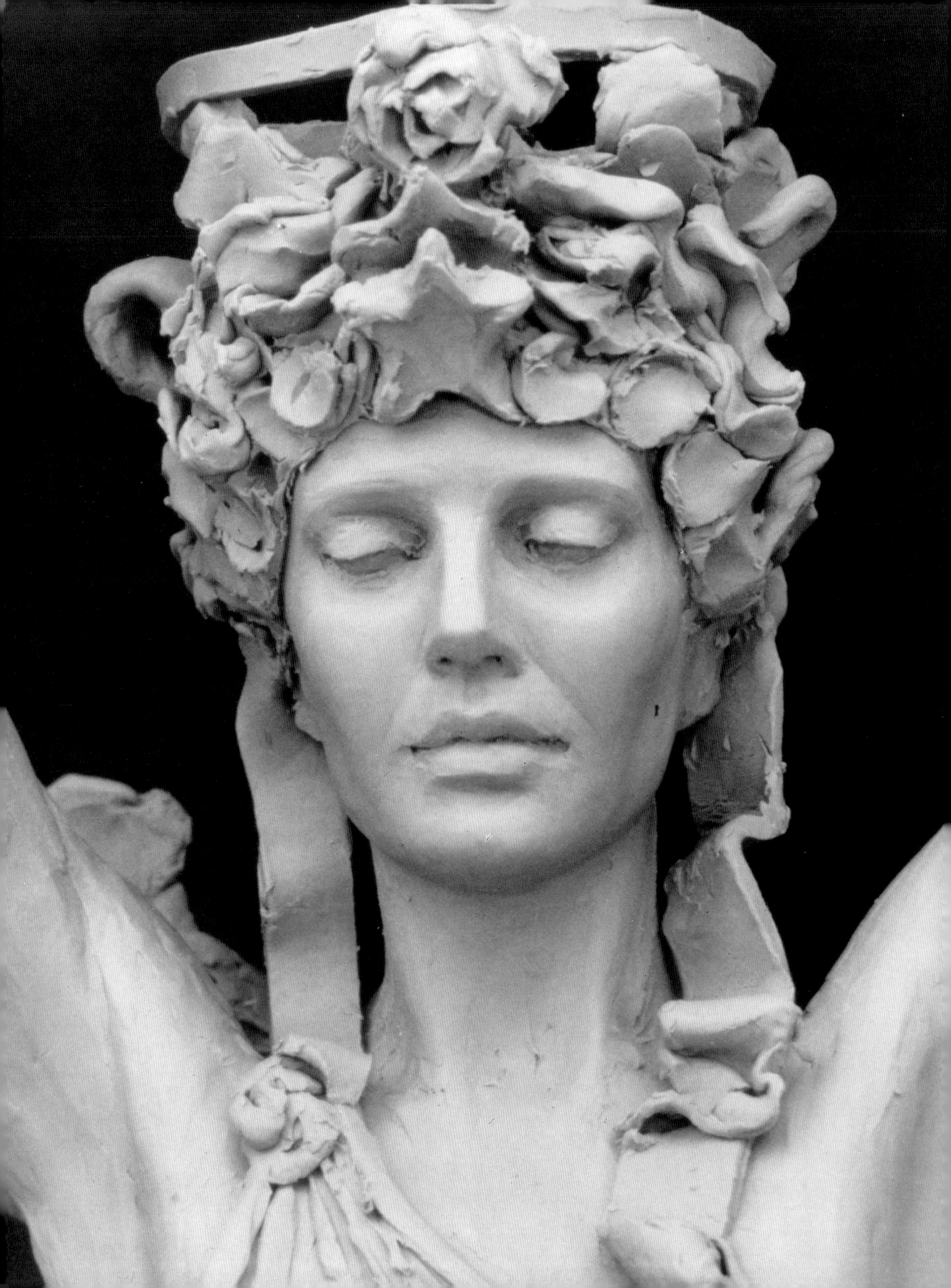

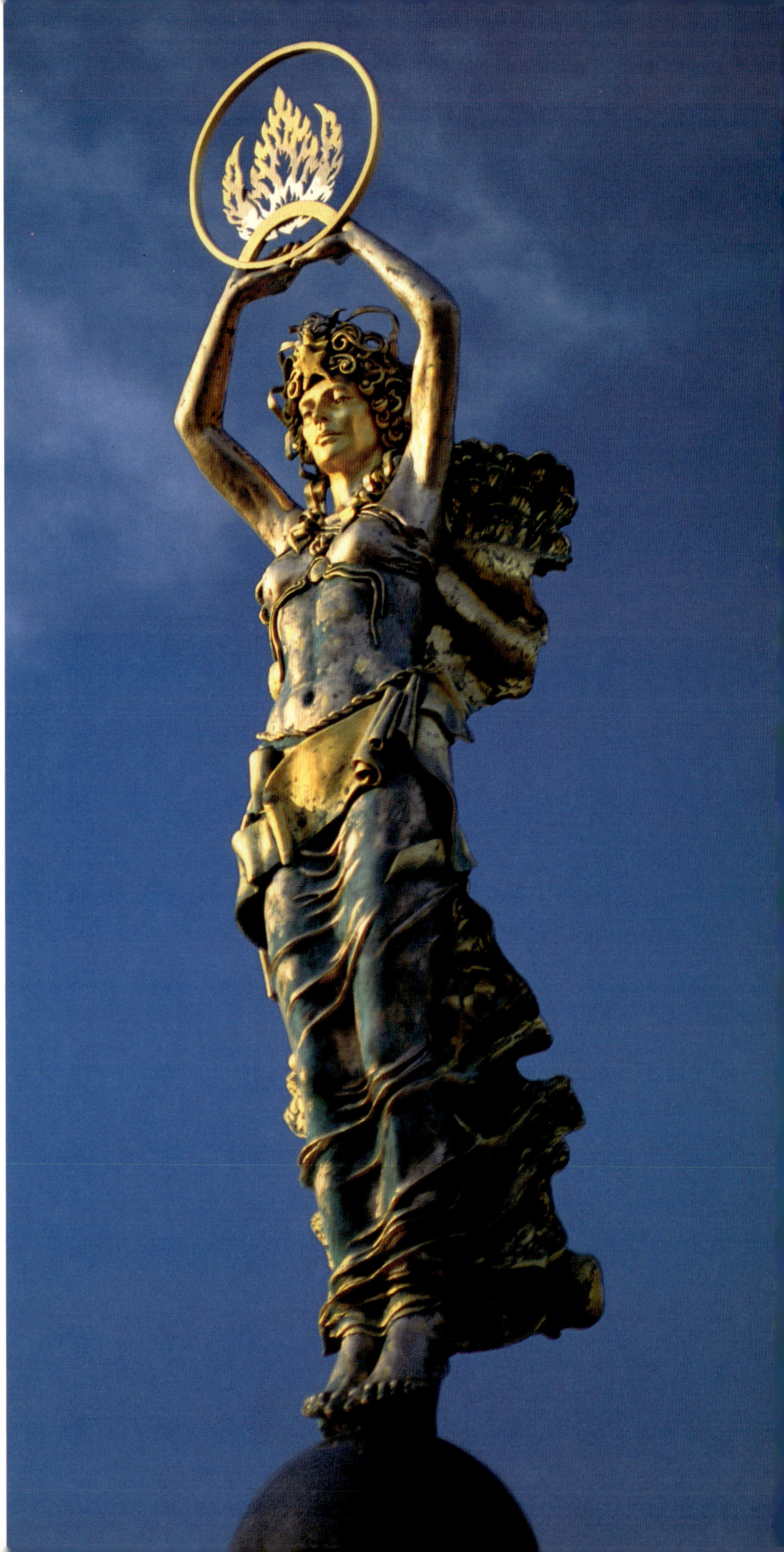

OPPOSITE:
Civitas: Four Visions (Gateway to the City of Rock Hill) (detail). 1988
Clay, Styrofoam, and cardboard maquette, height 54″ (with base). Now destroyed

Civitas: Four Visions (Gateway to the City of Rock Hill). 1990–91
Patinated and gilded bronze with black granite base, height 22′ (with base), 13′ (without base)
One of the four sculptures is shown here after installation at the Rock Hill Gateway, South Carolina, April 1991

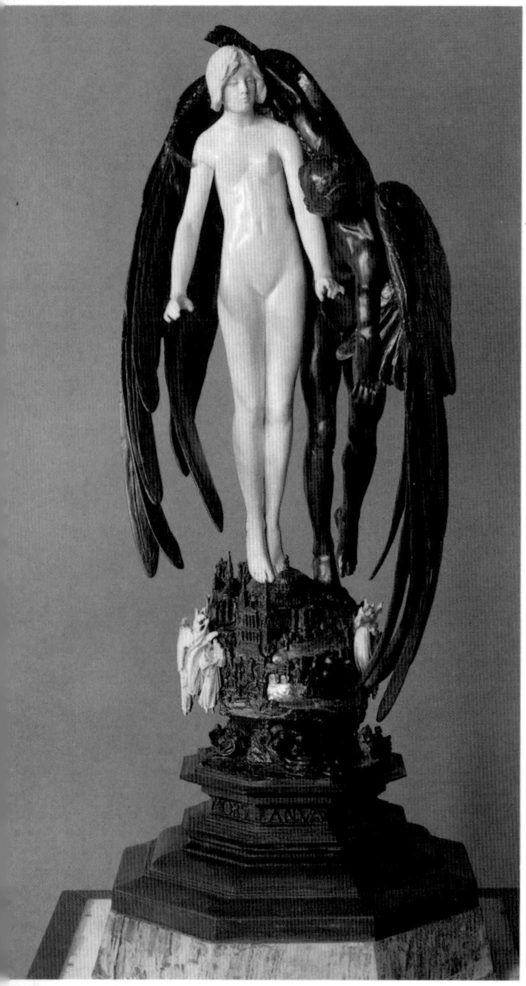

Harry A. Bates. *Mors Januae Vitae.* 1899
Bronze, marble, ivory, and mother-of-pearl, height 36″
Walker Art Gallery, Liverpool, courtesy The Board of Trustees of the National Museum & Galleries on Merseyside

OPPOSITE:
Victory (Earth Mother). 1990
Polychromed and gilded plaster, height 18″ (with base)
Collection the artist

Masonic temple that was razed in Charlotte, North Carolina. Each figure holds aloft attributes within a stylized circle that symbolize the city and its virtues.

Prior to its completion, this program known as *Civitas* existed only in maquette form of *Vision,* a bronze version, and as a full-size head. A statuesque six-foot "Amazon" female (who was also a marathon runner) modeled for the figure and was herself a personal embodiment of independence and strength. The large head has stars and a rose in her hair and slightly serpentine locks; the curly volutes that frame the largest star are derived in part from the *Pedestal of the Perseus.*[18] These modern mythmakers at Rock Hill also owe a debt of inspiration to late Victorian sculpture, particularly to Harry Bates' *Mors Januae Vitae* of 1899, a work that Flack actively sought out and studied when she went to Liverpool several years ago. The pose of being lifted heavenward—in Bates' piece the ivory-bodied female is about to be borne aloft by Death—is adapted from this late Victorian sculpture for the Rock Hill personification. A transformational usage of traditional nineteenth-century sculpture—respecting the naturalistic form yet offering an iconoclastic interpretation of the female figure, is moreover embodied in this comparison with Bates' work. In *Vision* Flack radically remakes the limp, helpless female figure being lifted by a male force into an assertive, independent entity who is formidable in her own right and exhibits clear self-control.

The *Visions* also inherently belong, of course, to a series of other international efforts to forge the female figure in colossal size—such as The Statue of Liberty in New York, the towering Soviet image, *The Motherland,* and *Ste. Nazaire* in Paris. Flack also knew of four nineteenth-century statues by Alfred Drury installed at Central Square, Leeds, and their serial aspect in part inspired the concept framework of the four *Visions.* As a result, in the *Gateway* the artist has attempted to create a sculptural series that is as appropriate and responsive to its site as, for example, Athena was for Athens. Accordingly, she studied the history of the town of Rock Hill, whose heritage includes many old textile mills. As Flack was well aware, the town was somewhat ambivalent about its textile background, at least as a basis for a work of art. Nevertheless, the artist has subtly integrated this historical element into her design, putting bolts of material blown onto the figures and adding ribbons to form the undulating wings and streamers in the hair. The bronze version stands on a granite ball, an earthlike orb, and has been gilded in nuances of color. Nitrous oxide was used to create this effect, with golden touches (twenty-three-carat and moon gold) moving up the torso in increasing amounts, culminating in a face that shines—as did *Islandia*'s—"like a Buddha."[19] Compared with the maquette, the final version of the thirteen-foot *Vision* was adjusted and enlarged in scale in several ways—with wider wings, more girth, and an increased billowing and energetic profile trailing behind the figure.

The colossal size, plus the specific rooting of imagery in local history, adds to the dignity of the figures and bestows a sense of civic pride and history on these textile motifs. Civic art is a matter of genuine concern to Flack, who feels fervently about the importance of orchestrating potentially sublime interreactions among sculpture, building, site, and human. She has designed other works with this in mind, although thus far they have not yet been realized in commissions. In this category are *Victory* (*Earth Mother*) of 1990 and *Sky Gateway* of 1989–90. In the former, the maternal figure is a metaphor

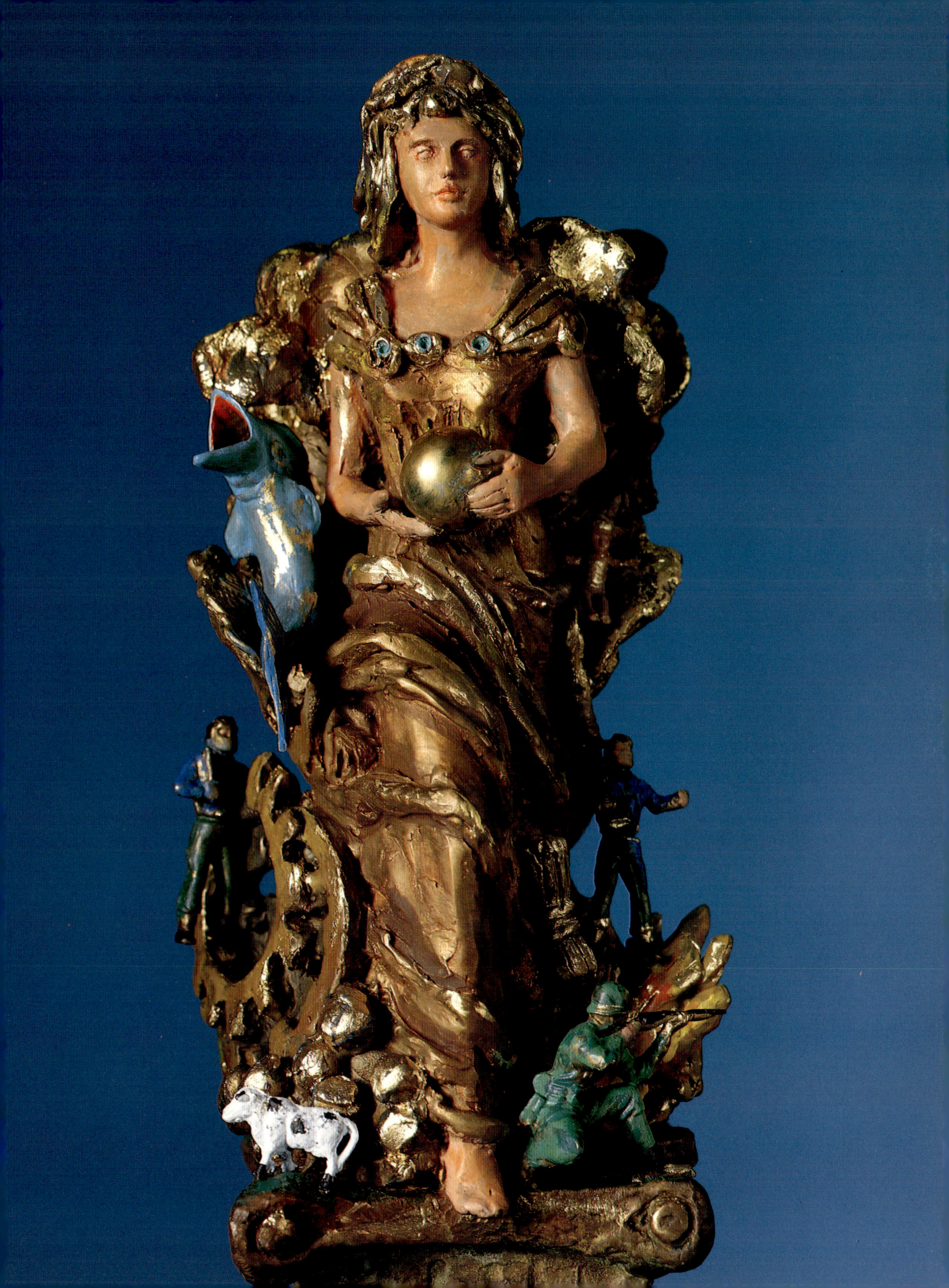

for the earth, which she also holds as a globe in her hands. She struggles to rise from the column that supports her but is weighed down by various burdens—a fish, cow, and other animals, along with people, a soldier, and a sheaf of wheat—that nestle or hide amid her drapery and pull her downward. Another sculpture that exists only in clay form, an unnamed "anima," seems a likely companion piece to *Earth Mother*, and her visual inheritance from *Islandia* and her ancient parallel *Nike* is overt. By contrast, the *Sky Gateway* sculpture consists of a pair of figures who stand alone and apart as they hold up a shared arc of the sky. The figure at left is thicker and more earthbound, while her counterpart is slimmer and more androgynous. Each has snaky locks and a phallic airplane that forms an erection over their drapery, reminiscent of *Egyptian Rocket Goddess.*

Other feminized mythologies have been distilled into the essence of human personality, the face and head. The best example is Flack's amazing large head of *Medusa*, which the artist has observed has already caused some male viewers to experience a form of aesthetic agony, arguably even terrified misogyny. The theme and character of Medusa has long had a history in art, as the 1987 "Magic of Medusa" exhibition in Vienna (at the Wiener Künstlerhaus, which held 250,000 visitors spellbound) attests.[20] Flack was well aware of this tradition, and in fact knew Benvenuto Cellini's rendering of Perseus holding the head of the doomed Medusa in *Perseus and Medusa* of c. 1545–54 (Loggia dei Lanzi, Florence), Giovanni-Lorenzo Bernini's marble head *Medusa* of 1630 (Capitoline Museum, Rome), and also the famed Rondanini *Medusa*. She was sensitive as well to Victorian permutations of this subject in paintings and sculpture, for example, George Frederick Watts' marble sculpture of *Medusa* of 1873 (Manchester, Whitworth Art Gallery), and may have had some of these images in mind when synthesizing her conception of Medusa's stony, potentially soul-destroying, visage. While artists such as Josef Müllner painted Medusa as masculinized virago, other nineteenth-century artists depicted her as a predatory female unleashing bestial sexuality, her mouth half-parted or wide-open.[21] Flack herself created an earlier permutation of the angry *Medusa*, a bellowing, inhuman fury with even the snakes on her head seemingly enraged and piqued to turn men into stone. Freud interpreted the Medusa's decapitated head as a symbol of castration and thus castration anxiety or even male hysteria, an instrument of terror and horror for men.[22] Yet in the context of Flack's other female personifications, the agonizing scream of this small Medusa might be viewed as a reaction to all the suffering of women, a three-dimensional distillation of female pain and angst.

Medusa's saga and Flack's interpretation merit more probing examination partly because of the centrality of this mythological figure in recent feminist literature.[23] The artist, aware of these intellectual investigations, was especially conscious of and sensitive to the issue of Medusa's beauty. The historical presupposition of Medusa's ugliness to her is "damning, contributing to the two versions of her character as either non-threatening or as a bellowing, raging fury with her head cut off." According to standard legends, Medusa's mother gave birth to three Gorgon daughters, monstrous twin sisters, and the exquisite Medusa. However, Medusa's innocent beauty was imperiled after Poseidon espied and then raped her in Athena's temple. Angered by this transgression, Athena (whose mother was Metis, possibly Medusa herself), ironically "punished" the victimized Medusa by turning her hair to snakes, an act of destruction that on some levels can be equated with

Sky Gateway. 1989–90
Terra-cotta-colored fiberglass, height 19¼″ (with base)
Collection the artist

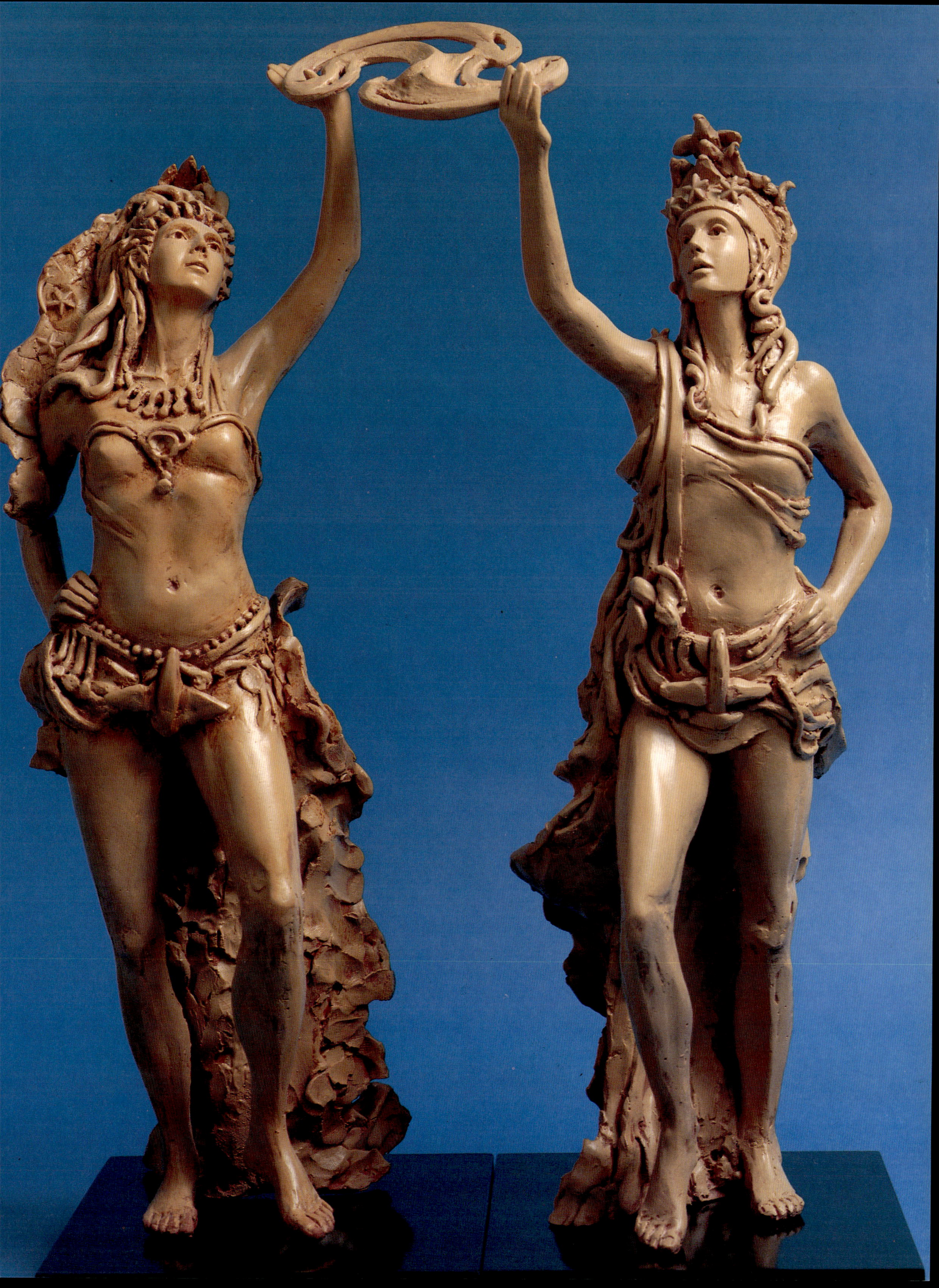

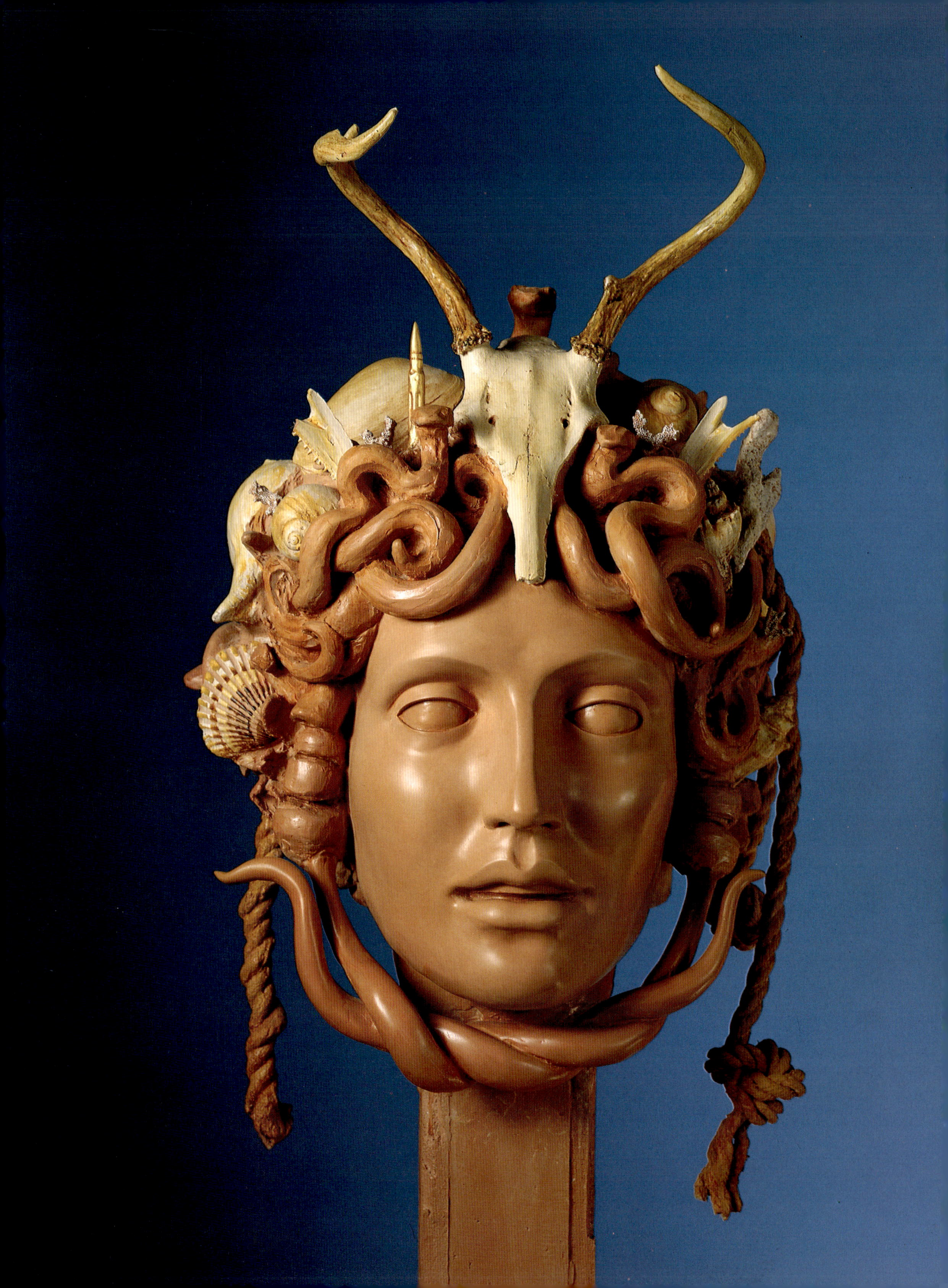

either matricide or suicide. Flack believes this male myth of fickleness and jealousy is a misconstruing of character, "since Athena was usually very fair, not jealous. Nor was the ancient Medusa vindictive. . . . When her hair became snakes, these may have been the signs of intelligence and wisdom and not merely death threats." Medusa's beauty functioned as both a blessing and a curse, causing her to be doubly victimized by Perseus, who raped and beheaded her. Flack maintains that in some respects Medusa's situation parallels the rape of the earth, "since some men can't leave the earth or female beauty alone without ruining it." Medusa's plight, as symbolized by her severed head, thus becomes a metaphor for that of the earth itself, innocent yet nonetheless unfairly ravished, vulnerable yet potentially vengeful. In the large head *Medusa* this meaning is further heightened by the embedding of a real bullet in the frontal locks, suggesting how this female is a victim of violence—both sexual and homicidal.

Furthermore, according to some versions of the tale, Medusa's blood became the coral in the sea and, in addition to menstrual connotations, had healing and apotropaic powers as protection from the evil eye that ally her with other priestess figures by the artist.[24] In Flack's vision, the large *Medusa* has various shells on her head, including a phallic one on the right side, and ropes on both sides that connote murder and possibly represent umbilical cords.[25] On her head are deer horns, not the ominous type in Georgia O'Keeffe's desert visions, but emblems instead of a gentle, vulnerable side. Deer were always considered magically endowed, and horned deer were deities as well as sacrificial creatures.[26] The twin curl on each side of the antlers may refer to her Gorgon twin sisters, while those framing her chin suggest a masculinizing, beardlike growth and add an androgynous note to her character. In Flack's large *Medusa* Pegasus emerges from the back of the head, alluding to the winged horse's birth from Medusa only after her head was cut off by Perseus. In some legends, the snake coiled within the female pelvis until it rose to the head, where it became life giving and a sign of wisdom. As one writer has recently suggested, snakes represent female wisdom of the past, present, and future, and here the writhing tresses are signs of intelligence and not simply grasping phallic tentacles.[27] They also connote immortality due to the regeneration possible by the shedding of skin, and in Egyptian and Indian beliefs the female serpent is celebrated as a sacred embodiment of wisdom, in contrast to Christian connotations of the snake as a diabolic seducer of Eve.[28] Medusa's serpentine locks also symbolize menstrual secrets, and in some ancient lore men could be turned into stone at the sight of menstrual blood, just as they faced the same fate if they made eye contact with a Gorgon.[29] The colossal *Medusa*'s face betokens the demeanor of a serene modern sphinx: her eyes are seeing yet unseeing and her mouth remains questioning, mysterious, struggling to speak. Paradoxically, in a way quite different from her shamanistic "sisters," the destructive Medusa became an artist by turning her victims into stony sculptures. Perseus had to traverse a world of petrified beings in order to reach Medusa and challenge her, and he risked the penalty of death for meeting her gaze. At least in the artist's studio, modern viewers also have to "fight" through a visual field of Flack's sculptures in order to encounter and confront Medusa and her immobilized form and beauty. On another level this choice of subject may also signify the paradoxical triumph and danger of the female gaze, an illuminating role reversal of the typical male gaze of the past.

Colossal Head of Medusa. 1990
Polychromed terra-cotta-colored fiberglass, height 33″ (without base)
Private collection

Inspired in part by the dread force of Medusa's expression even in death, Flack has been working on a colossal female head known as *Daphne*. This huge head is also sphinxlike, with staring eyes and slightly parted lips that seem about to impart some secret to the viewer. The name Daphne means "bloody one" (further linking her with Medusa), and in mythological lore she was a priestess delivered from Apollo's attempts to rape her by Mother Earth, who changed her into a laurel tree. Later the laurel branch became synonymous with victory wreaths proffered to athletes and poets, but in Flack's stark vision the branch is bare and seems to wound *Daphne*'s head like a stabbing knife frozen in an act of violence. Like Medusa, Daphne, too, is a female victim whose imminent loss of virginity by force makes her, as feminist Nancy Huston has remarked of other mythological Amazon types who resist bondage or submission to males, an "irredeemably permeable, irreversibly vulnerable" embodiment of female existence and principles.[30]

In the years since Flack's canvases were first exhibited, much has happened to female imagery in contemporary painting and sculpture. The paramount development has been the veritable explosion of feminist dialogues exploring gender and semiotic issues of the female body and its multivalent associations as object and subject in past cultures.[31] This "rewriting the female body" in political and cultural terms has also wrought a revolutionary impact on artists. Indeed, Flack's decade of sculpture-making seems to crystallize some of these critical upheavals and altering levels of awareness, above all by challenging ways of looking at and responding to the female figure as well as giving new life to contemporary sculpture in a classicizing mode.

As the artist herself is well aware, the reception of a work of art is never indifferent or neutral, and how it is read helps to determine meaning for both the artist and the spectator.[32] Innumerable revisionist scholars such as Laura Mulvey, Monique Wittig, Helene Cixous, Norman Bryson, and others have speculated about the sexual differences in perceiving female images, and in art this gender differential is predicated on the spectacle of the active masculine gaze and the female passive state of "to be looked-at-ness." In general, Flack seems to align her approach more with recent British (vs. French) feminist theorists, e.g., extending some of the concepts espoused by Beverly Brown and Parveen Adams about "the unity of the body, the unity of sexuality, the unity of control, the overarching unity of the individual . . . , and ultimately, a unity of the body of women."[33] The artist moves such arguments into another medium (especially evident in sculptures such as *Medusa* or *Rock Hill Gateway*, although her screen image of *Marilyn* may also fit into this category), couching these principles in traditional realistic form while simultaneously modifying, even reversing, certain prevailing assumptions. She breaks through convention —even in her honest way of using female sitters—and she does not spy on, exploit, or consume models purely for her own artistic needs. Instead, in her creative process she respects and deliberately becomes attuned to their individuality and allows their personal qualities and innate dignity and presence to dictate content to some degree. In addition, Flack deals with the vexing problem of female allegory and figuration on her own terms, for the past decade working through her own ideas and those of others. As a result, hers are not eroticized images of the female body on display for men to enjoy; instead they are often pared down paragons of supple musculature and strength, feminine and even androgynous in some cases. In essence, she has deployed male signifiers of body strength and assertiveness within the female

Head of Medusa. 1989
Patinated bronze,
height 10″ (with base)
Collection Jane Bryant Quinn

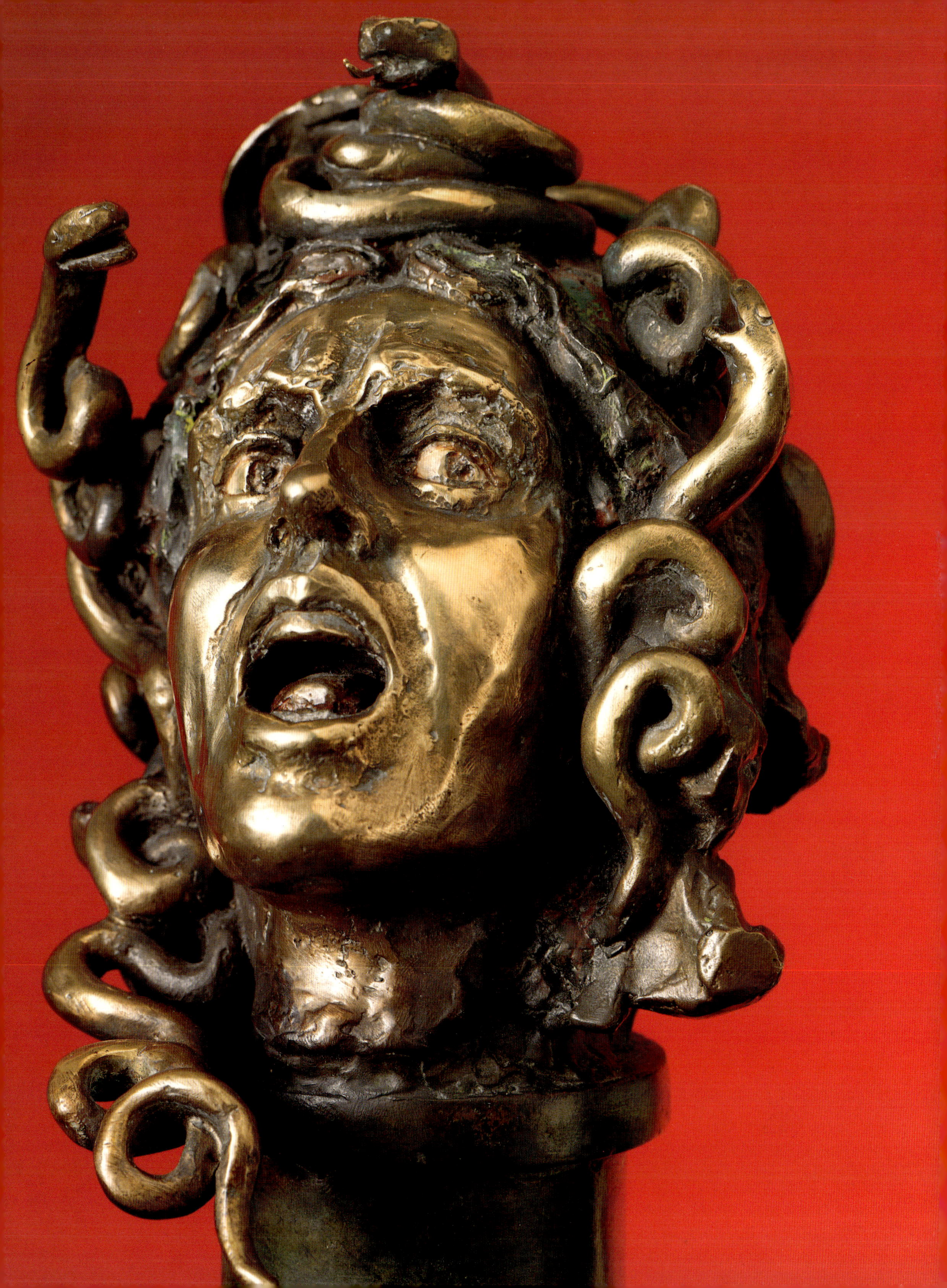

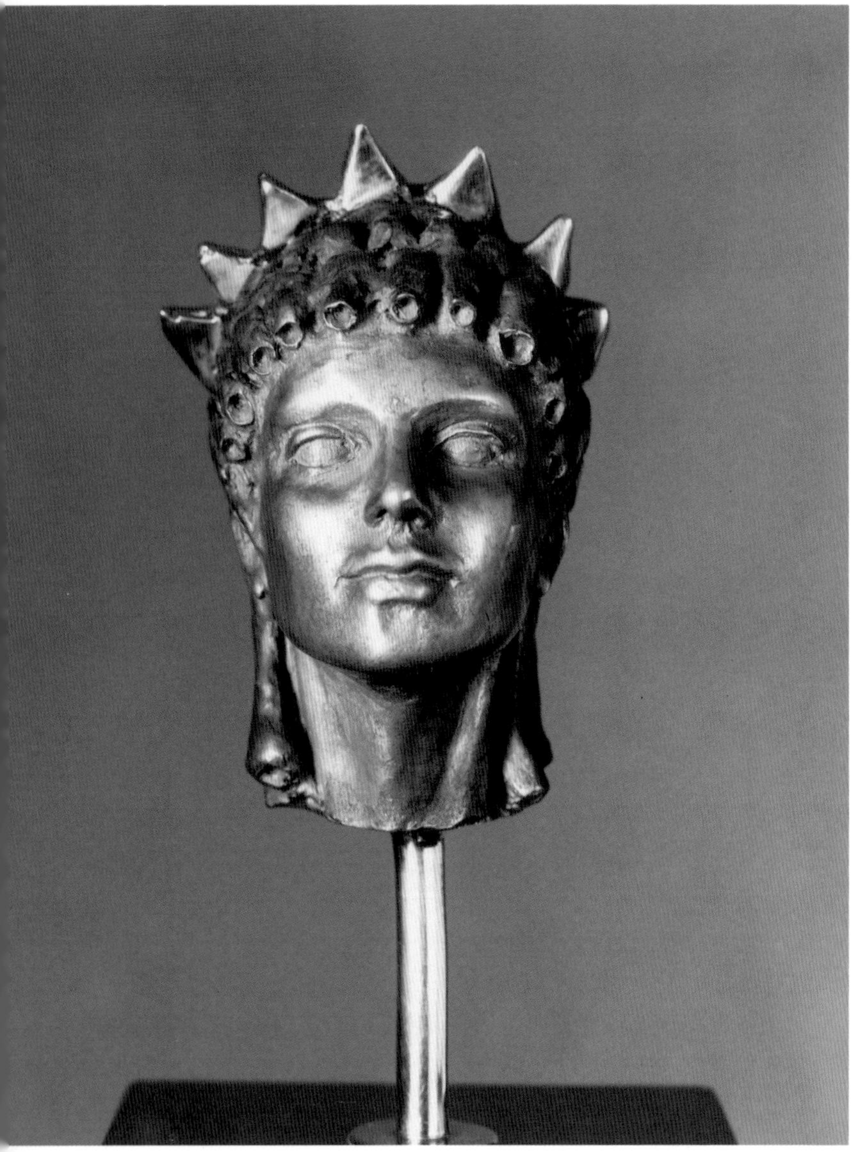

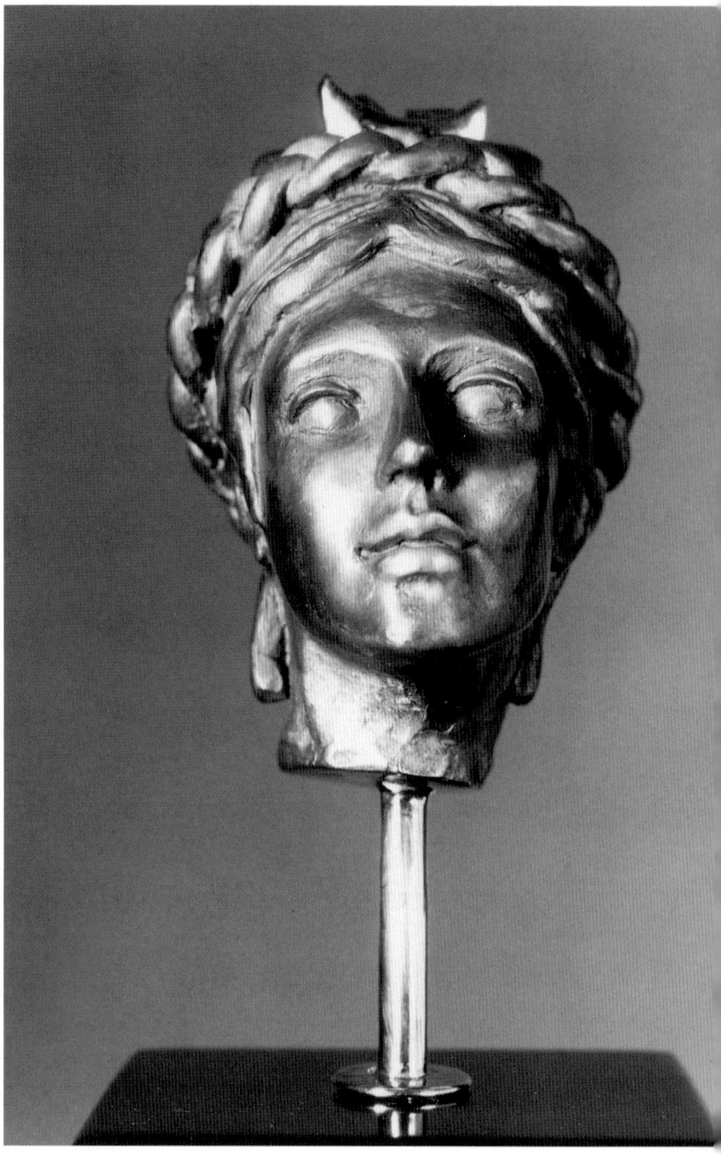

Head of Art Muse. 1991
Patinated bronze,
height 6″ (with base)
Private collection

RIGHT:
Head of Diana. 1991
Patinated bronze,
height 7″ (with base)
Private collection

body, inverting and eroding past prejudices and misconceptions about female submissiveness and male supremacy.

Confrontation between the viewer and goddess or personification is unavoidable, and in some ways Flack has implied a volatile opposition between the sexes in their potential reactions to these figures. Flack's figures are makers, not solely carriers, of meaning, and they accumulate new meaning as they are encoded by a late-twentieth-century audience. To some degree the artist has arguably "remade" masculinity and femininity, engineering a postmodernist irony that enlists naturalism and mythology, two traditional sources of inspiration, to interrogate and illuminate the sexual differences of looking at sculpture and the transformational power of these relationships. Instead of producing a mirror of relationships between the sexes, she has created an imaginary dialectic, in the process raising the issue of the acceptance or rejection of femininity as filtered through subject matter, scale, and gesture as well as the politics of empowerment.

Quintessentially Flack celebrates the female body yet endows it with the differential of male power and strength. These are demanding, charismatic creatures who populate the artist's all-female sanctuary—in fact their freedom and potential to dominate, certainly to control their own destinies, underscores their threat and thus speaks the unspoken taboo concerning the female desire for power. All in one room or space (their ideal setting), the effect is overpowering, a summoning to private and public responses in a magical domain that constitutes a genuine gynaeceum or "place of women" presided over by shaman artists. Viewed as an ensemble, they transmit their greatest energy, healing, and magnetism. The issue of gendered spectatorship also arises and exposes a revealing latent polarity of response: to many women the individual and collective impact of Flack's sculptures is energizing, while some men feel enervated and intimidated. Others are disturbed by a sense of alienation and an unspoken fear that these potent goddesses could somehow destroy or replace everyday reality. The power of images to disarm spectators is often denied or neglected, but the relationship here between the sculptures and the audience is highly charged, with aesthetic distance from their meaning "crowded out" by covert fear about the danger they pose.[34] Flack's deities and personifications stir up strong feelings, especially anxiety about art, about tales of men and statues—Pygmalion and otherwise—and their potential intimacy and threat. Not surprisingly, viewers continue to experience feelings in front of these sculptures that linger long after they have left their presence.

The very subject of goddess figures, icons of reverence and fear, has sparked debate and feminist research about ancient cultures and the status of female deities, by some accounts later suppressed or taken away by men. As this pantheon of female personifications attests, Audrey Flack has boldly, even audaciously, chosen to create matrilineal "anachronisms" for her time and paradoxically to use myth simultaneously as a means of visual exorcism of sexual stereotyping and as a means of visual empowerment. She does not simply restate timeless interests in the goddess figure; instead, she partly reinvents the subject, mobilizing an impressive visual injunction for viewers. In doing so, she reverses and subverts the traditional male way of perceiving the female form in sculpture, instilling in her own figures a sovereignty and superiority, a self-possession and assurance, that sustains these remythologized beings as they invade our space and we enter theirs.

A GATEWAY TO THE CITY OF ROCK HILL: CIVIC PRIDE IN A FRAGMENTED WORLD

Thalia Gouma-Peterson

Driving along Dave Lyle Boulevard as it crosses Gateway Boulevard at the edge of the city of Rock Hill, motorists are jolted by an unexpected sight: four large golden female figures hovering on black granite spheres, flanked by two gigantic columns, amidst clusters of bushes and trees. If they continue on their course, the motorists will within seconds have passed them; the speed of twentieth-century life often does not allow time for the thoughtful study of art. And yet, many of the people in the 17,000 cars that daily use the four-lane boulevard do return to look closely at the four commanding figures. Intentionally set at a very busy intersection of two highways, the sculptures provide a focal point in in a divided and fragmented passage.

The work, named the *Rock Hill Gateway*, stands at the edge of one of the historic centers of Rock Hill, South Carolina. A collaboration between architect Michael Gallis and sculptor Audrey Flack, it is a visual expression of the civic pride and aspirations of a small southern city. Subtitled *Civitas: Four Visions*, the complex bears testimony to a successful cooperation between architect, sculptor, and city government.

All the constituent parts of the *Gateway* complex have been laid out on a circular plan of 120-foot radius. The plan was calculated on multiples of six, a number derived by Gallis not from sacred geometry or abstract harmonic theory but from six specific objectives Rock Hill has set for itself during the next decade: to be known as a business city, historic city, functional city, educational city, cultural city, and garden city.

At the four corners of a sixty-foot square inscribed within the circle and crossed at right angles by the two boulevards—the square's east-west and north-south axes—are four landscaped and terraced islands. Bordered by the circle's circumference and overlapped by one of the corners of the square, each of these islands forms the setting for one of Flack's thirteen-foot female figures. These four *Visions* of *Civitas*, set on the circle's periphery on diagonally crossing radii, turn inward and look across the space they help define. The two on the west are flanked by sixty-foot Egyptian Revival columns from the Masonic Temple of Charlotte, North Carolina, demolished to make room for a bank. The columns also directly flank Dave Lyle Boulevard on the north and south and demarcate the actual point of entry into Rock Hill. These relics, carefully dismantled and saved by Gallis and the city, provide layered allusions to temples of Masonic brotherhoods and of Egyptian pharaohs but are combined in a novel and meaningful setting that specifically refers to Rock Hill.

On the black granite cubes that Flack and Gallis have designed as podia for the columns are inscribed the city's name and date of foundation (1852) and inscriptions that declare its aspirations to be "a garden city committed to the protection and enjoyment of its natural environment" and a city with "a commitment to preserve and enhance its history."

Civitas: Four Visions (Gateway to the City of Rock Hill). 1990–91
Patinated and gilded bronze with black granite base, height 22′ (with base), 13′ (without base)
One of the four sculptures is shown here after installation at the Rock Hill Gateway, South Carolina, April 1991
The statue is flanked by a sixty-foot Egyptian Revival column

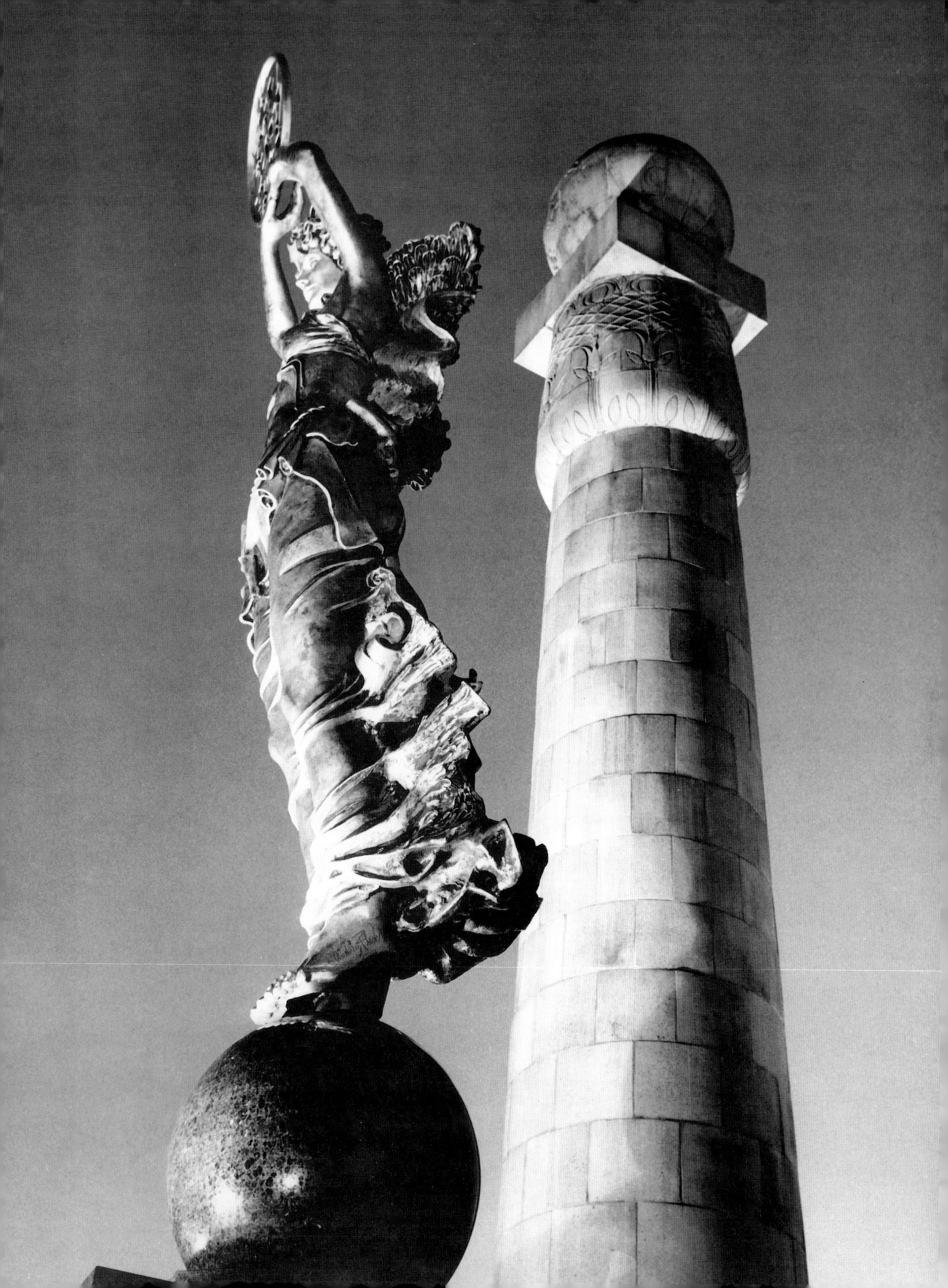

The four allegorical figures, modern equivalents of civic virtues, stand on black granite spheres—three feet in diameter—on top of six-foot black speckled granite cubes. Expressing Rock Hill's determination both to hold to the past and build toward the future, they hold aloft circular emblems symbolizing the city's goals: the gears of industry, the flames of knowledge, the stars of inspiration and creativity, and the lightning bolts of energy.

Taut, elegant, and athletic, these modern manifestations of *Civitas,* in patinated and gilded bronze and swathed in fluttering draperies, appear like visions that have just alighted on their spheres. The reflective gilded surfaces shimmering in the afternoon sun, the mobile and muscular bodies, and the fluttering wings cascading down as bolts of cloth (an allusion to Rock Hill's past as a textile city) and again becoming wings as they reach the feet suggest that the *Visions* are still in motion and might leave again. The goals of civic virtue have become elusive in a world of constant motion. The four images of *Civitas* embody Rock Hill's faith that these goals are attainable.

Traffic in a continuous stream speeds along Dave Lyle Boulevard, the major entry leading into Rock Hill from the highway that crosses the border from North into South Carolina. The boulevard, named in honor of a former mayor, also is the major east-west axis of the *Gateway.* Here the trajectories of life and art overlap. The axis of life with its speeding machines cuts through the sculpture and its intended meaning but the *Gateway* holds its own—a permanent presence amidst a stream of shifting mobility.

Thirteen feet tall and on their spherical and cubic bases rising to a height of twenty-two feet, the *Four Visions,* expressing human strength and durability, confront the cars and lumbering trucks that regularly go by. Brick paths, linking the corners of the complex and visibly demarcating the square inscribed within the circle, provide access to close-up views of each *Vision.* But the speeding vehicles on Lyle Boulevard have the right of way, and pedestrians crossing to look at the sculptures have to fight their way against these twentieth-century machines. The installation of traffic lights, not planned by Flack and Gallis but determined recently to be necessary for safety reasons, will be a regrettable visual intrusion.

Each *Vision* with its terraced landscape setting functions as a temporary refuge within which the pedestrian can slowly walk or, sitting on the stepped pedestals below the cubic bases, survey the layout of statues, columns, paths, and plantings. In front of each *Vision* Flack has designated an optimum viewing spot, formed by the apex of the corner of the central square. Only when standing in this spot can the viewer establish contact with the gaze of the figures.

Unlike the Caryatids of the Erechtheion on the Athenian Acropolis, which they bring to mind, the *Four Visions* are not part of a temple or temple complex nor are they rooted in a local mythic and religious tradition. Rather they are informed by a civic and contemporary mythology generated by what used to be a small southern textile mill city whose historic remnants, the J. P. Stevens textile mill and the modest homes of Mill Village, flank the *Gateway* on the west. North and south is the growing and carefully landscaped Tech Park, a commercial development housing American and foreign companies. This modern agora, which is not part of the civic center of Rock Hill, can be reached only by car from various residential areas of the city. It adds a north-

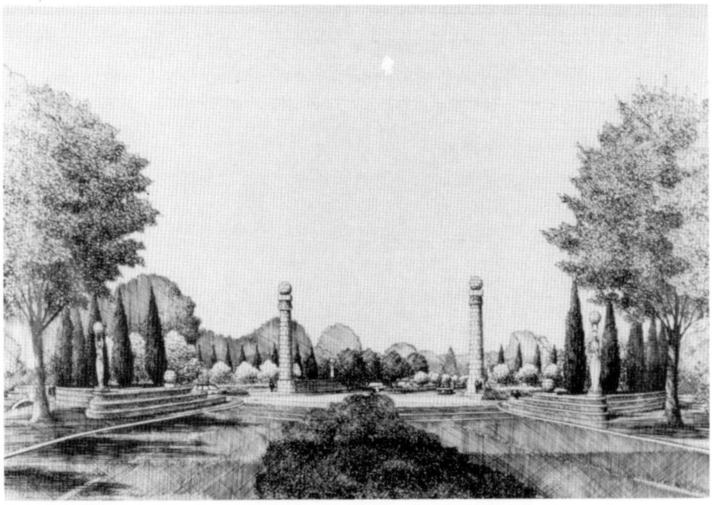

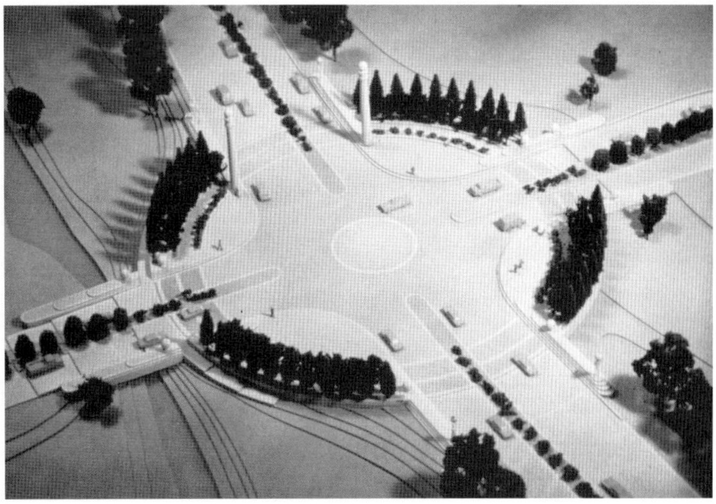

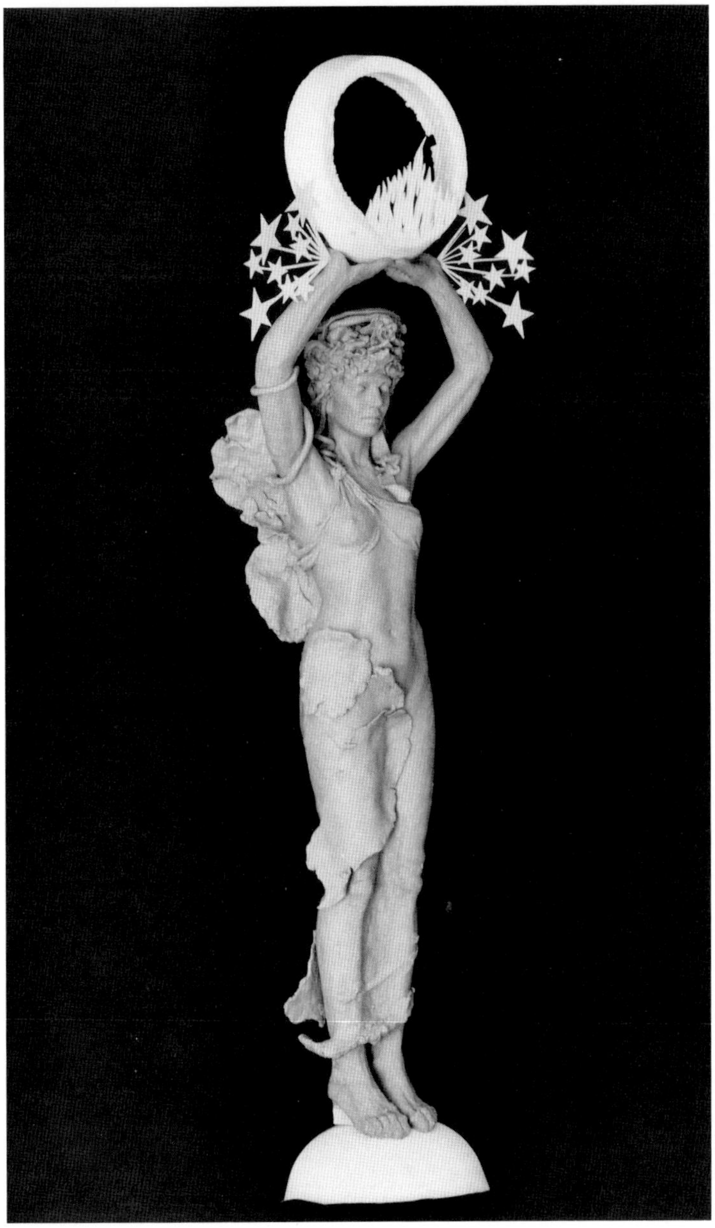

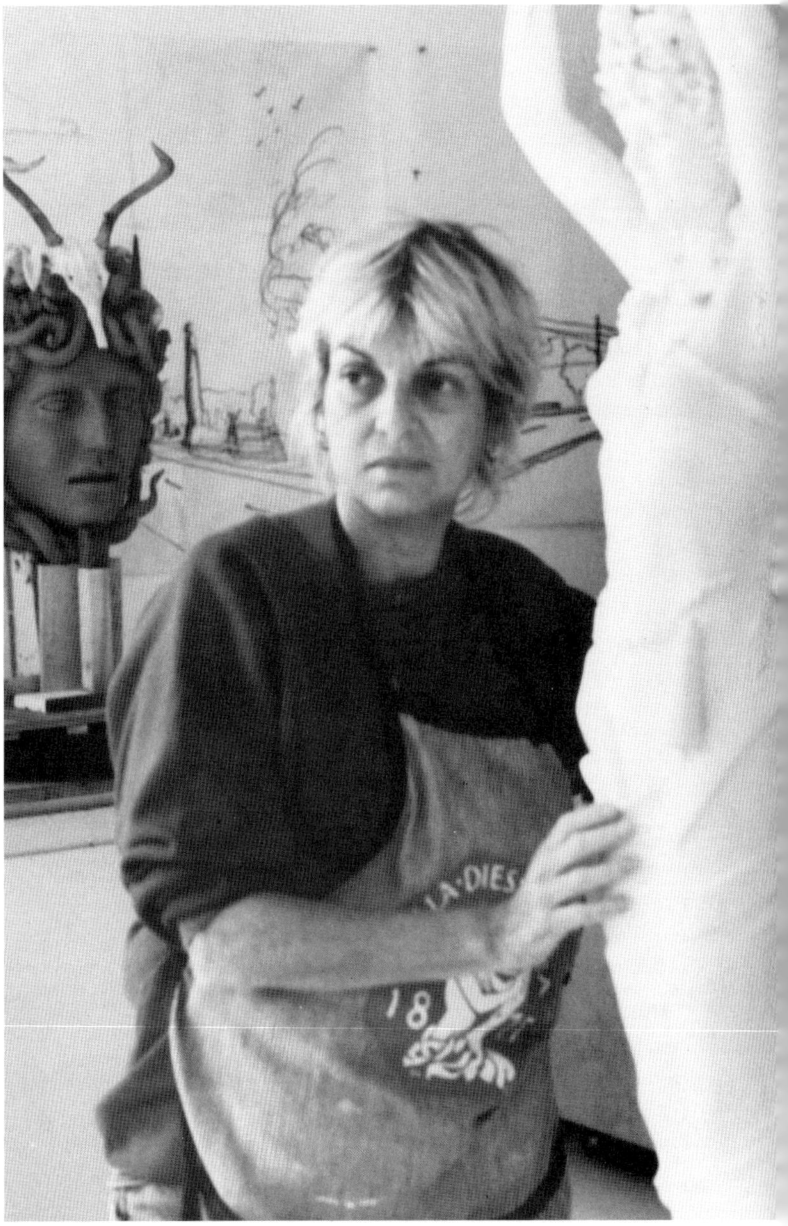

ABOVE, LEFT:
Early rendering of the plan for *Rock Hill Gateway*

ABOVE, RIGHT:
Architect Michael Gallis' scale model for *Rock Hill Gateway*

BELOW, LEFT:
Civitas: Four Visions (Gateway to the City of Rock Hill). 1988
Clay, Styrofoam, and cardboard maquette, height 45″ (without base)
This clay maquette, shown here in its early stages, was used to create the mold from which the plaster model of *Civitas* was made. The clay statue was destroyed in the process

BELOW, RIGHT:
The artist at work in her studio carving and sanding the 45″-tall plaster maquette of *Civitas,* which was later used for making the full-scale clay enlargement

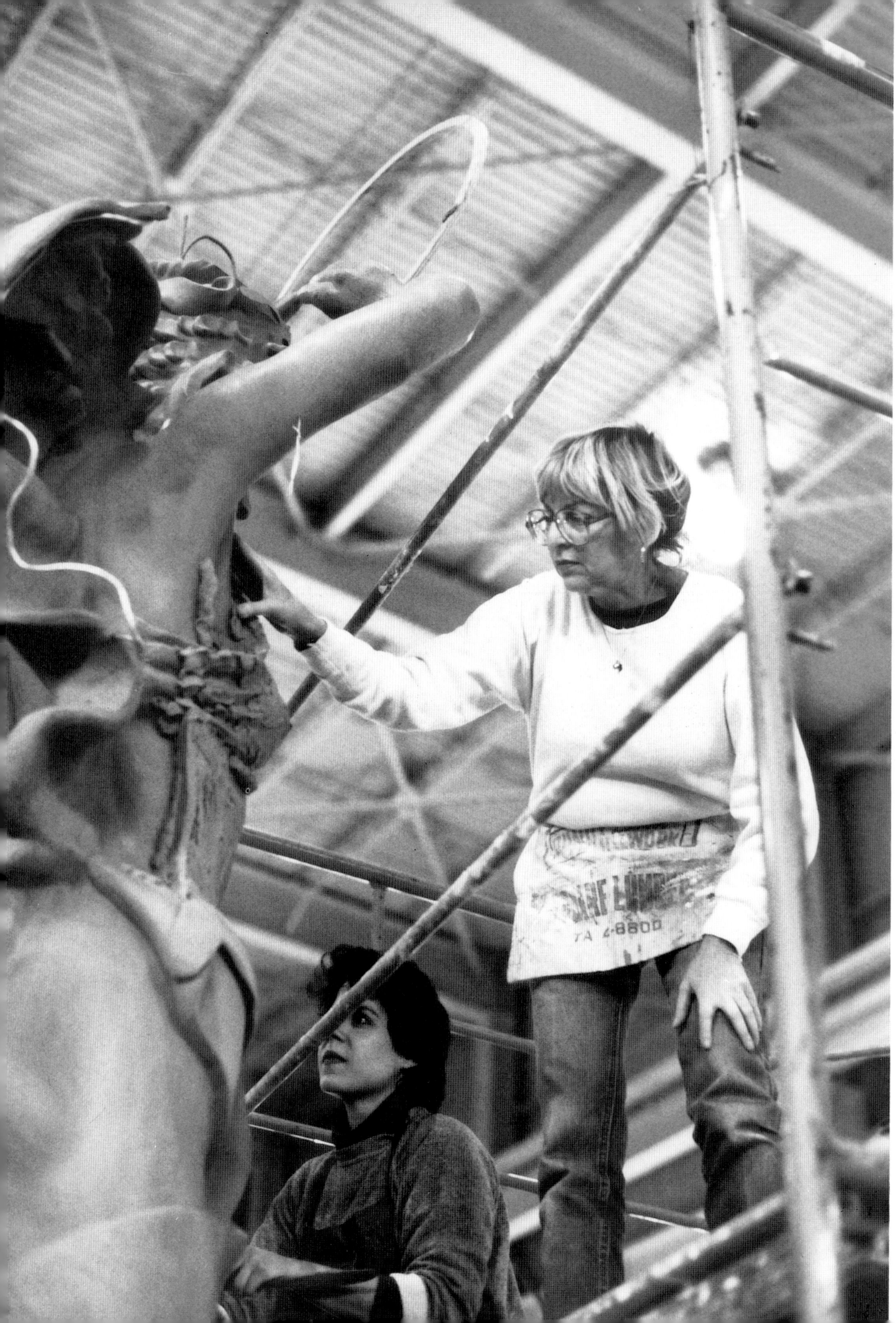
TA 4-8800

OPPOSITE:
Artist on scaffold expanding the armature for the wings on the full-scale clay enlargement of *Civitas*, Tallix foundry, Beacon, N.Y.

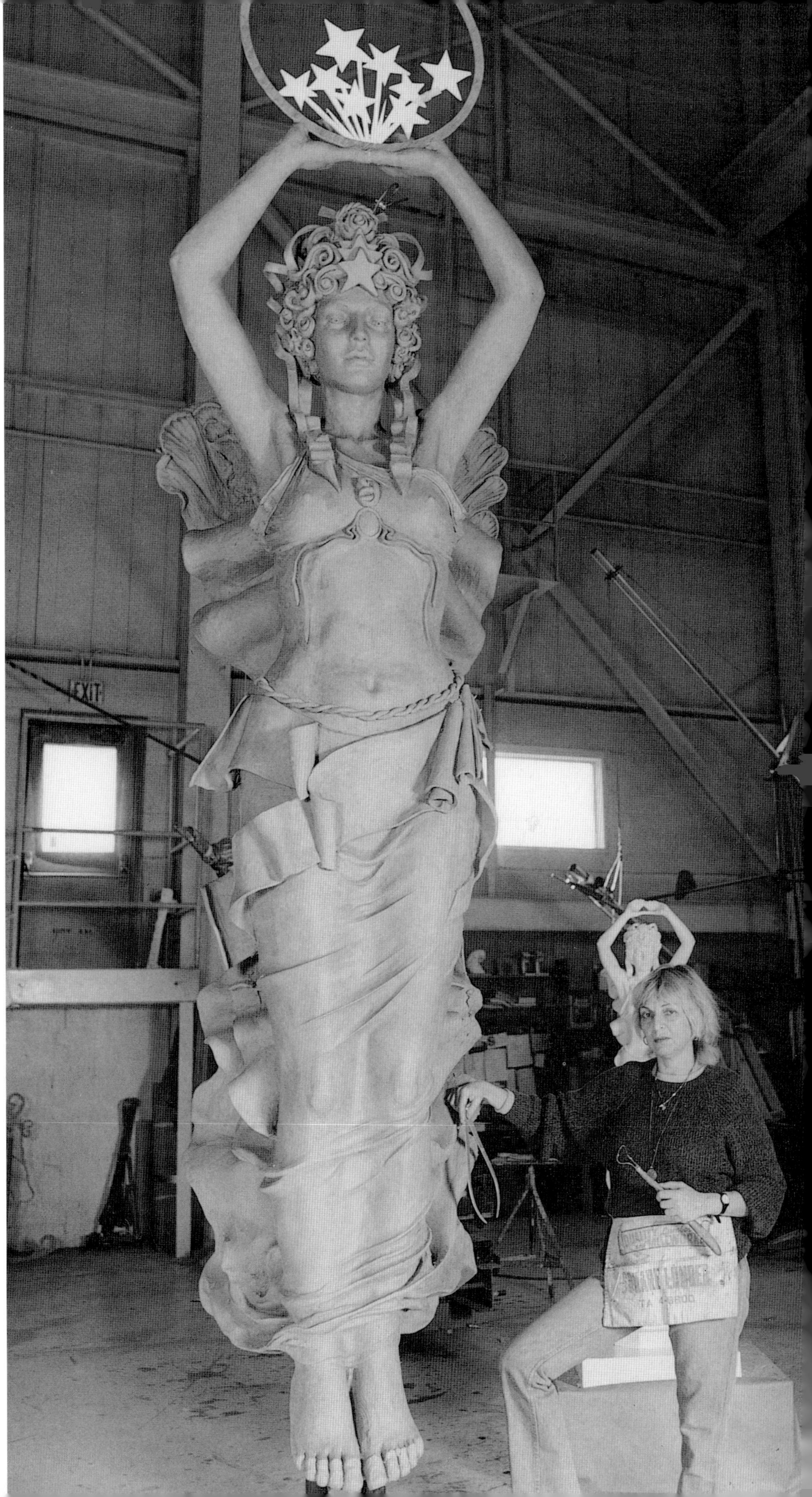

Artist standing beside the full-scale clay enlargement of *Civitas*, Tallix foundry.
The thirteen-foot-tall clay statue (now destroyed) was used to make the wax mold from which the final bronze was created

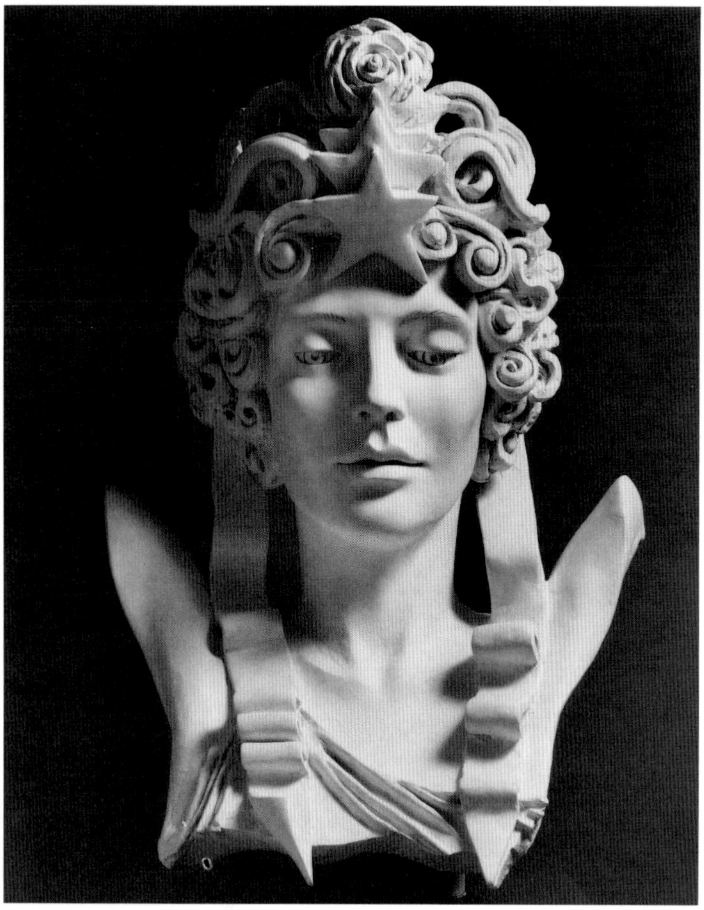

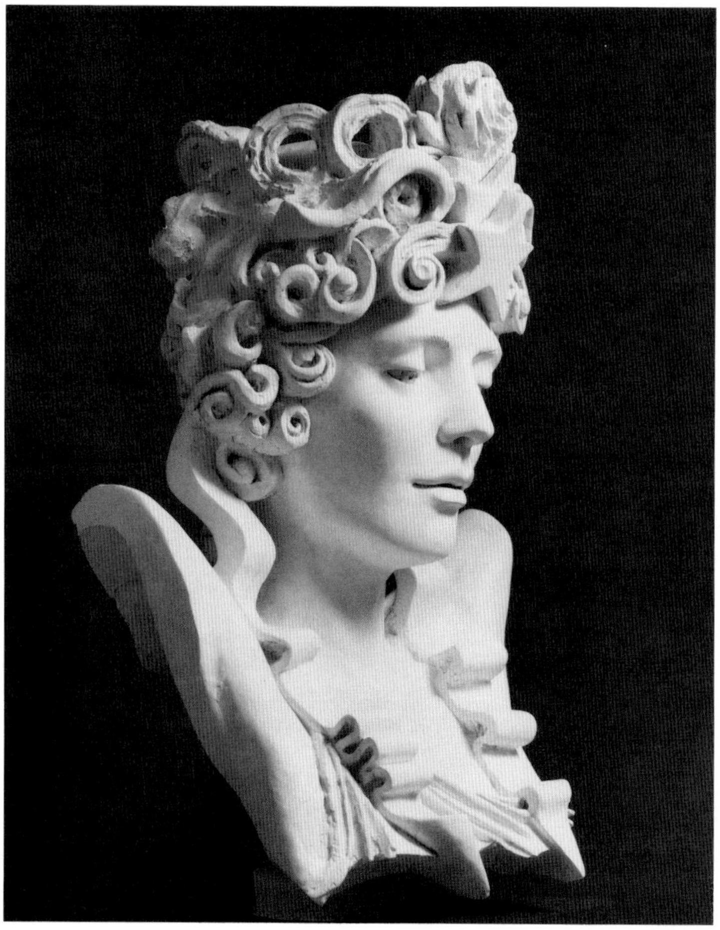

Civitas: Four Visions (Gateway to the City of Rock Hill) (head, two views). 1989
Polychromed plaster, height 32″ (without base)
Collection Andreas Bechtler
The artist cast this full-scale plaster head of *Civitas* from the original mold of the bronze

OPPOSITE:
Assembling the parts of the wax mold of *Civitas*, in order that corrections can be made before the final bronze is cast, Tallix foundry

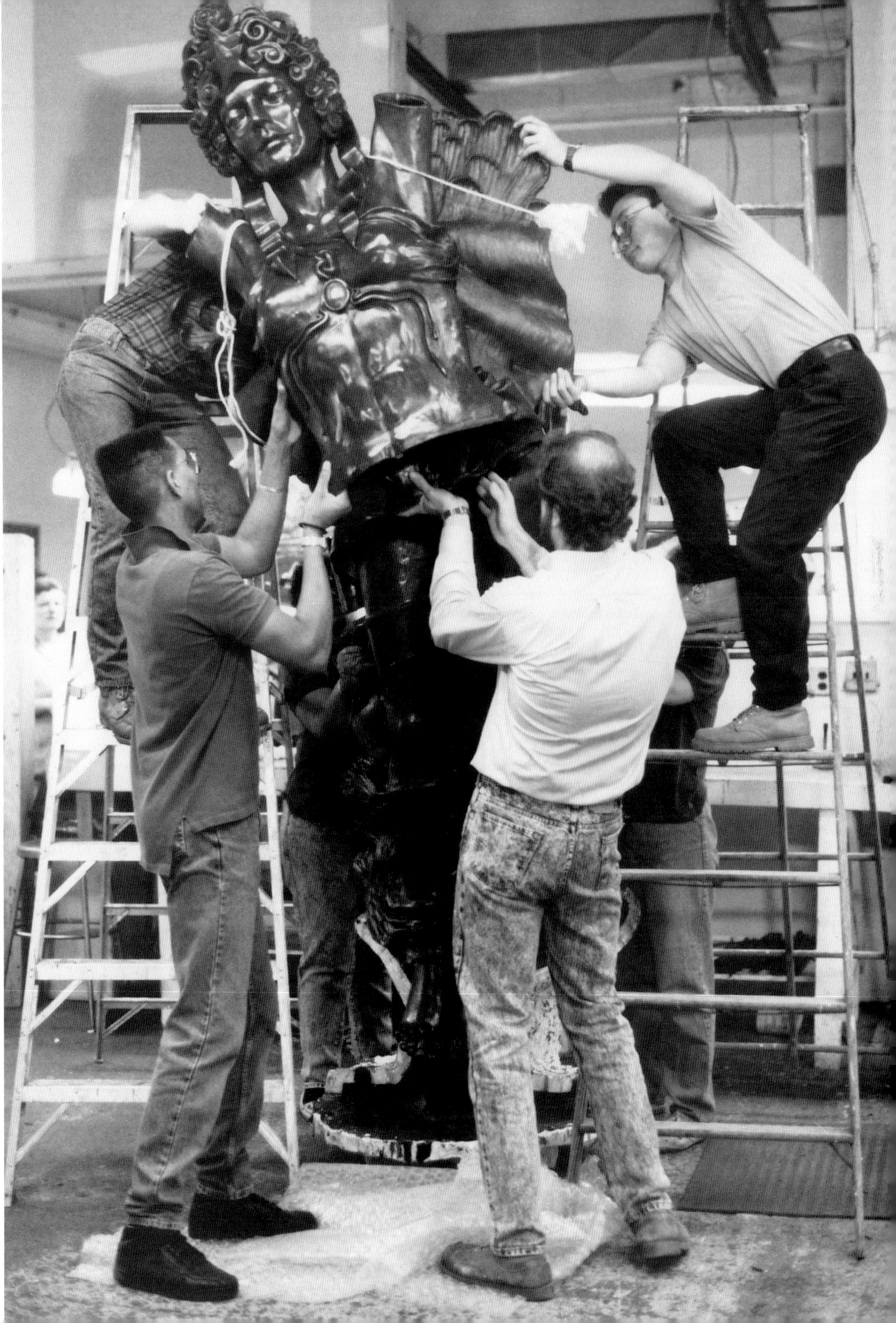

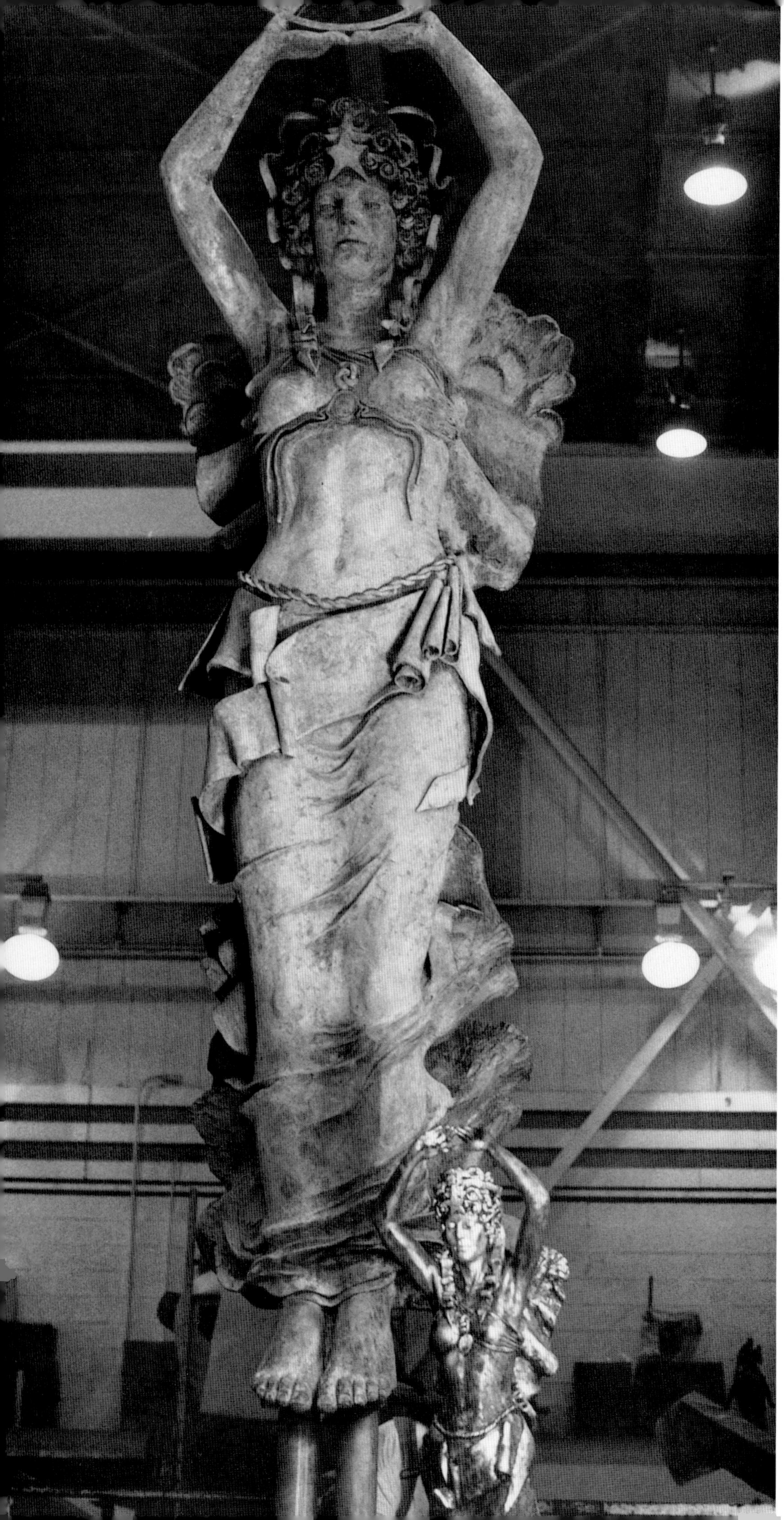

The final bronze figure of *Civitas* in early stages of patination with nitrous oxide before gold leaf is applied; in the foreground is a small-scale bronze maquette of the figure, Tallix foundry

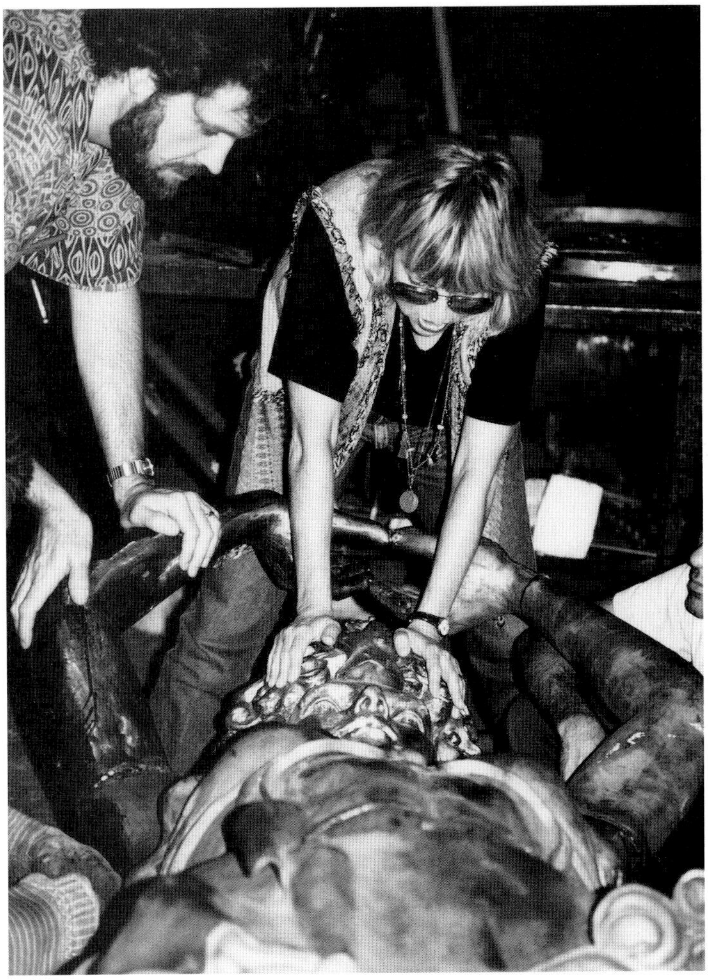

The artist checking the alignment
of the welded joints
of the final bronze *Civitas*

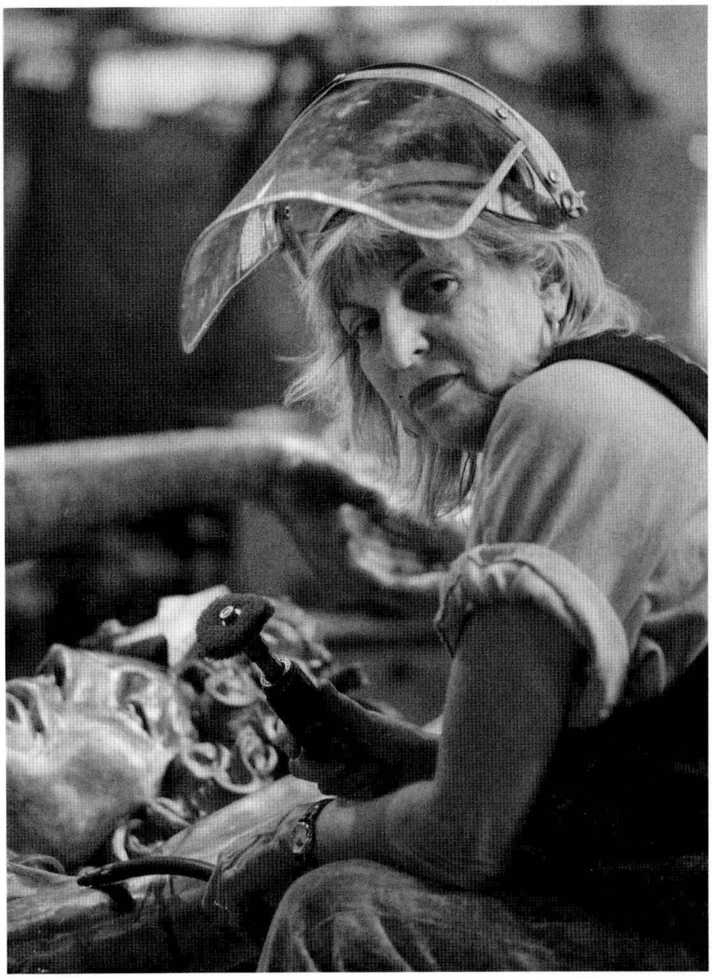

The artist at work
in the welding section
of Tallix foundry

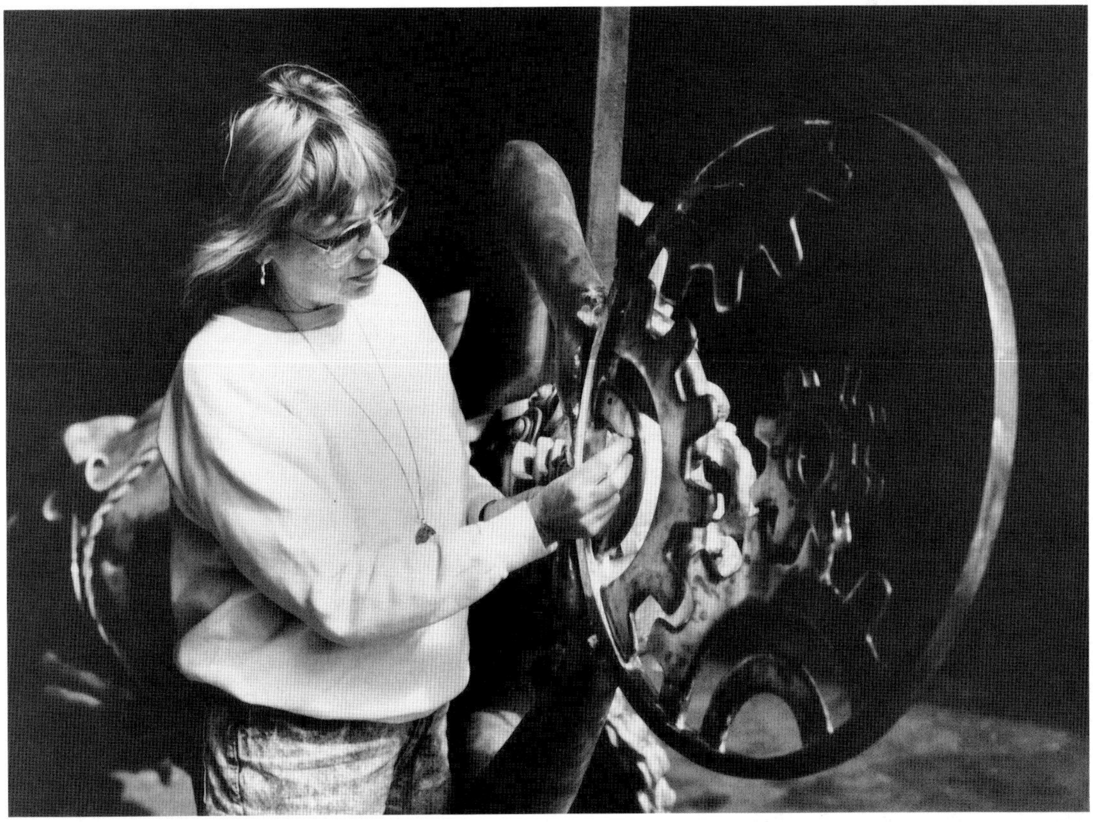

The artist bolting the gear emblems
to the top of one of the four
final bronze *Civitas* figures

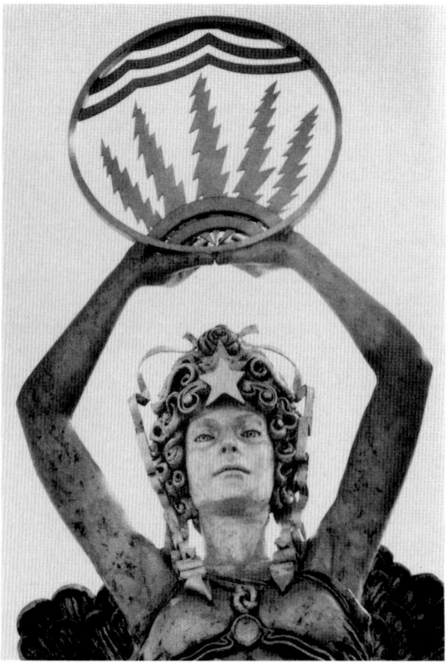

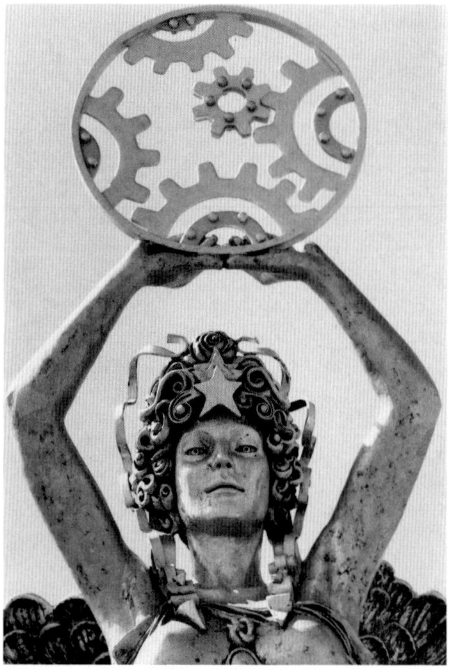

ABOVE AND OPPOSITE:
Details of the sculptures of *Civitas: Four Visions (Gateway to the City of Rock Hill)* showing the four symbolic emblems:
the lightning bolts of energy,
the gears of industry,
the flames of knowledge,
and the stars of inspiration and creativity

south stream of traffic that moves at right angles to Lyle Boulevard. In this flow and counterflow the *Visions* define a specific site that helps to focus fragmented twentieth-century realities.

The surroundings of the *Gateway* evoke multiple and diverse impressions: old textile mill and Mill Village, modern boulevards and business park, a small creek framing the village, and the constant movement of cars. The *Gateway* itself is a collage. The glazed-tile columns are historic landmarks—the sole surviving components of a once-functioning Masonic temple. Their Egyptian Revival style, including lotus bud capitals, alludes to the temple of Karnak. But the columns of the *Gateway* are not burdened by a roof. Rather, each stands freely and is crowned by a sphere, one symbolizing the earth (s-w) and the other the universe (n-w).

The statues, too, allude to earth and universe through the flames of fire, starry sky, and lightning bolts contained in the circular emblems they hold over their heads. As the columns refer to ancient temples so the statues recall a number of public monuments: the Athena Parthenos, the Caryatids, the *Venus de Milo*, the *Nike of Samothrace*, Michaelangelo's *David*, Giambologna's bronzes, and The Statue of Liberty, among others. But these modern *Visions* are unlike any of their predecessors. Though clearly female, their bodies—muscular and taut—are reminiscent of the idealized male bodies of ancient Greek and Renaissance sculptures. The frontality of their stance and the almost complete symmetry of their bodies also brings to mind sixth-century kouroi and korai. Like a number of these Archaic young men and maidens, the *Visions* make an offering, but unlike the ancient statues, to the living not to the dead. In their reinvention of the past these female figures reflect the contradictions of a present seeking a cultural identity through art.

On the day of the official dedication, April 5, 1991, traffic was diverted and the *Gateway Plaza*, as it is identified in local publications, resembled for a few hours the central square of an old European town, decorated with flower carts and a large, centrally placed bell, and filled by pedestrians carrying colorful umbrellas. It became a festive place for citizens to gather. Seen in this human context and devoid of cars, the circularity of the design became emphatically clear and its proportions acquired a new scale. The columns looked even taller. The *Visions* appeared larger and more permanently fixed on their spheres. But their size clearly had been scaled by Flack to the human beings.

People clustered around the *Visions*, walked along the landscaped paths, studied the symbolic emblems, stood and sat on the stepped platforms, and admired the beauty of the statues. At 12:10 p.m., as the governor and mayor began to speak, a torrential downpour broke, and the citizens ran to their cars or sought shelter under a large tent from which the *Gateway* was visible against the black and ominous sky shot through with lightning bolts. The lightning in the emblem held by one of the *Visions* had become reality, and *Civitas* was absorbed into the rhythms of nature.

Later that afternoon, the rain stopped and a cool light shone through the clouds and sharply defined the *Visions* against the gray sky. Only a few people were present—mainly small family groups with young children walking on the terraced islands. *Civitas* became almost a mythic presence emerging out of the past.

From the center of the now-empty *Gateway* complex, it became evident that the ground inclines down toward the north and that the figures and their bases are on stepped platforms of unequal height—from a minimum of two steps on the south to a maximum of six on the north. The *Gateway* is then site-specific, that is, "a work whose actual site and placement within that site form an essential part of its being."[1] It conforms to the topography of the site and the objects appear to rise from within the earth. Simultaneously, it is oriented toward the city and aligned with the main artery that leads into the city center. Its design has been structured around the city's goals, which inform both the placement of the objects and their symbolism. A civic sculpture set at the intersection of two boulevards, it stands in the midst of the flow of daily traffic and remains outside the fine-art context of museums, art parks, and galleries.

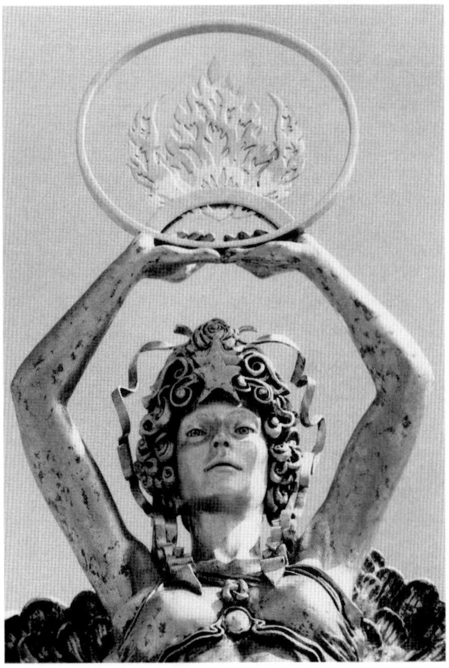

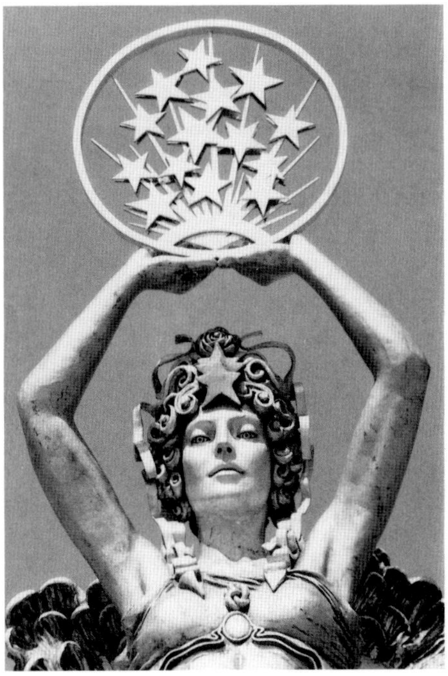

At midnight on that inaugural day the brightly spotlighted *Gateway* stood out sharply against the surrounding darkness. Depending on the angle from which they were seen, the *Visions* appeared either to have just alighted or to be about to take off. The few cars that sped by intermittently, enveloped in the darkness, were almost invisible, and their sounds became part of the flying *Visions*. Fog set in, covering *Civitas* in a milky dome with a central aperture. The dome of the Pantheon came to mind—nature imitating art whose initial inspiration she had been.

The silence was broken suddenly by four noisy, cigarette-smoking teenagers. "That's where our tax money went," they declared, no doubt echoing their parents' complaints. But they were clearly of several minds and protective of the work. They climbed the steps, jumped on the cubic bases, embraced and caressed the spheres. They said they came to see the new statues every night and had given them names. They thought they were about love and dared anyone to hurt them. Seemingly unimpressed when told that the woman they had been speaking with was the artist herself, they noisily departed in their delapidated car. Then they returned, waving their arms wildly and yelling "We love you"—to both artist and statues.

As we were about to drive away, we saw a woman ritualistically walking along the perimeter of the circle, followed by a man. The third time, she stopped at each statue and raised her hands, holding up a bowl-like object in a gesture of offering. She then crossed to the center of the circle and knelt on the ground. She said she was an astrologer and nature worshiper and in her monthly newsletter she had announced the dedication of the *Gateway*, "where the four of the five mothers stand," as a dedication "on a spiritual level to a new vision for all humanity."

One month later, on Mother's Day, a *New York Times* editorial described a similar ritual, led by a woman, on an Adirondack hillside. There the libation had been offered to a birch tree. The editorial commented: "Such is the practice of goddess worship, a new development in America's spiritual life, and one worth acknowledging on Mother's Day: it is rooted in reverence for the ultimate mother, for woman as the giver of life."[2] It added that goddess-based cultures cherished the earth as nurturer and that much goddess worship today centers on the classic elements of earth, water, wind, and fire. Recognizing that goddess worship has also prompted ridicule, the editorial concluded that it still warrants sympathy and respect, "for it proceeds from values of nurturing, peace and harmony with nature."

This also is the central message of the *Gateway:* the meeting of *civitas* and *natura* in a fragmented and mechanized modern world.[3]

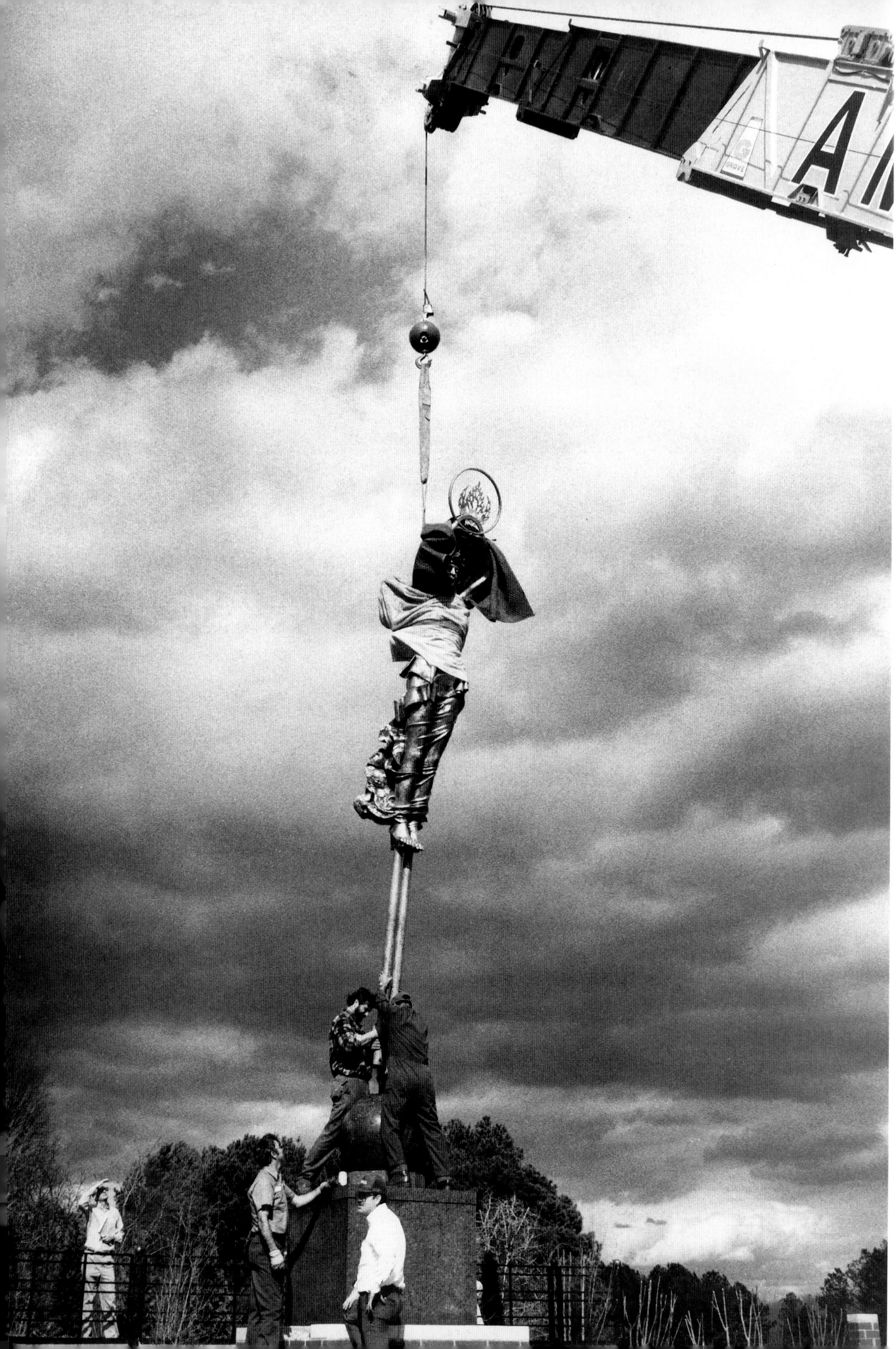

OPPOSITE:
Crane installing the first sculpture of *Civitas: Four Visions (Gateway to the City of Rock Hill)*, March 1991

View of the reverse of one of the sculptures of *Civitas: Four Visions (Gateway to the City of Rock Hill)* after installation at Rock Hill Gateway, South Carolina

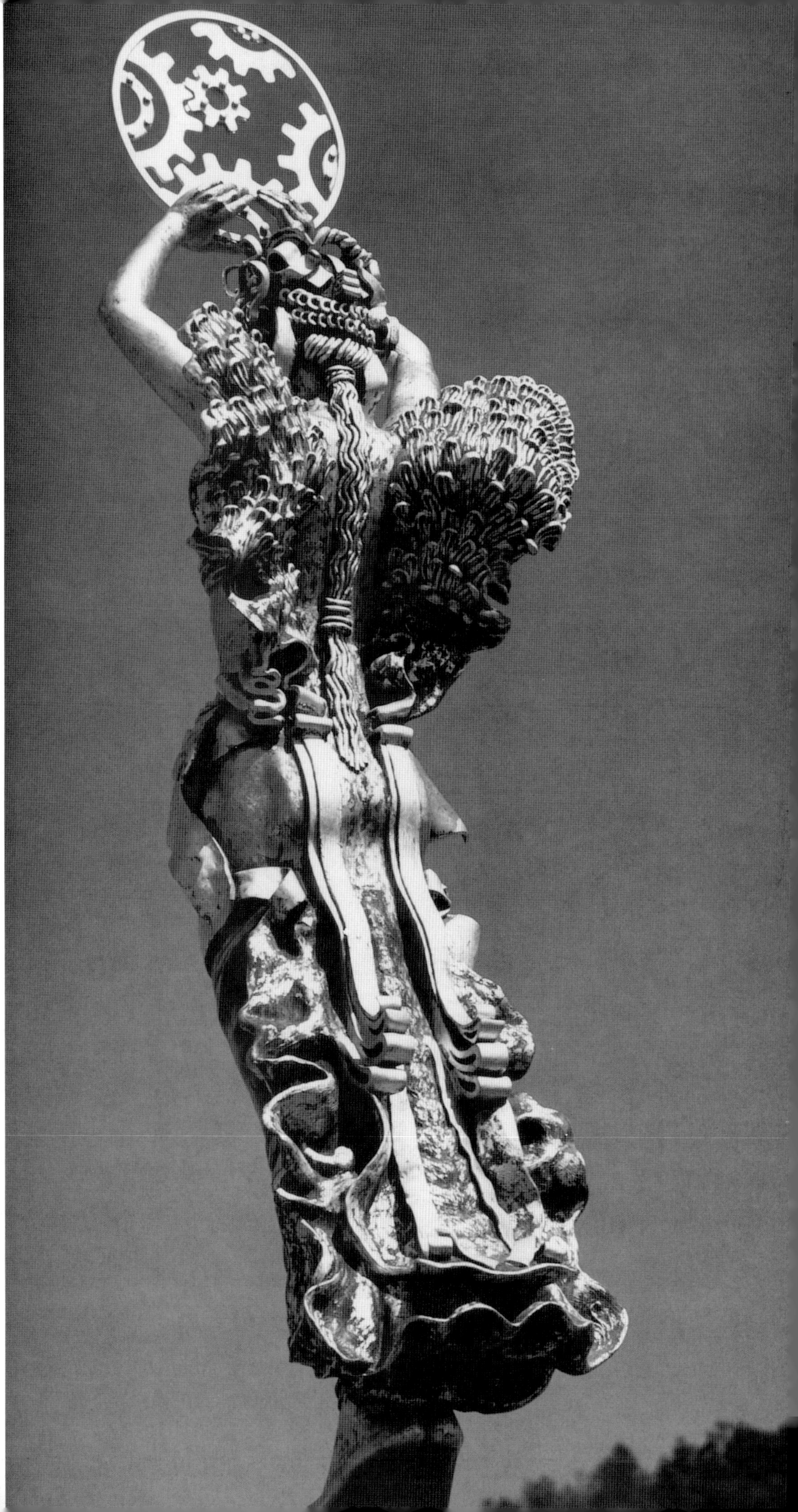

OVERLEAF:
Sky Gateway Introducing Diana
Grouping of three plaster figures, 1990
Collection the artist

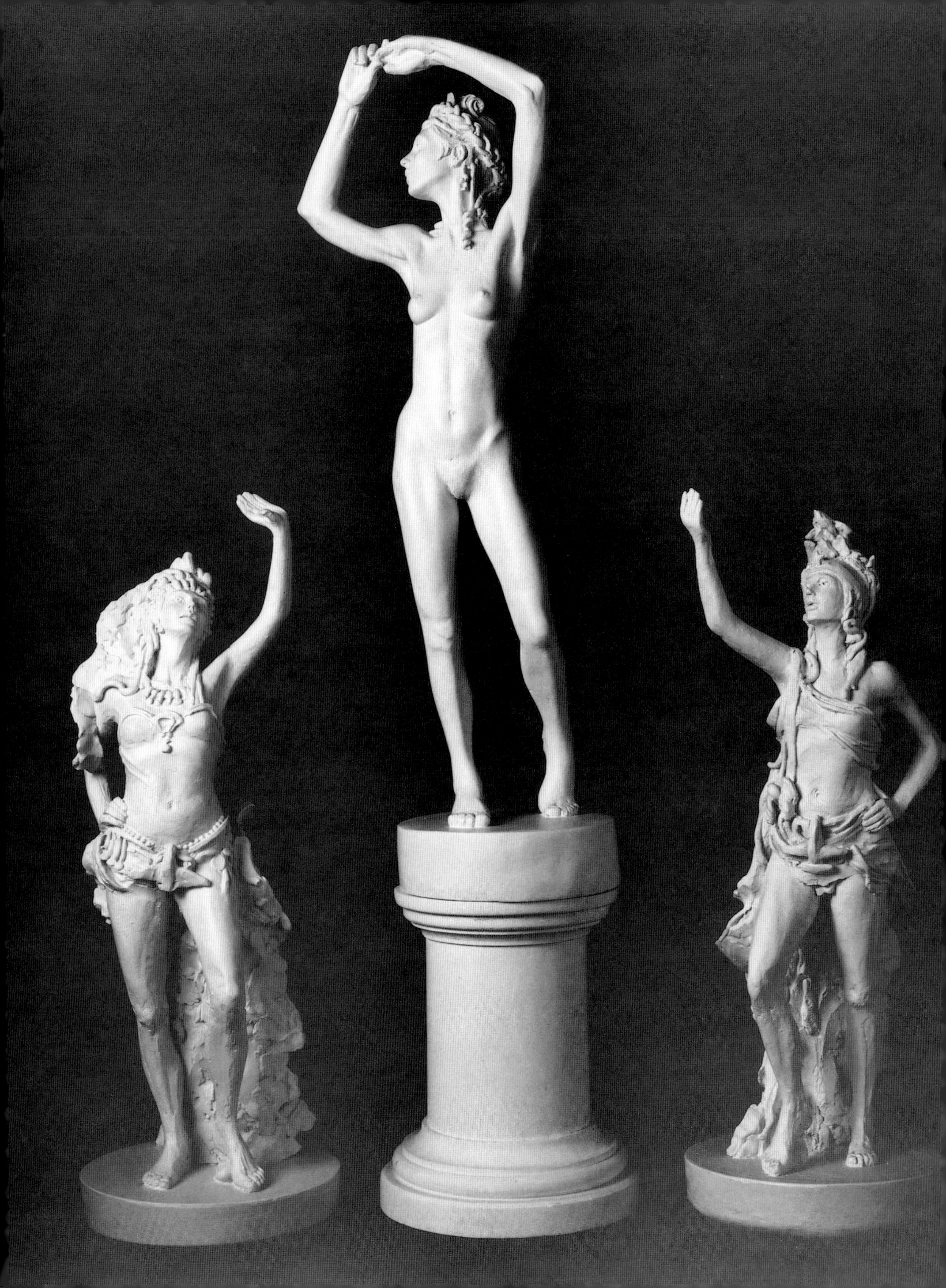

NOTES

INTRODUCTION

1 Audrey Flack's work was included in many exhibitions of American Photorealist (or New Realist) painting of the late sixties and early seventies. For example: "Painting from the Photograph" (Riverside Museum, New York, 1969), "Twenty-two Realists" (Whitney Museum of American Art, New York, 1970), "Phases of the New Realism" (Lowe Art Museum, University of Miami, Coral Gables, Fla., 1972), "Amerikansk realism" (Galleri Ostergren, Malmö, Sweden, 1973), and "Hyperréalistes américains" (Galerie Arditti, Paris, 1973).

2 See William C. Seitz, "The Real and the Artificial: Painting of the New Environment," *Art in America*, November–December 1972, pp. 64–72.

3 Lawrence Alloway, "Introduction," in *Audrey Flack On Painting* by Audrey Flack (New York: Harry N. Abrams, 1981), p. 27.

4 Gerrit Henry, "The Real Thing," *Art International*, Summer 1972, reprinted in Gregory Battcock, *Super Realism: A Critical Anthology* (New York: E. P. Dutton, 1975), p. 11.

5 Louis K. Meisel, *Photorealism* (New York: Harry N. Abrams, 1980), p. 241.

6 Matthew Kangas, "Rebirth of Venus: The Persistence of the Classical in Contemporary Sculpture," *Sculpture*, November–December 1990, pp. 49–55. The sculptors discussed in this article are Jim Dine, Manuel Neri, Judith Shea, and Nancy Mee, all of whom work from and with the ancient fragment.

REFLECTIONS IN A MIRROR

1 All statements by the artist and information about her life derive from interviews conducted in the summer of 1983 and from subsequent correspondence.

2 For *Marilyn*, see Audrey Flack, *Audrey Flack On Painting* (New York: Harry N. Abrams, 1981), pp. 84–89. *Golden Girl* was not included in Flack's book nor was it shown in her 1987 exhibition at the Louis K. Meisel Gallery, New York.

3 Flack, *On Painting*, pp. 84–89.

4 Laura Mulvey, "Visual Pleasure and Narrative Cinema," *Screen*, 16:3, pp. 6–18. Reprinted in Laura Mulvey, *Visual and Other Pleasures* (Bloomington, Indiana: Indiana University Press, 1989), pp. 14–26.

5 Flack, *On Painting*, p. 86.

6 Flack had an exhibition at the Roko Gallery in New York City in 1959 but did not include any of the self-portraits. Two of these early self-portraits were included in her 1983 exhibition at the Armstrong Gallery in New York City.

7 Sandra M. Gilbert and Susan Gubar, *The Madwoman in the Attic* (New Haven and London: Yale University Press, 1979), p. 15.

8 The full text of the first stanza of the poem reads as follows:

I sat before my glass one day,
And conjured up a vision bare,
Unlike the aspects glad and gay,
That erst were found reflected there—
The vision of a woman, wild
With more than womanly despair.

For the full text of the poem see Gilbert and Gubar, *Madwoman*, pp. 15–16.

9 For example, see Joanne S. Frye, *Living Stories, Telling Lives: Women and the Novel in Contemporary Experience* (Ann Arbor, Michigan: Michigan University Press, 1986).

10 See the essay by Patricia Hills, pp. 44–61 of this book.

11 Flack, *On Painting*, pp. 32–42. Flack commented in a 1986 interview with Lowery Sims: "There was a need for me to find a female goddess as a role model. A woman of sorrow for my sorrow." *Saints and Other Angels: The Religious Paintings of Audrey Flack*, Lowery Sims, Curator (New York: The Cooper Union, 1987). For a discussion of Flack's goddess sculptures see the essay by Susan Casteras, pp. 102–29 of this book.

12 See the essay by Lawrence Alloway, pp. 62–83 of this book.

13 On the bodily presence and vocal absence of women in representation, see Griselda Pollock, *Vision and Difference: Femininity, Feminism, and the Histories of Art* (London and New York: Routledge, 1988), pp. 170–71.

14 For further discussion of this painting see essay by Thalia Gouma-Peterson, "Iconic Images for a Secularized Age," pp. 84–101 in this book.

15 For the texts of these inscriptions see Gouma-Peterson's essay in this book, pp. 92–95.

THE PERSON, THE STUDIO, THE WORLD

1 This essay is based not only on the written sources, cited below, but also on conversations, during which I took notes, held with Audrey Flack on April 17, 1975; October 20, 1988; November 9, 1988; February 3, 1989; July 31, 1989; and August 22, 1990. More important, I have known the artist as a friend since the early 1970s and have followed her changes yet witnessed her constancy. I want to thank her here for her generosity in recalling events and for correcting factual errors. I also want to thank Kevin Whitfield and Patricia Johnston for carefully reading the manuscript and Amy Lyford for her assistance in tracking down some of the sources of Flack's paintings.

2 Cindy Nemser, *Art Talk* (New York: Scribners, 1975), 306–7.

3 Nemser, p. 309.

4 Nemser, p. 308.

5 Audrey Flack, *Audrey Flack On Painting* (New York: Harry N. Abrams, 1981), pp. 52–53.

AUDREY FLACK'S STILL-LIFE PAINTINGS IN THE 1970s

1 Lawrence Alloway completed this essay shortly before his death; it appears here in unedited form. The text incorporates material from two earlier pieces on Flack by Alloway: "Introduction" in Audrey Flack, *Audrey Flack On Painting* (New York: Harry N. Abrams, 1981); *Audrey Flack—Vanitas*, exhibition catalogue (New York: Louis K. Meisel Gallery, 1978).

2 This painting was known first by the date of Margaret Bourke-White's photograph, "April, 1945." Only later was the title changed to *World War II*.

3 Jeanne Hamilton in Flack, *On Painting*, pp. 96–104.

4 Flack, *On Painting*, p. 81.

5 Alfred B. Barr, Jr., *Picasso: Fifty Years of His Art* (New York: Museum of Modern Art, 1948), pp. 73, 291.

6 *Close to Home*, exh. cat., arranged by Lucy Sallick and Phyllis Floyd (New York: Genesis Galleries, 1976).

7 Francis Ponge, *Methodes* (Paris: Gallimard, 1961). Translation by Beth Archer, *The Voice of Things* (New York: McGraw Hill, 1974), p. 83. Ponge's earlier book, *Le Parti Pris des Choses*, is translated by Archer and partially by Cyd Corman in *Things* (New York: Grossman, 1971).

8 Linda Nochlin, in conversation with the author, c. 1975.

9 Ann Sutherland Harris and Linda Nochlin, *Women Artists 1550–1950* (Los Angeles: Los Angeles County Museum and New York: Alfred A. Knopf, 1976), p. 146.

10 For illustration see Harris and Nochlin, p. 76.

ICONIC IMAGES FOR A SECULARIZED AGE

1 Unless otherwise indicated, all quoted statements are derived from an interview with the artist (spring 1983) and subsequent correspondence and conversation. Some of the material in this article was published in *Arts Magazine*, November 1983, pp. 136–41.

2 See the 1986 interview with Lowery Sims in *Saints and Other Angels: The Religious Paintings of Audrey Flack* (New York: The Cooper Union, 1987).

3 Lawrence Alloway, introduction to *Audrey Flack—Vanitas* (New York: Louis K. Meisel Gallery, 1978).

4 Audrey Flack, "On Carlo Crivelli," *Arts Magazine*, June 1981, p. 92.

5 Flack, "Crivelli," p. 92. For two divergent recent discussions of contemporary American realism, see Linda Nochlin, "The Flowering of American Realism," *Real, Really Real, Superreal Directions in Contemporary American Realism* (San Antonio: San Antonio Museum of Art, 1981), pp. 25–35; and Donald B. Kuspit, "What's Real in Realism?" *Art in America*, September 1981, pp. 89–94. Though a number of critics have written about contemporary American realist art and several have attempted a more thorough and refined analysis, we still lack a systematic and coordinated discussion of this complex and varied contemporary movement. On this see Lawrence Alloway, "The Renewal of Realist Criticism," *Art in America*, September 1981, pp. 108–11. For an anthology of important essays on realism published in the late sixties and early seventies see Gregory Battcock, *Super Realism* (New York: E. P. Dutton, 1975).

6 Flack met Baba through a former student, Nancy Bundt, a photographer. Flack was won over by the silent holy man and knew that she had to paint him. She visited him in India and shot hundreds of photographs of him, but was not satisfied with any of them and ended up selecting a photograph by Nancy Bundt. She subsequently found out that Baba himself had instructed Bundt to photograph him for that particular shot.

7 Audrey Flack, *Audrey Flack On Painting* (New York: Harry N. Abrams, 1981), pp. 60–75.

8 In medieval icons the halo becomes the visible manifestation of spiritual energy. Flack's intent in this painting is very similar.

9 Flack, "Crivelli," p. 92.

10 She observed, "I haven't been able to make those kinds of mistakes in my other works. My paintings had to be perfect and were carefully prepared. I had to set up the still life, find the perfect set up, take the slides, identify the perfect slide . . . all that mechanical stuff. To go out and sit by the ocean and do watercolors . . . I had a need to keep doing them every day. I *had* to work, grab my kit and run in sunshine, rain, and snow."

11 On this group, which includes Fairfield Porter, John Button, Bill Sullivan, Neil Welliver, and Jane Wilson, among others, see Gerrit Henry, "Painterly Realism and the Modern Landscape," *Art in America*, September 1981, pp. 112–19.

12 From being afraid, at the beginning, to show them at all—"They are just little watercolors; they are small; they don't look like any other of my work; they are not monumental masterpieces"—Flack finally decided to include them in the 1983 show of her work at the Meisel Gallery.

13 "I am trying to say we are all one and who is to say that if you are dealing with the Italian Renaissance you can't deal with the Hopi Indians in the same breath?"

14 The texts are derived from Pandit Usharbuth Arya, *Meditation on the Art of Dying* (Honesdale, Pennsylvania: Himalayan International Institute of Yoga, Science, and Philosophy, 1979).

15 Flack often thinks of the title from the beginning. She feels that the earlier the title gets into a painting the better because it becomes part of the intent of the painting.

16 "I am now more concerned with healing colors than with light per se, the aura of the painting, the effect it will have on the observer."

17 Flack had been paired for this exhibition with Pintauro, whom she did not know. A former Jesuit and author of the play "Snow Orchid," Pintauro had lengthy discussions with Flack and read to her many of his poems, all of which she rejected. Finally he brought out of the files in his basement a poem he had written years ago and Flack responded immediately, "That's it."

18 "I dressed Hannah up in a red satin blouse and put a gypsy star on her forehead. I read the poem to her and told her you are a goddess. She got very much into it. Then things began happening. It was to be a very supernatural painting; a goddess that is alive eternally . . . I wanted *Hannah* to cast a healing aura." In keeping *Hannah* as a title, rather than only *Who She Is*, as originally planned, Flack focused more on the specific identity of the female image.

19 Flack, *On Painting*, pp. 32–42.

20 For a discussion of the sculptures see the essay by Susan Casteras in this book, pp. 102–29.

21 Flack, *On Painting*, p. 28.

22 Flack, *On Painting*, p. 28.

BREAKING THE MOLD

1 Indeed, New York City was full of prominent works by female sculptors in the past, ranging from Anna Hyatt Huntington's over-life-size monument of *Joan of Arc* on Riverside Drive to Evelyn B. Longman's huge *Genius of Telegraph (Electricity)* for the top of the 1916 Western Union Building.

2 Unless otherwise credited, all quotations in this text are derived from interviews with the artist conducted in fall 1989 and summer and fall of 1990.

3 Audrey Flack, *Art & Soul: Notes on Creating* (New York: E. P. Dutton, 1986), p. 26.

4 Audrey Flack, *Audrey Flack On Painting* (New York: Harry N. Abrams, 1981), p. 32.

5 Barbara G. Walker, *The Women's Dictionary of Symbols and Sacred Objects* (San Francisco: Harper & Row, 1988), pp. 221–22.

6 For the *Egyptian Rocket Goddess* Flack was partly inspired by Rupert Sheldrake's book *Morphogenetic Fields*, which espouses the view, according to the artist, that "everything that existed in the past still exists in some form of energy somewhere in the universe. Nothing disappears . . . and thus this figure, coming from the past through the present, can exist in all temporal planes simultaneously."

7 Barbara G. Walker, *The Women's Encyclopedia of Myths and Secrets* (New York: Harper & Row, 1986), pp. 101–2. The artist herself owns and has read a copy of this book.

8 Walker, *The Women's Dictionary*, pp. 341–42.

9 Marina Warner, *Monuments and Maidens: The Allegory of Female Form* (London: Pan Books, 1987), pp. 137–39 *passim.*

10 Flack, *Art & Soul*, p. 10.

11 Flack, *Art & Soul*, p. 98.

12 Flack, *Art & Soul*, p. 108.

13 Another rather self-possessed, heroic personification is *The Art Muse* of 1989, which exists in various media, including bronze and white resin. Her compact musculature and slim, even androgynous body ally her with *Diana* and seem to draw partial inspiration from Victorian sculpture such as Alfred Drury's bronze *Circe* of 1893–94 (Leeds City Art Gallery). Wearing a gem-encrusted headdress and a necklace of rhythmic snakelike motifs, *The Art Muse* looks ahead and up but not really at viewers. In actuality, there was no single goddess of the arts, and one wonders whether this figure is, consciously or not, partly a subtle parody of the notion of divine female inspiration.

14 Walker, *Myths and Secrets*, p. 233.

15 Walker, *Myths and Secrets*, p. 102.

16 The artist has suggested that *American Athena* would be an ideal addition to the iconography of the Capitol, specifically, atop the White House.

17 Flack, *Art & Soul*, p. 25.

18 As depicted and described in a book owned by the artist, Irene Fortuyn and Robert O'Brien, *Bon voyage voyeur. Thoughts about sculpture* (Amsterdam: privately printed, 1984).

19 Flack has painted a still life titled *Buddha*, with a sculpture of the seated god as the central figure.

20 See Wieland Schmied, Giorgio Manganelli, and Marina Warner, "The Fatal Glance," *FMR Magazine* (September/October 1988), pp. 47–70.

21 Bram Dijkstra, *Idols of Perversity. Fantasies of Feminine Evil in Fin-de-Siècle Culture* (New York and Oxford: Oxford University Press, 1986), pp. 310–11.

22 Warner, as quoted in *FMR*, p. 67.

23 Among other examples can be cited Monique Wittig's critical interpretations in *The Laugh of the Medusa* (London: The Women's Press, 1980).

24 Walker, *The Women's Dictionary*, p. 507.

25 Walker, *The Women's Dictionary*, pp. 129–30. In the Egyptian underworld, e.g., the magical cord signified the binding force of matriarchal law.

26 Walker, *The Women's Dictionary*, p. 370.

27 Walker, *Myths and Secrets*, p. 268.

28 Walker, *The Women's Dictionary*, pp. 387–88.

29 Walker, *The Women's Dictionary*, p. 255.

30 Nancy Huston, "The Matrix of War: Mothers and Heroes," in *The Female Body in Western Culture: Contemporary Perspectives*, ed. Susan Rubin Suleiman (Cambridge: Harvard University Press, 1986), p. 129.

31 Good examples of this include Suleiman, ed., *The Female Body in Western Culture;* Griselda Pollock, *Vision and Difference: Femininity, Feminism and the Histories of Art* (London: Routledge, 1988); E. Ann Kaplan, "Is the Gaze Male," in *Women and Film: Both Sides of the Cinema* (New York: Methuen, 1983); and Kate Linker, "Representation and Sexuality," in *Art After Modernism: Rethinking Representation*, ed. Brian Walis (New York: The New Museum of Contemporary Art, 1984).

32 Flack herself has written about the interaction between maker and viewer in the creative process, commenting in *Art & Soul* (p. 9) that "you are not just producing images, but provoking and being provoked by those images. You get involved in a metaphoric revelation, and witness metaphors emerging from the work. . . . The ultimate achievement is a transference of that revelation from private to public."

33 Beverly Brown and Parveen Adams, "The Feminine Body and Feminist Politics," *m/f*, 3 (1979), p. 44.

34 See, e.g., David Freedberg, *The Power of Images: Studies in the History and Theory of Response* (Chicago: University of Chicago Press, 1989).

A GATEWAY TO THE CITY OF ROCK HILL

1 This basic definition was recently proposed by Yve-Alain Bois, "*In Situ:* Site Specific Art in and out of Context," *The Journal of Art*, January 1991, 33.

2 "The Week in Review," *The New York Times*, Sunday, 12 May 1991, Section 4, p. 16.

3 I thank Professor Patricia Mathews of Oberlin College for her helpful critical comments on this chapter.

CATALOGUE RAISONNÉ OF PAINTINGS AND SCULPTURES

Unless otherwise noted, works are in the collection of the artist
* Indicates works in the exhibition *Breaking the Rules: Audrey Flack, A Retrospective 1950–1990*

PAINTINGS

Six Characters in Search of an Author. 1949–50. Oil on canvas, 43 × 55″
**Flashback.* 1949–50. Oil on canvas, 45 × 28″. Private collection
Stained and Painted Abstract. 1950. Oil on canvas, 48 × 34″
Abstract Portrait of Anita. 1950. Oil on canvas, 49 × 33″
Portrait of Nick Marsicano. 1950–51. Oil on canvas, 40 × 28″
**Black Graph Abstract.* 1951. Oil on canvas, 44 × 33″
**Diamonds and Sky (Abstract).* 1951. Oil on canvas, 50 × 34″
Abstract Landscape with Sky (Diamond Series). 1951. Oil on canvas, 26 × 28″
**Abstract Expressionist Landscape with Clouds.* 1951. Oil on canvas, 30 × 40″
Abstract Expressionist Landscape. 1951. Oil on canvas, 42 × 33″
Abstract Landscape (Sun and Earth). 1951. Oil on canvas, 32½ × 48″. Collection Eve and Stanley Queller, New York
Galaxies: Dark Brown Abstract. 1951. Oil on canvas, 40 × 42″
Monumental Lovers (Pink Abstract Expressionist). 1951. Oil on canvas, 43 × 60″
**Abstract Force: Homage to Franz Kline.* 1951–52. Oil on canvas, 49½ × 72″. Collection Norman and Sherry Bunin, New York
Abstract Expressionist Self-Portrait. 1952. Oil on canvas, 40 × 28″. Miami University Art Museum, Oxford, Ohio
Morris Flack. 1952. Oil on canvas, 36 × 24″
Portrait of Mother. 1952–53. Oil on canvas, 36 × 28″
Abstract Expressionist Landscape. 1953. Oil on canvas, 20 × 34″
Self-Portrait with Flower. 1953. Oil on canvas, 45½ × 29½″. Collection Beverly and Hyman Dolinsky, New York
Figure Group (Gorky). 1953. Oil on canvas, 36 × 50″
**Anatomy Lesson.* 1953. Oil on canvas, 42 × 50″. Miami University Art Museum, Oxford, Ohio
**Still Life with Apples and Orange.* 1953. Oil on canvas, 26 × 36½″. Collection Beverly and Hyman Dolinsky, New York
Still Life with Candle Stick. 1953–54. Oil on canvas, 25 × 28″. Collection Eve and Albert Stewertka, Long Island, N.Y.
Portrait of Gregory. 1953–54. Oil on canvas, 28 × 34″
Lyrical Still Life with Fruit. 1953–54. Oil on canvas, stained, 30 × 38″
**Black and White Still Life with Pompons, Chrysanthemums, and Wine Glass (For Franz Kline).* 1954. Oil on canvas, 25 × 36″. Collection H. Robert Marcus
Still Life with Pompons and Pear. 1954. Oil on canvas, 25 × 36″. Collection Beverly and Hyman Dolinsky, New York
Three Graces Study (unfinished). 1954. Oil on canvas, 28 × 34″
Self-Portrait with Glasses. 1954. Oil on canvas, 26 × 36″
Portrait of a Young Boy. 1954. Oil on canvas, 19¾ × 18″. Collection Pat and Al Stewart, East Hampton, N.Y.
Portrait of Anita. 1954. Oil on canvas, 36 × 52″. Collection Anita Bookey
Still Life with Red Peppers. 1954–55. Oil on canvas, 28 × 40″. Collection Beverly and Hyman Dolinsky, New York
Pat Ronson. 1955. Oil on canvas, 28 × 36″
Portrait with Mirror (Pre-Raphaelite). 1955. Oil on canvas, 50 × 36″
Beatrix (after Velazquez). 1955. Oil on canvas, 36 × 52″
Allegory of War (after Rubens). 1955. Oil on canvas, 38 × 53″
Oval Portrait: Beatrix. 1955. Oil on board, diameter 23″

Self-Portrait in Gown with Bow. 1955. Oil on canvas, 18 × 24″. Miami University Art Museum, Oxford, Ohio
**Self-Portrait with Anita.* 1955. Oil on canvas, 25 × 36″. Collection Thalia Gouma-Peterson and Carl A. Peterson, Oberlin, Ohio
Anita and Ted (Wedding Portrait). 1955. Oil on canvas, 36 × 50″
Beatrix. 1955. Oil on canvas, 15 × 18″
Still Life with Apples. 1955. Oil on canvas, 28 × 34″. Collection Charles Dimston, Long Island, N.Y.
Still Life with Apples and Teapot. 1955. Oil on canvas, 28 × 36″. Private collection
Self-Portrait with Grey Tunic. 1956. Oil on canvas, 36 × 28″. Private collection
**Self-Portrait Holding Charcoal Stick.* 1956. Oil on canvas, 40 × 28″. Miami University Art Museum, Oxford, Ohio
Self-Portrait in Tank Top. 1956–57. Oil on canvas, 70 × 48″. Miami University Art Museum, Oxford, Ohio
Portrait of Pat. 1957. Oil on canvas, 36 × 50″
Double Portrait of Debbie. 1957. Oil on canvas, 24 × 34″
Portrait of Frank Playing Cello. 1958. Oil on canvas, 28 × 42″
**Self-Portrait (the Memory).* 1958. Oil on canvas, 50 × 34″. Miami University Art Museum, Oxford, Ohio
**Self-Portrait in Underpants.* 1958. Oil on canvas, 52 × 48″. Miami University Art Museum, Oxford, Ohio
**Self-Portrait with Drafting Table.* 1958. Oil on canvas, 72 × 41″. Miami University Art Museum, Oxford, Ohio
Nude. 1957–58. Oil on canvas, 50 × 32″
**Vesalius Study (Anatomy).* 1958. Oil on canvas, 50 × 36″. Private collection
Self-Portrait at Easel: For Franz Kline. 1958. Oil on canvas, 28 × 40″. Miami University Art Museum, Oxford, Ohio
**Triple Self-Portrait.* 1958. Oil on canvas, 42 × 40″. Miami University Art Museum, Oxford, Ohio
Double Self-Portrait. 1958. Oil on canvas, 15 × 22″. Miami University Art Museum, Oxford, Ohio
Self-Portrait with Palette. 1958. Oil on canvas, 41 × 42″
Melissa and Me. 1959. Oil on canvas, 19 × 26″. Miami University Art Museum, Oxford, Ohio
Dance of Death. 1959. Oil on canvas, 6 × 8′
Self-Portrait: Dark Face. 1960. Oil on canvas, 18 × 14″. Miami University Art Museum, Oxford, Ohio
Portrait of Else in a Rocking Chair. 1960–61. Oil on canvas, 52 × 36″
Frank Playing Cello (with Melissa). 1961. Oil on canvas, 42 × 60″. Collection Steve Knapp, New York
Else. 1961. Oil on canvas, 18 × 14″
Portrait of Else (Small Head). 1961. Oil on canvas, 18 × 14″. Collection Beverly and Hyman Dolinsky, New York
**The Three Graces.* 1962. Oil on canvas, 67 × 40″. Private collection
**Four Horsemen of the Apocalypse.* 1962. Oil on canvas, 7 × 9′. University of Virginia Art Museum, Charlottesville
**Hannah and Annie.* 1962. Oil on canvas, 16 × 20″. Collection Hannah Flack Marcus, San Francisco
Small Head (model study). 1962. Oil on canvas, 8 × 10″. Riverside Museum, New York
Hannah in Sunsuit. 1962. Oil on canvas, 21½ × 18″. Collection Hannah Flack Marcus, San Francisco
Sailor's Head. 1962. Oil on canvas, 16 × 20″
Portrait of Hannah in Red Dress. 1962. Oil on canvas, 15 × 18″
**Matzo Meal.* 1962. Oil on canvas, 14 × 18″
**Royal Jello.* 1962. Oil on canvas, 9 × 12″
Cosmetic Still Life. 1962. Oil on canvas, 11 × 14″. Private collection, New York
**Hannah (Golden Head).* 1963. Oil on canvas, 12 × 9″. Collection Hannah Flack Marcus, San Francisco
Rockefeller. 1963. Oil on canvas, 30 × 40″. Greater Lafayette Museum of Art, Indiana
**Hitler.* 1963–64. Oil on canvas, 28 × 28″
Teheran Conference. 1964. Oil on canvas, 41 × 72″. Jimmy Carter Library
Truman's Teachers. 1964. Oil on canvas, 20 × 30″. Collection Beverly and Hyman Dolinsky, New York
**Kennedy Motorcade.* 1964. Oil on canvas, 38 × 42″. Private collection
Davey Moore. 1964. Oil on canvas, 36 × 30″. Private collection
Two Women Grieving over Kennedy Outside a Dallas Hospital. 1964. Oil on canvas, 36 × 28″. Collection Edward Lamb, Toledo, Ohio
Chief Spotted Feather Visiting the White House. 1964. Oil on canvas, 32 × 50″. Collection Mr. and Mrs. Bern Siler, New York
Portrait of Sarah Flichtenfeld (Grandmother Field). 1964. Oil on canvas, 36 × 30″
**Portrait of Melissa.* 1964. Oil on canvas, 15 × 10″
Marilyn Monroe. 1964. Oil on canvas, 24 × 18″
Carroll Baker. 1964. Oil on canvas, 20 × 16″. Private collection
The Carpetbaggers. 1964. Oil on canvas, 28 × 30″
Party Laugh (Melina Mercouri). 1965. Oil on canvas, 16 × 12″. Collection Mr. and Mrs. Ted Wasserman, Briarcliff, N.Y.
Hannah Marie (Mickey Mouse Hat). 1965. Oil on canvas, 10 × 8″. Collection Hannah Flack Marcus, San Francisco
**Sisters of the Immaculate Conception Marching for Freedom.* 1965. Oil on canvas, 38 × 70″. New York University, New York
Old Mexican Orange Seller. 1967. Oil on canvas, 20 × 26″. Collection Jerome Spiller, New York
Old Woman, Mexico. 1967. Oil on canvas, 8 × 10″. Collection Estelle and Marvin Goldman, New York
Orange Seller Laughing at Me for Taking Her Picture. 1967. Oil on canvas, 8 × 10″. Collection Steve Weil, Washington, D.C.
Dona Rosa the Potter. 1967–68. Oil on canvas, 10 × 8″. Collection Oriole Farb, Amherst, Mass.
**Young Mexican Farmer in Oaxaca Market.* 1967–68. Oil on canvas, 40 × 62″. Collection Sidney Singer
Mad Beggar Woman, Mexico. 1968. Oil on canvas, 10 × 12″
Two Weavers from Oaxaca. 1968. Oil on canvas, 20 × 24″. Collection Rosita Sarnoff, New York
Tante Feige. 1968. Oil on canvas, 30 × 25″. Collection Herman and Helen Greenberg, North Miami, Fla.
**War Protest March.* 1968. Oil on canvas, 20 × 30″. Collection Phil Desind, The Capricorn Gallery, Bethesda, Md.
**Farb Family Portrait.* 1969–70. Oil on canvas, 40 × 60″. Rose Art Museum, Brandeis University, Waltham, Mass.
Sunset. 1971. Oil on canvas, 20 × 28″. Private collection
Sunset. 1971. Oil on canvas, 24 × 30″. Private collection
**Sunset over Florence.* 1971. Oil on canvas, 46 × 66″. Collection H. Robert Marcus
**Siena Cathedral.* 1971. Oil on canvas, 66 × 46″. Collection Louis K. and Susan Pear Meisel, New York
Amiens Notre Dame. 1971. Oil on canvas, 66 × 46″. Private collection
Michelangelo's David. 1971. Oil on canvas, 66 × 46″. Private collection
Ammannati's Neptune Fountain. 1971. Oil on canvas, 26 × 40″. Butler Institute of American Art, Youngstown, Ohio (gift of Phil Desind)
**Piazza of Miracles.* 1971. Oil on canvas, 48 × 72″. Collection H. Robert Marcus
**Tower of Pisa.* 1971. Oil on canvas, 72 × 48″. National Museum of American Art, Smithsonian Institution, Washington, D.C.
Macarena Esperanza. 1971. Oil on canvas, 66 × 46″. Collection Paul and Camille Hoffman, Naperville, Ill.
**Macarena of Miracles.* 1971. Oil on canvas, 66 × 46″. The Metropolitan Museum of Art, New York (gift of Paul F. Walters)
**Dolores of Cordoba.* 1971. Oil on canvas, 70 × 50″. Collection Jane Rubin, New York
**Lady Madonna.* 1972. Oil on canvas, 78 × 69″. The Whitney Museum of American Art, New York (gift of Martin J. Zimet)
Cordoba Angel. 1972. Oil on paper, 30 × 20″. Private collection
San Giminiano Angel. 1972. Oil on paper, 30 × 20″. Private collection
Jolie Madame. 1972. Oil on canvas, 71 × 96″. National Gallery Australia, Canberra
Rich Art. 1972–73. Oil over acrylic on canvas, 36 × 50″. Private collection
Crayola. 1972–73. Oil over acrylic on canvas, 28 × 40″. Private collection, Switzerland
Shiva Blue. 1972–73. Oil over acrylic on canvas, 36 × 50″. Private collection, Switzerland
Spitfire. 1973. Oil over acrylic on canvas, 70 × 96″. Stuart M. Speiser Collection, Smithsonian Institution, Washington, D.C.
Royal Flush. 1973. Oil over acrylic on canvas, 70 × 96″. Private collection
Solitaire. 1974. Acrylic on canvas, 60 × 84″. Collection Joan and Barrie Damson, New York
Chanel. 1974. Acrylic on canvas, 56 × 82″. Collection Mrs. Morton G. Neumann, Chicago
Poundcake Sundae. 1974. Oil over acrylic on canvas, 38 × 50¼″. Private collection
Banana Split Sundae. 1974. Oil over acrylic on canvas, 38 × 50⅛″. Collection Donna and Neil Weisman, New Jersey
Strawberry Tart. 1974. Oil over acrylic on canvas, 24 × 30⅛″. Collection Bruce R. Lewin Fine Art, New York
Coconut Lemon Cake. 1974. Oil over acrylic on canvas, 24 × 30″. Collection Bruce R. Lewin Fine Art, New York
Self-Portrait. 1974. Acrylic on canvas, 80 × 64″. Collection Marcus Kutter, Basel, Switzerland
**Strawberry Tart Supreme.* 1974. Oil over acrylic on canvas, 54 × 60¼″. Allen Memorial Art Museum, Oberlin, Ohio (National Endowment for the Arts Museum Purchase Plan)
Spaced Out Apple. 1974. Acrylic on wet sanded canvas, 58 × 60¼″. Collection Mr. and Mrs. Jerome Westheimer, Ardmore, Okla.
Parrot Still Life. 1975. Acrylic on paper, 24 × 16″. Private collection, New York
**Buddha.* 1975. Oil over acrylic on wet sanded canvas, 70 × 96″. Saint Louis Art Museum (Purchase and Contemporary Art Society Fund)
**Leonardo's Lady.* 1975. Oil over acrylic on wet sanded canvas, 74 × 80″. Collection, The Museum of Modern Art, New York (Purchased with funds from the National Endowment for the Arts and an anonymous donor)
Grand Rosé. 1975. Oil over acrylic on wet sanded canvas, 90 × 90″. Private collection, Calif.
Untitled (Drape and Beads). 1975. Oil and acrylic on canvas, 36 × 30¼″. Akron Art Museum, Ohio
**Queen.* 1975–76. Acrylic on wet sanded canvas, 80 × 80″. Collection Louis K. Meisel Gallery, New York
**Gambler's Cabinet.* 1976. Oil over acrylic on canvas, 83 × 78″. Collection Louis, Susan, and Ari Meisel, New York
Dutch Still Life. 1976. Acrylic on canvas, 60 × 60″. The Solomon R. Guggenheim Museum, New York
Petits Fours. 1976. Acrylic on illustrator's board, 16 × 24″. Collection Louis K. and Susan Pear Meisel, New York
Golden Banana Split Sundae. 1976. Acrylic on illustrator's board, 16 × 24″. Collection Mr. and Mrs. William Jaeger, New York
Mother Cake. 1976. Oil on acrylic on canvas, 22 × 30″. Collection Mr. and Mrs. Dale Jones, New York
**World War II (Vanitas).* 1976–77. Oil over acrylic on canvas, 96 × 96″. Collection Mr. and Mrs. David Pincus, Philadelphia
**Wheel of Fortune (Vanitas).* 1977–78. Oil over acrylic on canvas, 96 × 96″. Collection Louis K. Meisel Gallery, New York
**Marilyn (Vanitas).* 1977. Oil over acrylic on canvas, 96 × 96″. University of Arizona Art Museum, Tucson
Hers (Hershey's Kisses). 1977. Acrylic on museum board, 16 × 23″. Collection Louis K. and Susan Pear Meisel, New York
Sadat. 1977–78. Acrylic on canvas, 40 × 32″. Collection Jihan Sadat, Cairo, Egypt
Marilyn: Golden Girl. 1978. Oil over acrylic on canvas, 48 × 60″. Private collection
Parrots Live Forever. 1978. Oil over acrylic on canvas (spot varnished), 83 × 83″. National Gallery of Victoria, Melbourne, Australia

Bounty. 1978. Oil over acrylic on canvas, 80 × 67″. Collection Bellbranch Road Foundation, North Carolina
Time to Save. 1979. Acrylic and oil on canvas, 80 × 64″. Private collection
Sojourner Truth. 1980. Acrylic and oil on canvas, 62 × 48″
Monarch and Rose. 1980. Acrylic on paper, 15 × 21½″. Private collection, New York
Velvet Flowers. 1980. Acrylic on paper, 23½ × 15½″. Collection Mr. and Mrs. David Moscow, Chicago
**Self-Portrait.* 1980. Oil and crayon on paper, 32½ × 20″. Collection R. Wesley Mutchler, Jr., Oakland, Calif.
**Energy Apples.* 1980. Acrylic and oil on canvas, 47¾ × 48¼″. Collection Susan Pear Meisel, New York
We Are All Light and Energy. 1981. Acrylic and oil on canvas, 46 × 66″. Private collection, Switzerland
**Hannah: Who She Is.* 1982. Acrylic and oil on canvas, 84 × 60″. National Museum of Women in the Arts, Washington, D.C.
**Invocation.* 1982. Acrylic and oil on canvas, 64 × 80″. Collection Louis K. Meisel Gallery, New York
A Pear to Heade and Heal. 1983. Acrylic and oil on canvas, 38 × 56″. Collection Mr. Glenn Golenberg, Los Angeles
Rainbow Christ. 1983. Acrylic and oil on canvas, painted wooden frame, 31 × 17½ × 6½″
**Roman Beauties.* 1983. Acrylic and oil on canvas, 54 × 74″. Collection Mr. and Mrs. Sydney Besthoff III, New Orleans
**Isis.* 1983. Acrylic and oil on canvas, 60 × 60″. Private collection
Fruits of the Earth. 1983. Acrylic and oil on canvas, 54 × 74″. Private collection
**Baba.* 1980–83. Acrylic and oil on canvas, 7½ × 13′. Collection Mr. and Mrs. Barry Hirschfeld, Denver
Roman Beauties (small version). 1985. Oil and acrylic on canvas, 24 × 34″. Collection Mr. and Mrs. Dale Jones, New York

SCULPTURES

**Angel with Heart Shield.* 1981. Bronze, height 9″ (with base). Collection Ari Ron Meisel, New York
Black Medicine. 1981–82. Clay, height 17¾″ (without base)
Islandia: Goddess of the Healing Waters. 1987. Polychromed and gilded plaster, height 5′ (without base). Samuel P. Harn Museum of Art, University of Florida, Gainesville
**Islandia: Goddess of the Healing Waters.* 1987. Polychromed and gilded plaster, height 5′ (without base)
Islandia: Goddess of the Healing Waters. 1988. Patinated and gilded bronze, height 5′9″ (with base). Collection New York City Technical College, Brooklyn
**Islandia: Goddess of the Healing Waters.* 1988. Patinated and gilded bronze, height 5′ (without base). Collection Louis K. Meisel Gallery, New York
Diana. 1987–88. Gilded plaster, height 21⅝″ (without base)
**Diana.* 1988. Cast marble with jewels, height 23⅛″ (with base). Collection Mr. and Mrs. Marvin Padover
**Diana.* 1988. Gold-plated bronze with jewels, height 21⅝″ (without base). Private collection
Head of Diana. 1988. Plaster, height 7½″ (with base)
The Art Muse. 1987–88. Plaster, height 16½″ (without base)
The Art Muse. 1988. Manzini poured marble, height 16½″ (without base)
**The Art Muse.* 1988. Gold-plated bronze with jewels, height 16½″ (without base). Private collection
Head of Art Muse. 1988. Plaster, height 6⅝″ (with base)
**Medicine Woman.* 1989. Patinated and gilded bronze, height 19″ (with base). Private collection
**Head of Medusa.* 1989. Patinated bronze, height 10″ (with base). Collection Jane Bryant Quinn
**Colossal Head of Medusa.* 1990. Polychromed terra-cotta-colored fiberglass, height 33″ (without base). Private collection
**American Athena.* 1989. Patinated bronze with gilded ornament and mother-of-pearl inlay, height 37″ (with base). Collection Donna and Neil Weisman, New Jersey
Civitas: Four Visions (Gateway to the City of Rock Hill). 1988. Plaster maquette, height 45″ (without base)
**Civitas: Four Visions (Gateway to the City of Rock Hill).* 1989. Patinated and gilded bronze maquette, with cast glass flame and marble orb, height 54″ (with orb). Collection Donna and Neil Weisman, New Jersey
Civitas: Four Visions (Gateway to the City of Rock Hill) (head). 1989. Polychromed plaster, height 32″ (without base). Collection Andreas Bechtler
**Sky Gateway.* 1989–90. Terra-cotta-colored fiberglass, two figures, height 19¼″ (with base)
Dismembered Statue. 1990. Painted plaster, 18¾ × 10¼ × 5″ (with frame)
Receiver of the Sun (Sun Goddess). 1989–90. Plaster, height 33½″ (with base)
**Receiver of the Sun (Sun Goddess).* 1989–90. Polychromed resin with objects, height 33½″ (with base). Collection Janet Lehr
Egyptian Rocket Goddess. 1990. Patinated bronze, height 42″ (with base). Private collection, Ontario
Victory (Earth Mother). 1990. Polychromed and gilded plaster, height 18″ (with base)
Daphne (head). 1990. Clay over plaster, height 6′ (without base)
Palladian Keystone Muse (head). 1990. Polychromed plaster, height 14″ (without base)
Anima. 1990. Clay, height 18″ (with base)
Civitas: Four Visions (Gateway to the City of Rock Hill). Four figures, 1990–91. Patinated and gilded bronze, height of each 22′ (with base); 13′ (without base). Rock Hill, S.C.
Civitas: Four Visions (Gateway to the City of Rock Hill). 1990–91. Patinated and gilded bronze, height 13′ (without base). Rock Hill City Hall, S.C.
Civitas: Four Visions (Gateway to the City of Rock Hill). 1990–91. Patinated and gilded bronze, height 13′ (without base). Collection Louis K. Meisel Gallery, New York; installed at Sagaponack, N.Y.
Sky Gateway Introducing Diana. 1990. Plaster, three figures, heights 19¼″ and 21⅝″
**Victory (Earth Mother).* 1991. Polychromed and gilded bronze, height 18″ (with base)
Black Medicine. 1991. Polychromed and gilded bronze, height 19″ (with base). Collection Pamela Roseneau, New York
Colossal Head of Medusa. 1991. Patinated and gilded bronze, height 35½″ (with base)
Head of Diana. 1991. Patinated bronze, height 7″ (with base). Private collection
Head of Art Muse. 1991. Patinated bronze, height 6″ (with base). Private collection
Amulet. 1991. Bronze, silver, or gold, 3 × 2⅛″
Civitas Maquette (Miniature). 1988. Patinated and gilded bronze, height 18¾″ (with base)

BIOGRAPHY

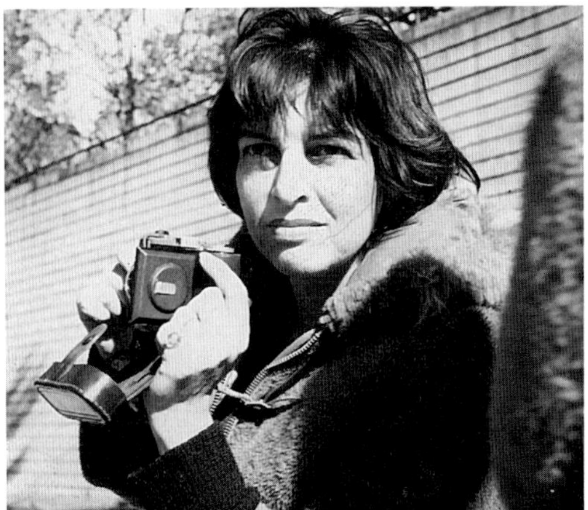

Audrey Flack, c. 1964

1931 Born: New York

EDUCATION

1951 Graduated from Cooper Union, New York
1952 B.F.A., Yale University, New Haven, Conn.
1953 New York University, Institute of Fine Arts

TEACHING

1960–68	Pratt Institute, New York New York University
1966–67	Riverside Museum Master Institute, New York
1970–74	School of Visual Arts, New York
1975	Albert Dorne Professorship, University of Bridgeport, Conn.
1982	Mellon Professor, Cooper Union, New York
1986	Master Workshop, Atlantic Center for the Arts, New Smyrna Beach, Fla.
Since 1987	National Academy of Design, New York
	Visiting professor and lecturer at universities and colleges throughout the U.S. and abroad

AWARDS AND HONORS

1974	Butler Institute of Art Award of Merit
1977	Cooper Union Citation and Honorary Doctorate
1982	Saint-Gaudens Medal, Cooper Union
1985	Artist of the Year Award, New York City Teachers Association
1989–93	Member of the Board of Directors, College Art Association of America

PUBLIC COMMISSIONS

1988	New York City Technical College, Brooklyn, N.Y. *Islandia: Goddess of the Healing Waters.* Bronze, height 5′
1991	Rock Hill, S.C. *Civitas: Four Visions (Gateway to the City of Rock Hill).* Designed in collaboration with architect Michael Gallis; 4 bronze figures, height of each, 13′

EXHIBITION HISTORY

SOLO EXHIBITIONS

1959 Roko Gallery, New York
1963 Roko Gallery, New York
1972 French and Co., New York
1974 Joseloff Gallery, University of Hartford, Conn.
Louis K. Meisel Gallery, New York
1975 Carlson Gallery, Arnold Bernhard Arts Center, University of Bridgeport, Conn.
1976 "Audrey Flack—The Gray Border Series," Louis K. Meisel Gallery, New York, April 10–May 1
1978 "Audrey Flack—Vanitas," Louis K. Meisel Gallery, New York, March 23–May 4
1981 "Audrey Flack: Works on Paper, 1950–1980," Fine Arts Gallery, University of South Florida, Tampa; Art and Cultural Center, Hollywood, Fla.
1982 "Audrey Flack: Drawings and Prints," Gallery Eleven, Tufts University, Medford, Mass., September 30–October 23
1983 "Audrey Flack—Light and Energy," Louis K. Meisel Gallery, New York, November 5–December 3
"Audrey Flack, The Early Years 1953–1968," Armstrong Gallery, New York, November 8–December 3
1984 Hewlett Art Gallery, College of Fine Arts, Carnegie-Mellon University, Schenley Park, Pa., February 4–March 2
Tomasulo Gallery, Union College, Cranford, N.J., November 2–24
1986 "Dye Transfer Photographs and Prints," Atlantic Center for the Arts, New Smyrna Beach, Fla.
1986–88 "Saints and Other Angels: The Religious Paintings of Audrey Flack," traveling exhibition sponsored by Cooper Union, New York: The Cooper Union, New York, October 28–November 18, 1986; Alexander Brest Museum, Jacksonville University, Fla., January 21–March 20, 1987; Gallery of Fine Arts, Daytona Beach Community College, Fla., April 6–May 3, 1987; Philip Johnson Center for the Arts, Muhlenberg College, Allentown, Pa., June 18–July 26, 1987; The Hoyt L. Sherman Gallery, Ohio State University, Columbus, August 17–October 4, 1987; The College of Wooster Art Museum, Ohio, October 15–November 30, 1987; Charleston Heights Arts Center, Las Vegas, December 20, 1987–February 3, 1988; Irvine Fine Arts Gallery, University of California, Irvine, February 14–March 15, 1988; Danforth Museum of Art, Framingham, Mass., April 22–July 10, 1988
1990 "Civitas," Belk Building, Town Center Mall, Rock Hill, S.C., October
1991 "A Pantheon of Female Deities," Louis K. Meisel Gallery, New York, April 27–July 12
"Audrey Flack: Islandia, Goddess of the Healing Waters," The Parrish Art Museum, Southampton, N.Y., June 7–September 15

SELECTED EXHIBITIONS

1948 "Seventh Annual Exhibition," National Academy of Design, New York
1952 Yale University Art Gallery, New Haven, Conn.
1954–57 Tanager Gallery, New York
1956 Collectors Gallery, New York
1960 "Christmas Show," Karnig Gallery, New York
Stable Gallery Annual, New York
1963 Boston University Gallery of Fine Arts
1963–64 "Nine Realist Painters," Robert Schoelkopf Gallery, New York
1964 "Ten West Side Artists," Riverside Museum, New York
1965 "Six Women," Fischbach Gallery, New York
"Sixty-five Self-Portraits," School of Visual Arts, New York
1967 Goddard-Riverside Community Center, New York
1969–70 "Paintings from the Photograph," Riverside Museum, New York, December 9–February 15
1970 "New Realism, 1970," Headley Hall Gallery, St. Cloud State College, Minn., February 13–March 11
"Twenty-two Realists," Whitney Museum of American Art, New York
1972 "Annual Exhibit of Contemporary American Paintings," Whitney Museum of American Art, New York, January 25–March 19
"Artists for CORE," Grippi and Waddell Gallery, New York
Clark Polak Gallery, Los Angeles
"L'Hyperréalistes américains," Galerie des Quatre Mouvements, Paris
"New Accessions U.S.A.," Colorado Springs Fine Arts Center, Colo., August 14–October 1
"Painting and Sculpture Today, 1972," Indianapolis Museum of Art, April 26–June 4
"Phases of the New Realism," Lowe Art Museum, University of Miami, Coral Gables, Fla., January 20–February 20
"Realism Now," New York Cultural Center, New York, December 6–January 7
"Thirty-two Realists," Cleveland Institute of Art
Warren Benedek Gallery, New York
"Women in Art," Brainerd Hall Art Gallery, State University College, Potsdam, N.Y., March 3–28
1973 "American Drawings 1963–1973," Whitney Museum of American Art, New York
"Amerikansk realism," Galleri Ostergren, Malmö, Sweden, September 8–October 14
"The Emerging Real," Storm King Art Center, Mountainville, N.Y.
"Hyperréalistes américains," Galerie Arditti, Paris, October 16–November 30
"Objects and Eight Women Realists," University of Massachusetts, Amherst, November 18–December 14
"Photo-Realism," Serpentine Gallery, London
"Realism Now," Katonah Gallery, Katonah, N.Y.
"The Super-Realist Vision," DeCordova and Dana Museum, Lincoln, Mass., October 7–December 9
"Women Choose Women," New York Cultural Center, New York, January 12–February 18
1973–78 "Photo-Realism 1973: The Stuart M. Speiser Collection," traveling exhibition: Louis K. Meisel Gallery, New York; Herbert F. Johnson Museum of Art, Cornell University, Ithaca, N.Y.; Memorial Art Gallery, University of Rochester, N.Y.; Addison Gallery of American Art, Andover, Mass.; Allentown Art Museum, Allentown, Pa.; University of Colorado Museum, Boulder; University Art Museum, University of Texas, Austin; Witte Memorial Museum, San Antonio, Tex.; Gibbes Art Gallery, Charleston, S.C.; Brooks Memorial Art Gallery, Memphis, Tenn.; Krannert Art Museum, University of Illinois, Champaign-Urbana; Helen Foresman Spencer Museum of Art, University of Kansas, Lawrence; Paine Art Center and Arboretum, Oshkosh, Wis.; Edwin A. Ulrich Museum, Wichita State University, Kans.; Tampa Bay Art Center, Tampa, Fla.; Sewall Art Gallery, Rice University, Houston, Tex.; Tulane University Art Gallery, New Orleans; Smithsonian Institution, Washington, D.C.
1974 "Amerikaans fotorealisme grafiek," Hedendaagse Kunst, Utrecht; Palais des Beaux-Arts, Brussels
"Ars '74, Ateneum," Fine Arts Academy of Finland, Helsinki, February 15–March 31
"Art 5 '74," Basel, Switzerland, June 19–24
"Aspects of Realism," Moos Gallery, Toronto, September–October
"Contemporary American Painting and Sculpture, 1974," Krannert Art Museum, University of Illinois, Champaign-Urbana
"Contemporary Portraits by American Painters," Lowe Art Museum, University of Miami, Coral Gables, Fla., October 3–November 10
"11th Tokyo Biennale, '74," Tokyo Metropolitan Museum; Kyoto Municipal Museum; Aichi Perfectual Art Museum, Nagoya
"From Teapot Dome to Watergate," Everson Museum of Art, Syracuse, N.Y., May 2–12
Moos Gallery, Montreal
"New Image in Painting," Tokyo International Biennale, June
"New Photo-Realism," Wadsworth Atheneum, Hartford, Conn., April 10–May 19
"New Realism Revisited," Brainerd Hall Art Gallery, State University College, Potsdam, N.Y.
"New York Eleven," C.W. Post Art Gallery, Long Island University, Brookville, N.Y.
"Thirty-eighth Annual Midyear Show," Butler Institute of American Art, Youngstown, Ohio, June 30–September 2
"Women's Work: American Art 1974," Museum of the Philadelphia Civic Center, April 27–May 26
1975 "Art: A Woman's Sensibility," California Institute of the Arts, Valencia
"Image, Color and Form—Recent Paintings by Eleven Americans," Toledo Museum of Art, Ohio, January 12–February 9
"Kent Bicentennial Portfolio: Spirit of Independence," exhibited in 105 museums, 50 states (commissioned print is in possession of 100 museums throughout the United States)
"The New Realism: Rip-Off or Reality?" Edwin A. Ulrich Museum, Wichita State University, Kans.
"Photo-Realists," Louis K. Meisel Gallery, New York
"Report from SoHo," New York University, Grey Art Gallery, New York
"Watercolors and Drawings—American Realists," Louis K. Meisel Gallery, New York, January
"The Year of the Woman," Bronx Museum of the Arts, New York, January 16–February 20
1975–76 "Photo-Realism, American Painting and Prints," New Zealand traveling exhibition: Barrington Gallery, Auckland; Robert McDougall Art Gallery, Christchurch; Academy of Fine Arts, National Art Gallery, Wellington; Dunedin Public Art Gallery, Dunedin; Govett-Brewster Art Gallery, New Plymouth; Waikato Art Museum, Hamilton
"Super Realism," Baltimore Museum of Art, November 18–January 11
1976 "American Artists '76: A Celebration," Marion Koogler McNay Art Museum, San Antonio, Tex.
"Artists and East Hampton," Guild Hall Art Gallery, East Hampton, N.Y., August 14–October 3
"Art 7 '76," Basel, Switzerland, June
Lowe Art Museum, University of Miami, Coral Gables, Fla.
"Realism (Paintings and Drawings)," Young Hoffman Gallery, Chicago
Roko Gallery, New York
"Troisième foire internationale d'art contemporain," Grand Palais, Paris, October 16–24
1976–77 "The Aubrey Cartwright Foundation Exhibition of Contemporary Religious Art," Cathedral Church of St. John the Divine, New York, November 18–January 2
1976–78 "Aspects of Realism," traveling exhibition sponsored by Rothman's of Pall Mall Canada, Ltd.: The Gallery/Stratford, Ont., June 8–

September 5, 1976; Centennial Museum, Vancouver, B.C., September 16–October 17, 1976; Glenbow-Alberta Institute, Calgary, Alta., October 29–November 28, 1976; Mendel Art Gallery, Saskatoon, Sask., December 10, 1976–January 9, 1977; Winnipeg Art Gallery, Man., January 20–February 20, 1977; Edmonton Art Gallery, Alta., March 1–April 1, 1977; Art Gallery, Memorial University of Newfoundland, St. John's, April 14–May 14, 1977; Confederation Art Gallery and Museum, Charlottetown, P.E.I., May 26–June 26, 1977; Musée d'Art Contemporain, Montreal, Que., July 7–August 7, 1977; Dalhousie University Museum and Gallery, Halifax, N.S., August 18–September 18, 1977; Windsor Art Gallery, Ont., September 29–October 23, 1977; London Public Library and Art Museum and McIntosh Memorial Art Gallery, University of Western Ontario, London, Ont., November 3–27, 1977; Art Gallery of Hamilton, Ont., December 8, 1977–January 8, 1978

1977 "Alumni Exhibition," Houghton Gallery, Cooper Union for the Advancement of Science and Art, New York
"Breaking the Picture Plane," Tomasulo Gallery, Union College, Cranford, N.J.
"The Chosen Object: European and American Still Life," Joslyn Art Museum, Omaha, Nebr., April 23–June 5
"New in the '70s," University Art Museum, Archer M. Huntington Gallery, University of Texas at Austin, August 21–September 25
"New Realism," Jacksonville Art Museum, Fla.
"Photo-Realists," Shore Gallery, Boston
Rice University, Houston
"Washington International Art Fair," Washington, D.C.
Woman's Caucus for Art, New York
"Works on Paper II," Louis K. Meisel Gallery, New York

1977–78 "Illusion and Reality," Australian traveling exhibition: Australian National Gallery, Canberra; Western Australian Art Gallery, Perth; Queensland Art Gallery, Brisbane; Art Gallery of New South Wales, Sydney; Art Gallery of South Australia, Adelaide; National Gallery of Victoria, Melbourne; Tasmanian Museum and Art Gallery, Hobart
"June Blum, Audrey Flack, Alice Neel: Three Contemporary American Women Realists," Miami-Dade Community College, South Campus Art Gallery, Miami, Fla., December 5–6, 1977, January 4–19, 1978
Tulane University, New Orleans

1978 "Art About Art," traveling exhibition: Whitney Museum of American Art, New York; North Carolina Museum of Art, Raleigh; Frederick S. Wight Art Gallery, University of California, Los Angeles; Portland Art Museum, Ore.
"Artists Look at Art," Helen Foresman Spencer Museum of Art, University of Kansas, Lawrence, January 15–March 12
"Aspects of Realism," Guild Hall Art Gallery, East Hampton, N.Y., July 22–August 13
Brookdale Community College, N.J.
The Center of Jewish Community, Stamford, Conn.
"Drawing the Line," Montclair Art Museum, Montclair, N.J., January 22–March 19
Monmouth Museum, Lincroft, N.J.
"Perspective '78: Works by Women," Freedman Art Gallery, Albright College, Reading, Pa., October 8–November 15
"Photo-Realism and Abstract Illusionism," The Arts and Crafts Center of Pittsburgh, Pa.
"Photo-Realist Printmaking," Louis K. Meisel Gallery, New York
Tolarno Galleries, Melbourne, Australia
"Washington International Art Fair," Washington, D.C.
Woman's Interart Center, New York

1978–80 "American Painting of the 70s," Albright-Knox Art Gallery, Buffalo, December 8, 1978–January 14, 1979; Newport Harbor Art Museum, Balboa, Calif., February 3–March 18, 1979; Oakland Museum, Calif., April 10–May 20, 1979; Cincinnati Art Museum, July 6–August 26, 1979; Art Museum of South Texas, Corpus Christi, September 9–October 21, 1979; Krannert Art Museum, University of Illinois, Champaign-Urbana, November 11, 1979–January 2, 1980

1979 Country Art Gallery, Locust Valley, N.Y.
Jewish Community Center of Washington, Rockville, Md.
"Narrative Realism," The Art Association of Newport, R.I., August 18–September 16
"The New American Still Life," Westmoreland County Museum of Art, Greensburg, Pa., June 3–July 15
"The Opposite Sex: A Realistic Viewpoint," University of Missouri Art Gallery, Kansas City
"Photo-Realism: Some Points of View," Jorgensen Gallery, University of Connecticut, Storrs, March 19–April 10
"Realist Space," C. W. Post Art Gallery, Long Island University, Brookville, N.Y., October 19–December 14
"Selections of Photo-Realist Paintings from N.Y.C. Galleries," Southern Alleghenies Museum of Art, St. Francis College, Loretto, Pa., May 12–July 8
Vision Gallery, Boston
Washington International Art Fair, Washington, D.C., May 2–7
"Women Artists of Eastern Long Island," Guild Hall, East Hampton, N.Y.

1979–80 "Genesis of a Gallery, Part 2," Australian National Gallery, Canberra, to travel throughout Australia
The Vice President's House, Washington, D.C.

1980 "Directions in Realism," Danforth Museum, Framingham, Mass., May 17–August 24
Great Lake College Association, New York
Hartford Jewish Community Center, West Hartford, Conn.
"The Language of Symbols," Landmark Gallery, New York, March 29–April 17
"The Morton G. Neumann Family Collection," National Gallery of Art, Washington, D.C., August 31–December 31
National Academy of Art, New York
New York Art Fair, New York
"Photo Realism," Kauffman Galleries, Houston
"69th Annual Exhibition," Randolph-Macon Woman's College, Lynchburg, Va.
"Still Life: A Collection of Contemporary Paintings," Kent State University, Kent, Ohio
"20th Century Self Portrait Show," Harold Reed Gallery, New York
University of Cincinnati

1980–82 "Art in Our Time," HHK Foundation for Contemporary Art, Inc.: Milwaukee Art Museum, Wis.; Contemporary Arts Center, Cincinnati; Columbus Museum of Art, Ohio; Virginia Museum of Fine Arts, Richmond, Va.; Krannert Art Museum, University of Illinois, Champaign; High Museum of Art, Atlanta; University of Iowa Museum of Art, Iowa City; Brooks Memorial Art Gallery, Memphis, Tenn.; University Art Museum, University of Texas, Austin

1981 Art and Culture Center of Hollywood, Hollywood, Fla.
"Changes 1881/1901," Marquette University, Marquette, Wis.
"Distinguished Graduates," Yale University, New Haven, Conn.
"Heresies Benefit Exhibition," The Grey Art Gallery, New York
"The Image in American Painting and Sculpture—1950–1980," Akron Art Museum, Ohio, September 12–November 8
"Images of Labor," District 1199 Traveling Exhibition
"Insights," The New Gallery of Contemporary Art, Cleveland, Ohio
"Seven Photorealists from New York Collections," Solomon R. Guggenheim Museum, New York, October 6–November 8
Shepherd College, Shepherdstown, W.V., March 28–April 10
"Toyama Now, 1981," Museum of Modern Art, Tokyo, July 5–September 23
"Women and Art," Suzanne Brown Gallery, Scottsdale, Ariz., January 21–February 4

1981–82 "Real, Really Real, Superreal," traveling exhibition: San Antonio Museum of Art, Tex.; Indianapolis Museum of Art; Tucson Museum of Art, Ariz.; Museum of Art, Carnegie Institute, Pittsburgh, Pa.

1981–83 "Contemporary American Realism Since 1960," traveling exhibition: Pennsylvania Academy of the Fine Arts, Philadelphia, September 18–December 13, 1981; Virginia Museum of Fine Arts, Richmond, Va., February 1–March 28, 1982; Oakland Museum, Oakland, Calif., May 6–July 25, 1982; *USICA Sponsored Tour:* Gulbenkian Foundation, Lisbon, September 10–October 24, 1982; Salas de Exposiciones, Madrid, November 17, 1982–January 8, 1983; Germanishes National Museum, Nuremberg, February 11–April 10, 1983

1981–82 "Joseph Albers: His Art and His Influence," The Montclair Art Museum, Montclair, N.J., November 15, 1981–January 17, 1982

1981–83 "American Super Realism: From the Morton G. Neumann Family Collection," Kalamazoo Institute of Arts, Kalamazoo, Mich., September 1–November 1, 1981; The Art Center, Inc., South Bend, Ind., November 22, 1981–January 3, 1982; Springfield Art Museum, Springfield, Mo., January 16–February 28, 1982; Dartmouth College Museum and Galleries, Hanover, N.H., March 19–May 2, 1982; De Cordova and Dana Museum, Lincoln, Mass., May 9–June 20, 1982; Des Moines Art Center, Iowa, July 6–August 15, 1982; Terra Museum of American Art, Chicago, November 4, 1982–December 7, 1983
"Deja Vu: Masterpieces Updated," Western Association of Art Museums traveling exhibition: El Paso Museum of Art, Tex., February 1–March 1, 1981; Cheney Cowles Memorial Museum, Spokane, Wash., April 15–May 15, 1981; Arapaho Community College, Littleton, Colo., July 8–August 14, 1981; Roanoke Fine Arts Center, Va., October 1–30, 1981; Colorado State University, Fort Collins, November 20–December 18, 1981; Dayton Art Institute, Ohio, February 13–March 21, 1982; Pacific Union College Art Gallery, Angwin, Calif., April 20–May 20, 1982; Art Center, Inc., South Bend, Ind., August 15–September 12, 1982; Beaumont Art Museum, Beaumont, Tex., October 1–30, 1982; University of Hawaii, Honolulu, November 15–December 15, 1982; Santa Fe Community College Art Gallery, N.M., January 10–February 15, 1983; Bass Museum, Miami Beach, Fla., March 1–29, 1983; The Fine Arts Center, Nashville, Tenn., April 19–June 13, 1983

1982 "The Artist and the Airbrush," San Jose State University, Calif., February 1–March 12
Contemporary Art Center, New Orleans, October 9–November 7
"Contemporary Realism," a three-gallery exhibition, January–February: "Still Life," The Gallery at Hastings-on-Hudson, N.Y.; "Landscape," The Museum Gallery, White Plains, N.Y.; "The Figure," The Castle Gallery, New Rochelle, N.Y.
"Cranbrook U.S.A., 15 Artists' Painting and Sculpture" (Alumni Show), Cranbrook Academy of Art Museum, Bloomfield Hills, Mich., January 31–March 28
"Louis K. Meisel Gallery in Brussels," Galerie Isy Brachot, Paris, January 13–March 6
"Photographs by the Photorealists," Fort Wayne Museum of Art, Ind., January 8–31; Cleveland Museum of Art, Ohio, February 11–28; Ball State Museum, Muncie, Ind., March 7–31
"Photo-Realisme Dix Ans Après," Galerie Isy Brachot, Brussels, April 22–May 22
"Realism 1982," The Munson-Williams-Proctor Institute, Utica, N.Y., February 15–April 15
"Women's Art: Miles Apart," Valencia Community College, Orlando, Fla.; Aaron Berman Gallery, New York, March 12–April 20

1982–83 "25: Namuth and Twenty-four Artists," Phoenix II Gallery, Washington, D.C., December 7, 1982–January 29, 1983

1983 "The American Photorealists," Fischer Fine Art, London, May 6–June 3
"Faces Since the Fifties," Center Gallery, Bucknell University, University Center Gallery, Lewisburg, Pa., March 5–April 17
"P.C.A. Invites: An Exhibition of Work by Artists in the Historical Archives of the Women's Inter-Art Center in N.Y.C.," Philadelphia College of Art, February 11–March 19
"Printed by Women—A National Exhibition of Photographs and Prints," The Port of History Museum at Penn's Landing, Philadelphia, February 17–March 27
"10th Anniversary Exhibition," Louis K. Meisel Gallery, New York, October 8–29

1983–84 "American Still Life: 1945–1983," traveling exhibition: Contemporary Arts Museum, Houston, September 17–November 20, 1983; Albright-Knox Art Gallery, Buffalo, N.Y., December 10, 1983–January 25, 1984; Columbus Museum of Art, Ohio, April 7–May 20, 1984; Neuberger Museum, Purchase, N.Y., June 7–September 15, 1984; Portland Art Museum, Oreg., October 9–December 9, 1984
Museum of Fine Arts, Boston, November 10, 1983–January 29, 1984
"Update: Cranbrook," Robert Kidd Associated Galleries, New York, December 10, 1983–January 28, 1984

1983–85 "Assignment: Aviation—The Stuart M. Speiser Photo-Realist Collection," Smithsonian Institution Traveling Exhibition: Anchorage Historical & Fine Arts Museum, January 1–31, 1983; Denver Museum of Natural History, Colo., July 23–September 4, 1983; Maryland Science Center, Baltimore, September 24–November 6, 1983; Columbus Museum of Arts & Sciences, Ga., November 26, 1983–January 8, 1984; Neville Public Museum, Greenbay, Wis., January 28–March 11, 1984; The Dane G. Hansen Memorial Museum, Logan, Kans., March 31–May 13, 1984; Longview Museum & Art Center, Tex., June 2–July 15, 1984; Colorado Springs Fine Arts Center, August 4–September 16, 1984; Springfield Art Museum, Mo., October 6–November 18, 1984; Fine Arts Center at Cheekwood, Nashville, Tenn., December 8, 1984–March 24, 1985; Historical & Creative Arts Center, Lufkin, Tex., April 13–May 26, 1985; Amarillo Art Center, Tex., June 15–July 28, 1985; Santa Fe Community College Art Gallery, Gainesville, Fla., October 19–December 1, 1985

1984 "American Women Artists Part I: 20th Century Pioneers," Sidney Janis Gallery, New York, January 12–February 4
Columbus Museum of Art, Ohio, April 7–May 20
"Design in America: Cranbrook Alumni," Herman Miller Gallery, New York, April 17–June 17
"A Feast for the Eyes," Museum of Modern Art for: Dancer, Fitzgerald, & Sample, Inc., Chrysler Building, New York, March 30–July 30
"Flower as Image," Wave Hill, Bronx, N.Y., February 8–May 7
Hewlett Art Gallery, Carnegie-Mellon University, Schenley Park, Pa., February 4–March 2
Judith Posner & Associates, Milwaukee, July 7–August 15
"Major Contemporary Women Artists: In Celebration of Simone de Beauvoir," Suzanne Gruss Gallery, Philadelphia, March 27–April 28
"Photorealism," Walter Moos Gallery, Toronto, September 15–October 15
Tomasulo Gallery, Union College, N.J., November 2–24
University of Bridgeport, Bridgeport, Conn., February 25–April 1

1984–85 "New Realism," Robert Kidd Gallery, Birmingham, Mich., December 15, 1984–January 19, 1985
"Nine Realist Painters Revisited: 1963–1984," Robert Schoelkopf Gallery, New York, December 8, 1984–January 2, 1985

1985 "Academy—Institute Purchase Exhibition," American Academy & Institute of Arts and Letters, New York, November 18–December 15
"American Realism: The Precise Image," traveling exhibition: Isetan Museum of Art, Tokyo, June 25–August 19; The Daimura Museum, Osaka, Japan, October 9–28; Yokahama Takashimaya, Yokohama, Japan, November 7–12
"The Drawing Center Show," Elaine Benson Gallery, Inc., Bridgehampton, N.Y., June 15–July 2
"49th Annual National Mid-Year Show," Butler Institute of American Art, Youngstown, Ohio, June 30–August 25
"9th Annual Small Works Show," 80 Washington Square Galleries, New York University, February 2–March 1

1985–86 "American Art: American Women," Stamford Museum & Nature Center, Stamford, Conn., December 15, 1985–February 16, 1986
Beaux Arts Collectors Gallery, Columbus Museum of Art, Ohio, January 24, 1985–January 1986
"A Decade of American Realism: 1975–1985," Wichita Art Museum, Kans., December 7, 1985–January 5, 1986

1985–87 "American Realism—20th-Century Drawings and Watercolors from the Glenn C. Janss Collection," San Francisco Museum of Modern Art, November 7, 1985–January 12, 1986; DeCordova & Dana Museum & Park, Lincoln, Mass., February 13–March 6, 1986; Archer M. Huntington Art Gallery, University of Texas, Austin, July 31–September 21, 1986; Mary & Leigh Block Gallery, Northwestern University, Evanston, Ill., October 23–December 14, 1986; Williams College Museum of Art, Williamstown, Mass., January 15–March 8, 1987; Akron Art Museum, Ohio, April 9–May 31, 1987; Madison Art Center, Madison, Wis., July 26–September 20, 1987

1986 "An American Renaissance: Painting & Sculpture Since 1940," Museum of Art, Fort Lauderdale, Fla., January 12–April 1
"The Figure in 20th Century American Art—Selections From The Metropolitan Museum of Art," Colorado Springs Fine Arts Center, February 9
"Sacred Images in Secular Art," Whitney Museum of American Art, New York, May 1–July 13
"Signs of the Times," traveling exhibition sponsored by Artrain, Detroit, February 1–December 20
Vered Gallery, East Hampton, N.Y., June–July

1987 "American Art Today: The Portrait," The Art Museum, Florida International University, Miami, May 8–June 3
"Contemporary Editions: Prints/Sculpture," Elaine Benson Gallery, Bridgehampton, N.Y., August 15–September 3
"Mainstream America: The Phil Desind Collection," The Butler Institute of American Art, Youngstown, Ohio, March 1–April 5
"New Works: Drawings," Danforth Museum of Art, Framingham, Mass., January 18–March 1
"Realism: The New Generation," R.H. Love Modern, Chicago, June 5–July 13
Vered Gallery, East Hampton, N.Y., August 15–September 3

1987–88 "Art and the Law," traveling exhibition sponsored by West Publishing Co., Saint Paul, Minn.: Plaza Gallery, Bank of America World Headquarters, San Francisco, August 3–14, 1987; Albrecht Art Museum, St. Joseph, Mo., August 25–September 27, 1987; Muscarelle Art Museum, College of William & Mary, Williamsburg, Va., November 21, 1987–January 17, 1988; Minnesota Museum of Art, St. Paul, February 5–April 3, 1988
"The Artist's Mother: Portraits and Homages," Heckscher Museum, Huntington, N.Y., November 14, 1987–January 3, 1988; National Portrait Gallery, Smithsonian Institution, Washington, D.C., March 25–June 5, 1988
"Contemporary Still Life," Vault Gallery, The Boston Company, Boston, December 1987–February 1988

1988 "Classical Myth and Imagery in Contemporary Art," The Queens Museum, Flushing, N.Y., April 15–June 12
"Drawing on the East End: 1940–1988," Parrish Art Museum, Southampton, N.Y.
"Just Like a Woman," Greenville County Museum of Art, Greenville, S.C., March 15–May 15
"Selections from the Ellen and Jerome Westheimer Collection," Oklahoma Art Center, Oklahoma City, April 15–July 3
"This Was Pratt: Former Faculty Centennial Exhibition," Pratt Manhattan Gallery, New York, March 12–April 16; Schafler Gallery, Pratt Institute, Brooklyn, N.Y., June 13–July 8
"20th Anniversary (15 in SoHo)—Artists & Movements from Our First Two Decades," Louis K. Meisel Gallery, New York, November 5–26

1989 "Amerikansk Fotorealism," Art Now Gallery, Gothenburg, Sweden, October 20–November 25
"Color in Art: American Expressions from the Mid-Twentieth Century to the Present," Samuel P. Harn Museum of Art, University of Florida, Gainesville, September 22–December 2
"Images of Death in Contemporary Art," Haggerty Museum of Art, Marquette University, Milwaukee, March 22–June 3
"Making Their Mark: Women Artists Today," traveling exhibition: Cincinnati Art Museum, February 2–April 2; New Orleans Museum of Art, May 5–June 18; Denver Art Museum, July 15–September 10; Pennsylvania Academy of the Fine Arts, Philadelphia, October 20–December 31
"Objects Observed—Contemporary Still Life," Gallery Henoch, New York, February 13–March 10
"The 79th Annual Exhibition," Maier Museum of Art, Randolph-Macon Woman's College, Lynchburg, Va., April 1–May 20

1991 "In Sharp Focus: Super Realism," Nassau County Museum of Art, Roslyn, N.Y., April 15–July 7
"Motion as Metaphor: The Automobile in Art," Virginia Beach Center for the Arts, Virginia Beach, Va., April 13–June 16
Vered Gallery, East Hampton, N.Y., July

PUBLIC COLLECTIONS

Akron Art Museum, Ohio
Albright-Knox Art Gallery, Buffalo, New York
Allen Memorial Art Museum, Oberlin College, Ohio
Australian National Gallery, Canberra
Butler Institute of American Art, Buffalo, New York
Capricorn Gallery, Baltimore
Dallas Museum of Fine Arts
Greater Lafayette Museum of Art, Indiana
Solomon R. Guggenheim Museum, New York
Samuel P. Harn Museum of Art, University of Florida, Gainesville
HHK Foundation for Contemporary Art, Inc., New York
Louis K. Meisel Gallery, New York
Metropolitan Museum of Art, New York
Miami University Art Museum, Oxford, Ohio
Mint Museum of Art, Charlotte, North Carolina
Museum of Modern Art, New York
National Gallery of Victoria, Melbourne, Australia
National Museum of American Art, Washington, D.C.
National Museum of Women in the Arts, Washington, D.C.
New York University Collections, New York
Riverside Museum, New York
Rose Art Museum, Brandeis University, Waltham, Massachusetts
Saint Louis Art Museum
San Francisco Museum of Fine Art
Stuart M. Speiser Collection, Smithsonian Institution, Washington, D.C.
University of Arizona, Tucson
University of Texas at Austin
Wadsworth Atheneum, Hartford, Connecticut
Walker Art Center, Minneapolis
Whitney Museum of American Art, New York

SELECTED BIBLIOGRAPHY

ARTICLES

1959 Mellow, James R. "Audrey Flack." *Arts Magazine* (February 1959).
Sandler, Irving. "New Names This Month." *Art News* (February 1959).
1963 Raynor, Vivien. "Audrey Flack." *Arts Magazine* (March 1963).
1964 Adler, Robert. "West Side Artists: A New Awareness." *West Side News*, 1 October 1964, p. 3.
1966 "Art Tour: The Galleries—A Critical Choice." *New York Herald Tribune*, 19 March 1966.
1969 Alloway, Lawrence. "Art." *The Nation*, 29 December 1969, pp. 741–42.
Baumgold, Julie, ed. "Best Bets." *New York Magazine*, 8 December 1969.
Gaynor, Frank. "Photographic Exhibit Depicts Today's U.S." *Newark-Sunday-News*, 14 December 1969, Sec. 6, p. E18.
Perreault, John. "Get the Picture?" *The Village Voice*, 18 December 1969.
1969–70 Nemser, Cindy. "Paintings from the Photograph." *Arts Magazine* (December–January 1969–70).
1970 Alloway, Lawrence. "In the Museums, Paintings from the Photo." *Arts*, 1 December 1970.
Coleman, A. D. "Latent Image." *The Village Voice*, 1 January 1970.
Deschin, Jacob. "Photo Into Painting." *The New York Times*, 4 January 1970.
Genauer, Emily. "On the Arts." *Newsday*, 21 February 1970.
Lichtblau, Charlotte. "Painter's Use of Photographs Explored." *The Philadelphia Enquirer*, 1 February 1970.
Lord, Barry. "The 11 O'Clock News in Color." *Arts/Canada* (June 1970): 4, 21.
The New York Times, Sec. II, 8 November 1970, pp. 6, 25.
Ratcliff, Carter. "22 Realists Exhibit at the Whitney." *Art International* (April 1970): 105.
Stevens, Carol. "Message Into Medium: Photography as an Artist's Tool." *Print*, Vol. XXIV, No. III, 6 May 1970, pp. 54–59.
Stevens, Elizabeth. "The Camera's Eye on Canvas." *The Wall Street Journal*, 6 January 1970.
1971–72 "Acquisitions by the Museum 1971–72." *The Whitney Review*, 1971–72.
Whitworth, Sarah. "Journeys in Art: Audrey Flack: 3 Views." *The Ladder* (December–January 1971–72): 32–35, cover.
1972 Benedict, Michael. "Audrey Flack." *Art News* (April 1972).
Borsick, Helen. "Realism to the Fore." *Cleveland Plain Dealer*, 8 October 1972.
Canaday, John. "Audrey Flack." *The New York Times*, 4 March 1972.
Henry, Gerrit. "The Real Thing." *Art International* (Summer 1972): 87–91.
Karp, Ivan. "Rent Is the Only Reality, or the Hotel Instead of the Hymn." *Arts Magazine* (December 1972): 47–51.
Kirkwood, Marie. "Art Institute's Exhibit Represents the Revolt Against Abstraction." *Sun Press* (Ohio), 12 October 1972.
Naimer, Lucille. "The Whitney Annual." *Arts Magazine* (November 1972): 54.
Nemser, Cindy. "New Realism." *Arts Magazine* (November 1972): 85.
———. "Close-Up Vision: Representational Art." *Arts Magazine* (May 1972): 44–48
Pozzi, Lucio. "Super Realisti U.S.A." *Bolaffiarte* 18 (March 1972): 54–63.
Seitz, William C. "The Real and the Artificial: Painting of the New Environment." *Art in America* (November–December 1972): 64–72.
Wasmuth, Ernest. "La revolte des réalistes." *Connaissance des Arts* (June 1972): 118–23.
Wooten, Dick. "Something New? Real Pictures?" *The Cleveland Press*, 17 October 1972, p. 9.
1973 Allen, Barbara. "In and Around." *Interview Magazine* (November 1973): 36.
"Amiens Notre Dame." *Kunstforum International*, 4 March 1973, p. 158.
Art Now Gallery Guide (September 1973): 1–3.
Azara, Nancy. "Artists in Their Own Image." *Ms. Magazine* (January 1973): 57.
Beardsall, Judy. "Stuart M. Speiser Photorealist Collection." *Art Gallery Magazine* 17, no. 1 (October 1973): 5, 29–34.
Bell, Jane. "Stuart M. Speiser Collection." *Arts Magazine* (December 1973): 57.
Drexler, Rosalyn. "Audrey Flack." *The New York Times* (January 1973).
"Goings on About Town." *The New Yorker*, 1 October 1973.
Gold, Barbara. "Sisterhood in New York." *The Baltimore Sun*, 4 February 1973.
Guerico, Antonio del. "Iperrealismo tra 'pop' e informale." *Rinascita* 8, 23 February 1973, p. 34.
Henry, Gerrit. "A Realist Twin Bill." *Art News* (January 1973): 26–28.
"L'Hyperréalisme américain." *Le Monde de Grandes Musiques*, No. 2 (March/April 1973): 4, 56–57.
Lubell, Ellen. "Women Choose Women." *Arts Magazine* (March/April 1973).
Mizue (Tokyo) 8, no. 821, 1973.
"Neue Sachlichkeit-Neuer Realismus." *Kunstforum International*, 4 March 1973, p. 114–19.
Perreault, John. "Airplane Art in a Head Wind." *The Village Voice*, 4 October 1973, p. 24.
———. "Winning a Place in the Show." *The Village Voice*, 25 January 1973.
"Realism Now." *Patent Trader*, 26 May 1973, p. 7A.
"Reviews and Previews." *Art News* (March 1973).
Sheridan, Lee. "'Women-Women' Contains Spirit." *Springfield Daily News*, 9 February 1973, p. 14.
"Shop Around." *The Evening Standard*, 30 March 1973.
1974 Coleman, A. D. "From Today Painting Is Dead." *Camera 35* (July 1974): 34, 36–37, 78.
"Collection of Aviation Paintings at Gallery." *Andover Townsman* (Mass.), 28 February 1974.
Forman, Nessa. "Goodbye to the Femme Fatale." *Art News* (Summer 1974): 65–66.
Frackman, Noel. "Audrey Flack." *Arts Magazine* (May 1974): 70.
Frank, Peter. "Audrey Flack." *The SoHo Weekly News*, 11 April 1974.
"Gallery Notes." *Memorial Art Gallery of the University of Rochester Bulletin* 39, no. 5 (January 1974).
Goldenthal, Jolene. "Look at Art: Photo-Real Show at Atheneum." *The Hartford Courant*, 14 April 1974, p. 12F.
Goldenthal, June. "Look at Art: Audrey Flack, Photorealist." *The Hartford Courant*, 9 May 1974.
Henry, Gerrit. "Reviews and Previews." *Art News* (May 1974): 91–92.
Hill, Richard. "The Technologies of Vision." *Art Magazine* (Toronto) 6, no. 19 (Fall 1974): 10.
Hughes, Robert. "An Omnivorous and Literal Dependence." *Arts Magazine* (June 1974): 25–29.
Kozloff, Max. "Audrey Flack." *Artforum* (June 1974): 65.
"Letter to the Editor." *The SoHo Weekly News*, 18 April 1974.
Levin, Kim. "Audrey Flack at Meisel." *Art in America* (May/June 1974): 106.
Nemser, Cindy. "Conversations with Audrey Flack." *Arts Magazine* (February 1974): 34–38.
———. "Letter to Audrey Flack Re: Kozloff on Audrey Flack." *The Feminist Art Journal* 3, no. 3 (Fall 1974).
"New York Eleven." *North Shore Commentary*, 14 February 1974.
Perreault, John. "Glints of Glass, A Whiff of Poetry." *The Village Voice*, 4 April 1974.
———. "Reading a Monumental Still Life." *The Village Voice*, 2 May 1974, p. 45.
Picard, Lil. "In . . . Out . . und in Again." *Kunstforum International*, 2 January 1974, pp. 215–17.
Progresso Fotografico (December 1974): 61–62.
"Reviews and Previews: Audrey Flack." *Art News* 71, no. 2 (April 1974).
Saradoff, Lucia. "Outraged Women Artists. . . ." *The SoHo Weekly News*, 16 January 1974, pp. 2, 4, 5, 16.
School of Visual Arts Catalog (Spring 1974): cover.
Stubbs, Ann. "Audrey Flack." *The SoHo Weekly News*, 4 April 1974.
Vlack, Carol. "Photo Realist Audrey Flack Displays Works at MAG." *University of Rochester Campus Times*, 18 January 1974, p. 9.
Walsh, Sally. "Paintings That Look Like Photos." *Rochester Democrat and Chronicle*, 17 January 1974.
Zabel, Joe. "Realistic Works Predominate in 1974 Mid-Year." *The Jambar* (Youngstown State University, Ohio), 11 July 1974, p. 7.
1974–75 Spear, Richard. "Acquisitions 1973–1974." *Allen Memorial Art Museum Bulletin* (Oberlin College, Ohio) 23 (1974–75): 17.
1975 "Audrey Flack Named Visiting Professor of Art." *Bridgeport Sunday Post*, 9 February 1975.
Bruner, Louise. "Brash Paintings Stimulate Thinking Rather Than Passive Thoughts." *The Blade* (Toledo, Ohio), 12 January 1975, p. 4.
Cowart, Jack. "Acquisitions: Three Contemporary American Paintings." *St. Louis Art Museum Bulletin* (September–October 1975): 88–95.
DeMarino, Marg. "Art Makes Life More Liveable." *New Haven Register*, 21 March 1975.
———. "Photo-Real Paintings Newest Art Style." *The Hartford Times*, 21 March 1975, p. 17.
Dubrow, Marsha. "Female Assertiveness: How a Pussycat Can Learn to Be a Panther." *New York Magazine*, 28 July 1975, p. 42.
"Growing Up." *Crawdaddy* (June 1975): 42–43.
Loercher, Diane. "Soho, the New World." *Christian Science Monitor*, 15 October 1975, p. 30.
McNamara, T. J. "Photo-Realist Exhibition Makes Impact." *New Zealand Herald* (Auckland), 23 July 1975.
"Major Art Event: Painting Sold to MOMA." *The New Haven Register*, 11 April 1975.
Mikotajuk, Andrea. "American Realists at Louis K. Meisel Gallery." *Arts Magazine*, 23 January 1975, pp. 19–20.
Nemser, Cindy. "Audrey Flack, Photorealist Rebel." *The Feminist Art Journal* 4, no. 3 (Fall 1975): 5–12.
Normile, James. "Contemporary Portraiture." *Architectural Digest* (July–August 1975).

Perreault, John. "Putting His Finger in Butter," *The Soho Weekly News*, 16 October 1975.
Perry, Jean. "They're Displayed for Art's Sake," *The Daily News*, 18 January 1975, p. 15.
"Photographic Realism." *Art-Rite* 9 (Spring 1975): 15.
"Photo-Realism Exhibit is Opening at Paine Sunday." *Oshkosh Daily Northwestern*, 17 April 1975.
"Photo-Realism Flies High at Paine," *The Milwaukee Journal* (May 1975).
"Photo-Realists at Paine." *View Magazine*, 27 April 1975.
Richard, Paul. "Whatever You Call It, Super-Realism Comes on with a Flash." *The Washington Post*, 25 November 1975, p. B1.
Toledo Museum of Art Bulletin (January 1975).

1975–76 Lanser, Fay. "Book Review-Art Talk: Conversations with 12 Women Artists." *Feminist Art Journal* (Winter 1975–76): 40.
"1975–76 Cultural Programs: Photo-Realist Audrey Flack To Appear At C.S.U." *Colorado State University Bulletin* (1975–76) 22.
Weatherspoon Gallery Association Bulletin (University of North Carolina, Greensboro), (1975–76).
"The World Food Population Crisis." *Cross Talk* 4, part 1 (December–February 1975–76): 14.

1976 Alloway, Lawrence. "Alex Katz's Development." *Artforum* (January 1976): 45.
———. "Art." *The Nation*, 1 May 1976, pp. 539, 541.
———. "Audrey Flack." *The Nation* (April 1976).
———. "Close To Home." *The Nation*, 30 October 1976, p. 446.
"At Meisel Gallery." *The East Hampton Star*, 29 April 1976, Sec. 11, p. 7.
Bourdon, David. "Photography Comes to Still Life." *The Village Voice*, 26 April 1976, p. 128.
———. "Why Photographers Like Artists." *The Village Voice*, 23 February 1976, p. 103.
The Bulletin Board (San Antonio) 1, no. 1 (May 1976).
Chase, Linda. "Photo-Realism: Post Modernist Illusionism." *Art International* 10, no. 3–4 (March–April 1976): 14–27.
"Female Art Show." *San Antonio Express*, 5 February 1976, p. 9F.
Forgey, Benjamin. "The New Realism, Paintings Worth 1,000 Words." *The Washington Star*, 30 November 1976, p. G24.
Glasser, Penelope. "Aspects of Realism at Stratford." *Art Magazine* (Toronto) 7, no. 28 (Summer 1976): 22–29.
Grove, Nancy. "Audrey Flack." *Arts Magazine* (June 1976): 24.
Henry, Gerrit. "Audrey Flack." *Art News* (Summer 1976): 170.
Hoelterhoff, Manuela. "Strawberry Tarts Three Feet High." *The Wall Street Journal*, 21 April 1976.
Jones, Nancy Scott. "Celebrating Women in Art." *San Antonio Express News*, 23 May 1976, p. 3E.
Kramer, Hilton. "The Current Backlash in the Arts." *The New York Times*, 23 May 1976.
Lanser, Fay. "Book Review—Art Talk: Conversations with 12 Women Artists." *The Feminist Art Journal* (Winter 1976): 40.
Lion Art Magazine (Taipei), (January 1976): 47.
"NcNay Planning Major Exhibition." *Northside Recorder* (Texas), 5 February 1976, p. 5NE.
Moorman, Adelaide. "Women's Show." *Houston Breakthrough* 1, no. 6 (June/July 1976): 13.
Nemser, Cindy. "More on the Arts Backlash." *The New York Times*, 30 May 1976.
"News from the Southwest." *Women's Caucus for Art Newsletter* (April 1976): 8.
Pension World (July 1976): cover.
Perreault, John. "Getting Flack." *The Soho Weekly News*, 22 April 1976, p. 19.
———. "Photo-Shock." *The Soho Weekly News*, 22 January 1976, p. 16.
Perry, Art. "So Much For Reality." *Province*, 30 September 1976.
"Photography: Art & Process." *Visual Dialog* 1, no. 4 (June–August 1976): 18.
"Planning Major Art Show." *San Antonio Light*, 5 February 1976, p. 5D.
Rappaport, Jody. "Audrey Flack Art in Soho." *State University of New York at Stonybrook Journal* (June 1976).
San Antonio Express, 21 May 1976, p. 14A
Shirey, David. "A Mark of Independence." *The New York Times*, 25 July 1976, p. 16.
———. "It Was a Very Good Hundred Years." *The New York Times*, 19 September 1976, p. 26.
Sieberling, Dorothy. "Real Big: An Escalation of Still Lifes." *New York Magazine*, 26 April 1976, pp. 42–44
Siegel, Jeanne. "Audrey Flack's Objects." *Arts Magazine* (June 1976): 103–5.
Tucker, William G. "Louis K. Meisel: Audrey Flack." *Artists Review Art* 1, no. 4 (April 1976).
———. "Sugar on the Optic Nerve." *The Villager*, 15 April 1976, p. 11.
"Weekly Guide to Culture: Happenings in San Antonio." *San Antonio Express News*, 23 May 1976.
Womanschool 2, no. 2 (Fall 1976): 13.

1976–77 Greenwood, Mark. "Toward a Definition of Realism: Reflections on The Rothman's Exhibition." *Arts/Canada* 24, no. 210–11 (December–January 1976–77): 6–23.

1977 Battcock, Gregory. "Dinner for Eighty." *The Soho Weekly News*, 10 November 1977.
Borlase, Nancy. "In Selecting a Common Domestic Object." *Sydney Morning Herald*, 30 July 1977.
Carmalt, Susan. "Huntington Displays New Trends." *Daily Texan* (Austin), (August 1977).
"Commencement 1977." *At Cooper Union* 9, no. 2 (Spring 1977).
Edelson, Elihu. "New Realism at Museum Arouses Mixed Feelings." *Jacksonville Journal* (Florida), (February 1977).
———. "New Realism Shows Varying Degrees." *Jacksonville Journal*, 26 February 1977, p. 18.
"For the Record." *The Art Gallery Magazine* (Summer 1977): 80.
Pequod 11, no. 3 (Summer 1977): cover.
Glueck, Grace. "The 20th Century Artists Most Admired by Other Artists." *Art News* 76, no. 9 (November 1977): 84.
Graves, Jack. "The Star Talks to Audrey Flack, Super Realist." *The East Hampton Star*, 4 August 1977, p. 11.
Grishin, Sasha. "An Exciting Exhibition." *The Canberra Times*, 16 February 1977.
"Illusion and Reality." *This Week in Brisbane* (June 1977).
Langer, Gertrude. "Realising Our Limitations in Grasping Reality." *Brisbane Courier Mail*, 28 May 1977.
Lynn, Elwyn. "The New Realism." *Quadrant* (September 1977).
McGrath, Sandra. "I Am Almost a Camera." *The Australian* (Brisbane), 27 July 1977.
McIntyre, Mary. "70's Art Comes to Town." *The Austin American-Statesman*, 28 August 1977, pp. 7, 8.
Makin, Jeffrey. "Realism from the Squad." *The Sun* (Melbourne), 19 October 1977, p. 43.
Morrison, C. L. "Strong Works," *Artforum* (December 1977).
"The Museum of Modern Art." *Art in America*, 10 September 1977, pp. 93–96.
Perreault, John. *The Soho Weekly News* (January 1977).
"Photo-Realism and Related Trends." *The New York Times*, 4 February 1977.
"Prints Exhibition for D'port." *Examiner* (New Zealand), 7 September 1977.
Russell, John. "Photo-Realism and Related Trends." *The New York Times*, 4 February 1977, p. 16C.
"Some Artists' Ideas on Eating Well." *The New York Times*, 21 December 1977, p. C5.
"Spotlight." *America Illustrated* (U.S. Information Agency, Washington, D.C.), no. 247 (1977): 56.
Thomas, Daniel. "The Way We See Now." *The Bulletin*, 10 September 1977.
Tufts, Eleanor. "The Veristic Eye." *Arts Magazine* (December 1977): 142.

1978 Adams, Laurie. "Intimations of Morality." *Ms. Magazine* (May 1978): 24.
Art Now Gallery Guide 8, no. 8 (April 1978): 17.
"Audrey Flack." *Art World*, April 15–May 15, 1978, p. 13.
Bannon, Anthony. "A Slice of American Painting from the 1970's." *Buffalo Evening News* (Buffalo, N.Y.), (November 1978).
Battcock, Gregory. "Thinking Decently: Two Audacious Artists in New York." *New York Arts Journal*, 5 April 1978, pp. 24–26.
Bell, Jane. "Art about Art about Art. . . ." *New York Arts Journal*, no. 11 (September–October 1978): 28.
Bongard, Willie. *Art Aktuell* (Cologne, West Germany), (April 1978).
Devanely, Sally. "Kaleidoscope." *Art Gallery Magazine* (October–November 1978): 25.
Edwards, Ellen. "Eyes Have It in Portrait Show." *The Miami Herald*, 8 January 1978, p. 3L.
Englehart, Nina. "Audrey Flack Portrays Man of the Year." *Women Artists News* 3, no. 8 (February 1978).
Glueck, Grace. "Greater Soho-Spring Guide to Downtown Art World." *The New York Times*, 31 March 1978, p. C12.
———. "Soho in Springtime." *The New York Times*, 31 March 1978, p. C1.
Harnett, Lila. "Beyond Reality." *Cue*, 14 April 1978, p. 21.
———. "Photo-Realist Prints: 1968–1978." *Cue*, 22 December 1978, p. 23.
Harris, Helen. "Art and Antiques: The New Realists." *Town and Country* (October 1978): 242, 244, 246–47.
Jacobson, Carol. "Two Exhibits of Major Interest at Lincroft Sites," *The Daily Register* (Lincroft, N.J.), 1 February 1978.
Jordan, George. "Photo Realism Show at Tulane." *The Times-Picayune* (New Orleans) Sec. 1, 23 February 1978, p. 21.
Kline, Katy. "Painting of 70's Exhibit Has Variety." *Courier Express* (Buffalo, N.Y.), (1978).
Kramer, Hilton. "A Brave Attempt to Encapsulate a Decade." *The New York Times*, 17 December 1978, p. 39.
Lubell, Ellen. "Phototransformations." *The Soho Weekly News*, 28 September 1978, p. 80.
Mackie, Alwynne. "New Realism and the Photographic Look." *American Art Review* (November 1978): 72–79, 132–34.
"Man of the Year." *Time Magazine*, 1 January 1978, cover.
The New Republic Magazine, 24 June 1978, cover.
O'Conor, Mary. "Eight Artists." *The East Hampton Star*, 17 July 1978, p. 14.
Perreault, John. "A Painting That Is Difficult to Forget." *Art News* (April 1978): 150–51.
———. "Audrey Flack: Odds Against the House." *The Soho Weekly News* 5, no. 25, 23–29 March 1978, pp. 19–21, cover.
———. "Photo Realist Principles." *American Art Review* (November 1978): 108–11, 141.
"Photo Journalism and Photo Realism." *Milwaukee Journal*, 10 December 1978.

Raynor, Vivien. "Audrey Flack." *The New York Times*, 14 April 1978, p. C22.
Richard, Paul. "New Smithsonian Art: From 'the Sublime' to Photo Realism." *Washington Post*, 30 November 1978, p. G21.
"Segunda Guerra Mundial." *Artes Visuales*, no. 18 (Summer 1978).
Shirey, David. "Drawings: A Show with More than One Meaning." *The New York Times*, 5 February 1978, p. NJ-19.
———. "More Real Than Real." *The New York Times*, 6 August 1978, p. LI-14.
"Special from Broadway." *The East Hampton Star*, 20 July 1978, p. 13.
"Style Hampton-Style." *East Hampton Summer Sun*, 27 July 1978, p. 11.
Thill, Mary. "Photorealist Flack Visits Brookdale." *The Stall* (Brookdale, N.J.) 17, no. 2, 17 February 1978, p. 5.

1978–79 Goodman, Vera. "Surprise Them with Art." *New Directions for Women* (Westwood, N.J.) 7, no. 4 (Winter 1978–79): 13, 22.
"American Painting in the Seventies." *Bulletin-Krannert Art Museum* (University of Illinois) 5, no. 1 (1979): 2–3, 5.
Glueck, Grace. "Painting: Ludwig Sander's Passion for Color." *The New York Times*, 7 December 1979, p. C20.
Goodman, Vera. "Surprise Them with Art." *New Directions for Women* (Westwood, N.J.) 7, no. 4 (1979): 13, 22.
Houck, Catherine. "Women Artists Today." *Cosmopolitan* (January 1979): 198–99, 220–221, 258, 266.
Lewis, Jo-Ann. "Jewish Women—Their Voices From the Past." *The Washington Post*, 16 December 1979.
Melcher, Victoria Kirsch. "Vigorous Currents in Realism Make up Group Show at UMKC." *Kansas City Star*, 11 March 1979, p. 3E.
Perreault, John. "New Life for the Still Life." *The Soho Weekly News*, 12 April 1979, p. 54.
———. "New Museum? For Real? It Figures." *The Soho Weekly News*, 20 September 1979, p. 43.
Preston, Malcom. "Art Review: Realist Space at C. W. Post." *Newsday*, 12 December 1979.
Sozanski, Edward. "Narratives Boldly Stated Preface Untold Stories." *Providence Sunday Journal*, 19 August 1979, p. H1.
"Statues Don't Hit Back." *The New York Times*, 16 February 1979, p. C23.
Weintraub, Linda. "Perspectives '78: Works by Women." *Arts Exchange* (Philadelphia) 3, no. 1 (January–February 1979): 25.
"What's On In Washington." *Women Artists News* (January 1979): 2.

1980 Bourdon, David. "Made in U.S.A." *Portfolio* (November–December 1980): 45–47.
Bulletin (Krannert Art Museum, University of Illinois), (1980).
Bulletin (Ulrich Museum of Art, Wichita State University, Kans.), (Summer 1980): 4.
MacBean, J. P. "Soho: It Boasts the Finest Collection of Cast Iron Architecture in America." *Horizon* (1980): 57.
McClelland, Elizabeth. "Is the Future Still?" *Dialogue: The Ohio Arts Journal* (July–August 1980): 16.

1981 *Arts Report* (WUSF–FM radio) 8 January 1981.
Blass, Ruth. "The Illusion of Reality." *Art News* (December 1981): 79.
Braun, Ruth. "Arizona Exhibits Photomurals, Women Artists Aid Nursery." *Tempe Daily News*, 21 January 1981, p. 84
Carnegie Magazine (Carnegie Institute, Pittsburgh) 55, no. 8 (October 1981): cover.
Dietrich, Linnea S. "Audrey Flack at U.S.F." *Art Visions Inc.* (1981).
Forgey, Benjamin. "Aviation Art at Home in its Hangar." *The Washington Review*, 21 May 1981.
Kohen, Helen C. "Shutterbug Superrealism: Flack's Photo Images Strike Familiar Chord." *The Miami Herald*, 8 March 1981.
Kotrozo, Donnell C. "Women and Art." *Arts Magazine* (March 1981): 11.
Kuspit, Donald B. "What's Real in Realism?" *Art in America* (1981): 84, 93.
Matthew, Lyn. "Networking Can Work For Women Too." *Scottsdale Progress*, 28 January 1981.
Montini, Ed. "Crisis Nursery Gets Artful Support." *Arizona Republic*, 28 January 1981.
1981 Annual Report (The Solomon Guggenheim Museum, New York), p. 11.
Nochella, Sam. "Contemporary American Realism Since 1960." *The Bulletin* (The Pennsylvania Academy of Art, Philadelphia) 20 September 1981.
"On Audrey Flack." *Arts Magazine* (June 1981): 96–97.
Perreault, John. "Photorealing in the Years." *The Soho Weekly News*, 20 October 1981, p. 64.
Reith, Stephanie J. "Must-Sees." *Arizona Arts and Lifestyle* (January 1981).
Rodriguez, Milani Joanne. "Audrey Flack, Mistress of Manipulation." *The Tampa Tribune*, 29 January 1981.
Soloman, Linda. "The Art of McLaughlin, Flack: Eloquent Sentience." *Oracle* (1981).
"Superrealism: One View." *Airbrush Digest* (August 1981): 14.
Towar, Judy. "Women and Art Support Crisis Nursery." *Arizona Living* (March 1981).
"Women and Art, Selected Pick-Hits for This Week." *New Times Weekly*, 21–27 January 1981, p. 19.
"Women Join the Mainstream." *Artweek* (January 1981).
Yoskowitz, Robert. "Photos by the Photorealists." *Arts* (March 1981): 25.
Zimmer, William. "Shiny American Things." *Arts News* (November 1981).

1982 *Archives of American Art Newsletter*, no. 1/2, (1982): 2.
Boettger, Suzaan. "Real Life Art." *The Museum of California—The Oakland Museum* 5, no. 5 (May/June 1982): 9–10.
Bourdon, David. "Contemporary Still Life Painting." *America Illustrated* (November 1982): 20–27, 24–25.
Burkhart, Dorothy. "Airbrush Paints Diffuse Portrait of Spray-On Art." *San Jose Mercury*, 4 February 1982, p. 3E.
Colby, Joy Hakanson. "The Cranbrook 15 Return in High Style." *The Detroit News*, 7 February 1982, p. 4E.
"Cranbrook Marks 50th Anniversary." *Oakland Press*, 2 March 1982, p. A8.
Delatiner, Barbara. "Art to Read as Well as See." *The New York Times*, 4 July 1982.
Foreman, B. J. "Exhibits Focus on Paintings." *Cincinnati Post* (November 1982).
Frueh, Joanna. "Re-Vamping the Vamp." *Arts Magazine* (October 1982): 98–109. 99.
Gillemon, Daniele. "Une Galerie Bruxelloise a l'heure New-Yorkaise." *Le Soir* (Brussels), 12 May 1982.
Krebs, Betty Dietz. "The Lively Arts." *Dayton Leisure*, 14 February 1982, p. 13.
———. "See It—'Deja Vu: Masterpieces Updated.'" *Dayton Leisure*, 14 February 1982.
Meisel, Louis K. "On Plagens, On Flack." *Art in America* (May 1982): 5.
Miro, Marsha. "Celebration of a Legacy at Cranbrook." *Detroit Free Press*, 21 February 1982, p. 8C.
Morera, Daniela. "Fotorealismo." *Italian Vogue* (October 1982): 634–39, 700.
"New York a Bruxelles et Vice-Versa." *Libre Belgique* (Brussels), 7 May 1982.
Plagens, Peter. "Painting." *Art in America* (February 1982): 21, 23.
Ray, Stephane. "La Galerie Brachot et La Galerie Louis K. Meisel." *Echo de la Bauru* (Brussels), 9 May 1982.
Shore, Charles. "An Impressive Show of Airbrush Painting." *Tribune Today*, 28 February 1982, p. I24.
Tannenbaum, Barbara. "Audrey Flack on Painting." *Women's Art Journal*, book review (Spring/Summer 1982).
Tomkins, Calvin. "The Art World: The Truth of Appearances." *The New Yorker*, 5–11 September 1982, pp. 103–8.
Vaizey, Marina. *The Artist as Photographer* (1982): 112.
Weiner, Judith. "Cranbrook Exhibit Honors Its Alumni." *Oakland Press*, 14 March 1982.

1983 Bannon, Anthony. "Still Life Exhibition Offers a Moving Treat." *The Buffalo News*, 14 December 1983.
"Creative Women in New York." *Cordier Essence* (Fall 1983): 34–35.
De Rouleaux, Margaret. "Hamptons' Magic Charms Artists." *Sunstorm* (August 1983): 9.
———. "Seducing The Viewer." *Sunstorm* (September 1983).
Gouma-Peterson, Thalia. "Icons of Healing Energy: The Recent Work of Audrey Flack." *Arts Magazine* (November 1983): 136–41, cover.
Johnson, Patricia C., "Still Life Show at Contemporary Arts Museum." *The Houston Chronicle*, 25 September 1983, p. 14.
Kalil, Susie. "Painting: Still-Life 1945–1983." *The Houston Post*, 25 September 1983, pp. 1F, 10F–11F.
Lewis, Jo Anne. "Picture Perfect." *The Washington Post*, 17 March 1983.
Russell, John. *The New York Times*, 11 November 1983.
Taylor, Angela. "The Evening Hours." *The New York Times*, 18 November 1983, p. B8.
Urban, William. "Audrey Flack—An Interview." *Airbrush Digest* (September–October 1983): 12–17, 49–55, cover.

1984 Bass, Ruth. "Audrey Flack." *Art News* (January 1984): 149.
Beals, Kathie. "Museum Displays Frames of Reference." *Weekend*, 22 June 1984, p. 11.
Eliasoph, Philip. "Museum Exhibit Shows Still Life Can Be Moving Art." *Southern Connecticut Newspaper*, 8 July 1984, pp. F1–3.
Gibson, Eric. "American Still Life." *The New Criterion* 3, no. 2 (October 1984): 70–75.
Glueck, Grace. "Art: Tracing the Flower in American Painting." *The New York Times*, 2 March 1984.
Hall, Jacqueline. "Still Life Exhibit Full of Vitality." *The Columbus Dispatch*, 29 April 1984, p. D7.
Hayakawa, Alan R. "Still Life Exhibit at Art Museum Shows Influence of Techniques." *The Oregonian* (Portland, Oreg.), 5 October 1984, p. E1.
Henry, Gerrit. "Audrey Flack at Meisel." *Art in America* (April 1984): 184, 186.
Mays, John Bentley. "Realism in the Abstract." *The Globe and Mail* (Toronto), 27 September 1984, p. E7.
Miller, Donald. "Flack's Realism Is Intense." *Pittsburgh Post-Gazette*, 11 February 1984, p. 22.
Olivastro, Dominic. "A Die Has Many Faces." *The Sciences* (September–October 1984): 67.

1985 Dalphonse, Sherri. "Artist Audrey Flack Sees Too Much Flack in The Art World Today, and Proposes Taking a Little Bit Out by Having Art Go Unsigned." *Hamptons Newspaper*, 25 July 1985, p. 10.

1986 Henry, William. "Artist Ponders Creativity." *The Southampton Press* (N.Y.), 16 October 1986, p. B4.
Omni Magazine (October 1986): 100.
"Women Artists Will Have Their Own Museum." *The New York Times*, 23 November 1986.

1987 Braff, Phyllis. "New Directions in Prints." *The New York Times*, 23 August 1987, p. 28.
———. "Recent Work on East End." *The New York Times*, 30 August 1987, p. 28.
Delatiner, Barbara. "Exploring the Artist-Mother Bond." *The New York Times*, 8 November 1987.
Hall, Jacqueline. "Works by Flack Express Her Religious Convictions." *The Columbus Dispatch* (Ohio), (September 1987).
Ligocki, Gordon. "Photorealism Holds on to 1980's Audiences." *The Times* (Hammond, Ind.), 3 July 1987, p. B7.
Lipson, Karin. "Rare Viewings of Mothers." *Newsday*, 13 November 1987, p. 25.
Martin, Judy Wells. "Saints and Other Angels—Jacksonville University Exhibits Religious Art of Audrey Flack." *Times-Union/Journal* (Fla.), 31 January 1987, p. 6.
1988 "Angels Take Wing at Danforth." *The Middlesex News* (Boston), 19 April 1988.
Daly, Matthew. "Rock Hill Envisions One-of-a-Kind Gateway." *The Charlotte Observer* (S.C.), pp. 1A, 11A.
Day, Meredith Fife. "Up Close And Spiritual—The Accessible Saints of Audrey Flack." *The Middlesex News* (Boston), 13 May 1988, pp. 1C, 4C.
Delatiner, Barbara. "The Spotlight Shines on Drawings." *The New York Times*, 11 September 1988.
The East Hampton Times, (N.Y.), 28 July 1988.
Fitzgerald, Pat. "Art Community Likes Concept of Gateway Plaza." *The Herald* (Rock Hill, S.C.), 13 July 1988.
———. "Golden Women to Greet Public." *The Herald* (Rock Hill, S.C.), 12 July 1988, pp. 1A, 7A.
Garfield, Ken. "Artist Falls in Love with Rock Hill." *The York Observer* (York County, S.C.), 24 July 1988.
Handal, Chris. "Gateway Plaza with Sculptures to 'Set Tone For City.'" *The Herald* (Rock Hill, S.C.), 12 July 1988, pp. 1A, 7A.
The Journal of the American Medical Association (Chicago), 260, no. 11, 16 September 1988, p. 1508, cover.
Larson, Kay. "An Artist's Sense and Sensibility: Audrey Flack in Manhattan and East Hampton." *Architectural Digest* (March 1988).
Maksymowicz, Virginia. "Children & Creativity Make For Tough Mix." *New Directions For Women*. (Englewood, N.J.) (July/August 1988): 6.
Maschal, David, and Dykes, David. "Temple's Historic Facade May Become City Entrance." *The Charlotte Observer* (S.C.), 16 June 1988, pp. 1A, 8A.
Museum School News (School of the Museum of Fine Arts, Boston), May 20th commencement address (Fall 1988).
Polak, Maralyn Lois. "Audrey Flack—A Firm Grip on Her Art." *The Philadelphia Inquirer Magazine*, 17 July 1988, pp. 9–10.
The Sciences (The New York Academy of Sciences, New York), (September/October 1988): 53.
Stapen, Nancy. "Religious Art Works Mix Humanity and Spirituality." *The Boston Herald*, 17 June 1988, p. 55.
Taylor, Robert. "Audrey Flack Offers Diverse Layers of Meaning." *The Boston Sunday Globe*, 26 June 1988, p. 91.
Twardy, Charles A. "Rock Hill Hopes to Share Identity with Art." *The State* (Columbia, S.C.), 13 July 1988.
1990 Burnham, Sophy. "Portrait of the Artist as a Woman." *New Woman* (June 1990): 94, 96, 99.
Greene, Trisha. "Jubilee '90 Is Step Toward Greatness." *The York Observer* (S.C.), 4 October 1990, p. 9Y.
Handal, Chris. "Art and Music Launch City's First Fall Festival." *The Herald* (Rock Hill, S.C.), 5 October 1990, pp. 1A, 10A.
———. "Civic Statues Show Art of Compromise." *The Herald* (Rock Hill, S.C.), 5 October 1990, pp. 1A, 10A.
———. "'Civitas' a Hit at Unveiling." *The Herald* (Rock Hill, S.C.), 5 October 1990, pp. 1A, 10A.
———. "Statue Sculptor Feels Work Will Draw Notice to City." *The Herald* (Rock Hill, S.C.), 4 October 1990, pp. 1A, 11A.
Nel, Francois Pierre. "Gateway Sculpture Unveiled: 'It's Beyond Most Vivid Imagination.'" *The York Observer* (S.C.), 4 October 1990, p. 1Y.
Plumb, Terry C. "Monument to the City." *The Herald* (Rock Hill, S.C.), 4 October 1990, p. 10A.
Seawright, Sandy. "Audrey Flack Super Realist." *Break Magazine* (Charlotte, N.C.), 17 October 1990, pp. 21–22.
1991 *CAA News* 16, no. 3 (May/June 1991): 7.
"Expo." *Hamptons* (1991): 32.
Goldowsky, Barbara. "Symbol of Long Island: A Welcoming Goddess Greets Museum Visitors." *The Southampton Press* (N.Y.), 6 June 1991.
Harn Museum of Art Monthly Bulletin (University of Florida, Gainesville) (April 1991): cover.
Hurwitz, Laurie S. *American Artist* (September 1991).
The Parrish Art Museum Calendar (Southampton, N.Y.) (June/August 1991).
"The Virgin Forest." *The Village Voice*, 2 July 1991.

BOOKS

1972 Coke, Van Deren. *The Painter and the Photograph*. Albuquerque: University of New Mexico Press.
Kultermann, Udo. *New Realism*. New York: New York Graphic Society.
1973 Kortlander, William. *Paintings with Acrylics*. New York: Van Nostrand Reinhold Co.
Sager, Peter. *Neue Formen des Realismus*. Cologne: Verlag M. DuMont Schauberg.
Who's Who in American Art. New York: R. R. Bowker & Co., Inc.
1974 *Art—A Women's Sensibility: The Collected Works and Writings of Women Artists*. Valencia: California Institute of the Arts.
Chase, Linda. *Hyperrealisme*. New York: Rizzoli.
Kamarck, Edward. *Arts in Society: Women and the Arts*. Madison, Wis.: University of Wisconsin Extension.
Kultermann, Udo. *Neue Formen des Bildes*. Tubingen, West Germany: Verlag Ernst Wasmuth.
Nemser, Cindy. *Art Talk*. New York: Charles Scribner's Sons.
Pomeroy, Ralph. *The Ice Cream Connection*. London: Paddington Press Ltd.
Rose, Barbara. *Readings in American Art, 1900–1975*. New York: Praeger Publications.
1975 Alloway, Lawrence. *Topics in American Art Since 1945*. New York: Norton.
Battcock, Gregory. *Super Realism: A Critical Anthology*. New York: E.P. Dutton.
1976 Peterson, Karen, and J. J. Wilson. *Woman Artists*. New York: Harper & Row.
Who's Who in American Art. New York: R. R. Bowker & Co.
1977 Melville, Keith. *Marriage and Family Today*. New York: Random House.
Rose, Barbara, and Jules D. Brown. *American Painting*. New York: Skira/Rizzoli.
Selleck, Jack. *Faces*. Worcester, Mass.: Davis Publications.
1978 Lipman, Jean, and Richard Marshall. *Art About Art*. New York: E. P. Dutton.
Saff, Donald, and Deli Sacilotto. *Printmaking*. New York: Holt, Rinehart & Winston.
Walters, Margaret. *The Nude Male: A New Perspective*. New York: Paddington Press.
1979 Chaet, Bernard. *Artist's Notebook: Techniques and Materials*. New York: Holt, Rinehart and Winston.
Lucie-Smith, Edward. *Super Realism*. Oxford: Phaidon Press.
Saff, Donald, and Deli Sacilotto. *Screenprinting History and Process*. New York: Holt, Rinehart and Winston.
Seeman, Helene Zucker, and Alanna Siegfried. *SoHo*. New York: Neal-Schuman.
1980 Curtis and Hunt. *A History and Technique: The Air Brush Book*. London: Orbis Pubio.
Lindey, Christine. *Superrealist Painting and Sculpture*. New York: William Morrow Company.
Lucie-Smith, Edward. *Art in the Seventies*. Oxford: Phaidon Press.
Meisel, Louis K. *Photorealism*. New York: Harry N. Abrams.
1981 Flack, Audrey. *Audrey Flack On Painting*. New York: Harry N. Abrams.
Krantz, Les. *The New York Review of Art*. New York: The Krantz Co.
1982 *Australian National Gallery—An Introduction*. Canberra: The Australian National Gallery.
Johnson, Ellen. *American Artists on Art, 1940–1980*. New York: Harper & Row.
Messer, Tom. *25 Artists—Photos by Hans Namuth*. Frederick, Md.: University Publishing of America.
Rubinstein, Streifer, Charlott. *American Women Artists*. Boston: G. K. Hall.
Paschal, Robert. *Air Brushing for Fine and Commercial Artists*. New York: Van Nostrand Reinhold.
1983 Milman, Miriam. *Trompe L'Oeil Painting*. New York: Rizzoli International Publications.
1984 Robbins, Corinne. *The Pluralist Era, 1968–1981*. New York: Harper & Row.
Van Wagner, Judy Collischan. *Women Shaping Art*. New York: Praeger.
1985 Brommer, Gerald F., and George K. Horn. *Art in Your Environment*. Worcester, Mass.: Davis Publications.
———. *Art In Your World*. Worcester, Mass.: Davis Publications.
Hunter, Sam, and John Jacobus. *Modern Art (Second Edition)*. New York: Harry N. Abrams.
Krantz, Les. *American Art Galleries*. New York: Facts on File Publications.
Krantz, Les. *American Artists—An Illustrated Survey of Leading Contemporary Americans*. New York: Facts on File Publications.
McCarter, William, and Rita Gilbert. *Living with Art*. New York: Alfred A. Knopf.
Paschal, Robert W., and Robert R. Anderson. *The Art of the Dot: Advanced Airbrush Techniques*. New York: Van Nostrand Reinhold Company.
Pelfrey, Robert, and Mary Hall. *Art and Mass Media*. New York: Harper & Row.
Russo, Alexander. *Profiles on Women Artists*. Frederick, Md: University Publications of America.
1985–86 Lucie-Smith, Edward. *American Art Now*. New York: William Morrow and Company.
1986 Arnason, H. H. *History of Modern Art (Third Edition)* New York: Harry N. Abrams.
Flack, Audrey. *Art and Soul*. New York: E. P. Dutton.
Janson, H. W. *History of Art (3rd Edition)*. New York: Harry N. Abrams.
Martin, Alvin. *American Realism: 20th-Century Drawings and Watercolors from the Glenn C. Janss Collection*. New York: Harry N. Abrams.

Siegel, Peter. *The Complete Airbrush Book.* New York: Leon Amiel Publisher.
1987 Heller, Nancy G. *Women Artists—An Illustrated History.* New York: Abbeville Press.
National Museum of Women in the Arts. New York: Harry N. Abrams.
1988 Krantz, Les. *The New York Art Review.* Chicago: American References.
Landa, Robin. *Inspired by Faith—A How-to Guide to Religious Oil Paintings.* Old Tappan, N.J.: Fleming H. Revell Company.
1989 Fichner-Rathus, Lois. *Understanding Art (Second Edition).* Englewood Cliffs, N.J.: Prentice Hall.
Gadon, Elinor W. *The One & Future Goddess.* San Francisco: Harper & Row Publishers.
Preble, Duane and Sarah. *Artforms.* New York: Harper & Row.
Rosen, Randy, and Catherine C. Brawer. *Making Their Mark: Women Artists Move into the Mainstream, 1970–85.* New York: Abbeville Press.
Ward, John L. *American Realist Painting 1945–1980.* Ann Arbor, Mich.: UMI Research Press.
1990 Cirlot, Lourdes. *Las Ultimas Tendencias Pictoricas.* Barcelona: Ediciones Vicens-Vives.
Goddard, Donald. *American Painting.* New York: Hugh Lauter Levin Associates.
Nash, Gary B. *The American People: Creating a Nation and a Society, (Second Edition).* New York: Harper and Row.

EXHIBITION CATALOGUES

1963–64 *Nine Realist Painters.* Robert Schoelkopf Gallery, New York.
1969–70 Farb, Oriole. *Paintings from the Photograph.* Riverside Museum, New York.
1970 Monte, James. *22 Realists.* Whitney Museum of American Art, New York.
Wallin, Lee. *New Realism, 1970.* Headley Hall Gallery, St. Cloud State College, Minn.
1972 Baratte, John J., and Paul E. Thompson. *Phases of the New Realism.* Lowe Art Museum, University of Miami, Coral Gables, Fla.
Whitney Review 1971–72.
Baur, John H. *1972 Annual Exhibit of Contemporary American Paintings.* Whitney Museum of American Art, New York.
Goldsmith, Benedict. *Women in Art.* Brainerd Hall Art Gallery, State University College, Potsdam, N.Y.
Naeve, Milo M. *New Accessions U.S.A.* Colorado Springs Fine Arts Center.
Warrum, Richard L. *Painting and Sculpture Today, 1972.* Indianapolis Museum of Art.
1972–73 Amaya, Mario. *Realism Now.* New York Cultural Center, New York.
1973 Alloway, Lawrence. *Amerikansk realism.* Galleri Ostergren, Malmö, Sweden.
———. *Photo-Realism.* Serpentine Gallery, London.
Hogan, Carroll Edwards. *Hyperréalistes américains.* Galerie Arditti, Paris.
Lamagna, Carlo. *The Super-Realist Vision.* DeCordova and Dana Museum, Lincoln, Mass.
Lippard, Lucy. *Women Choose Women.* New York Cultural Center, New York.
Meisel, Louis K. *Photo-Realism 1973: The Stuart M. Speiser Collection.* Louis K. Meisel Gallery, New York.
Mochon, Anne, and Miriam Levin. *Objects and Eight Women Realists.* University of Massachusetts, Amherst.
Sims, Patterson. *Realism Now.* The Katonah Gallery, Katonah, N.Y.
Solomon, Elke M. *American Drawings 1963–1973.* Whitney Museum of American Art, New York.
1974 Alloway, Lawrence. *New York Eleven.* C. W. Post Art Gallery, Long Island University, Brookville, N.Y.
Amerikaans fotorealisme grafiek, Hedendaagse Kunst, Utrecht, Palais des Beaux-Arts, Brussels.
Aspects of Realism. Moos Gallery, Toronto.
Campbell, Alan. *From Teapot Dome to Watergate.* Everson Museum of Art, Syracuse, N.Y.
Cowart, Jack. *New Photo-Realism.* Wadsworth Atheneum, Hartford, Conn.
Goldsmith, Benedict. *New Realism Revisited.* Brainerd Hall Art Gallery, State University College, Potsdam, N.Y.
Gruen, John. *Contemporary Portraits by American Painters.* Lowe Art Museum, University of Miami, Coral Gables, Fla.
Perreault, John, Kawakita Michiak, and Sir Roeland A. Penrose. *Tokyo Biennale '74.*
Chase, Linda. *New Image in Painting.* 11th Tokyo International Biennale.
Sarajas-Korte, Salme. *Ars '74 Ateneum.* Fine Arts Academy of Helsinki.
Thirty-eighth Annual Midyear Show. Butler Institute of American Art, Youngstown, Ohio.
Walthard, Dr. Frederic P. *Art 5 '74.* Basel, Switzerland.
Woman's Work: American Art 1974. Museum of the Philadelphia Civic Center.
1975 Baur, John H. *Kent Bicentennial Portfolio: Spirit of Independence.*
Meisel, Susan Pear. *Watercolors and Drawings—American Realists.* Louis K. Meisel Gallery, New York.
Metzger, Deena. *Art: A Woman's Sensibility.* California Institute of the Arts, Valencia.
Phillips, Robert F. *Image, Color and Form: Recent Paintings by Eleven Americans.* Toledo Museum of Art, Ohio.
Von Baron, Judith. *The Year of the Woman.* Bronx Museum of Arts, N.Y.
1975–76 Richardson, Brenda. *Super Realism.* Baltimore Museum of Art.
1976 *Artists and East Hampton.* Guild Hall Art Gallery, East Hampton, N.Y.
Felluss, Elias A. *Washington International Art Fair.* Washington, D.C.
Gervais, Daniel. *Troisième foire internationale d'art contemporain.* Grand Palais, Paris.
Meisel, Louis K. *Audrey Flack—The Gray Border Series.* Louis K. Meisel Gallery, New York.
Simkins, Alice C. *American Artists '76: A Celebration.* Marion Koogler McNay Art Museum, San Antonio, Tex.
Walthard, Dr. Frederic P. *Art 7 '76.* Basel, Switzerland.
1976–77 Ratcliff, Carter. *The Aubrey Cartwright Foundation Exhibition of Contemporary Religious Art.* Cathedral Church of St. John the Divine, New York.
1976–78 Chase, Linda. *U.S.A.—Aspects of Realism.* Rothman's of Pall Mall Canada, Ltd.
1977 Cloudman, Ruth H. *The Chosen Object: European and American Still Life.* Joslyn Art Museum, Omaha, Nebr.
Dempsey, Bruce. *New Realism.* Jacksonville Art Museum, Fla.
Felluss, Elias A. *Washington International Art Fair.* Washington, D.C.
Seabolt, Fred. *New in the '70s.* University Art Museum, Archer M. Huntington Gallery, University of Texas at Austin.
1977–78 *June Blum, Audrey Flack, Alice Neel: Three Contemporary American Women Realists.* Miami-Dade Community College, South Campus Art Gallery, Miami, Fla.
Stringer, John. *Illusion and Reality.* Australian Gallery Director's Council, North Sydney.
1978 Alloway, Lawrence. *Audrey Flack—Vanitas.* Louis K. Meisel Gallery, New York.
Hennessey, William. *Artists Look at Art.* Helen Foresman Spencer Museum of Art, University of Kansas, Lawrence.
Koenig, Robert J. *Drawing the Line.* Montclair Art Museum, Montclair, N.J.
Meisel, Susan Pear. *The Complete Guide to Photo-Realist Print-Making.* Louis K. Meisel Gallery, New York.
Schwartz, Therese. *Perspective '78: Works by Women.* Freedman Art Gallery, Albright College, Reading, Pa.
Young, Mahonri Shapr. *Aspects of Realism.* Guild Hall Art Gallery, East Hampton, N.Y.
1978–80 Cathcart, Linda L. *American Painting of the 70s.* Albright-Knox Art Gallery, Buffalo.
1979 Chew, Paul A. *The New American Still Life.* Westmoreland County Museum of Art, Greensburg, Pa.
Cooper, Marve H. *Narrative Realism.* The Art Association of Newport, R.I.
Gerling, Steve. *Photo-Realism: Some Points of View.* Jorgensen Gallery, University of Connecticut, Storrs.
Felluss, Elias A. *Washington International Art Fair '79.* Washington, D.C.
Miller, Wayne. *Realist Space.* C. W. Post Art Gallery, Long Island University, Brookville, N.Y.
Steuber, Michael. *Selections of Photo-Realist Paintings from New York City Galleries.* Southern Alleghenies Museum of Art, St. Francis College, Loretto, Pa.
1979–80 Mollison, James. *Genesis of a Gallery, Part 2.* Australian National Gallery, Canberra.
1980 Brown, J. Carter. *The Morton G. Neumann Family Collection.* National Gallery of Art, Washington, D.C.
Hills, Patricia, and Roberta Tarbell. *The Figurative Tradition and the Whitney Museum of Art: Paintings and Sculpture from the Permanent Collection.* University of Delaware Press, Newark, Del.
The Language of Symbols. Landmark Gallery, New York.
Perreault, John. *Aspects of the 70's: Directions in Realism.* Danforth Museum, Framingham, Mass.
Spear, Richard. *From Rembrandt to Christo.* Allen Memorial Museum, Oberlin College, Ohio.
1980–82 Perreault, John. *Art in Our Time.* HHK Foundation for Contemporary Art, Inc.
1981 Brown, Suzanne, and Erma Bombeck. *Women and Art.* Suzanne Brown Gallery, Scottsdale, Ariz.
Dietrich, Linnea S., *Audrey Flack—Works on Paper, 1950–80.* Fine Arts Gallery, University of South Florida, Tampa; Art and Cultural Center, Hollywood, Fla.
The Image in American Painting and Sculpture—1950–1980. Akron Art Museum, Ohio.
Perreault, John. *Joseph Albers: His Art and His Influence.* The Montclair Art Museum, Montclair, N.J.
Real, Really Real, Superreal. San Antonio Museum of Art, Tex.
Toyama Now, 1981. Museum of Modern Art, Tokyo.
1982 *The Artist and the Airbrush.* San Jose State University, Calif.
Cranbrook U.S.A. Cranbrook Academy of Art Museum, Bloomfield Hills, Mich.
Women's Art: Miles Apart. Aaron Berman Gallery, N.Y.
1983 *American Super Realism: From the Morton G. Neumann Family Collection.* Terra Museum of American Art, Chicago.

Perreault, John. *Audrey Flack—Light & Energy.* Louis K. Meisel Gallery, New York.
Printed by Women—A National Exhibition of Photographs and Prints. The Port of History Museum at Penn's Landing, Philadelphia.
1984 *American Women Artists Part I: 20th Century Pioneers.* Sidney Janis Gallery, New York.
1985 *Modern American Printmaking.* Amerika-Haus Hannover, Hannover, West Germany.
1985–86 *American Art: American Women.* Stamford Museum & Nature Center, Stamford, Conn.
1986 *Sacred Images in Secular Art.* Whitney Museum of American Art, New York.
1986–88 Sims, Lowery S. *Saints and Other Angels: The Religious Paintings of Audrey Flack.* Traveling exhibition organized by Dominique Mazeaud and Cooper Union, New York.
1987 *American Art Today: The Portrait.* The Art Museum, Florida International University, Miami.
Art and the Law. West Publishing Co., Saint Paul, Minn.
The Artist's Mother: Portraits and Homages. Heckscher Museum, Huntington, N.Y.
1988 *Just Like a Woman.* The Emrys Foundation and The Greenville County Museum of Art, Greenville, S.C.
Matilsky, Barbara C. *Classical Myth and Imagery in Contemporary Art.* The Queens Museum, Flushing, N.Y.
1990 *Civitas.* Belk Building, Tower Center Mall, Rock Hill, S.C.
1991 Casteras, Susan P. *Audrey Flack—A Pantheon of Female Deities.* Louis K. Meisel Gallery, New York.
Schwartz, Constance. *In Sharp Focus: Super Realism.* Nassau County Museum of Art, Roslyn, N.Y.

BOOKS AND ARTICLES BY AUDREY FLACK

1978 Flack, Audrey. "Luisa Ignacia Roldán," *Women's Studies* 6, Gordon and Breach Science Publishers Ltd., Great Britain
1979 Flack, Audrey. "The Haunting Images of Luisa Roldán." *Helicon Nine A Journal of Women's Arts and Letters* (1979).
1981 Flack, Audrey. "On Carlo Crivelli." *Arts Magazine* (June 1981): 92–95.
Flack, Audrey. *Audrey Flack On Painting.* New York: Harry N. Abrams.
1986 Flack, Audrey. *Art and Soul.* New York: E. P. Dutton.
1989 Flack, Audrey. *Audrey Flack: The Daily Muse.* New York: Harry N. Abrams.

INDEX

Titles of works are in *italics*. All works are by Flack unless otherwise indicated. Page numbers in *italics* refer to pages on which illustrations appear.

A

B

C

D

E

F

PHOTOGRAPH CREDITS

Unless otherwise noted photographs for this book were provided courtesy the artist or Louis K. Meisel Gallery, New York. Other photograph credits appear below:
 Nancy Bundt: 119, 140, 141, 143; Ann Chwatsky: 6, 134, 135, 137, 138; D. James Dee: 35; Thalia Gouma-Peterson: 12, 22, 25, 65; Bruce C. Jones: 29, 49 top left and right and bottom right, 54 top right and bottom, 62, 67 top, 72, 79, 81, 82; Steve Lopez: 1, 2, 8, 10, 11, 14, 15, 20 top left and bottom, 23, 24, 28, 31, 45, 49 bottom left, 53, 59 bottom right, 68, 69, 114, 117, 127, 128; John Mills Photography Limited: 120; Daniel Ranalli: 58 bottom; Stan Ries: 104, 107, 108, 118, 121, 123, 124; Roko Gallery: 46 bottom; Walter Rosenblum Photographer: 16; Penny Young: 131, 142.

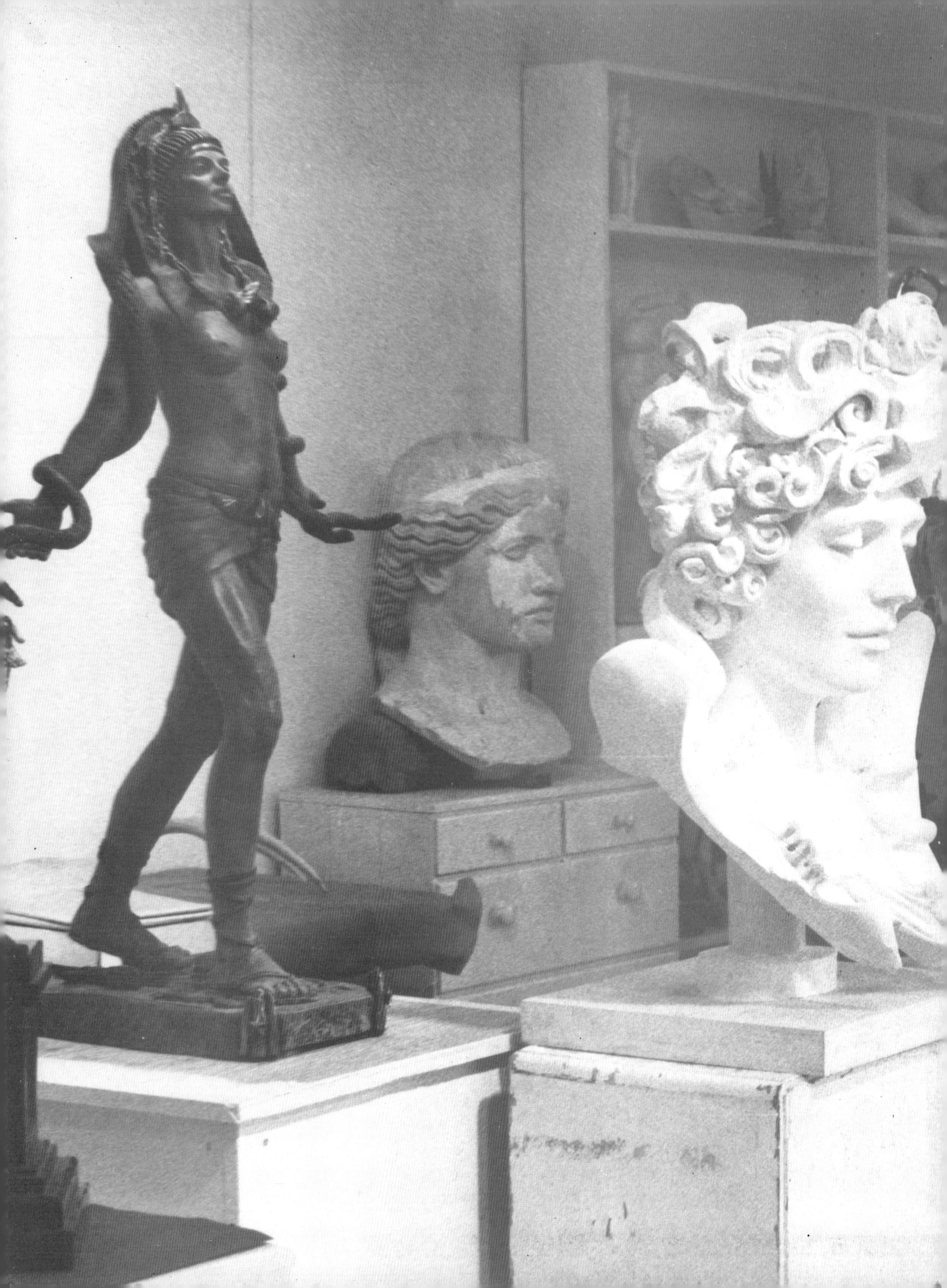